To

DR. WHITNEY

BEST WISHES

Bernie & Ilana

Head in the Clouds
Feet on the Ground

Bernard Loewenthal, Jr.

Publisher's Page

Head in the Clouds—Feet on the Ground
by Bernard Loewenthal, Jr.

ISBN 978-0-9894028-0-4 54995

Produced and packaged by:

Book design:	imageProjektions Design Group, Chris Rabkin
Editing:	Vision Communications, Stacie Jennings
Cover design:	Opus Studio, Inc., Becky Kiel

Dedication

My autobiography is dedicated to my wife's parents, Mr. and Mrs. Immanuel Mirkin. The Mirkins were instrumental in enabling me to attain what I have achieved in my life. They provided me with the love, support and food that my family did not. They unfailingly supported my wife Ilana, our daughter Bonnie, her family, and me, in more ways than anyone could ever have imagined; totally unselfishly, and beyond the call of duty, for many years. The Mirkins were wonderful people and I miss them. May they rest in peace.

My wife's parents, Marion and Immanuel Mirkin

Table of Contents

Foreword 6

Prologue 7

Introduction 8

Chapter 1 1938-1952
The Early Years 9

Chapter 2 1952-1960
High School, Working, College, and Marriage 30

Chapter 3 1960-1970
Dental School, The Air Force, Post-Graduate Training, and Farming 50

Chapter 4 1970-1995
Periodontics, Meteorology, Inventing, Farming, and New Adventures 70

Chapter 5 1995-2013
Retirement and Beyond 116

Epilogue 124

Supplement

Curriculum Vitae 126

Periodontal Career 131

The PerioWise® Probe 144

Weather 167

Fishing 188

Gardening Fun 202

Cooking 218

President Coolidge in the Oval Office

Persistence...

"Nothing in the world can take the place of persistence. Talent will not; nothing is more common than unsuccessful men with talent. Genius will not; unrewarded genius is almost a proverb. Education will not; the world is full of educated derelicts. Persistence and determination alone are omnipotent."

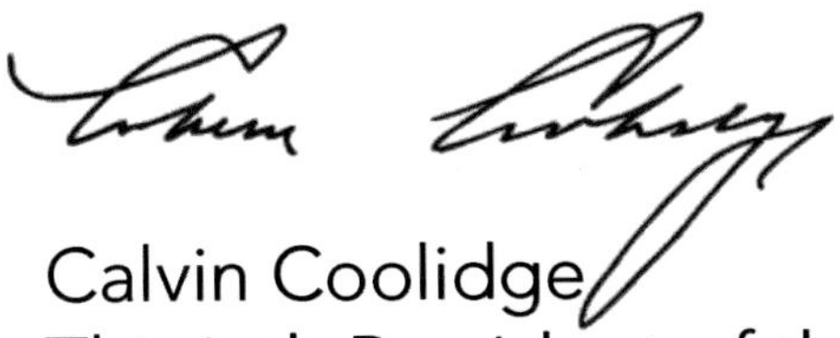

Calvin Coolidge
Thirtieth President of the United States

Foreword

On the wall of Dr. Bernard Loewenthal, Jr.'s home office in Naples, Florida, hangs a distinctive commemorative plaque, a gift from his wife, Ilana. It reads:

Renaissance Man
Periodontist
Implantologist
Meteorologist
Inventor
Fisherman
Farmer
Hunter

Dr. Loewenthal ("Bernie" to his family and friends) is indeed one of those rare individuals who has not only attained a broad base of experiential knowledge, but is also skilled in multiple disciplines. His autobiography, "Head in the Clouds—Feet on the Ground" is the account of an ordinary boy who became this extraordinary man, despite facing frequent and seemingly insurmountable ***challenges*** throughout his life.

In this candidly honest narrative, the author describes the troubled home life he and his family experienced. The loss of his father's business accentuated the family's problems. It was while he was very young that young Bernie first developed fascinations with weather, fishing, and hunting. From his account of school days at Flushing, New York's P.S. 20 to his Tom Sawyer-like fishing adventures with his friend Malcolm in the Catskill Mountains of New York State, Bernie vividly portrays what life was like for a boy growing up in the 1940s. By the time Bernie had become a young man, he'd already taken responsibility for his life, working throughout his high school years, beginning at fifty cents an hour at a local supermarket, and then making his own way through college. With a less than stellar collegiate academic record, Bernie seemed destined for a life of mediocrity. Until, that is, he was required to attend a summer make-up French class. It was there that he met the stunning blonde Ilana Mirkin, the woman who a few years later became his wife.

With the support of his loving wife and the encouragement of her devoted parents, who treated their son-in-law as if he were their own, Bernie successfully pursued and fulfilled his professional dream of becoming a periodontist.

Throughout the years, his love of learning and his fascination with the weather and nature never waned. In addition to running a thriving periodontal practice, Bernie was also forecasting the weather for the city in which he lived, for a Fortune 500 company, and appeared as the meteorologist on the local television station. He also created and operated his own vegetable farm. Perhaps his most notable professional contribution was the invention of a flexible, color-coded periodontal probe that enables dentists and hygienists to more accurately, and more comfortably for the patient, diagnose periodontal disease.

The book you now hold in your hands is Bernard Loewenthal, Jr.'s gift to you in celebration of his seventy-fifth birthday. You'll laugh a little, you'll learn a lot, and you most certainly will be inspired by this true-life story of one very special and quintessential renaissance man: Bernard Loewenthal, Jr.— ***Stacie Jennings, Editor***

Prologue

I was about twelve years old and my mother and I were hiding in my bedroom. A crazed man ran into the room shouting profanities. He charged at my mother, swinging a baseball bat at her. I jumped on him and was able to wrestle the bat from his grip, and it fell to the floor. The alcohol stench coming from his mouth was disgusting.

I managed to push my drunken father out of my bedroom, and close the door. He was enraged, pounding on the door as hard as he could trying to get back into the room. The door had no lock. I leaned against it as hard as I could to prevent him from getting back into the room. I held my ground and he eventually went away.

My mother was on the floor, with tears running down her reddened face, sobbing, ***"I can't take this anymore. I want to die."*** ***"Mom, I am so sorry,"*** I said. ***"When Dad drinks I get scared too, and run away from the house."*** She said, ***"I know. I wish I could leave too."***

1943 "I Am Junior!"

1945 Junior

Introduction

I am not really certain why I decided to write my autobiography. My life's story is probably of interest only to my family, my friends and me. It will however, leave a record of my life, as a legacy for future generations of my family.

My story is of being an unexpected child, born into a very dysfunctional family, and growing up predominantly on my own. Lack of love, family financial ruin, and my parents' egocentric existence left me with deep and unhealed wounds. I have been trying to heal them, with only modest success. I hope that you enjoy reading about my life's adventures.

My name is Bernard Loewenthal, Jr. I was called Junior until I was a teenager, except in grammar school, where I was known as Bernard. My parents did not give my needs, or me, as much thought or attention as I would have liked. They did provide shelter, clothing, and adequate food until I was fourteen years old, and I am thankful to them for that. I was basically on my own from a rather early age, and then entirely from age fourteen until I was married at age twenty-one.

I learned by dint of hard work, and virtually no parental guidance, to progress through my life by being ***persistent***, and by learning about life from a multitude of diverse people, many of them experts in their fields.

I have also learned that ***chance***, ***persistence***, ***challenge***, and ***fear*** have all played significant roles in my life. They were intertwined, and have been part of a recurring theme. ***Fear*** has always been a powerful motivator for me.

My life's philosophy has been, and remains: ***Much of life happens for the best and for our highest good and learning. Undesirable and bad things do happen, but occasionally they have a positive effect—given time.***

Chance - (adjective): accidental, occurring by ***chance***, serendipitous, unforeseeable, random, unplanned

Persistence - (noun): perseverance, tenacity, determination, doggedness, commitment

Challenge - (noun): a task or situation that tests someone's abilities

Fear - (verb): be afraid of, be scared of, live in ***fear*** of, and be anxious about

I will try to connect, by example, how ***chance, persistence, challenge, fear,*** and ***my philosophy about life***, have pertained to my life. I will use anecdotes, pictures, and documentation where possible, to try and make this autobiography completely factual, engrossing reading, and perhaps amusing at times.

As I look back over my life, many of its facts amaze me. I am fully aware of how my life could have turned out profoundly differently.

Chapter 1

1938-1952: The Early Years

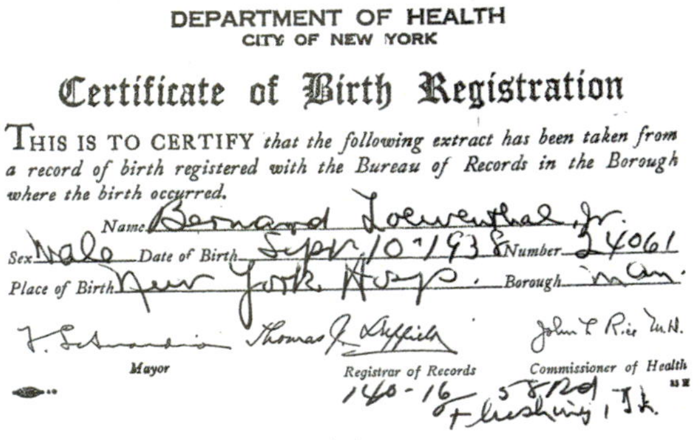

DEPARTMENT OF HEALTH
CITY OF NEW YORK

Certificate of Birth Registration

THIS IS TO CERTIFY *that the following extract has been taken from a record of birth registered with the Bureau of Records in the Borough where the birth occurred.*

Name Bernard Loewenthal Jr.

Sex Male Date of Birth Sept. 10 1938 Number 24061

Place of Birth New York Hosp. Borough Man.

Mayor Registrar of Records Commissioner of Health

140-16 58 Rd Flushing, L.I.

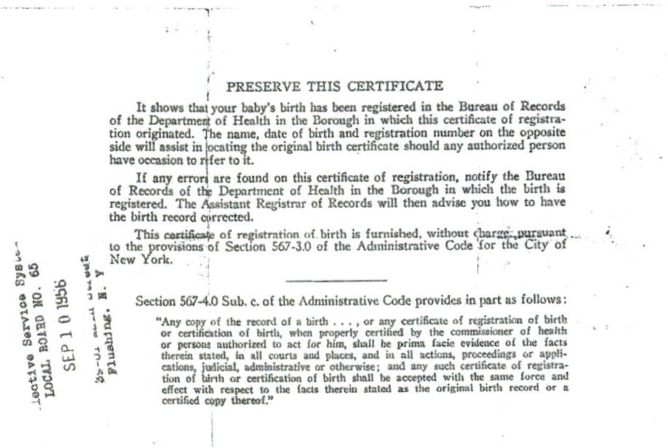

PRESERVE THIS CERTIFICATE

It shows that your baby's birth has been registered in the Bureau of Records of the Department of Health in the Borough in which this certificate of registration originated. The name, date of birth and registration number on the opposite side will assist in locating the original birth certificate should any authorized person have occasion to refer to it.

If any errors are found on this certificate of registration, notify the Bureau of Records of the Department of Health in the Borough in which the birth is registered. The Assistant Registrar of Records will then advise you how to have the birth record corrected.

This certificate of registration of birth is furnished, without charge, pursuant to the provisions of Section 567-3.0 of the Administrative Code for the City of New York.

Section 567-4.0 Sub. c. of the Administrative Code provides in part as follows:

"Any copy of the record of a birth . . . , or any certificate of registration of birth or certification of birth, when properly certified by the commissioner of health or persons authorized to act for him, shall be prima facie evidence of the facts therein stated, in all courts and places, and in all actions, proceedings or applications, judicial, administrative or otherwise; and any such certificate of registration of birth or certification of birth shall be accepted with the same force and effect with respect to the facts therein stated as the original birth record or a certified copy thereof."

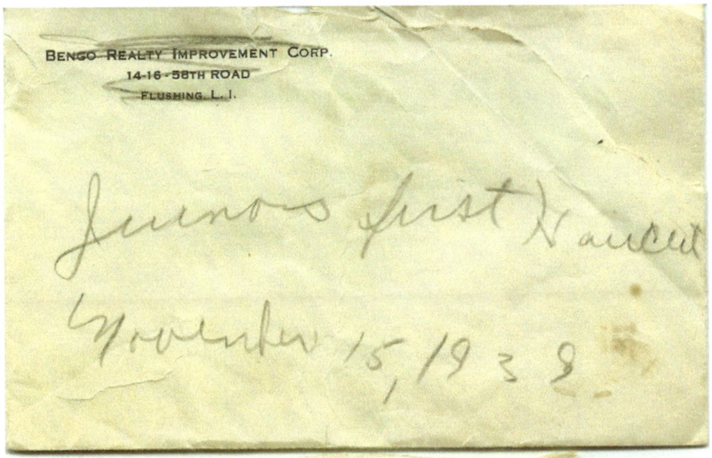

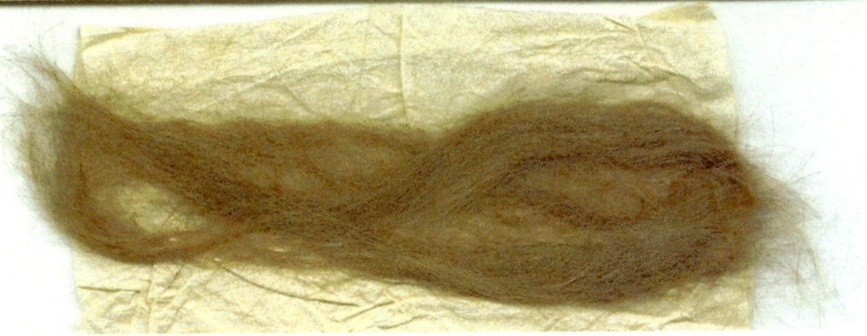

I was born, by ***chance,*** on September 10, 1938. The Hurricane of 1938, a devastating storm, was born at the same time. I was born in New York City. The hurricane was born in the far eastern tropical Atlantic. I have often wondered if there was any significance to this ***chance,*** simultaneous birth, because my entire life, as you will read, has been significantly influenced by the weather.

Until I was thirteen years old, my family lived in three different locations each year, requiring me to attend three different grammar schools. This was a problem for me because the schools were very different in their curricula, and I didn't live in one place long enough to make meaningful friendships.

I lived in New York City primarily during the winter in the town of Flushing, in a first floor apartment of a six story brick apartment house. Part of some winters were spent in Coral Gables, Florida, and in the early spring, summer and early fall, I spent time in Loch Sheldrake, which is located in the Catskill Mountains of New York State. Living in Flushing was routine, Florida was just okay, but my summers spent in Loch Sheldrake provided me with many of the happiest and most memorable days of my life. Those memories remain vivid and joyful.

Family

My parents

My family consisted of my parents and my two older sisters, June and Connee. June was fifteen years, and Connee ten years older than I. Both sisters married: June to Stanley Lanes, a professional engineer, and Connee to Edwin Silbert, an executive in marketing women's clothing.

Both of my brothers-in-law became significant in my life, but for entirely opposite reasons. Both of my sisters had children. June had a girl, Barbara, and a son, Bradley. Connee had two girls, Sheryl and Pamela, and a boy, Brian. All of the children but one have grown up nicely and have their own families. The exception was June's son, Bradley, who died before the age fifty from heart disease, caused by drugs and alcohol. He was not married. My parents, my sister June, and both brother-in-laws have died.

My parents were married for thirty-eight years. Those years were frequently miserable ones for everyone, and over time, home life became extremely unpleasant.

June and Stanley

My parents continually quarreled, and their fighting and screaming was terribly frightening for me. This environment led my sister Connee to marry at the tender age of seventeen. She told me that she had to get away from the house—permanently. I stayed away from the house as much as I could, but since I was just a boy, I was unable to leave.

Connee and Edwin

My sisters and I

My parents did not provide any guidance for me regarding any of my activities. They never discussed my daily living, schooling, religion, my life's ambitions, sex, or anything else with me.

I was told that my father had a tainted history, and that he had spent time in prison. Once wealthy in the 1920s, he went bankrupt during the Great Depression. He could not find work, and never made a financial comeback. He was not a bad person, and when not drinking was reasonable and smart. In his later years, financial ruin and alcohol abuse were the decisive factors in his daily life. When he drank he became dangerous, and his abominable temper took over. He simply went completely out of control at those times.

In the late 1930s, he took a ***chance*** and borrowed six hundred dollars to build a single bungalow in the hamlet of Loch Sheldrake, which lies in the Catskill Mountains of New York State. Back then it was a five-hour drive to there from New York City.

This bungalow was the first of many that he built, creating a large bungalow colony of over one hundred units. It was called "Loewenthal's Bungalow Colony." The bungalows produced rental income from New York City residents who wanted to get out of the hot City during the summer and enjoy the more comfortable and cooler mountain weather. He used the rental income, plus borrowed money, to live on and to keep enlarging the bungalow colony. Poor management, decreasing rental income, and my parents living above their means caused another bankruptcy.

The loan sharks, from whom the money was borrowed, seized the bungalow colony and our house in Loch Sheldrake in 1952. This was a devastating blow to me for many reasons. Following this loss, my father tried to put together other business ventures, but none worked. Depressed for years, he spent his days wandering the streets of New York City, usually ending up talking for hours with anyone who would listen. By day's end, he would find himself back home in Flushing, starting to drink.

One of the main issues that my parents argued about was money. My father accused my mother of stealing money, in concert with his business partner, Gene. He also accused her of having an affair with Gene. I have no idea if this was true. In later years, my mother married Gene. My father died in 1962, at the age of seventy-two, living with his new wife, Sylvia, who I believe was an old girlfriend.

I did not feel close to my mother, I felt that I never received her loving attention. My sister Connee took over many of my mother's responsibilities helping to raise me when I was a child; I am very thankful to her for doing so. My mother was a nice looking woman; she smoked, loved to entertain, and was a fine cook. She prepared her finest meals to entertain friends. Many times I wanted to eat something that she had made for company, but she warned me not to touch any of the food; "It was for company!"

My mother was a very unhappy woman, locked in a rotten marriage. She did make lunch for me when I came home from grammar school. I attended P.S. 20 in Flushing, which was about three blocks from our apartment. Lunch usually consisted of Campbell's Tomato Soup, made with milk, and loaded with homemade rice. Sometimes I would have an "egg in the nest," or two. An egg in a nest is a slice of bread with a hole in the middle, an egg yolk in the hole, fried in butter, with a bit of salt. I still love to eat them!

"Eggs in their nests"

I never met my father's parents. My mother's parents were not living together. Her father, Benjamin Goldsmith, lived in Bloomingburg, New York, with a woman named Lil. He was a house painter, and a heavy smoker. I only remember seeing him a few times before he became ill and was moved into my bedroom in Flushing. I was moved into the living room. He died from lung cancer.

My maternal grandmother, Anna Goldsmith, lived in Monticello, New York, near Loch Sheldrake, with her common-law husband, Dan Spinelli. I vividly remember Anna and Dan visiting us on Sundays in Loch Sheldrake. Dan frequently brought live minnows and took me fishing in the nearby lake.

I clearly remember fishing with him because we always had a great time catching bass and pickerel. We fished while standing on large spruce trees that had fallen into the lake. The trees created a perfect habitat for fish to spawn, and to hide from predators. Dan's set-up for fishing was to use a red and white bobber with a live minnow attached to the hook. The minnow would make the bobber twitch a little, but when a fish struck the minnow, the bobber would go down—an exciting sight. We were thrilled at that moment, and the fight was on. ***That's a great memory!***

My family considered itself to be Jewish, but I don't know why. We were never members of, or worshipped at a Jewish synagogue. I never attended a Jewish service, not one. I was never taught a word about Judaism. None of the Jewish holidays were ever observed or celebrated, and my father continually ridiculed all forms of religion. However, we did celebrate Christmas— tree, tinsel, presents, and all. My sister Connee took charge of this holiday. I remember her putting me to bed early, many times, so Santa could deliver my presents.

When I was twelve years old, my mother asked me if I wanted to have a Bar Mitzvah. I didn't know what that meant, because I knew nothing about Judaism. I said okay, although I don't think that my mother cared about me "becoming a man" in the Jewish tradition. I think that the real reason my mother wanted me have a Bar Mitzvah was so that she could entertain. My brother-in-law Eddie bought me my first suit, for the occasion. Eddie was a wonderful and caring person, and I miss him dearly.

A ***chance*** meeting occurred between my sister Connee and a dentist, Dr. Lind. They were both eating in a luncheonette, strangers to each other. Connee was sixteen and had graduated from high school. She was working as a secretary. Dr. Lind offered her a job as a dental assistant. His offer was five dollars a week more than she was making. Connee had no experience in dentistry, but Dr. Lind didn't care. She took the job and worked with him for decades. Dr. Lind became my dentist. It appeared to me that the work he did was interesting, easy and he apparently made a lot of money. These observations started me thinking about becoming a dentist. This ***chance*** meeting changed my life forever.

Today, at age eighty-five, Connee remains strong, sharp as a tack, and works full time as Executive Vice President for her son Brian's real estate company, Silbert Realty and Management Company, Inc., in New Jersey.

Ring bearer for my sister's wedding

Living in Florida

My first recollection of Florida is sitting on a small toy train locomotive. I also remember liking pony rides, even though the ponies frightened me for some reason.

As I got older, I frequently played tackle football. At first I was afraid of getting hurt, but quickly learned that the grass was very thick and soft, so when I was tackled it almost felt like falling on a mattress.

My father took me fishing from a bridge once in Biscayne Bay, near Miami. We caught about ten fish. My father put the fish into the trunk of his car, which was parked near the water. At least I thought I saw him do that. When I turned around, I saw all of the fish floating away. My father said he didn't know what happened, nor did I.

I had a paper route and I delivered papers to houses using my bike. I also sold them to people in cars at a busy intersection. I worked on commission. If I had extra papers, my father bought them, so I earned a little more money than I really deserved.

Going to School on My Bike.

Tooth Decay on the Way

While in Florida, I developed a ritual on Monday, Wednesday, and Friday evenings. At 7:30 p.m. I would climb into my bed with a package of chocolate covered graham crackers. I would turn on the radio and begin listening to "The Lone Ranger."

Then, I would start eating the crackers in my unique way. I could see all of my crackers because they were wrapped in a cellophane package. I ate them at a pace that would allow me to finish the last cracker (yes, I ate the whole package of crackers) just as the program ended. My mind was satiated with the exciting story, and my stomach with all of the crackers; it was now time to go to sleep.

There was a big problem with my ritual, and I found out about it the hard way. I didn't brush my teeth before I went to sleep, and no one noticed. I developed rampant tooth decay because of this habit. My first dentist never used local anesthetic when he drilled into a tooth. He used a slow speed, belt driven drill, and this was true torture. I still shudder when I think of it.

Loch Sheldrake, Thunderstorms, School, and Stories

All of my summers were happily spent in Loch Sheldrake, until 1952, when I was thirteen years old. That was the year my father's bungalow colony was seized and our house in Loch Sheldrake taken away. Loch Sheldrake and its lake were my favorite places on earth. One important reason it was wonderful living there, is that it gave me the freedom to get away from my parents constant quarreling, which was terrifying to me.

I learned how to fish in Loch Sheldrake Lake, which was small in area, but very, very deep. So deep, in fact, that Murder Incorporated, an organized crime group in the 1930s and 1940s in New York State, buried bodies in the lake. They tied heavy weights, sometimes slot machines, to the bodies so that they would not float to the surface. Connee remembers walking by a body that was taken out of the lake by the New York State Police.

Loch Sheldrake Lake

Red Apple Rest

During the 1940s and early 1950s, in the spring, my parents spent all of the weekends at the bungalow colony, trying to rent bungalows. We traveled to and from there on Fridays and Mondays, so I often missed school on those days. During our drive to Loch Sheldrake I got more excited and happier with each passing mile. During our long trip we always stopped at The Red Apple Rest, where we used the facilities and got something to eat—usually a hot dog for me.

Eggs

When I was three or four years old, I did not like eggs, and I refused to eat them. One day my father brought home a live, squirming and cackling chicken. He fenced off a small area in our back yard for the chicken. I thought it was a pet for me.

A few days later, at breakfast time, my father came in with an egg from my chicken, encouraging me to eat it. He said that it would taste great because it was so fresh, and the egg came from my own chicken! He was right. For the rest of that summer I ate a yummy egg almost every morning. The egg was soft boiled, served in a cup with some white bread, a dab of butter, and a little salt. Who wouldn't like to eat that? Years later, I learned from my family, than my chicken had been a rooster!

My Egg Laying Rooster

Making a Thunderstorm

The weather in Loch Sheldrake was always a major turn-on for me, and I mean major! I loved the frequent, and sometimes severe, late afternoon thunderstorms. I noticed that the thunderstorms always seem to come from the same direction, the far side of the lake.

When only about five or six I learned that clouds and thunderstorms needed water to form. So, one day, I sat down on the hot sidewalk and poured a glass of water onto it, hoping to make a thunderstorm, or at least a cloud. The water quickly dried up and the sky remained clear. These were the first indications of my interest in the weather.

A Pickle Dunking

There was an old-fashioned country store in Loch Sheldrake, Kove's General Store. My parents had a charge account there, and then food was readily available. The store always smelled great to me, especially the kosher dill pickles, which were being fermented in a large open wooden barrel. I have always really loved kosher dill pickles, and the more garlic the better!

One day that I'll never forget, the owner of the store, Irving Kove, grabbed me by my ankles, turned me upside down, and put me headfirst into the pickle barrel, but not low enough to get my head wet. I was scared, but the smell was fabulous! Pickles became somewhat important to me later in life, as you will find out.

Fishing

Me, age 13

In Loch Sheldrake, fortunately for me, I found interest in healthy activities. I enjoyed watching the weather, fishing, playing softball, swimming, hunting small game, and playing the pinball machines. After about age seven I was able to leave my house on my own and go about my activities. I caught my first fish one evening after dinner. I remember leaving the dinner table, taking a fishing rod, a pail, a few worms, and going to the lake, which was only a few blocks away. I caught my first fish, a sunfish, perhaps four inches long. I was excited and proud! Someone took the fish off the hook for me and put water in the pail, along with the fish. I ran home, pail in hand with water splashing on me, but I didn't care. When I got home I showed my family my catch. The fish was swimming around happily. I put the pail on the back porch, planning to play with the fish the next morning. When morning came, the fish was floating on its back.

As I got older, the first thing I did when I got to Loch Sheldrake each spring was to get ready to go fishing. I would get a shovel, a coffee can, and go to my favorite spot to dig worms. My worm place was next to a white picket fence behind a particular bungalow. The soil was always moist there, and I never had trouble getting all the worms I wanted for bait.

My next step was to get my ten-foot wooden rowboat ready to use. Before I could use the rowboat, I had to make it watertight. The boat lay overturned for the winter on the shore, so the deck boards dried up and contracted, leaving spaces between the boards. The boat would sink when put into the water. While sunk, the water would expand the boards, and they would become watertight. This took a day or two and then the boat was safe to use. I fished from shore while my boat was becoming floatable. When the boat was ready, I would gather my fishing gear, which consisted of a tackle box, a spinning rod, my can of worms, and two oars. I walked to my boat carrying all of this gear. Fishing was always great in the spring. I would often catch over fifty yellow perch in just a few hours. Many times, the bottom of my rowboat would become totally covered with fish, and it became hard for me to move around. I put the fish on stringers made from lily pads. I took the stringers home loaded with fish. My mother was not interested in cooking the fish, so they were given away.

My niece Sheryl and I, at Loch Sheldrake Lake

Malcolm

My best buddy Malcolm and I had great fun together. Malcolm was a curly redhead with a round face along with acres of freckles on his entire body. His parents rented a bungalow every summer for as long as I can remember.

Malcolm and I fished together several times a week. He was a fantastic fisherman, always out-fishing me, and I was pretty good. I remember one evening in particular. We were trolling our fishing lines while rowing to the far end of the lake, to a place called Chinese Alley.

I have no idea where that name came from, but it stuck. The Alley was quite shallow, and filled with water lilies. There was always a sweet marshy scent there, and the Alley was home to legions of pickerel and bass; it was a great place to fish. That evening, while we were trolling, Malcolm caught three nice size bass. He was fishing on the shoreline side of the boat.

My line was on the outside, and I did not have one tug on my line, let alone catch a fish! Malcolm always seemed to catch more fish than I. We both caught some fish in Chinese Alley, and when it began to get dark, we started rowing back. I said to Malcolm, "I want to fish on the shoreline side on the way back, and you can fish on the outside." You guessed it: Malcolm caught a few more bass on our trip back, but no fish ever thought of looking at my line!

During the daytime when Malcolm and I fished, usually in Chinese Alley, we got pretty hot. We always planned to cool off by swimming when we got back. We would take turns rowing on our way back. By design, regardless of who was rowing, an oar would somehow splash water on the other guy, who would shout, "Hey, watch out, you got me wet!" We both knew that the splash was intentional, and that there would be many more splashes. By the time we got back, both of us would be totally drenched, a bit cooler, and ready to jump into the lake with our clothes on. We had a fabulous time as you can imagine, kids with no responsibilities, planning their next adventure.

One day, I received a surprise when I got home. I called it "blue balls." When I took my dungarees (now called jeans) off, my very private parts had turned blue! I believe that this happened because the dye in the dungarees wasn't "fixed," and the blue dye bled onto my skin. This sight was scary to see, but it has made for an interesting memory. I have tried very hard to find Malcolm using the Internet, but I have not succeeded.

One day, when I was twelve, I was in my rowboat, alone. I was about one hundred fifty feet out from the beach, which was crowded with mothers and children, many of them in the water. An old, second-hand, four-cylinder, five and a half horsepower Evinrude outboard motor was propelling my boat. Suddenly, my motor burst into flames. I knew that you could not put out a gasoline fire with water, but I splashed the engine with water a few times anyway. The flames grew bigger. I shouted as loud as I could to the people on the beach, "Fire! Fire! Get out of the water. Clear the beach."

Frightened, I jumped out of the boat, pushing it away from the shore, and swam to shore as fast as I could. I helped people get out of the water and got the others to leave the beach. My motor exploded a few minutes later. The explosion ripped off the back of my rowboat, and the motor sank to the bottom of the lake.

As it turned out, there was really little danger to anyone in the water or on the beach. Firemen from the Loch Sheldrake Volunteer Fire Department arrived, but there was nothing for them to do. My rowboat had floated away and was eventually found and repaired, but I rowed the boat from then on. No more used, cheap, second-hand motors for me!

Softball

Another great activity for me was playing on our bungalow colony's softball team. On weekends our colony's softball team played teams from surrounding hotels.

We had an excellent team, and at the age of twelve I was a member, primarily because my brother-in-law Eddie was the captain. Eddie had been a professional baseball player before he was called up to the Army to serve in WWII.

Our team was outstanding and we had terrific games, frequently beating teams from prominent surrounding hotels. Those weekend ball games were fabulous, and have created great memories for me.

Junior at Bat

A Very Young Driver

There was an old, unregistered, 1936 Pontiac parked next to our house in Loch Sheldrake. It may have once belonged to my grandmother, and the car still ran. I got the key for it when I was eleven years old. The car had a memorable damp and musty smell, and a three-speed stick-shift transmission; I taught myself how to drive it. During the fall and spring, when the bungalow colony was empty, I drove that car like a Nascar racer! Since my father owned the land, the bungalow colony, and its streets, there didn't appear to be a legal issue, and no one objected to my driving. The streets were unpaved and had a red shale or gravel surface, so the tires made a neat, crunchy sound while I drove. I spent a lot of time zipping and zooming up and down all of the streets; that really was a blast!

My first car!

Hurleyville School

School in the Mountains

When living in Loch Sheldrake during parts of the fall and spring, I attended fifth, sixth and seventh grades in a one room schoolhouse, in the nearby town of Hurleyville. My transportation was a school bus. Our classroom desks were moveable, and our teacher, Mr. Nathan Gainen, was a mandolin player. Every day at 11:30 a.m. it was time to square dance. We would move our desks to the side of the room, creating space for a dance floor. Mr. Gainen would start strumming on his mandolin, and we were taught to square dance. This half an hour was a lot of fun. From noon to 1:00 p.m., we had lunch in a small cafeteria in the basement. I remember the food as always being tasty.

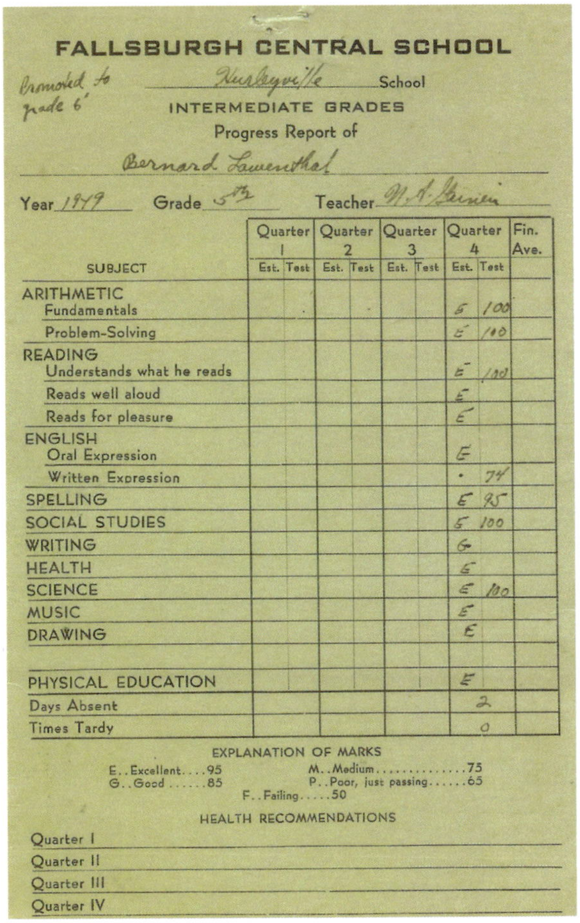

FALLSBURGH CENTRAL SCHOOL

Promoted to grade 6

Hurleyville School

INTERMEDIATE GRADES

Progress Report of

Bernard Lowenthal

Year 1949 Grade 5th Teacher N. A. Gainen

SUBJECT	Quarter 1 Est.	Quarter 1 Test	Quarter 2 Est.	Quarter 2 Test	Quarter 3 Est.	Quarter 3 Test	Quarter 4 Est.	Quarter 4 Test	Fin. Ave.
ARITHMETIC Fundamentals							E	100	
Problem-Solving							E	100	
READING Understands what he reads							E	100	
Reads well aloud							E		
Reads for pleasure							E		
ENGLISH Oral Expression							E		
Written Expression							•	74	
SPELLING							E	95	
SOCIAL STUDIES							E	100	
WRITING							G		
HEALTH							E		
SCIENCE							E	100	
MUSIC							E		
DRAWING							E		
PHYSICAL EDUCATION							E		
Days Absent							2		
Times Tardy							0		

EXPLANATION OF MARKS

E..Excellent....95 M..Medium..............75
G..Good......85 P..Poor, just passing......65
F..Failing.....50

HEALTH RECOMMENDATIONS

Quarter I
Quarter II
Quarter III
Quarter IV

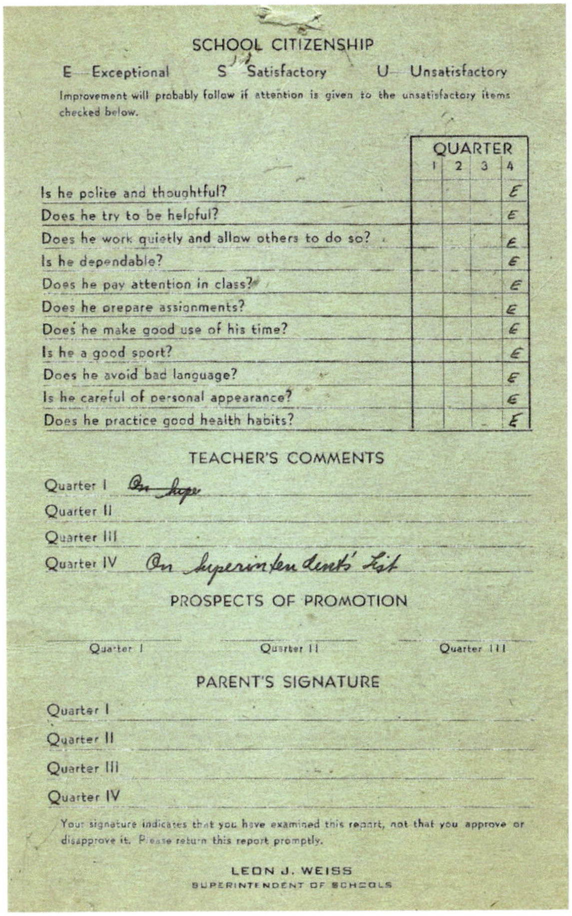

SCHOOL CITIZENSHIP

E—Exceptional S—Satisfactory U—Unsatisfactory

Improvement will probably follow if attention is given to the unsatisfactory items checked below.

	QUARTER 1	2	3	4
Is he polite and thoughtful?				E
Does he try to be helpful?				E
Does he work quietly and allow others to do so?				E
Is he dependable?				E
Does he pay attention in class?				E
Does he prepare assignments?				E
Does he make good use of his time?				E
Is he a good sport?				E
Does he avoid bad language?				E
Is he careful of personal appearance?				E
Does he practice good health habits?				E

TEACHER'S COMMENTS

Quarter I [illegible]
Quarter II
Quarter III
Quarter IV On Superintendents' List

PROSPECTS OF PROMOTION

Quarter I Quarter II Quarter III

PARENT'S SIGNATURE

Quarter I
Quarter II
Quarter III
Quarter IV

Your signature indicates that you have examined this report, not that you approve or disapprove it. Please return this report promptly.

LEON J. WEISS
SUPERINTENDENT OF SCHOOLS

My 5th Grade Report Card from Mr. Gainen

A Party

I was invited to attend a party, on a Friday night, at a classmate's house, near Loch Sheldrake. I had no idea what to expect, and I was a little nervous because I was the new kid in town. There were about eight to ten sixth and seventh grade boys and girls at the party. We sat down to play Spin the Bottle, the first time ever for me, and I was a quick learner! After that, some slow music was turned on, and a girl, Audrey, asked me to dance.

Audrey was very thin, cute, had short dark hair, and was and full of energy. We'd danced for just a minute, and then the lights went out! Audrey grabbed me, and started kissing me—ferociously. This was the first kiss I ever received from a non-relative, and it was a truly memorable experience, dating back sixty-three years now!

Young Love

During my last summer in Loch Sheldrake, I met an absolutely gorgeous, blonde, thirteen year-old girl, Billie. She was mature for her age, and had a figure that belied her thirteen years. She was a ballet dancer with very attractive muscular legs. We became friendly, and I invited her to roast marshmallows with me and another couple, after dark. I planned to go to a secluded area in the woods near the lake, one that I frequented, and knew very well. Of course, besides the marshmallows I had other things in mind. I was not quite sure exactly what the other things were.

One evening, I led our two couples down a dirt road, and into the woods. It was getting dark, and chilly. I built a small campfire, and the four of us huddled around it. We toasted marshmallows, and I moved closer to Billie. I bent over to give her a kiss, and she drew closer to me. ***The kiss was fabulous,*** and it was the second kiss I was ever given by someone not related to me!

A few minutes later I heard a siren far off in the distance. It seemed to be getting louder. Being an anxious person, I had this foolish thought that maybe the police were looking for us; how silly! I was becoming more concerned as the siren grew still louder, and I put the fire out. The four of us got back on to the road, and started walking toward home. All of a sudden, the bright headlights and the flashers on the top of a police car were heading right at us. My ***fear*** was realized; ***the police were looking for us!*** The police car stopped right in front of us, and I was really scared. A policeman and Billie's father jumped out of the car, and ran toward us. Billie and her father, who was screaming at her, were put in the back seat, and I was put in the front seat. The other couple just walked away.

I was taken home, where my father was waiting for me. I'd never had a real conversation or any advice from him, and I was afraid of his temper. I was trembling when I saw him. He had me sit down on the edge of a bed where he was sitting. His total advice for me was this (I remember it word for word): ***"A gentleman never takes a lady into the woods at night."***

That was it, not another word! It was, and remains, the only advice I remember ever receiving from him.

The next morning, while I was at the lake, Billie's father found and accosted me. He screamed at me using foul language, pushed me up against a concrete wall, and threatened me with bodily harm if I ever spoke to Billie again. I didn't.

Attempted Suicide

After school one day, as I got off the school bus, I saw a number of people, along with a group of uniformed New York State Police, standing in front of a bungalow near my house. I learned that, in an attempt to commit suicide, my mother had hanged herself, in a closet, in the bungalow—but she was still alive. She went on living until age ninety-two, smoking and all.

A Rifle

I still have my first rifle

When I was ten years old, I convinced my father to buy me a .22 caliber rifle from a friend of his. I was ecstatic. Neither my father or his friend knew anything about guns. I was able, on my own, to learn all about guns and gun safety. I spent many days each summer, alone in the woods and fields, hunting squirrels, crows (I was never able to shoot a crow), woodchucks, and rabbits. I meandered all around the area's woodlands, where I found fields that most people probably did not know existed, and small streams that held fish. I felt like a true explorer! My parents had no clue where I was most of the time, but I always turned up for lunch and dinner. We did have plenty of food when we lived in Loch Sheldrake.

Late one fall day, after all the renters had gone home and the bungalows were empty, I started to hunt for rabbits around the bungalows. My father asked his handyman, Walter, to follow me to make sure that I was safe. I don't know why my father did this, but I laughed to myself because I knew that Walter was an irresponsible, toothless old drunk. I walked slowly down "Laurel Lane," rifle in hand, to hunt rabbits. I turned around surreptitiously several times to see how Walter was doing. He was doing just fine, stumbling along with his head tilted back, while sucking on a bottle of whiskey! A while later, I found Walter lying on the ground, sleeping and snoring, so I went happily on my way hunting rabbits.

I had no idea why I wanted to shoot rabbits, or anything else; perhaps because it was a ***challenge***? No one ever told me that hunting was cruel. I came to this conclusion myself much later in life, and I haven't hunted for years. I treasure life, all animals, and I have a strong aversion to having any animal harmed. I do enjoy target shooting. I remember taking some rabbit's feet home to my apartment in Flushing and putting them in my socks drawer for good luck. It seems to have worked!

In the wintertime, my father occasionally took trips to Loch Sheldrake. I always asked him to take me with him, which he sometimes did. I wanted to be in the snow! I really loved snow, and usually Flushing had very little. During these trips I kept looking carefully for any snow. We traveled north from New York City into southern New York State, where I frequently would see small accumulations of snow. Further north, in Loch Sheldrake, there would almost always be a lot of snow, the lake would be frozen, and it might even be snowing! This was paradise for me; the only problem was that we were going back home the same day, so my fun was short lived. As time went on, the weather, particularly snow, influenced my life, as you will learn.

My Idol, Stan Musial

My Idol

At about age nine, although I didn't understand it at the time, I was looking for a father figure. Stan Musial, an outstanding baseball player, and a gentleman, turned out to be the man for whom I was searching.

I became enthralled with Stan to such a great extent that it is hard for me to describe. I learned about him and his illustrious career using newspapers, the radio, and television. I read countless articles and books written about his life, and to this day I watch videotapes about him. Stan Musial is my hero, and my true idol. I was attracted to him not only because of his baseball skills, but just as importantly, because of his gentlemanly conduct both on and off the baseball field. Stan Musial, unlike almost all other baseball players, was never ejected from a baseball game. He was elected to the Baseball Hall of Fame the first year in which he was eligible.

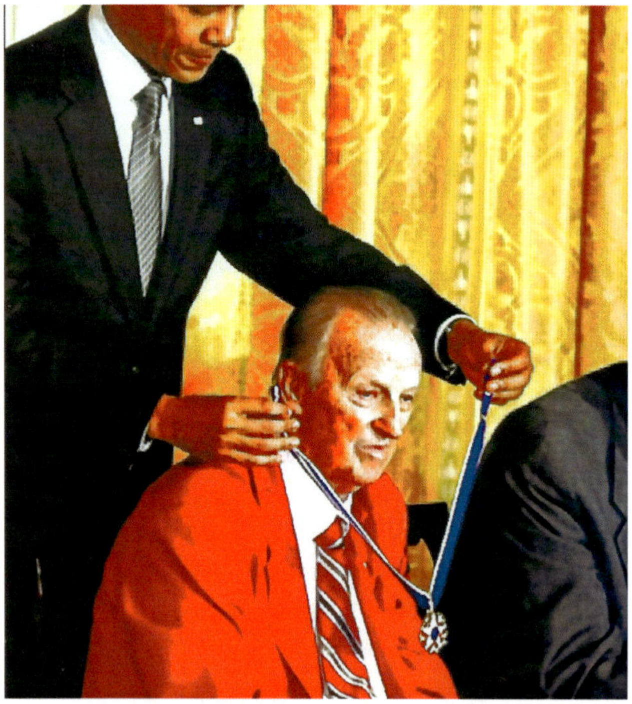

Receiving The Presidential Medal of Freedom

Stan Musial

It is said that emulation is the sincerest form of flattery, and I wanted to emulate Stan Musial, on and off the field. Stan was a left-handed hitter, and I was a right-handed hitter. I taught myself how to hit left-handed. Here's how I did it: There was large pile of small stones, maybe one inch or so in diameter, near the lake in Loch Sheldrake. I started my left-handed hitting training by hitting these rocks, left handed, into the lake. Splash!

Hitting left-handed was difficult at first, but I got better and better. While holding a bat in my left hand, I would toss a stone into the air with my right hand. While the stone was up a foot or two in the air, I would grab the bat with my free right hand, and swing it at the stone with both hands, "left handed." I did this training many times a week, performing hundreds of "at bats." My timing got so good that I could toss a stone into the air, and with my eyes closed, swing the bat and hit the stone pretty consistently.

I would play games, the right-handed swing vs. the left handed swing. Eventually, for reasons I don't understand, I could hit the stones (later baseballs) further left-handed than right-handed. I was becoming ***persistent*** at an early age.

In 1976 I had the extraordinary and wonderful pleasure of meeting Stan in his St. Louis restaurant. As you can imagine, I was nervous, happy, and awed, all at the same time. Stan Musial was awarded The Presidential Medal of Freedom in 2011. This medal is given for "especially meritorious contribution in cultural or other significant or private endeavors." ***My childhood instincts were right on the money!***

My man-cave is filled with his memorabilia, most of it signed by him. In 1963 Stan Musial announced his retirement. I knew that this would happen some day, but I wasn't prepared for it. I was twenty-five years old when I learned about this, and I cried all night. Stan Musial passed away as I was writing about him for this book.

Living in Flushing

Some of my fondest school memories from Flushing are from the seventh and eighth grades at P.S. 20, where I had rather unique experiences. My teacher for both years was Mrs. Helena Lake. Mrs. Lake was a pleasant, gray-haired, and soft-spoken teacher. I was a very quiet, introverted, and a shy young boy. Somehow or another, over those two years I became "the teacher's pet," and an important part of P.S. 20's day-to-day functioning. We had a school assembly held in the school auditorium on Tuesday mornings. When our national anthem was played, a color guard marched onto the auditorium's stage. I was appointed the captain of the color guard, and I carried the American flag for two years of our assemblies.

The girls in the seventh grade began flirting with me. Gail Collura, a very sweet and quiet girl, became my girlfriend—until we started high school. Gail had a fine soprano voice and sang in our school plays. She once sang "La Vie en Rose," staring at me intensely for the entire song. I was chosen to play the male lead role in two plays. I was Frosty the Snowman in seventh grade, a role I loved because I loved snow. I was costumed as a snowman, covered with large sheets of white crepe paper, along with a top hat and a pipe. All I had to do was turn around slowly, as my classmates sang "Frosty the Snowman."

In the eighth grade I had the lead role in a comedy that involved my on-stage sister, played by Gail. I still remember one line I had to say, a pun, in a pretty silly story. It seemed that my sister's boyfriend might have been poisoned. The boyfriend was unresponsive, and my sister said, "Maybe he has ptomaine poisoning." My line was, "Why don't you take off his shoes and see?"

Special Student

During the eighth grade I was for some reason considered to be a special student. The school principal, Mr. Louis W. Phillips, assigned me to be in charge of the school's audio-visual system. This meant that I would have to leave my classroom frequently to show films to other classes, or to prepare the school's audio system for audio feeds to the classrooms for talks by Mr. Phillips, or for radio broadcasts.

The school's 16mm. movie projector was quite heavy. I had a helper, Richard Walker—a big, strong, soft-spoken friend—who would frequently accompany me. Guess who carried the projector? This all evolved into the fact that I had the run of the school! I could leave my classroom at any time, without a pass, no questions asked. No one ever questioned Bernard, at any time, when he was walking in the halls or anywhere else! This was amazing; I felt that I had teachers' privileges.

"Too Sick to Play Ball?"

I became excellent at playing baseball and basketball, usually with boys older than I. When sides were being chosen, I felt good to be picked first most of the time. After school, while I was playing basketball in my schoolyard, an older lady would occasionally come by and say hello to me. I wasn't sure who she was; I thought that perhaps she was a relative. I found out, after she died, that she was my Aunt Norma, my mother's sister. She left me five thousand dollars in her will. I was told that she left me the money because I stopped playing and took the time to talk to her. I was the only person in my family that Norma recognized in her will.

In June of my final year at P.S. 20, I became ill with a bad sore throat. A doctor gave me an injection of penicillin, and I stayed home in bed for a number of days. My class, Class 8-1, was scheduled to be in a softball playoff game with another class for the school championship. Around noon, the day of the game, my doorbell rang. When I opened the door, a few of the players from my class's softball team were standing there. They said that they needed me, and they urged me to come and play in the championship game. I agreed to play; I loved to play ball!

I got dressed, put on my sneakers, grabbed my baseball glove and bat (I had to use my own bat; the school's bats weren't good enough for this rising star), and I went to the schoolyard, where the game was to be played. Mrs. Lake was there watching her class team getting ready to play. She was probably wondering how Bernard, who didn't attend class that morning because he was sick, was well enough to play ball. I was a shortstop and switch hitter. I doubt Mrs. Lake knew that her teacher's pet was also a good athlete, but she was about to find out.

I switch hit, and I went to bat a number of times. I got a hit every time; it was very easy for me, and I fielded flawlessly at shortstop. My team won by a large margin. That was the end of my activities at P.S. 20, except for graduation. Graduation was not memorable; my parents did not attend it, the only family member who came to my eighth grade graduation was my sister Connee.

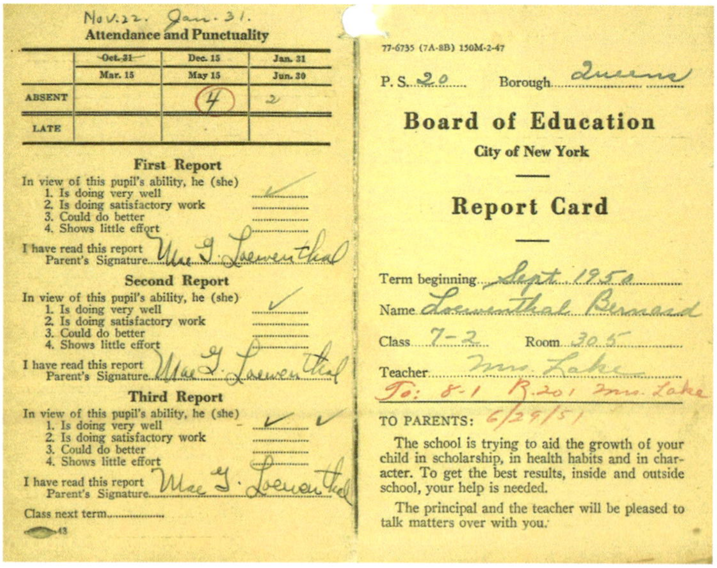

Nov. 22. Jan. 31.

Attendance and Punctuality

	Oct. 31 / Mar. 15	Dec. 15 / May 15	Jan. 31 / Jun. 30
ABSENT		4	2
LATE			

First Report
In view of this pupil's ability, he (she)
1. Is doing very well ✓
2. Is doing satisfactory work
3. Could do better
4. Shows little effort

I have read this report
Parent's Signature Mae G. Loewenthal

Second Report
In view of this pupil's ability, he (she)
1. Is doing very well ✓
2. Is doing satisfactory work
3. Could do better
4. Shows little effort

I have read this report
Parent's Signature Mae G. Loewenthal

Third Report
In view of this pupil's ability, he (she)
1. Is doing very well ✓ ✓
2. Is doing satisfactory work
3. Could do better
4. Shows little effort

I have read this report
Parent's Signature Mae G. Loewenthal

Class next term

43

77-6735 (7A-8B) 150M-2-47

P. S. 20 Borough Queens

Board of Education

City of New York

Report Card

Term beginning Sept. 1950

Name Loewenthal Bernard

Class 7-2 Room 305

Teacher Mrs. Lake

To: 8-1 R. 201 Mrs. Lake

TO PARENTS: 6/29/51

The school is trying to aid the growth of your child in scholarship, in health habits and in character. To get the best results, inside and outside school, your help is needed.

The principal and the teacher will be pleased to talk matters over with you.

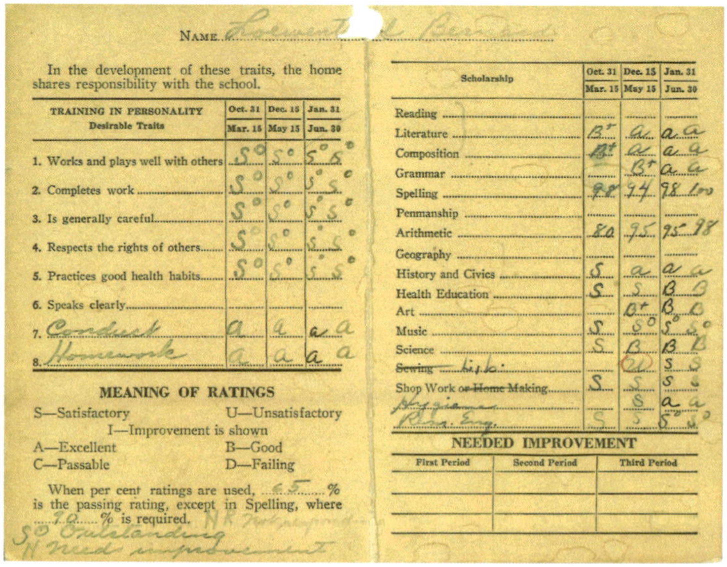

NAME

In the development of these traits, the home shares responsibility with the school.

TRAINING IN PERSONALITY Desirable Traits	Oct. 31 / Mar. 15	Dec. 15 / May 15	Jan. 31 / Jun. 30
1. Works and plays well with others	S°	S°	S° S°
2. Completes work	S°	S°	S° S°
3. Is generally careful	S°	S°	S° S°
4. Respects the rights of others	S°	S°	S° S°
5. Practices good health habits	S°	S°	S° S°
6. Speaks clearly			
7. Conduct	a	a	a a
8. Homework	a	a	a a

MEANING OF RATINGS

S—Satisfactory U—Unsatisfactory
I—Improvement is shown
A—Excellent B—Good
C—Passable D—Failing

When per cent ratings are used, 65 % is the passing rating, except in Spelling, where 90 % is required.

Scholarship	Oct. 31 / Mar. 15	Dec. 15 / May 15	Jan. 31 / Jun. 30
Reading			
Literature	B+	a	a a
Composition	B+	a	a a
Grammar		B+	a a
Spelling	98	94	98 100
Penmanship			
Arithmetic	80	95	95 98
Geography			
History and Civics	S	a	a a
Health Education	S	S	B B
Art		B+	B B
Music	S	S°	S° S°
Science	S	B	B B
~~Sewing~~			S S
Shop Work ~~or Home Making~~	S	S	S S
Hygiene		S	a a
	S	S	S° S°

NEEDED IMPROVEMENT

First Period	Second Period	Third Period

My 7th Grade Report Card

In my eighth grade graduation picture ***I am the last boy on the right, in the top boy's row. Gail Collura (my girlfriend), is second from the right, in the bottom girl's row.***

My 8th Grade Class

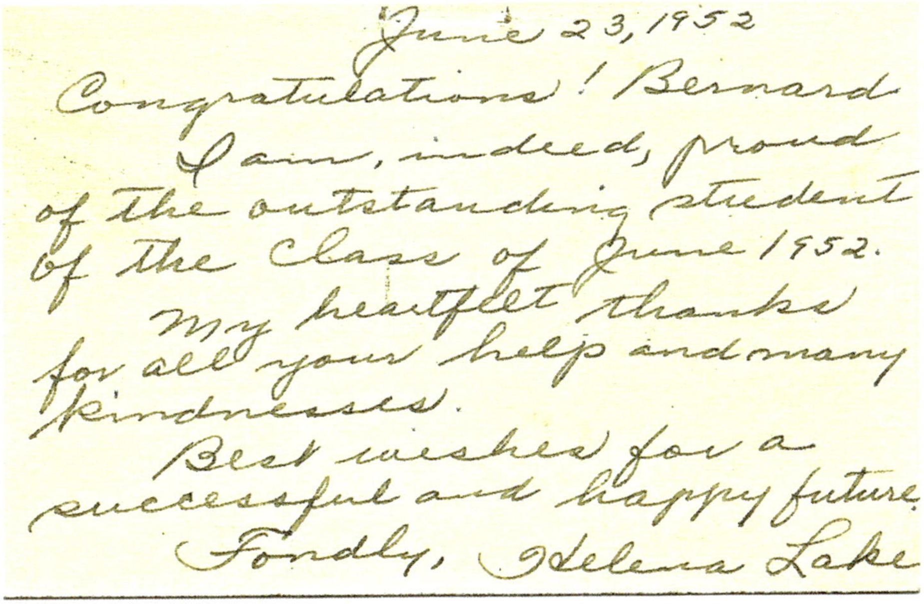

June 23, 1952
Congratulations! Bernard
I am, indeed, proud
of the outstanding student
of the Class of June 1952.
My heartfelt thanks
for all your help and many
kindnesses.
Best wishes for a
successful and happy future.
Fondly, Helena Lake

An Unexpected Card From My Teacher After Graduation

My Last Happy Summer in Loch Sheldrake

After my eighth grade graduation it was off to Loch Sheldrake for the summer. It was to be my last summer living in my house there, but I didn't know it. My sore throat returned, along with a high fever, soon after I arrived. The local country doctor, Dr. Jacobs, administered another injection of penicillin. My sister June was with me that day. The penicillin injection turned out to be life threatening. The timing of the injection, just a few weeks after my previous injection, created a violent allergic reaction.

I broke out in hives, starting on my abdomen, and they spread to my whole body. My itching was relentless. The skin over my belly got bright red and thickened remarkably. I had to vomit, and I got to the bathroom, vomited, and then fainted. When I fell, I knocked the bathroom door closed, and my sister could not open the door. I eventually was put back into bed, and Dr. Jacobs came back and injected me with adrenalin. I felt better not long afterward. This was a dreadful start to my summer.

During that summer I met Arnee, who was a few years older than I. We met by ***chance*** while playing softball. I played shortstop. Arnee played third base, and we were a good combination.

I was about to enter Flushing High School that fall, and Arnee told me that he worked in a supermarket near my high school. He asked me to visit him. As you will read, this visit greatly impacted my life because I got my first real and memorable job because of it.

Loss of the Bungalow Colony

My parents' loss of their bungalow colony late in 1952, their only source of income, remains one of the most traumatic events in my life. Nothing was ever the same after that occurred. Food became scarce, and I lost my ability to spend my summers in Loch Sheldrake, where the happiest times of my life had been spent. I was truly devastated, and I had to find a job.

My parents were never going back to Loch Sheldrake. However, I felt compelled to go back the following summer; I just needed to be there. I found a job as a lifeguard at a small hotel, The Brookside, only a quarter of a mile from my old house, on the same side of the road.

At age fourteen I didn't really have the necessary skills to be a lifeguard, but I could clean the pool. I slept in a shack with the waiters and busboys, and I was allowed to eat in the dining room after the guests had eaten (reminiscent of home). Food had become a very important issue for me.

Sometimes I would walk down the road, passing by my old house. I was jealous of the new family that I could see living in what was my house only a year before. I would meet a few friends, mostly adults, who couldn't understand why I was there. When I was alone, feeling very alone indeed, I sometimes cried. I don't believe my parents missed me or cared where I was that summer, I was on my own.

Fifty years later, I went back to Loch Sheldrake. I should not have done that. To my sorrow, I found the house that I'd cherished so much, lay in ruin. Roads and houses replaced the woods and fields I loved so much as a boy. The bungalows remained, now privately owned. They had not changed very much, but everything looked much smaller to me.

My old house lay in ruin

Chapter 2

1952-1960: High School, Working, College, and Marriage

In 1952, when I started high school, my home life was becoming even worse as a result of my parents losing their only source of income. Our apartment was usually empty and quiet, with very little food. I frequently did not know where my parents were, except at night, when they were usually at home.

My sister Connee lived with her husband, Eddie, and her children, a few subway stops away from Flushing. I loved to visit them, and Connee probably noticed that I showed up usually around dinnertime. I was welcome, and I always had an excellent dinner. I do not believe that Connee realized that there was a lack of food at home.

I knew that I had to get a job, but I had no idea where or how to start looking. I walked anxiously to my first day of high school, unsure of what to expect. I registered and got my class schedule. When I finished, I walked up Union Street, beyond the high school, to see if I could find the supermarket where Arnee worked, and I found it. The store was large and modern, owned by a supermarket chain named Daitch Shopwell. I walked into the store timidly, looking for Arnee, but I didn't see him.

I was about to walk back out when a tall man with curly red hair, wearing a blue store jacket, asked if he could help me. I told him that I was looking for Arnee, and he said that Arnee wasn't working today. He looked me up and down, and then said, "Are you looking for a job?" I immediately said yes. I was hired right on the spot—talk about ***chance***!

The man, Norman Weinberg, was the manager of the store. He asked me if I had working papers; I didn't know what those were. He said that I had to get working papers because of my young age. He told me where to go to apply for them, which I did immediately. Since one of my parents had to sign the papers, one or both of them knew I had a job.

With working papers in hand, I went back to the store to start my job. Norman talked with me, showed me around the store, and then told me what my duties and wages would be. My job was to sweep the floor, put returned soda bottles in their proper places, and bring in the shopping carts from outside. I knew that I could handle these tasks easily. He told me that my salary would be fifty cents an hour. The store was open every day, except Sunday. It closed at 6:00 p.m. daily, but stayed open until 9:00 p.m. on Thursdays and Fridays.

We decided that I would work after school every day, and until the store closed on Thursdays and Fridays, and all day Saturday. I averaged working about twenty-four hours a week. I was able to walk to school, then to the supermarket, and then back home. The walk home was long; it was the distance to school plus the distance to the supermarket, about two miles.

I attended Flushing High School for four years. I felt like an insignificant student, with only a few friends from P.S. 20. I did not have time to study, and I did poorly in my French class. My French teacher's name was Mrs. Worms. Every time I heard her name I thought about fishing! In French class, I did my best to slump way down in my seat, with my French book hiding my face, in the hope that Mrs. Worms wouldn't call on me. French was always a real struggle for me, but my philosophy that: ***Much of life happens for the best and for our highest good and learning. Undesirable and bad things do happen, but occasionally they have a positive effect—given time***, proved to be quite accurate for me in a few years.

While in high school, I had very little time for myself. The days of frequent baseball and basketball games were pretty much gone. On Sundays, if I saw people playing basketball in the park across the street from my apartment, rather than choosing to study, I would put my sneakers on and run out to play. Albert Lanes, Stanley Lanes' younger brother, was a good friend, and we played sports together. Albert was several years older than I. We usually played basketball or stickball with a few friends of his, who later became good friends of mine. Albert lived a block away from me.

One of the nicest memories I have is going to a delicatessen, "The Laurel," with Albert after playing ball. We always had hot dogs with deli mustard, relish, sauerkraut, and a Dr. Brown's soda. I don't know who savored these times more, Albert or me.

Infatuation

There was a girl named Ann in many of my high school classes. She was a cute, petite blonde, incredibly intelligent, and always scoring nineties or higher on all of our tests. I was attracted to her and I ***persistently*** watched her ponytail bobbing around for three years. But I was simply too shy to talk to her. I only had enough courage to say hello when we passed in the hall.

Finally, after three years of yearning to spend some time with her, I got up the courage to ask her for a date, and she said yes. She gave me her address and I went to her house by bus for our date; we decided to go to a movie. We took a bus to the theatre. I bought tickets and popcorn and we took our seats. There was an ice cream parlor called Jan's next to the theatre and after the movie I asked Ann if she would like an ice cream soda. She said that would be nice, so we went to Jan's and had sodas.

I took Ann home on the bus, and said good night to her at her front door. A goodnight kiss just didn't feel right to me, so I got on a bus and went home. I don't know what chemistry was missing, but following my first date with Ann, I had no desire to see her again. Go figure?

I had a narrow escape from having a serious physical beating by Joe Marconi, a guy in my high school gym class; Joe was very muscular, and had huge biceps. I didn't know anything about him. An incident occurred in my outdoor gym class. The boys were lined up single file, in parallel rows. Joe was standing on my right, in the row next to me, and he spit on my sneaker. I looked at him and said, as a ***challenge***, something like, "Don't ever do that again!" Thankfully he didn't.

A few weeks later, after school, a large crowd gathered in front of the school. There was going to be a fight, and Joe was one of the fighters. Joe pummeled the other person into a bloody mess. I thought how lucky I was not to have been the other guy! It turned out that Joe was a boxer, a known bully, with ties to the mob. ***Whew, was I lucky!***

"BLT Down, Hold the Grass!"

I had lunch at a Whelan's Drug Store luncheonette occasionally. I loved bacon and I always ordered the same sandwich. I said for my order, "I'd like a bacon, lettuce, and tomato sandwich, on toast, with mayo, but no lettuce please."

The man that took my order always shouted back to the cook, ***"BLT down, hold the grass, mayo."*** I learned that this meant bacon, lettuce, and tomato; "hold the grass" meaning no lettuce, and "down" meaning toast. Boy, was I smart!

I still don't want "grass"

The Supermarket

I continued to work in the supermarket through my four years of high school and part of college. I ***persistently*** worked as hard as I could. Exactly two weeks after I began working, Norman came over to me while I was sweeping the floor and said, "You're doing a good job, and I'm giving you a raise to sixty-five cents an hour."

I was very happy to know that I as doing well, and I surely liked the raise. As the years went on, I did better and better in Norman's eyes. I advanced, and my duties changed. I was put in charge of the soda and candy aisles. I kept the shelves in these aisles filled and looking good. Every once in a while a candy package containing my favorite candy, chocolate covered malted milk balls, or Raisenets, would somehow get opened "accidentally," and I ate some. Today I would surely have to pay for anything that "accidentally" got opened and eaten.

I was promoted to work with the full-time employees in the grocery department. I was a good, fast worker, and the men appreciated me. One nice man, Sid, was of particular help to me with regard to bowling, as you will find out.

Norman again changed my responsibilities, giving me another promotion. He assigned me to write the lists that were used for stocking the grocery shelves. When I wasn't there, the men working full-time did this. I know that there was a little resentment having me, a kid, doing this, but I was simply following orders.

At this time, circa 1956, in New York City, it seemed as if all of the cashiers in the supermarkets were women. I was surprised when Norman asked me to learn how to become a cashier! I may have been the first male cashier in New York City, but I cannot be certain of this. I did very well as a cashier, and I learned how to give the correct amount change back, accurately, and very rapidly. I have retained this ability. Today, cash registers show the cashier how much change is due. When I am paying with cash, I know exactly what is due back, as I wait for my cashier and the machine to catch up!

Norman promoted me one more time. This time it was to be in charge of counting the day's receipts on Saturdays. He taught me how to go to each cash register, take the cash and checks, put them into an envelope, and mark the envelope appropriately.

When all of the cash registers were completed, I think there were ten of them, I would take all of the money up to the office, and I would start counting it. When everything jibed, I made out a deposit slip and put all of the money in a moneybag. Norman would drive us to the bank and, using a key, I would put the moneybag into a deposit vault on the bank's outside wall. This trip always required two people for safety; I believe Norman might have been carrying a gun. He had to drive since I was too young to have a license to drive.

Pranks

I always have, and still love to play practical jokes. I played a few on my boss, Norman. One evening, just before closing, I tied together about ten shopping carts and hitched them to the back of his car, which was parked behind the store. He drove away, but did not immediately notice the shopping carts noisily trailing him. When, he heard the rattle of the carts, he stopped, got out of his car, and looked in amazement at what someone had done! He laughed at his predicament, and I helped him put the carts back inside the store.

Another time, I attached a harmless smoke bomb to the engine of Norman's car. The bomb was connected to two spark plugs, so when the ignition was turned on, the bomb would whistle loudly and smoke. When Norman started his car, the bomb worked perfectly. He jumped out of his car, looking concerned, trying to figure out what was going on. I was there to calm his nerves, and we laughed while we watched the smoke drift away. The only other prank I played on him was to put marbles in his hubcaps. I was such a naughty boy!

I had developed a very close and comfortable relationship with Norman. One day, completely unexpectedly, he told me that he was being transferred to manage another store. I was heartbroken. I sobbed a little, and he comforted me, but this felt like a disaster. Norman left; I was never to see him again. I have tried diligently for over fifty years to locate him, without success.

New Store Manager

The new manager was John Santarpia, a big-bellied man. John was pleasant, and he allowed me to continue on as I had been, except I no longer counted the money on Saturdays. However, he and I did something strange, for fun, on Thursday and Friday nights, after the store closed.

John was an expert rubber band shooter, and he taught me how to shoot. We took candles, matches, and rubber bands to the dairy food case. We stuck candles on the case by melting their bottoms. The candles were then lit, and John would shoot out the flames with rubber bands. I was really impressed! I learned how to shoot rubber bands, but I never approached his level of expertise.

Bowling

While a freshman in high school, I went on a bowling double date with my previous girlfriend, Gail. She dated a fellow I didn't know. He was a good bowler, out-bowled me badly, and I was embarrassed by my incompetence. I couldn't let that performance stand, so I went to work on my bowling skills, and I was ***persistent***.

A fellow worker at the supermarket, Sid, was a bowling expert. I told him about my poor bowling, and he told me that he could help. He said the first thing to do was to get me my own bowling ball. We went to a store where they sold and custom drilled bowling balls to fit the bowler's hand. Sid, and the experts at the store, encouraged me to get something called "easy lift," which was a special design, inside the finger holes, that helped the bowler lift the ball more easily. I got a ball with this feature.

Sid gave me bowling lessons; there was a lot to learn. Over time I became a reasonably good bowler, and I tried out for the high school bowling team. The tryouts were held in a bowling alley near the school. Mr. Larson, a gym teacher, was the coach. There were about ten other boys trying out. Those with the highest scores would make the team.

When it was my turn to bowl, I nervously took my new ball, followed Sid's instructions as best I could, rolled the ball down the alley, and knocked out nine pins. Then I knocked down the last pin, giving me a spare in the first frame. My next eight frames were extraordinary; I got eight straight strikes!

At this point the entire bowling alley became quiet. Everyone came over to watch me bowl my tenth frame, and I was nervous. I carefully took my place on the approach to the lane, lined myself up using the marks on the floor, and promptly threw a noisy gutter ball! I managed to get a few more pins, giving me a score of two hundred fifty-six, something I've never come close to again. The manager of the bowling alley presented me with a gold colored tiepin that was engraved with "250 Club."

Mr. Larsen made me captain of the bowling team. I bowled a few matches for the school, did reasonably well, but I had to quit the team because I couldn't take the time from work. My ego, not the bowling team, was the reason I wanted to learn how to bowl. I wanted to show Gail that I could bowl well, and beat her new friend at bowling. So, the same two couples went on another bowling date. After a few games it became obvious that I was a good bowler as I outscored the other fellow easily. That was my last meeting with Gail. She was a lovely person.

College

My graduation from high school was unremarkable. Once again, my parents did not attend my graduation, and the only family member that attended was my sister Connee.

During my senior year in high school I took a test to apply for admittance to the City University of New York, the public university system of New York City. I wanted to go to college, but I could not consider any other colleges because of their cost. The wonderful part about all of the City Colleges was that there was no tuition! Students only had to pay for their books, laboratory, and gym fees!

At that time there were four, four-year City Colleges: Queens College, City College, Brooklyn College, and Hunter College, ranked academically in that order. Queens College was ranked as the tenth leading liberal arts college in the country, and it was only a mile from my apartment. Admittance to Queens College required a ninety percent high school average, or a very high ranking in a competitive citywide examination that I had taken. My high school grades were just okay, certainly not ninety percent. I still didn't know whether I wanted to become a dentist or a meteorologist.

In the summer of 1956 I received a letter from the City University of New York. It said that I was accepted to City College! That was wonderful. However, attendance there required almost two hours of commuting each way, by bus and subway. Going to Queens College would have obviated this travel. City College also had a fine reputation, and it had a meteorology program. I loved the idea of weather forecasting. However, I knew that most of the jobs in meteorology were government jobs, whose salaries were considered to be low. I was also sensitized about, and ***feared***, not having money, because of my parent's bankruptcy and its consequences. Dentistry offered me an opportunity to do better financially. It also would allow me to be my own boss, which appealed to me. The possibility of becoming a dentist was far in the future. It would require me to finish college with high grades, and then to be able to pay for, and graduate from, dental school.

Later that same summer, I received another letter from the City University of New York. I was surprised and elated to read that, because I did very well on the competitive examination, I was accepted to Queens College! I could almost, but not quite, walk there, and now I didn't have to spend hours commuting.

I began attending Queens College in the fall of 1956, traveling to and from there by bus, just a ten-minute ride. The first few days were taken up by registering for classes. I had no idea what classes I needed, and I stumbled through the experience, not sure if I had registered for the right ones.

My parents knew virtually nothing about my college situation, my working, or my plans for the future. Although we all lived in the same apartment, it was empty most of the time, and I had very little contact with either of them. I think that my mother was working, because someone was paying the rent. My father did have a car, which he used infrequently, and I drove it to college from time to time. I had learned to cook for myself quite handily, and I still enjoy my homemade "BLTs hold the grass." The ability to cook has worked out well for me.

I tried out for the Queens College freshman baseball team, and I made the team as a shortstop. I will always remember the coach saying to me, ***"I like the way you move, Loewenthal."*** But, as was the case with the high school bowling team, I could not afford the time to play baseball, so I had to quit the team. My once important dream of becoming a major league shortstop was over.

Poor Grades

After a year of college, I decided that I wanted to become a dentist. However, my grade point average was a very poor 2.0. I had failed French, and I had to take a make-up French class in summer school. The failing of the French class was bad, but it turned out to validate my philosophy that: ***Much of life happens for the best and for our highest good and learning. Undesirable and bad things do happen, but occasionally they have a positive effect—given time.*** The failing also validates, as you will read, how very important ***chance*** was in my life.

I continued working at the supermarket; however, other working opportunities were becoming available. My brother-in-law Stanley asked me if I would like to work for him as a draftsman. Stanley and his brother, Albert, worked in Stanley's engineering practice, which was quite busy and successful. I took the drafting job, and I did some beginner's drafting work.

A few months later, Stanley called me into his private office, and said that he wanted to have a serious talk with me. He did all of the talking. I will always remember this talk; it had a profound affect on me. Stanley said, "***What are you going to do with your life? You have poor grades, no money, and your family cannot help you.***" I said very simply, ***"I am going to be a dentist."*** I don't remember his exact reply, but it was something like, ***"you will never succeed."*** The talk was over. His words angered and ***challenged*** me! This set the tone for me to work harder than ever. ***Thank you, Stanley!***

My Make-Up French Class

My make-up French class was given on Tuesday and Thursday evenings. Students could take any seat in the classroom, and I always got to class early. I have a need to be a little early for everything, and I simply hate it when someone is late. I guess this is a symptom of my Type A personality.

On the first evening of class I watched the students enter the classroom. I saw an extremely attractive young woman come into the room. She had a big smile, a nice looking blonde "pageboy" hairstyle, and she had a gorgeous figure. During the class, the teacher called her "Miss Mirkin." I was still much too shy to say anything at all to Miss Mirkin.

But I was ***persistent***. I managed to sit next to her at every class. Finally, I got a ***chance*** to see her contact information. Miss. Mirkin's notebook was open, and I saw her name, address, and telephone number, and I sneakily copied all of that information. I felt that I could probably summon up enough courage to call her on the telephone, which was much easier for me than talking to her in person.

Very nervously, one evening I called her from a pay phone. Her father answered; he had a foreign accent. I said, ***"This is Mr. Loewenthal.*** I am in your daughter's French class. May I speak with her?"

Miss Mirkin

He stopped me cold by saying, ***"How can you be low and tall at the same time?"*** Oh my, was I stymied; he had made fun of my name! Without another word he put his daughter on the phone and I said, ***"Hi. This is Mr. Loewenthal; I sit next to you in French class."*** I lamely said, ***"I have lost my assignment, and I'm wondering if you can help?"*** She said, ***"Are you the redhead?"*** I said, no, and then I said, rather aggressively for me, "***Do you think I could come over and get the assignment?"*** There was a long pause, and she said, ***"Please wait, I have to ask my parents." The answer was yes!***

I ran home, got my father's car, and slowly made my way to her house in Laurelton, New York, about a thirty-minute drive.

I rang the doorbell and was greeted by Miss. Mirkin. Her given name was Ilana (pronounced Elana). Her parents were standing behind her, and they introduced themselves as Mr. and Mrs. Mirkin.

The house was quite small and was very neatly kept. Just beyond the tiny entrance foyer, on the left, was a small dining room with a table, four chairs, and a stand-alone television set. Ilana and I sat down at opposite ends of the table with our French books, paper, and pens, while her parents disappeared. This arrangement felt very awkward, probably for both of us. It was an exciting and pleasant evening.

As the summer progressed, Ilana and I started dating. We went to movies, I took her fishing once, and we got to know each other better and better. By the time the fall semester began, I was eating dinner regularly at her house, and that was truly wonderful! Her parents treated me very nicely.

The Police Car

Jerry and I, on occasion, rode around in his father's official looking black car. The car looked like an unmarked police car. There was a telephone handset in the glove case, its wire not attached to anything but air.

For fun, Jerry would pull up next to a car on our right, while I put the handset next to my ear and pretended that I was talking, while I was staring at the driver in the car next to me. When the driver saw me, he or she would instantly slow down to a crawl, for ***fear*** we would pull their car over for some reason. ***What fun!***

A Kind Family

Jerry's mother invited me for dinner from time to time. After dinner, Jerry and I would study in his room. Jerry's family members were very observant Jews. I guess you could say that he was somewhat observant too. I remember one time when I went to High Holiday Services with Jerry, his family, and his girlfriend. After the services, we went back to his house and had the customary holiday meal. Jerry's father had a wonderful voice and sang the prayers for the meal. After the meal, Jerry disappeared with his girlfriend; I think to his bedroom, I am sure, to discuss religion.

The Earthquake

At the end of my junior year my grades remained the same, as did Jerry's. He was destined for medical school anywhere he wanted to go. I was very proud of him, and a bit envious. In May, when the school year ended, Jerry came up with a novel idea. It was for three guys to drive to Yellowstone National Park in August, for an outdoor adventure. This sounded fabulous to me. I talked with Ilana about the trip; she knew Jerry very well, and it was a "go" for me as far as Ilana was concerned. I told Jerry to count me in!

The three people for the trip included Hal, a friend of Jerry's, Jerry, and myself. We took Hal's father's car for the trip. We brought pup tents, sleeping bags, food, duffle bags, personal items, and I took fishing my gear. The first day of our trip, on August 15, 1959, was very long. We arrived in Chicago late at night, and stayed at the YMCA. The next night we camped out under the stars in a Nebraska cornfield.

The third day of our trip was eventful. I was driving the last leg of the trip, through Cody, Wyoming. We were climbing in altitude as we entered the Rocky Mountain range. Lightning was creating a wondrous, and eerie scene all around us, and I loved it! At about 1:00 a.m., extremely tired, we approached the eastern entrance of Yellowstone. I rolled down my driver's window so I could talk to the ranger maintaining the entrance. He quickly informed us that the park was closed due to an earthquake. I asked the ranger where we could sleep, and he directed us back down the mountain a few miles, to an area where we could sleep, in the forest.

We found the area, got in to our sleeping bags, and tried to sleep. The ground shook every once in a while, and that shook us up. The next morning we drove back to the park, which was only partially open. We saw large cracks in the road, and we were told that we could not drive to the west side of the park, where the epicenter of the earthquake was, because the road was closed.

I learned later that this earthquake was quite powerful. We did not realize the earthquake's severity while vacationing in the park. It occurred on August 17, 1959, only a few hours before we reached the park. The magnitude of the quake was 7.5 on the Richter scale.

The quake caused a huge landslide and over twenty-eight fatalities. It left $74 million in damage, in today's money. The quake blocked the flow of the Madison River, resulting in the creation of Quake Lake.

Our first day in the park, was cloudy, damp, and cool. We bought sandwiches and sodas to eat in a nearby area, where there were picnic tables and restrooms. We put our lunches on a table, and the three of us went to use the restroom. When I exited the restroom, I looked at our table, and much to my surprise, a bear was eating my lunch! I decided not to intervene, because I never told a bear what to do. The other fellows agreed. Bottom line: lunch for the bear, not for us.

We pitched our tents in a designated area, and kept all of our valuables locked in the car. We drove around and enjoyed the sights on one side of the park. We could not see Old Faithful, because it was on the side of the park that was closed. We rented a rowboat and fished in Yellowstone Lake, using worms for bait. We each caught several very pretty cutthroat trout. While we were fishing, Hal started complaining that he had a toothache. The toothache got worse, and it was decided that Hal needed to see a dentist.

The nearest dentist was one hundred miles north, in Livingston, Montana. After driving for three days across the country, the one hundred miles did not seem like very much, so we headed to Livingston in search of a dentist. When we got to Livingston it was very hot, with temperatures in the nineties, and there was a rodeo in progress. Our first task was to find a dentist, which we did. The dentist was an older, friendly man. He could not find a problem in any of Hal's teeth and his toothache had gone. We left the dentist's office, got some Cokes, and watched the rodeo.

We left Livingston about 5:00 p.m. and headed into the mountains, back to Yellowstone. I noticed, with excitement, that thunderstorms were building. When we got back to the park, it was raining hard and getting colder, a huge change from the sunshine and ninety degree temperatures we just had left. We crawled into our tents, then into our sleeping bags, and went to sleep. About 2:00 a.m. I was awakened, and startled, as my tent fell down on me! The tent had caved in because of an accumulation of heavy wet snow!

Another Bear

We decided to rent a log cabin for the last few days of our trip. The first night we were in the cabin, Jerry and Hal went into nearby Canyon City to look around. I remained in the cabin. I seemed to have a cold or an allergy, and I was sneezing a lot. I sat on my bed, reading; I didn't like to be alone. The cabin shook slightly a few times. I assumed that this was caused by aftershocks from the earthquake. I was really glad when my friends returned.

I was still sneezing and my nose was dripping. I had a bottle of Coricidin, an allergy medicine, in the car's glove case, and I went to get it. I walked down the front steps of the cabin to the car; it was very dark. When I opened the passenger door, a dim overhead light went on, and I sat down. My right leg was dangling out of the car, with my foot resting on the ground, and I opened the glove case. While I was searching for my medicine I saw Jerry, backlit in the cabin's doorway, but he could not see me. I found the Coricidin, and I had the bottle in my hand when I sensed "something" next to me. I turned my head slowly to the right, and saw a large bear's head sniffing at my leg. Yikes!

I started quaking, so now there were at least two quakes this week. I tried to shout, "help" to Jerry, but no sound came out of my mouth. In a minute or two, although it felt like an hour, the bear meandered away. I jumped out of the car and ran up the stairs, past Jerry, and into the cabin, breathless. Jerry asked me what was going on; he had seen nothing.

A few days before we were scheduled to drive home, I realized that I had not called Ilana, so I did. I should have called sooner; she and her parents were concerned about all of us. The serious earthquake was well publicized, and I apologized for not calling her sooner.

On the way home, while Jerry was driving, there was a very frightening incident. We were on a two-lane highway; the speed limit was "reasonable and proper." We were going about 90 mph when we saw a dark speck far ahead, in our lane. It soon became apparent that this speck was a car speeding right at us. We thought that the driver probably had fallen asleep. Jerry was going to have to make a decision that meant life or death. To avoid a collision he had to make a choice between swerving to the left or holding his ground in the hope that the driver of the oncoming car would awaken; there were no soft shoulders to allow our car to be pulled off to either side of the road. Jerry decided to hold his ground. At the last possible second, the other car swerved into the other lane and missed us. The incident was quite traumatic, and remains embedded in my mind. I don't know why Jerry did what he did, neither does he.

The Painter

I went into the painting business with an older friend, Bobby Gilmartin. My first job was to paint the interior of Ilana's house. I finished the job in a few weeks and everyone was pleased. Her parents were generous, as usual.

We contracted a small job from my sister June; it was to paint her upstairs bathroom. The bathroom was located at the top of a staircase. June was a very particular and demanding person. She had picked out a special pink semi-gloss paint and a paint roller with a bubble design on it, along with some black paint to use on the roller. Her instructions were to create stylish looking black bubbles on pink walls. We had a spray can of black paint so we could touch-up areas. We painted the bathroom one evening when June and Stanley were both out.

The pink paint went on easily and dried quickly. We painted the walls, the front of the drawers, and the vanity doors. Then we applied the black bubbles on the walls very carefully, using the roller, and the walls looked great. The front of the drawers and the vanity doors were difficult to paint with the roller because of the handles. We didn't remove the handles, and we decided to "freehand" the bubbles around the handles, using the spray can of black paint.

Well, wouldn't you know it, things got out of control! We sprayed big and little black circles at the top, bottom, and sides of drawers and doors. When they were opened, part of a bubble would be stationary and one part moved. When the drawer or door was closed, the bubble would be whole again. Pretty neat! We did not drink one drop of alcohol. We were just two energetic, not-so-bright painters having fun, but who were soon to get their comeuppance.

Stanley came home first, and he started walking up the staircase to see the newly painted bathroom. When almost to the top, he looked into the bathroom and began to laugh. He laughed harder and harder. He laughed so much that not able to climb the last stair.

He slowly sunk down onto the staircase, holding on to the rail, unable to get up, because his laughter had drained all of his self-control and energy. When my sister came home, things went bad in a hurry. She looked at the bathroom, screamed at her two painters, and kicked us out of her house. Only one person was allowed to come back to repaint everything, her brother!

Our next job was to paint the inside of an apartment house, located in an undesirable and rundown neighborhood in Brooklyn, New York. Bobby had seen the place and estimated how much paint we would need, and how long it would take to paint all of the apartments, and he negotiated a contract. There were about fifteen apartments. We went to buy the paint. Bob went into the paint store while I waited in his car. He came out with really good news. He said that there was a new kind of paint called latex, which dried in only a few hours. And, he said that the paint was so advanced that it only required one coat to cover any old paint. It was August, and the temperature was in the nineties with unbearable humidity; fortunately, we would be painting inside.

Bobby's '55 green and white Chevy

We loaded up all of our materials into Bobby's '55 green and white Chevy. We had many gallons of the special latex paint, ladders, drop cloths, extra pails, rollers, paintbrushes, rags, a freezer chest with food and water, and a battery operated radio. It took about an hour to get to the place, which was unlocked and neglected. We went inside, and the first thing we noticed was the stench of cat urine and feces; it was horrible. The place was filthy; there were feral cats everywhere—inside and outside. And it was hot! We unloaded our painting gear, made a game plan, and started painting.

The apartment walls were painted red, orange, blue, and some were even black! Our ***challenge*** was to paint all of the walls and the ceilings white. By lunchtime we had finished painting several walls. After a quick lunch, we both noticed that the latex paint had dried quickly, as promised. However, we could see the underlying color of the walls, almost as if we did not paint them!

We immediately realized that this job was not going to turn out as planned. We repainted all of the walls we had painted, and then we pooped out. It turned out that to look good, every wall needed three coats of paint. We were taking a financial hosing on the project.

One day, we were sitting on the floor having lunch, dejected, and Bobby said to me, ***"So, you're in college, your grades are poor, and you have no money. What are you going to do with your life?"*** I said, ***"I'm going to be a dentist."*** Bobby laughed and said, ***"I'll bet that you won't be." "Okay,"*** I said. ***"Let's bet five dollars,"*** to which Bobby, agreed.
We eventually finished painting the place, thankfully.

We had another painting adventure that winter. Bobby got a contract to paint a one-story duplex bungalow in the town of New Paltz, New York. New Paltz lies in the lower Hudson valley of New York State. Bobby figured that if we left Flushing in the evening, we could get to the bungalow before midnight, and then start painting early the next morning.

It was a rainy, foggy, cold, and miserable night as we drove north to New Paltz. Temperatures were in the low thirties. We had a lot of trouble finding the place. It was deep down in the valley, the visibility was very poor, and there were no road signs. We finally found the bungalow around midnight. We had sleeping bags, food, and all of our painting gear. There was a large house with a few lights on across the yard from the bungalow. We hadn't known that this house existed.

The rain began to freeze, coating everything with a layer of ice. The door to the bungalow was locked, so Bobby went to the house and knocked on the door. A man answered, puzzled why anyone would be here so late at night. Bobby explained the situation. This man knew nothing about a paint job, but he did have a key for the bungalow, which he gave to Bobby.

When all of our gear was inside we felt relieved and opened up two cans of beer. We didn't feel tired, so we started painting. There was no heat, and it was cold. The paint was so cold, and so thick, that it could not be used. Bobby had brought a Coleman stove. He lit it and began heating a can of paint. The paint cooperated and thinned out enough so that it could be applied. We painted for a while, and heated more paint. We finally called it quits around 3:30 a.m., but left the stove burning for heat. That was a big mistake.

We crawled into our sleeping bags and went to sleep. We came close to dying because of lack of oxygen; the stove had used it up. The paint never dried on the cold walls, and kept emitting fumes, which made us sick. We woke up, realized what was happening, and raced out of the bungalow. We drove to a diner, had coffee, and eventually went back to paint—feeling lousy. We spoke to the man who lived in the house and explained our situation to him. He was very understanding and helped us by supplying some electric heaters to warm up the bungalow. The nicest thing this man did for us was to let us sleep in his house that night. We finished painting the next day, drove home, and I went to bed. That was the very last time I picked up a paintbrush!

Life and College Continue

My relationship with Ilana and her parents was growing stronger. Her parents primarily spoke Hebrew. This proved to be awkward for me because I did not understand a word of Hebrew. Ilana and I did go to the Jewish Theological Seminary in Manhattan and took Hebrew lessons. I was invited to go to High Holiday Services with the Mirkins. I went, but I felt extremely out of place and very uncomfortable because of my lack of knowledge about Judaism, and my inability to read Hebrew.

I was always very nervous ***fearing*** that I might be called upon to participate in the service, whereupon I would probably embarrass myself. I was very relieved when the services were over. Following the services we had a traditional holiday meal in Ilana's home. Ilana's mother's matzo balls were hard enough to use as cannon balls. I never said a word.

My poor grades continued as I entered my junior year of college. I finally finished my French requirements with a D average, but I didn't realize that my ***challenge*** with the French language was not completely over. My guidance counselor was professor Donald Lancefield. He discussed my grades, and cautioned me that my low grades would likely prevent my admission to any dental school. He was correct.

I began applying for admittance to dental schools early in 1959, for admission to a class beginning in 1960. The applications were long and all required a transcript of grades, plus a fee, to pay for the review of my application. I applied to almost every dental school in the country, with little hope of being accepted.

In addition to a transcript of grades, each applicant was required to take "the Dental Aptitude Test," now called "the Dental Admission Test," which is administered by the American Dental Association. I had taken the examination and had found it difficult. I took it at the New York University College of Dentistry. Predictably, I was not accepted for admission to any dental school.

A glimmer of hope for me came from Dr. Lind, my dentist, who was a graduate of the New York University College of Dentistry. He said that he might be able to help me. In the fall of 1959, Dr. Lind asked me to go with him to visit the Assistant Dean of his former dental school. The Assistant Dean's name was Dr. Earl O. Butcher. Dr. Butcher was also Chairman of the Department of Anatomy.

We entered the Dean's office, and naturally I was very nervous. This meeting represented my last ***chance*** of ever becoming a dentist. We were there to discuss if there was any way I could be accepted as a student at this dental school. Dean Butcher was very straightforward. He explained that my grades were simply too low for acceptance, but that my score was quite high on my Dental Aptitude Test. Then Dr. Butcher made to me what I considered to be an astounding offer. He told me that if I could maintain a B average for the current college semester, I could have a place in the next class. Talk about a ***challenge***! I could hardly believe this, and I thanked the Dean and Dr. Lind profusely for giving me a ***chance***.

Down to Studying

Assistant Dean Earl O. Butcher

A College Dinner Dance

I immediately stopped working, and I devoted my time to studying. My grades shot up, and I got all A and B grades that semester.

I promptly sent my transcript of grades to Dean Butcher in early January 1960. I waited anxiously for the mail each day, but I did not receive a letter from the dental school. After a month went by, I called Dean Butcher. I told him about my good grades, and reminded him of what he had told me. He said that he remembered me, and if what I had told him about my grades was accurate, I would have a place in the next class.

It was the first week of February when I re-submitted my transcript, and I waited again. I didn't have to wait very long. On Saturday, February 20, 1960, at 11:15 a.m., I received a letter from the New York University College of Dentistry, Office of the Assistant Dean, which said that I was accepted for admission to the next class! I was alone and I cried, because I was so very happy.

That Saturday was also very important for another reason. I called Ilana and told her about the dental school acceptance. She was of course overjoyed and said, ***"I'll see you here for dinner."*** That evening I was at the dinner table with Ilana and her parents. I had a bowl of my favorite salad in front of me. I fiddled with it, pushed the salad around with my fork, but I just couldn't eat because I was so nervous. The reason being that I planned to ask Ilana's father for her hand in marriage, now that I was admitted to dental school.

Her father was sitting to my left, at the head of the table. He looked at my still uneaten salad and asked me if I was sick. I said, ***"I'm okay, but I have to ask you an important question."*** Ilana did not know that the question was coming. I said, ***"I want to ask your permission to marry Ilana."*** He immediately said, ***"What took you so long?"*** We all were relieved and very happy; the answer was a hearty yes! This greatest event in our lives was going to require a lot of planning.

I still had the spring semester to finish in order to graduate with my B.S. degree. I had forgotten about a mandatory test, "the French senior reading test," which was a requirement for me to pass in order to graduate and earn my B.S. degree. I trembled at the thought of having to read French, and either answer questions or translate what I had read into English. I thought about not taking the test because I was already accepted at dental school.

NEW YORK UNIVERSITY
COLLEGE OF DENTISTRY
421 FIRST AVENUE
NEW YORK 10, N.Y.

OFFICE OF THE ASSISTANT DEAN

TELEPHONE: OREGON 9-1880

February 17, 1960

Dear Sir:

I take pleasure in informing you that your application for admission into New York University College of Dentistry has been accepted by the Admissions Committee for the September 1960 class.

Inasmuch as the number of students we can accept into our Freshman Class is strictly limited, it will be necessary for you, in order to reserve a place for yourself in the class to make a deposit of two hundred dollars ($200) which will be applied to your tuition fees of next year. It is understood that this deposit is a guarantee of good faith on your part and obligates the school to reserve a place for you. This deposit is refundable only for withdrawal in case of serious illness.

If this deposit is not paid by March 15, 1960 we shall assume you are not coming and shall cancel our acceptance of your application.

Sincerely,

Earl O. Butcher

EARL O BUTCHER, Ph.D
Assistant Dean

Mr. Bernard Lowenthal
42 20 Kissena Blvd
Flushing 55, New York

My College Graduation

However, Jerry convinced me that it would be foolish at this point not to have my B.S. degree. So, I took the French senior reading test, and to my amazement, I passed it!

My graduation from Queens College was uneventful. No one from my family attended the ceremony. Ilana and her parents did attend.

Our wedding date was set for August 20, 1960, only a few short months away. Ilana and her parents did most of the preparations for the wedding. Our plan was for me to live with Ilana in her home's one-room attic while I attended dental school and Ilana finished college. I was concerned about fitting in with my new family. I only had a few belongings. I brought some clothing and my chest of drawers to Ilana's house, packing everything into my father's car. My socks drawer was the upper right drawer, and it still contained my lucky rabbit's feet. No one knew about them, not even Ilana, and they continued working!

Our wedding was lovely. We honeymooned in Nassau, Bahamas, for a week, courtesy of Ilana's wonderful parents.

Mr. and Mrs. Bernard Loewenthal

Studying in our attic apartment

Chapter 3

1960-1970: Dental School, The Air Force
Post-Graduate Training, and Farming

We returned home from our honeymoon the week before dental school began. Needless to say, I was very apprehensive about school, my new home, and what lay ahead.

We lived in the finished attic of Ilana's parent's house during my four years of dental school. The attic was one long narrow room, finished in plywood, with windows at each end. There was a desk at one end, and a folding bed at the other end. It was a quiet, pleasant place where I spent most of my time studying. After dinner, on Saturday evenings, Ilana and I usually watched television with her parents. Mission Impossible, Paladin, and The Jackie Gleason Show were some of our favorites.

After graduating from Queens College, Ilana taught early childhood classes in Plainview, Long Island, New York. She was our only source of income for four years. My tuition was paid for by her income and several government low interest educational loans.

Starting Our Life Together

Dental School

My commute to school took about ninety minutes each way by bus and subway. Registration and orientation took up the first few days of school. Fortunately, during this time, I met three second-year dental students who lived near me. They suggested that we create a carpool, along with another freshman student, Howie. We did, and the carpool worked nicely, cutting our commuting time almost in half. The car pool members alternated driving days. I used Mr. Mirkin's car when it was my turn to drive.

Another benefit of the carpool was that the two freshmen could learn about what to expect in school, based on the experiences of the three second-year students. The serious work finally began. I was ***fearful*** and very insecure because of how poorly I had done in college. I didn't know what would happen if I flunked out of dental school. Historically, there were about one hundred sixty dental students in each first year class. However, only an average of about one hundred thirty students graduated.

My first year classes included dental anatomy, human anatomy (including the dissection of human cadavers), histology, physiology, pathology, and microbiology. After about six weeks, we began having our first examinations. I was of course nervous about taking them, but I had studied very hard. The test scores were posted and the students were able to see each other's grades. I was very pleased to have gotten very high grades on all of the tests. This had not happened to me since grammar school. I hoped that my good grades would continue.

After my first two years, I had one of the highest grade-averages in my class, and I was ecstatic. My fellow classmates admired my accomplishments, and that felt very, very good. My success was, and still is, hard for me to accept. Howie, the other freshman in my carpool, was asked to leave school because of his failing grades.

In March of 1962, as I was getting into the carpool car, Ilana ran out of the house and shouted; "don't go". The fellows in the car asked, "What happened?" I said, "I think my father died." My father indeed had died. I have no idea how I knew this. Precognition, if there is such a thing?

I became ill with stomach problems soon after his death. I was tested and re-tested, but nothing wrong could be found. I was hardly eating, and I lost over ten pounds. I had to stop going to school, and now my finishing dental school was in jeopardy. My illness was probably an emotional reaction to my father's death.

Unbeknownst to me, Ilana's father went to see Dean Butcher. He inquired about my dental school future, because I had missed about two months of school. Dean Butcher told him that my grades were outstanding, and that if I could pass all of my final examinations at the end of the year, I could go on to my third year. My health slowly began to improve. I passed all of the final examinations, and went on to my junior year.

The third and fourth years of dental school were ***challenging***. I managed to finish all of my requirements, and I passed both the New York State and Northeast Regional Board examinations with high scores. Ilana and her father attended my graduation. Her mother was ill and could not attend. I graduated with high honors, and I was very proud to receive awards for academic excellence. Ilana and her parents were as thrilled as I.

One of the awards I received is the New York University Founders Day Award. I cherish this award, and it hangs on my ego wall. I still look at and read it from time to time, to remind myself that I really earned it.

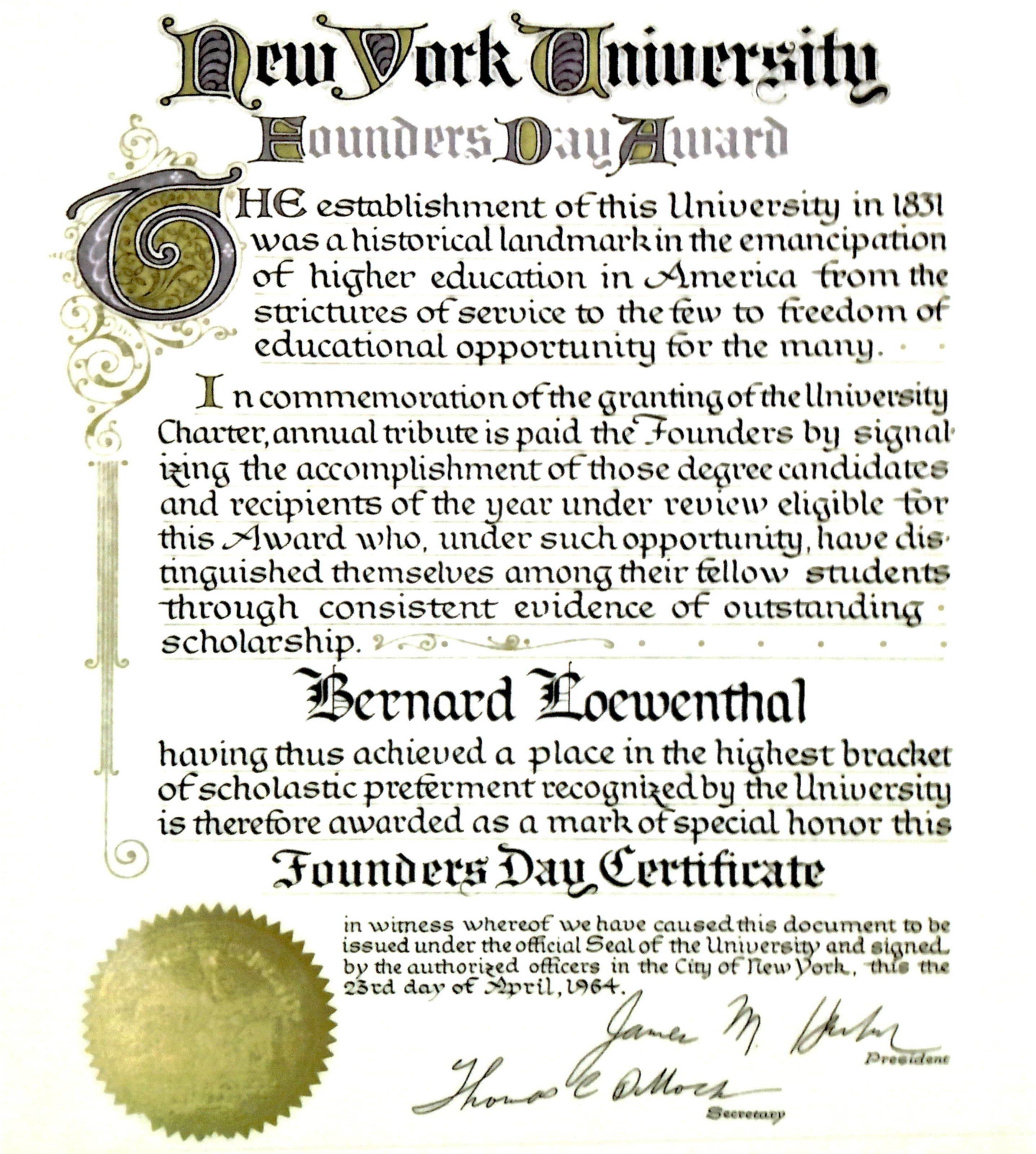

New York University

Founders Day Award

THE establishment of this University in 1831 was a historical landmark in the emancipation of higher education in America from the strictures of service to the few to freedom of educational opportunity for the many.

In commemoration of the granting of the University Charter, annual tribute is paid the Founders by signalizing the accomplishment of those degree candidates and recipients of the year under review eligible for this Award who, under such opportunity, have distinguished themselves among their fellow students through consistent evidence of outstanding scholarship.

Bernard Loewenthal

having thus achieved a place in the highest bracket of scholastic preferment recognized by the University is therefore awarded as a mark of special honor this

Founders Day Certificate

in witness whereof we have caused this document to be issued under the official Seal of the University and signed by the authorized officers in the City of New York, this the 23rd day of April, 1964.

President

Secretary

It remains hard for me to accept the fact that I earned this prestigious award.

A Bet Worth Losing!

My painting partner and good friend, Bobby Gilmartin, hosted a graduation party for me. He not only gave me the five-dollar bill I'd won from him, but he wrote on the bill, ***"In payment for a bet I was happy to lose."*** He framed the bill and later went on to frame my awards. He did a nice job and they are all hanging on a wall in my man-cave.

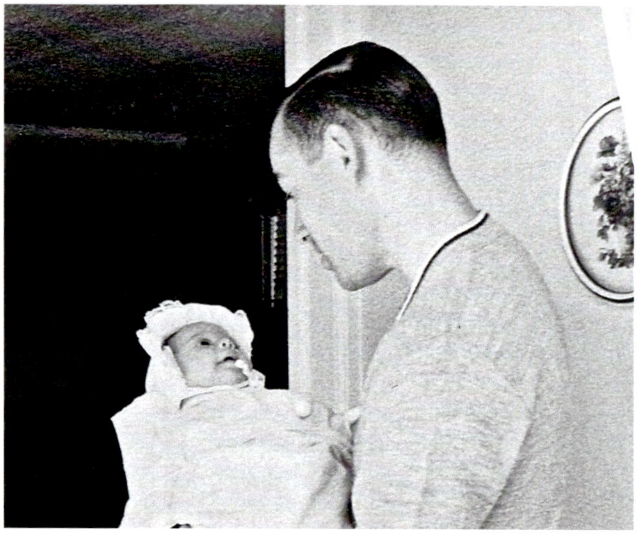

New Daddy

Bonnie Beth

Little Red Riding Hood

Surprise!

Chance once again was about to impact my life, this time in a very serious, irreversible, and blessed way. Despite all of my planning—and I planned carefully, with a good knowledge of the physiology of the female monthly cycle—and despite my high grades in physiology, the one and only time we had unprotected sex resulted in a pregnancy.

Our little surprise arrived on August 26, 1963: our daughter, Bonnie Beth. I was in my third year of dental school.

Bonnie

Bonnie became a wonderful young girl, a fine young lady, a hard working adult, a college graduate, and a superb wife and mother. She has blessed us with countless wonderful memories of her acting and dancing talents, and a fine family: more about Bonnie later.

Scott Air Force Base

Upon graduation, I was extremely fortunate to be chosen by the United State Air Force to become one of their few dental interns. This was a very difficult and prized position to obtain. It meant that my next three years, at a minimum, would be spent in the Air Force, as a dentist. These years turned out to be extraordinarily wonderful years for me.

I was assigned to Hospital Scott, at Scott Air Force Base, Belleville, Illinois. The Base was an hour's drive from St. Louis, home of the St. Louis Cardinals baseball team and my idol, Stan Musial. I drove to Scott alone so that I could get our apartment in order before Ilana and Bonnie arrived. The first afternoon I was there, before doing anything, I wanted to watch the Cardinals on television. I introduced myself to a neighbor, and asked him on which channel the Cardinal's games were televised. My neighbor said, "The who?"

Ilana and baby Bonnie were planning to follow me, soon. Ilana's mother, bless her heart, didn't want to part with her daughter or granddaughter. She said to Ilana, "If I had a little baby like Bonnie, I wouldn't take her out west where the Indians are." We lived in a nice apartment on the Air Force Base. Ilana and Bonnie did just fine with daily phone calls to and from Ilana's mother. No Indians, bows, or arrows were ever seen.

I was given a series of injections that would protect me from just about any disease, anywhere in the world, should the Air Force send me. But I never left the United States. There were four dental interns at Scott Hospital. We rotated singly through oral surgery, periodontics, restorative dentistry, and removable prosthetics. We received lectures from the hospital medical staff and the dental staff.

Captain Loewenthal

We rotated through several medical specialties including anesthesiology, otolaryngology, medicine, and radiology. We attended grand rounds and a CPC (clinical pathology conference), along with the medical staff at the hospital, on alternate Friday afternoons.

My first three-month rotation was in oral surgery. Dr. Dan Tolman was the oral surgeon. He was a marvelous surgeon and teacher. When I began my rotation, I was completely unprepared, and untrained, to perform oral surgery procedures. When my training was completed, I was able to perform advanced and complicated oral surgical procedures with confidence.

My next rotation was in periodontics, also for three months. Dr. Robert W. Spettel was the periodontist. Dr. Spettel was an incredibly gifted teacher and we had excellent chemistry. His training was so good that I decided to try and follow in his footsteps and become a periodontist. Bob and I have remained close friends and colleagues for the last forty-eight years. We served together on the Public Communications Committee of the American Academy of Periodontology. We now live close to each other in the winter, in Naples, Florida.

Makes Me Smile

During the year of my internship I had several amusing experiences. One time I was making a complete set of dentures for a General Richard. I looked out the window and saw thunderstorms building, and they were heading our way. I was excited because I loved to watch thunderstorms. I mentioned to the General that I believed that we were going to experience a thunderstorm.

He looked out the window and said, ***"I'm not so sure."*** After a few minutes I said, ***"How about a bet about the thunderstorm, General?"***

He wasn't sure if he wanted to bet. A little while later he excused himself so that he could use the men's room. He came back and took his seat in the dental chair, and after a few minutes he said, ***"Okay, how much do you want to bet about the thunderstorm?"*** I said, ***"My usual bet is a dollar."*** ***"Fine,"*** he said, and we shook hands.

The general won the bet; we did not get the storm, so I reached into my pocket and took out a dollar bill. The General said, ***"Well, I really didn't play fair. I did not go to the men's room; instead, I called the Air Weather Service here on Base. I was told that radar showed that the storms would miss us. Put the dollar back in your pocket."*** I thought, ***"That's why he is a General!"***

The interns got to know each other fairly well and my weather forecasting interest prompted a question and another bet. In August, one of the interns asked me if I could predict when we would have the first snowfall. Tongue in cheek, I boasted that I could, and I announced that the first one inch of snow would fall on November 19. They then **challenged** me with a bet that I accepted. If I was wrong, I would buy all of the interns drinks at the officer's club. And, if I was right, they would buy me drinks.

The months advanced, and November started with temperatures far above normal. On November 18, the temperature was in the sixties! I thought for sure that I would be buying the drinks. Suprisingly it snowed the next day! I was amazed, as was everyone else. They all wanted to know how I could predict this snowfall months in advance. The truth was that I thought that November 19 was Stan Musial's birthday, and that is why I picked that day. Until I wrote this book, only Ilana knew this. However, while checking my facts so I could be totally accurate for this book, I learned that I was wrong about Stan Musial's birthday; it is November 21st, not the 19th. So, because of my mistake, ***I won the bet!***

Ready to Practice Dentistry?

Following my internship I developed a strong opinion based upon my internship experience. I felt that no dental school graduate is prepared to practice dentistry, at a reasonable standard of care, without further significant training. I am a perfect example.

I had excellent grades in dental school, and I graduated with honors. I thought that I knew, and could do, just about everything I needed to do to begin practicing, but I was completely wrong. My internship showed me that I was ill prepared to practice. I think that an internship should be mandatory before a dentist is granted the privilege and license to practice.

Pease Air Force Base

My internship was drawing to a close in the spring of 1965. The interns were anxious to learn where they were going to be stationed next. I applied for three Air Force Bases in New England because I loved snowstorms, and what better place to be! I was ecstatic to be chosen, by ***chance***, to be stationed at Pease Air Force Base, in Portsmouth, New Hampshire. We lived there on the Base.

My commanding officer was Colonel Edwards. When I reported to the dental clinic for the first time, the colonel asked me what I would like to do, because I was the only dentist with extra training. I told him that I would like to practice periodontics. He said that was fine, but first he wanted me to act as the oral surgeon for my first six months and teach the other general dentists oral surgery techniques. Then I could practice periodontics, and that worked out just fine.

When I started practicing periodontics, I was given, for my use only, the last two treatment rooms on one end of the clinic. I could make my own schedule and appointments; it was almost like being in private practice.

Our Base Commander was a strange officer who I'll refer to as "Colonel Dumboy." One day after lunch, I was riding my bicycle from home, uphill, to the dental clinic. This commander pulled up next to me in his official blue Air Force car, pulled down the passenger side window, and shouted, "You're going too fast. I'm going to report you."

When I got to the dental clinic, Colonel Edwards looked at me and said, "You have been reported to the Air Police by the Base Commander for speeding." I explained that I was bicycling uphill in an area where the speed limit was 35 mph, and even if I tried, I could not get up to a speed of 20 mph. Nothing further ever happened because of this incident, but that jerk, Colonel Dumboy, had been serious.

Dr. Richter

I developed a bad itch and was treated by my friend, an internist, also in the Air Force, Michael Richter. I was not in pain, but I had a few blisters on my back; Michael said that I had shingles. He wanted to prescribe a pain medication, but I declined. I do not like to take medication unless absolutely necessary. A few days later I went back to Michael, in great pain, and got a prescription for Tylenol with codeine. Dr. Richter did my annual physical examinations, and he of course he always weighed me. I cannot get it out of my head that he used a "Richter" scale. Now, every time there is an earthquake, I think of Michael!

Farming Lessons

The nation's oldest family farm, founded in 1632, Tuttle's Red Barn, was located nearby in Dover, New Hampshire. The farm was famous for its vegetables, especially corn and tomatoes. Farming appealed to me a lot and I wanted to learn as much as I could about farming vegetables. The owner of the farm was Hugh Tuttle. Hugh was also previously the mayor of Dover, and he and his family operated the farm.

I saw Hugh on his tractor one day in the spring of 1966. He was harrowing a field. I caught up to him, introduced myself, and we talked about me learning vegetable farming. Hugh was very nice, cooperative, and suggested that I come back so we could talk and spend time walking through the fields.

I went back a few days later, armed with a yellow legal pad and a pen, and we began our tour. I wrote and wrote, and gleaned information and advice that would be difficult to find anywhere else. After several visits I thanked Hugh heartily for his time and effort. He gave me some special corn seed to try. We remained friends until he died many years later.

Air Force members could rent a plot of land for a garden on the Base for only five dollars for the summer. I rented two plots and started my farming career. At Hugh's suggestion, I concentrated on growing only corn and tomatoes.

To do this properly and efficiently was very time consuming, but fun. I carried this learning experience forward, as you will read.

Portsmouth

The Portsmouth area is beautiful. The ocean, bays, and rivers create breathtaking views and great fishing. ***I love to fish***, and fishing was literally around the corner. I took my father-in-law fishing in a small boat one day. He loved to eat fish, especially flounder, and we caught many fine looking flounder. His face lit up and he laughed heartily with every flounder he caught! We filled up two-bushel baskets with flounder that day. Guess what we ate for dinner? It was great fun for both of us.

Ilana and I were introduced to some excellent edible sea creatures, the best one being native shrimp. These shrimp are caught only during the winter. They are small, but ever so sweet and yummy; it's hard to describe their flavor. In the 1960s these shrimp cost, unpeeled, about a dollar per pound! Over time, like everything else, they went up in price, and they are now at least ten dollars per pound, unpeeled.

Eddie's 11-pound lobster

Dr. Poll, his office staff and I

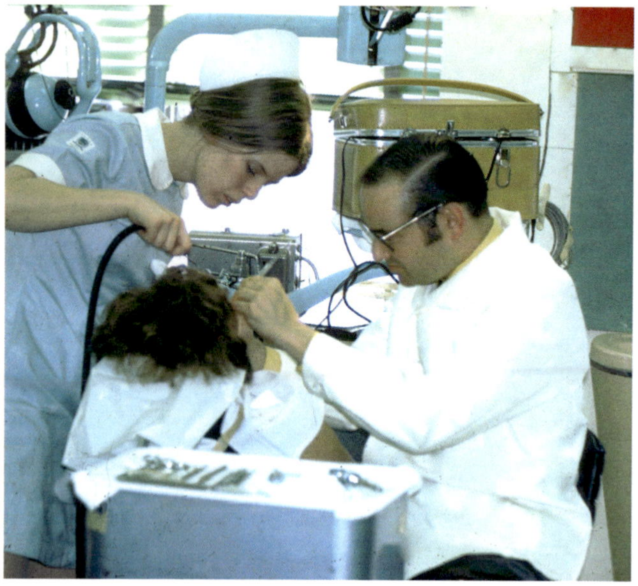

Working for Dr. Poll

We always loved lobster, and Portsmouth is a lobster lover's paradise. Lobsters there were reasonably priced, and plentiful. We dined on lobster too many times to admit! This reminds me about a tasty Air Force anecdote.

Some members of the dental clinic got a large number of lobsters, but had no place to cook them. There was a big autoclave next to my treatment rooms. Autoclaves are sterilizers that use steam and pressure to sterilize objects such as dental instruments. After work one day, I used the autoclave to cook the lobsters. ***Everyone enjoyed fantastic sterilized lobsters, until they were coming out of our ears. No one said a word.***

A Job

While still on active duty, needing money for my large educational loans, I found a job as a general dentist, on Saturdays, in Haverhill, Massachusetts. Haverhill is just over the New Hampshire border, about thirty miles south of Portsmouth, and about an hour's ride north of Boston. I worked for a Dr. Poll, and my income helped a little.

When my tour of duty ended, we moved to Haverhill. We rented the downstairs apartment in a two-family house, on a beautiful street, Lakeview Avenue. I began working full time for Dr. Poll. I was still hoping to become a periodontist, which meant going back to school for two years of specialty training. I had applied to two excellent schools in Boston: Tufts University School of Dental Medicine and Boston University School of Dental Medicine.

My mentor, Bob Spettel, had graduated from Tufts. Bob had told me stories about the very stressful program at Tufts, and the tough head of the periodontology department, Dr. Irving. The stories were hard to imagine, but I was ready because I love a ***challenge***!

My biggest problem was getting enough money for tuition. I was accepted at both schools but, unfortunately, I was not able to afford the tuition. I had to decline admission to both schools. It was 1967, and I continued to work for Dr. Poll full time.

Late that summer, to my surprise, the American Dental Association notified me that I had been awarded a full tuition teaching fellowship to attend Tufts University for my periodontology program. I was ecstatic, but I never used the scholarship. I will explain.

I introduced and performed periodontics in Dr. Poll's practice. I was paid a salary of about twelve thousand dollars per year, and I calculated that I generated income of about one hundred twenty thousand dollars per year, just in periodontal fees! I worked five days a week, Saturday mornings, and through most of my lunch hours when I did laboratory work while eating. It would be very advantageous for Dr. Poll to have me keep working instead of having me going back to school.

I didn't know it at the time, but Dr. Poll and Dr. Irving were good friends. When I notified Dr. Irving about my fellowship, he told me that there no longer was a place for me in this year's class. This was a huge disappointment, and meant that I had to decline the fellowship and continue working for Dr. Poll.

Dr. Loewenthal to Practice Dentistry Here

Dr. Bernard Loewenthal, Lakeview Avenue, will practice dentistry with Dr. Malvin Poll, 54 Merrimack Street, it was announced today. He graduated from Flushing High School, New York City, and received his Bachelor of Science degree in bio-chemistry from Queens College N.Y.

Dr. Loewenthal received his doctorate with high honors from the New York University College of Dentistry in 1964. He served a rotating dental internship at Scott Air Force Base, IL, and completed two years of active duty at Pease Air Force Base, Portsmouth N.H., where he headed the Department of Periodontology. He is married to the former Ilana Mirkin, New York City. They have a daughter, Bonnie Beth Loewenthal.

My Post-Graduate Training

I was ***persistent*** and insistent about becoming a periodontist, regardless of the financial consequences. I did get a place in the next class at Tufts, still unsure how I would be able to pay for my family's needs while becoming a full-time student again. I reapplied for the teaching fellowship the following year, but I was only a runner-up.

Armed for the stresses that were sure to come, I began my two-year training in periodontology in the fall of 1968, at Tufts, sans fellowship. I learned that the class ahead of mine was not filled, and there actually had been a place for me. I think I know what may have happened; can you guess? But, as you will read, my philosophy that: ***Much of life happens for the best and for our highest good and learning. Undesirable and bad things do happen, but occasionally they have a positive effect—given time*** proved to be true for me, once again.

The clinical part of my training was easy for me because I had so much experience in the Air Force. However, the bookwork and research were more difficult.

Ilana obtained a job in Haverhill, teaching fourth grade. Her salary was modest, but very helpful. I was able to get a one thousand dollar scholarship loan from the Haverhill Jewish Scholarship Loan Committee. I also obtained another federal educational loan with a low interest rate. I don't know how they did it, but my wife's parents sent us five hundred dollars a month while I was in school.

Connee told me that if we really needed financial help, she could send us some of the money that they had been saving for their son's Bar Mitzvah, but we declined. My sister June asked her husband, Stanley, to help us, but he declined, despite the fact that they were reasonably wealthy. Our pharmacist, Tom Valhouli, was very kind to us. He told me that we didn't have to pay our pharmacy bills until I opened my practice. That was a real help.

On Tuesday mornings, as had been the case for decades, Dr. Irving conducted his dreaded seminar. The students were distressed about this seminar because Dr. Irving frequently embarrassed a student in front of his or her classmates. It didn't matter how much the student knew, this was his way of teaching: by ***fear***. Dr. Irving had a way of making mature men—smart men, and gifted men—shake in their boots, as the saying goes. It was common to see these post-graduate students in the men's room, which was directly across the hall from the seminar room, either sitting down on the toilet because of a bowel problem or popping tranquilizers to help them get through the seminar.

I graduated from Tufts, somewhat traumatized. I taught there for a few years, leaving, following Dr. Irving's death.

Dr. Irving, seen here in the middle of the bottom row in the photo below, was probably the brightest researcher and periodontist of his time, but he was ***feared*** by his students. He died in October of 1972. I was rototilling my garden when his secretary called to inform me of his death; Ilana took the message. We attended his funeral in Boston.

Periodontology classes of 1970 and 1971

Thanksgiving at the Harbilas' Home

Gene and Jean became our closest friends. Gene was a crackerjack physician and he became our family doctor. The Harbilas duo was dynamic, sophisticated, and fun. Gene was a truly great chef, and Jean was not far behind him. They enjoyed life to its fullest and they introduced us to new and exciting activities.

We went on vacations and to concerts with them, always having a fun time. We played bridge frequently, usually at their home because of their young boys. We celebrated many holidays with them, usually at their house, including Thanksgiving, Christmas, and the Greek holidays. The celebrations always included a gourmet feast prepared by the two of them, and the finest wines money could buy. We learned cooking techniques and recipes from them, and enjoyed all kinds of new delectable foods.

Gene and I

Gene was a superb storyteller with a terrific sense of humor. I don't know how he could remember so many stories; I have trouble remembering just one or two! He had a funny saying, one that I still use. If someone said something bright or innovative, he would say, ***"Smart like two high schools."***

Gene was a heavy smoker and died from lung cancer in his early seventies. I will always feel indebted to Gene because he taught me so much about life. He was a brilliant person, and it was only by ***chance*** that we met because: ***Much of life happens for the best and for our highest good and learning. Undesirable and bad things do happen, but occasionally they have a positive effect—given time.***

These were wonderful times in our lives. I miss Gene dearly.

The Sting

On the night of a baseball all-star game in the late 1970s, Gene was in my kitchen with Ilana. He was sipping a glass of wine and he was barefoot. I was outside throwing a Frisbee for our beagle, Corky.

Corky our Beagle

Our yard was fenced in so Corky could not get out. I accidentally threw the Frisbee over the fence. It landed beneath a blueberry bush, one of several blueberry bushes that were on the lot I had recently sold to a neighbor. I ran around the fence and found the Frisbee. I kneeled down to get it, and when I looked up, I saw beautiful clumps of ripe blueberries, which were no longer mine. I said to myself, don't pick any blueberries; they're not yours anymore. I also said to myself, "oh...go ahead"; the new owner doesn't even know they exist.

So I reached up and tried to pick a few berries, but I couldn't, because, by ***chance***, a hornet stung my arm, and I fell to the ground, stunned. When I got up, I raced into my kitchen, grabbed Gene and said, "I've been stung. I feel very sick; please take me to the hospital immediately." He said, "Okay, I'll go home and get my shoes and my car."

I grabbed him by the arm and said, "No, take my car, and forget about the shoes," which he did. We got to the hospital quickly. My ears were clogged and I was itching all over, but my breathing was still all right. Gene steered me, while barefoot, right into the ER, where he was well known. He asked a nurse for a syringe with adrenalin. No paperwork was done, and he injected me. By this time huge hives were breaking out all over my body, I couldn't stop scratching and I could hardly hear.

After Gene observed me for about an hour, he took me home, put me to bed, and I went to sleep. When I woke up the next morning I felt weak. Gene prescribed a Medrol Dose Pack for me, which is a steroid drug given in decreasing doses over a period of a week. I started on the dose pack and rested for the remainder of that week.

Gene referred me to an allergist, where I had very sophisticated testing to determine to which stinging insects I was allergic. Very small doses of freeze-dried insect venom were injected subcutaneously to see how my body reacted. It turned out that I was severely allergic to several common stinging insects in the order of Hymenoptera. I was allergic to hornets, white-faced hornets, yellow jackets, and wasps...but not bees.

I began a desensitizing program that required many small injections of reconstituted freeze-dried venom from each of the offending insects. This treatment was dangerous, and could be life threatening, but I needed it, especially since I worked for long hours in my garden, where these insects were prevalent. I subjected myself to this procedure for over thirty years. I was injected every four to six weeks with a specific dose of venom from the four insect types. When I was outside, if one of these insects came anywhere near me, I reflexively jumped and ran away for fear of being stung. Someone watching me would no doubt wonder about me!

Allergy to Cold

The allergic reaction to the sting also resulted in another fairly unusual medical problem. I was doing some paperwork one morning, with my right forearm resting on top of my desk. My desk's surface was made out of slate, which feels cold to the touch. As I wrote, I absentmindedly began scratching the underside of my right arm; it itched. A few days later while I was shaving, my thighs were leaning against my porcelain sink, which was also cold to the touch. I began to itch where my thighs touched the sink, and they broke out in hives. Evidently my body had become allergic to "cold" because of my immune system's reaction to the sting.

About a week earlier I had been swimming in the ocean, where the water temperature was in the cold mid-sixties. When I got out of the water, my friend John Tucker said that my body was red everywhere. I didn't feel itchy, but I also had drunk a lot of beer. A few days later I checked out my strange reaction further. I took an ice cube and placed it on my arm for only about five seconds. A hive would form immediately, exactly where the ice cube had been.

My allergist explained to me that I had a fairly rare condition caused by the sting, called "acquired cold urticaria." This allergy to cold could be life threatening because it can cause a significant drop in blood pressure. This happens because blood vessels dilate when hives form. This drop in blood pressure could result in fainting, shock, and even death. This had been especially dangerous for me when I had been swimming because my whole body had been immersed in cold water. I was very lucky not to have had a life-threatening event! As time went on, the problem gradually disappeared, which was important because I lived in cold and snowy New England.

Giant Pumpkins

Although only slightly profitable, growing and selling vegetables became an important endeavor for me, which I enjoyed it a lot. My enjoyment of growing vegetables has continued, and has led me to other gardening ***challenges***. Years later, I saw huge pumpkins on display at an autumn fair. These monsters intrigued me, and I decided that I wanted the ***challenge*** of trying to grow one. The task of growing a giant pumpkin turned out to be much more complicated and time consuming than I had ever imagined.

Obtaining the very best seeds from other giant pumpkins was the first step. I found some of these seeds on the Internet. Then, learning from books specifically written about growing these huge pumpkins was essential. Intensive soil preparation, fertilization, germination of the seeds, heating the soil, adequate watering, sophisticated pest control, pruning the vines, control of pollination of each potential pumpkin by hand, tying the flowers closed before the bees got to them, and building a shade cover to protect the growing pumpkin from the sun all played vital roles in successfully growing a giant pumpkin.

My First Try— an 1100lb. pumpkin!

Smaller Pumpkins for Kids

Most people like pumpkins, especially children. If initials are carved into a small pumpkin, the initials will grow in size, along with the pumpkin. So, every summer I would carve the initials of children we knew onto small pumpkins. At harvest time the kids were thrilled to take home their own personal pumpkin.

Rachel and Geoffrey Ness with their personal pumpkins

Chapter 4

1970-1995: Periodontics, Meteorology, Inventing and New Adventures

Opening a Practice

My ***challenge*** now, after twenty-three years of schooling, was to open my periodontal practice. We were happy living in Haverhill, and decided that I would open my practice there. I found a site for my office and worked with a dental equipment company in Boston to set up and equip it.

This was all done expediently, and I was able to borrow twenty five thousand dollars to get my practice started. This new debt, piled on top of my large educational loans, was a tough nut to crack. I opened my practice on July 1, 1970.

BERNARD LOEWENTHAL, D.D.S.

ANNOUNCES THE OPENING OF HIS OFFICE FOR THE

PRACTICE OF PERIODONTICS

AT

444 MAIN STREET

HAVERHILL, MASSACHUSETTS 01830

Office Hours
By Appointment

Telephone
374-0114

A periodontist is dependent upon general dentists to refer patients. This made it essential for me to visit all of the dentists in the surrounding area. I cold-called on them, introducing myself and asking for referrals in a very nice way. This was a real ***challenge***. Dentists met me with mixed reactions. Some were interested, some didn't care that I was around, and some told me that they would never refer a patient because they just didn't refer patients to specialists. As the months went on, new patients slowly began to trickle in.

I used a spiral notebook to store all of a new patient's personal information. The patient was given a number; the referring dentist was noted, as was whether or not recent X-ray pictures were available. This book represented the life of my practice. When a new patient called for an appointment, I would always send a handwritten thank-you card immediately to the referring dentist. Whenever the telephone rang, I would listen to my secretary and hope that the call was from a new patient. My ***fear*** of not having enough business did not change, even after thirty years of practice. I think that some ***fears*** are so heavily ingrained that they cannot be overcome. It is said that ***fear*** is the supreme motivator, and it was for me. Because of this ***fear***, the philosophy of Napoleon Hill, author of "Think and Grow Rich", became incredibly meaningful to me. I took this quotation from his book, ***"Whatever the mind can see and believe, it can achieve."*** and made it my personal mantra. This quotation helped me look ahead and try as hard as I could to succeed; envisioning a flourishing and well respected practice.

I tried to practice at the cutting edge of my profession in every way that I could. I became a Diplomate of the American Board of Periodontology in 1976. A diplomate is a periodontist who has made significant achievements beyond the mandatory educational requirements of the specialty, and who is certified by The American Board of Periodontology. In lay terms this means ***"Board Certified."***

Only about five percent of periodontists achieved their Board certification when I did because the process was ***challenging***, extremely difficult, and time consuming. The examination process consisted of three parts: (1) a written examination, (2) the submission of five case reports showing the results of treatment of patients with complicated problems, documented with copies of the patient's record, X-ray pictures, colored clinical pictures of before, during, and after treatment, and (3) a combination a clinical examination including the execution of a surgical procedure and a ***challenging*** oral examination by Board examiners.

I remember vividly the day I found out the results of my examination. I was anxiously waiting for the result, and checking my mail every morning. When my secretary received "the" envelope, I snatched it from her hands and raced back to my private office. I opened it, saw that I had passed, and I was so happy that I cried!

After four years of practice in Haverhill, more and more patients were being referred to me from dentists in southern New Hampshire, and not from the Haverhill area. New Hampshire was growing rapidly as opposed to Haverhill, which was an older shoe-manufacturing city that was in decline. The handwriting was on the wall: the future of my practice was in New Hampshire.

I had to consider moving my practice to New Hampshire, specifically Portsmouth. That charming city, located on the ocean, contained lovely residential communities, fine cultural resources, and boasted many fine restaurants. Since we had lived in Portsmouth, we knew the area quite well and liked it a lot.

1974: Air Force Discharge and Practice Move

I was given my honorable discharge from the Air Force in 1974. I remained in the Air Force Reserve for many years.

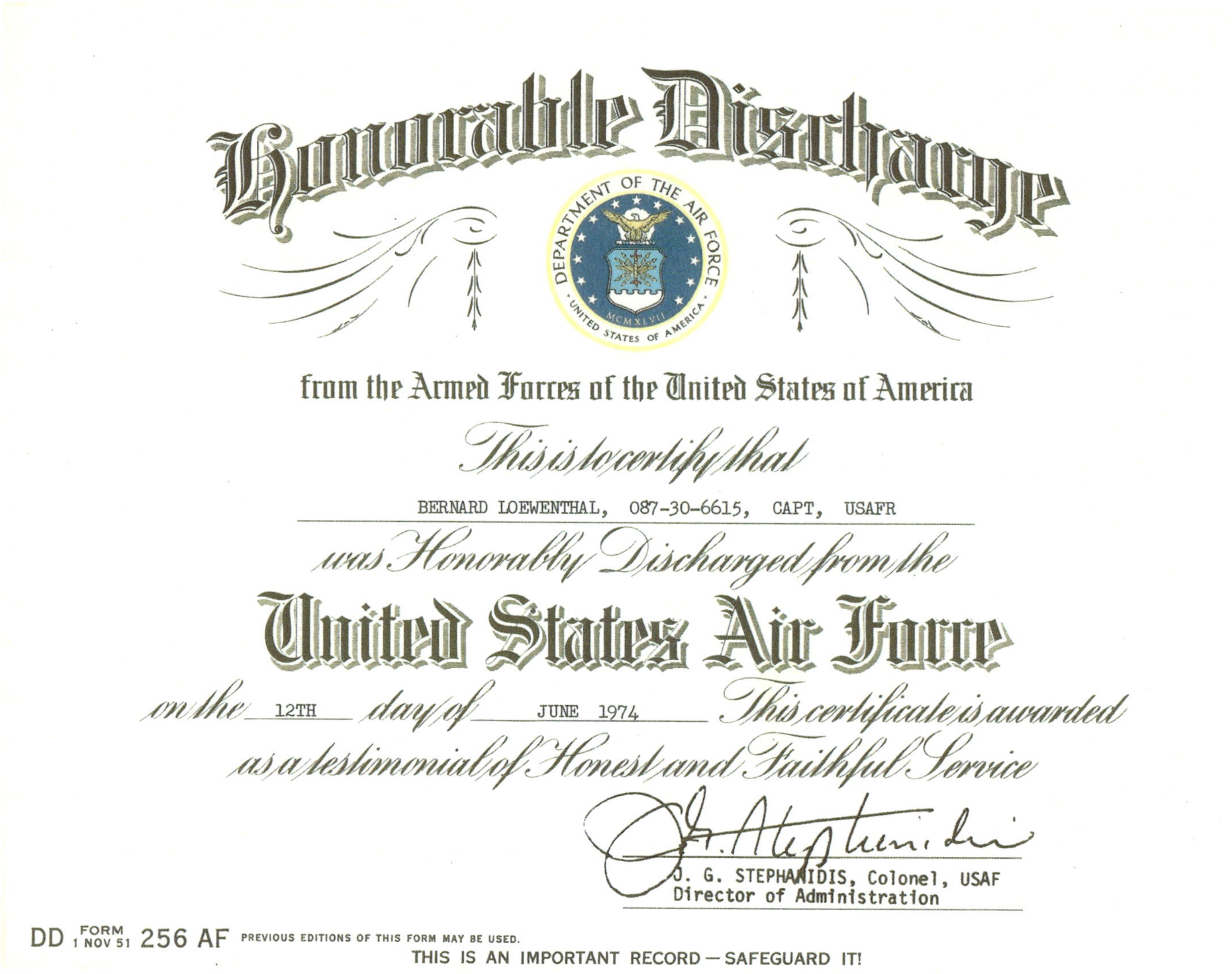

Honorable Discharge

DEPARTMENT OF THE AIR FORCE · UNITED STATES OF AMERICA · MCMXLVII

from the Armed Forces of the United States of America

This is to certify that

BERNARD LOEWENTHAL, 087-30-6615, CAPT, USAFR

was Honorably Discharged from the

United States Air Force

on the 12TH day of JUNE 1974 This certificate is awarded as a testimonial of Honest and Faithful Service

J. G. STEPHANIDIS, Colonel, USAF
Director of Administration

DD FORM 1 NOV 51 256 AF PREVIOUS EDITIONS OF THIS FORM MAY BE USED.

THIS IS AN IMPORTANT RECORD — SAFEGUARD IT!

I received an urgent telephone call in 1974 from a Portsmouth oral surgeon. He said, "Bernie, there's another periodontist looking around here, and he's planning to open a practice. If you are serious about coming up here, you'd better move your ass." That message sent shockwaves through me. A periodontist opening in Portsmouth would effectively cut off my referrals from New Hampshire.

Without delay, I got my foot in the door! I immediately called a general dentist friend of mine in Portsmouth, and I explained the situation to him. I asked him if I could, on a very temporary basis, rent one of his dental treatment rooms. He agreed to let me rent a room and I immediately made an announcement in the area's newspapers that I was opening a periodontal practice in Portsmouth. I began seeing patients in my rented room within a few days. By ***chance***, excellent office space opened up a few weeks later in the building next to where I was renting, and I grabbed it.

I renovated the office space, had all of my dental equipment installed, and started seeing patients there within a month. Both of my offices were two-day-a-week practices, and I kept both open. I spent Mondays and Wednesdays in Haverhill, and Tuesdays and Thursdays in Portsmouth. My staff and I commuted from Haverhill to Portsmouth. My office telephones were set up in such a way that no matter which office was being called, my secretary would answer, live. As expected, my Portsmouth office flourished.

After a few years I closed my Haverhill office and devoted full time to my busy Portsmouth office. I commuted from my home in Haverhill four days a week. My staff became tired of the commuting, so I eventually was forced to find new staff members.

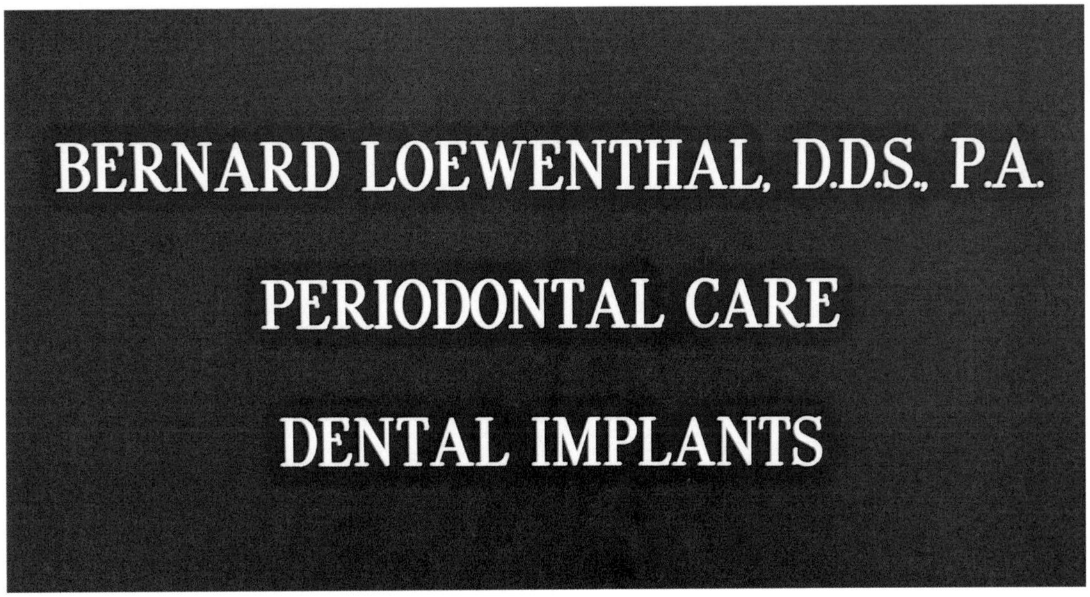

Bernard Loewenthal

Loewenthal speaks to military dentists

PORTSMOUTH — Dr. Bernard Loewenthal of Stratham was recently a guest lecturer at Walter Reed Army Hospital in Washington, D.C.

Loewenthal addressed Army, Navy, Air Force and civilian dentists. He was the featured speaker at an all week conference on periodontics.

His topic was "Providing Quality Care for Patients with Periodontal Problems Using Fixed Bridgework." Dr. Loewenthal discussed the importance of understanding each patient's specific needs, not only in terms of technical dentistry but in terms of the goals and values of the individual patient. He discussed the sequencing of treatment between the restorative dentist and periodontist to assure long-term predictable success.

Loewenthal is on the faculty of The Institute for Advanced Dental Studies, Swampscott, Massachusetts and is the only board certified periodontist in New Hampshire. He practices in Portsmouth.

Helping the Profession

I was privileged to have taught periodontics at Tufts University School of Dental Medicine, the Institute for Advanced Dental Studies, and I lectured at the New York University College of Dentistry. I also lectured on a national basis at locations such as the Walter Reed Army Hospital, the American Academy of Periodontology's annual meetings, the New York State Ninth District Dental Society, and a number of other venues.

I served on the Public Communications Committee of the American Academy of Periodontology for several years.

I published articles in several peer-reviewed professional journals on diverse subjects such as treatment planning using guided bone regeneration, dental implants, and the diagnosis of periodontal disease.

In 1983 I created a documentary television show that appeared on channel eleven, the New Hampshire PBS television station. The title of my show was "Periodontal Disease Fact and Fiction." My purpose in doing this was to help increase awareness about periodontal disease. Dr. Kathleen C. Swallow, the wife of a fellow dentist was the moderator, and my dental hygienist, Jan Knauss, appeared with me. We did it live and with no rehearsal. It was a fun project.

I founded and guided the "Great Bay Dental Study Group" in Portsmouth. Its mission was, and remains, helping dentists learn and improve their skills in all areas of dentistry. The club blossomed over time; others took over its reins when I retired. It remains a vital organization after twenty-eight years, continuing to mentor young dentists in the community.

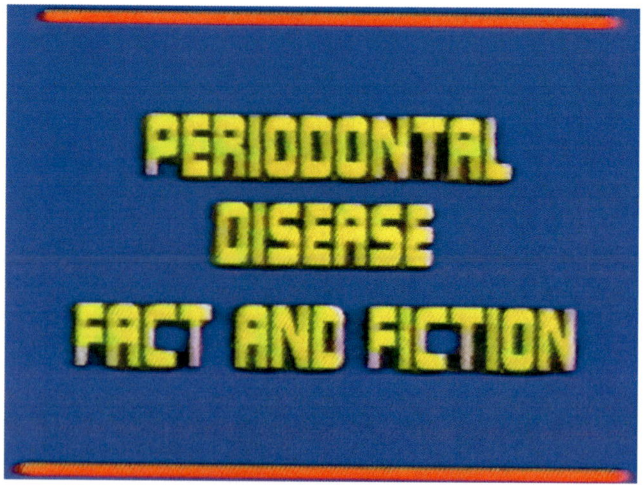

1983 PBS Segment
Periodontal Disease
Fact and Fiction

Foolish Bernie

When I moved my practice to Portsmouth in 1974, a dentist friend of mine advised me to never visit a Portsmouth dentist by the name of Tony Goodwin. He explained to me that Dr. Goodwin had the most prestigious dental practice in New Hampshire, and that Dr. Goodwin wouldn't even want to talk to me because he only refers his patients to a prominent periodontal practice in Swampscott, Massachusetts. He said that Dr. Goodwin and that periodontal practice did procedures that were too aggressive, and that all of their fees were unfair and much too high. Like a real dummy, I took his advice and never visited Dr. Goodwin.

About a year later, I attended a local dental society meeting being held in a Portsmouth restaurant. These meetings were well attended and provided a ***chance*** for me to meet and socialize with many of the dentists with whom I would like a professional relationship. As I was walking by the bar, totally by ***chance***, a tall, good looking man who was sitting on a bar stool looked down at me and said, "Are you Loewenthal, the new periodontist?" I looked up at him and said, "Yes, I am." He said, "Well, I'm going to test you." This person was Dr. Goodwin.

A few weeks later a new patient, Russell Davis, called my office to make an appointment. He said that Dr. Goodwin asked him to call for a consultation. Dr. Goodwin was evidently testing me, as he said he would. The patient arrived and I examined him, reviewed his X-ray pictures, and suggested a treatment plan to him. I told Mr. Davis that I would send Dr. Goodwin a report with my findings and recommendations, and that he should be hearing from Dr. Goodwin.

Dr. Goodwin received my report and called me. We discussed my plan briefly, but we did not agree on it. He suggested that we discuss things over dinner, so we made a dinner date. We met at The Library Restaurant, one of the nicer eateries in Portsmouth. I was a bit nervous because of Dr. Goodwin's reputation for being difficult and hard to get along with, and his unique affiliation with a world-renown periodontal practice in Massachusetts. My concerns were completely unwarranted. Dr. Goodwin was a pleasant, friendly, and well-spoken gentleman. We had a great discussion and dinner. This turned out to be one of the most important meetings of my life. We discussed many things well into the night. We were both scotch drinkers, and we kept our waitress busy long after the food was eaten.

I'll refer to Dr. Goodwin "Tony" because that's what I called him for the next thirty-five years. Tony was keenly aware that his referrals would be very important for me. He told me that the reason he ***challenge***d me by saying "I'm going to test you" was not that we needed to agree about a plan for any patients, but just the opposite. He was concerned that I would always try to agree with him, so as to encourage more referrals. When we had differing ideas about Mr. Davis, Tony was relieved. He said to me, "The last thing I wanted you to be was a ***yes man.***"

So began a wonderful and life-long friendship. Tony Goodwin has had a profound impact on my life, both professionally and personally. Tony's wife, Bonnie, was in all senses of the word a very, very fine lady. They had a daughter, Amy, and a son, Jonathan. Our two couples shared many marvelous times and family occasions together.

Wonderful Friends

In 1975, when my friendship with Tony began, I met some of his best friends: John Tucker, Lee Roper, Don Olen Sr., and Richard Peasley. I later met Don's son, Don Jr., his daughter, Liz, and Lee's sons, Brian, Marty, and Mark.

John and Lee were both local dentists. John was an endodontist, and Lee a general dentist. Don Olen Sr. was a salesman for a large dental supply company. He provided dental supplies to Tony, John, Lee, and me. Don worked out of his office in Portland Maine, not far from his home. He visited dentists in the Portsmouth area about every two weeks, on Tuesdays. Those Tuesdays were special because Tony, John, Don, and Bernie would have lunch together. I looked forward to those lunches because we had a ***chance*** to see Don, catch up on each other's lives, and make plans for upcoming events, including fishing and hunting trips. Richard Peasley worked for a paper company in Maine for many years. He is a childhood friend of Don's. Richard is a radio technician, and a private pilot as well.

By all standards I was a city-boy, despite the fact that I did some farming and hunting. My friendships with these men exposed me to real country-boy knowledge and experiences, for all of which I will be forever grateful. This knowledge and the experiences I had improved my life. Tony, Lee, Don, and Richard had been hunting and fishing buddies for many years, dating back to the 1960s. They all were true outdoorsmen, fine family men, and all were married for many decades. They are and were very responsible, honest, trustworthy, innovative, and very intelligent people. I will forever be indebted to them for the skills I learned, and for the experiences and camaraderie I have shared with them.

I learned skills about self-sufficiency. Most important was to be innovative and calm when faced with a problem of any kind in life, whether outdoors or indoors, and having total and complete trust and faith in close friends and in myself. I became proficient in skills such as surviving and navigating in the wilderness or on the water, and many other useful, know-how to do daily living skills.

These men traditionally held, an annual deer-hunting week during November at a camp in Maine. They went to either Don's camp or one belonging to Tony's father-in-law. The group was very tightly knit, and seldom invited a new person to hunt with them. If a new person was invited, he had to prove himself to be the same (excuse the pun) caliber of person as the others. He might not be invited back, if he did not fit in.

In 1980 my ego received a huge lift. Tony had conferred with the other men in the hunting group, and I was invited to their deer camp to hunt for that year. This was one of the best invitations I had ever received! For the next twenty-eight years I shared in the joy, fun, and camaraderie with these fine individuals every November, and on many other occasions as well.

In later years we hunted exclusively from a camp owned by Don and Don Jr. It was a remote camp in the mountains of northwest Maine, in the wilderness, only a few miles from the Canadian border. A small river, with a sometimes fast-moving current, had to be crossed to get to their camp. The Olens and Dick Peasley built an extraordinary raft, upon which we could cross the river with all of our gear, including all-terrain vehicles.

This innovative set-up was capable of floating a 650lb ATV and a 250lb man safely while crossing a VERY COLD river.

The raft was pushed by a two-horse outboard motor, which was attached to a small aluminum boat. There were eventually seven hunters, including Don Jr., and Lee's son, Brian. All these men were serious hunters and were usually in the woods very early, while it was still dark, and on a deer stand the minute it was legal to hunt. In the 1980s each of us, on his own, would head out into the mountains, bringing lunch, and usually not returning to camp until dark. As the years went on, some of the older folks would come back to camp for lunch and even take a snooze. By the year 2000, some of the senior members could be found snoring in their sleeping bags around 2:00 p.m., but still ready to go out to hunt for the last hour or two!

The magnificent seven!

Forgot to rotate the pie!

We ate like kings! Although everyone contributed to the menus, especially Lee who loved to cook Italian food, Tony and I, as the years went on, without objection, took over the week's menus. He and I had similar tastes, loved excellent food, and thought that we were chefs. We never felt that we had enough food for the week. I doubt that better food could be found in any five star restaurant!

Brian was in charge of the beer, including some that he brewed. Everyone brought their own booze. Tony's father always sent a fine bottle of scotch for the camp, usually Chivas Regal.

There was no electricity in this remote setting. We used propane or kerosene lamps, and we cooked with a wood burning or propane fueled stove. Tony always made a number of apple pies during the week. I usually peeled the apples after hunting, with either a scotch or a beer close at hand. The wood stove's oven cooked unevenly, so we had to rotate whatever was being cooked.

Tony cooking rib-roast with supervisor Lee

The week of hunting was only one aspect of the fun that the members of the group experienced. Many summers, Tony hosted a true New England clambake at his house. The families of the men were invited, along with a few other friends. He frequently cooked one hundred lobsters, a bushel of clams, five-dozen ears of corn, a few dozen eggs, and a similar number of hot dogs.

Scrumptious result!

Table setting after all the lobsters were cooked.

The cooking was done in a unique way. All of the food was placed and cooked in watertight, thirty gallon, galvanized trash barrels. The barrels were placed on cinder blocks that housed a hot wood fire. The bottom of the barrels had a few inches of water in them, so that steam would be created. The tops of the barrels were sealed tightly with wet canvas, which created a pressure cooker. After about forty-five minutes on the fire, the food was done, the table had been set, and everyone knew their task: eating! Being a good emulator, I copied Tony's technique and hosted clambakes at my house in subsequent years.

Cooking lobsters with Tony and John at my house

Dear friends Don and Marion Olen about to enjoy the feast

The guys feasted on the clams

Toothy Northern Pike

The group went on many fishing trips. Local trips took place in Maine, where one of us owned a camp. We fly fished for native brook trout and salmon. Away-trips included Alaska, Canada, the Rocky Mountains, Labrador, and the Bahamas. My good friend Mitch Kalter went on many of these trips. Some of my most memorable trips were to Labrador, where the largest brook trout in the world are found. The average trout weighed four to six pounds, and many six- to eight-pound fish were caught. All fish were released. There was also an abundance of northern pike in Labrador; pretty toothy critters.

On one trip to Labrador, our single engine plane was forced down by ***chance***, on a remote lake at 7:00 a.m. on June 12th, because of a snowstorm! Fortunately, the pilot knew where the only camp on the lake was located. He guided the plane to that camp, where we stayed all day while the snow continued to fall. The camp was new and very well equipped, with a gourmet kitchen run by a world class chef. The owner of the camp, the president of Labrador Airlines, and his staff treated us extremely well, and fed us fine food and drink. Just minutes before we were about to sit down to a gourmet roast beef dinner, our pilot notified us that we had to leave. It was getting dark, and we flew at a very low altitude to our destination at another lake.

World class-Brook Trout, Labrador

Mitch Kalter with huge Brook Trout

Plane forced down in snowstorm, June 12th

The Bahama fishing trips were primarily for bonefish. We fly fished, which made fishing much more challenging.

Bahama Bonefish

A Boat

My fishing enthusiasm created a desire in me to buy a boat to use in the large Portsmouth area bays and the nearby ocean. I bought a seventeen-foot Mako, center console boat, which was fine for fly fishing and very seaworthy. I named the boat ***"Cloudoc."***

I became a member of the Coast Guard Auxiliary after taking its Boating and Seamanship course, and then passing its comprehensive test. I donated my boat and time, on some weekends, to patrol the local waters and to help rescue boaters that were in harm's way. I went on to teach the Auxiliary's weather course.

U.S. Coast Guard Auxiliary

United States
COAST GUARD AUXILIARY
Presents this Certificate to
BERNIE LOEWENTHAL
For the successful completion of the subjects so indicated in the
BOATING SKILLS and SEAMANSHIP Course on 4 MAY '9

BS&S 6 Lesson Course DATE 4 MAY '92 FC	BASIC SAILING DATE 4 MAY '92 FC
PILOTING DATE 4 MAY '92 FC	WEATHER DATE 4 MAY '92 FC
MARINE ENGINES DATE 4 MAY '92 FC	RADIOTELEPHONE DATE 4 MAY '92 FC
MARLINSPIKE SEAMANSHIP DATE 4 MAY '92 FC	INLAND WATERWAYS, LOCKS and DAMS DATE FC

Contents approved by the National Association of State Boating Law Administrators and recognized by the United States Coast Guard

FLOTILLA 207 DISTRICT 1NR

FLOTILLA COMMANDER

Tony Goodwin doing what he liked best

Very sadly, Tony and Lee died when in their early 70s. Lee's death was caused by prostate cancer. Tony's death was shocking because it was completely unexpected. Tony was apparently very healthy. He hosted a clambake to say "good-bye" to the dying Lee. The day after the clambake, Tony had a stroke, and he died a week later. I remain extremely saddened because of their deaths.

1979: Moving to Stratham, New Hampshire

In 1979 we decided to move our residence to New Hampshire. We found land that was part of an apple orchard. The land was on top of a hill, which afforded great visibility looking south and west. This location was very important to me because of my weather interests. The location of the house enabled me to watch the sky from every direction.

We built a passive solar house, which was was a fifteen-minute drive to my office. The house had three levels, including a basement where I had my man-cave. It didn't feel like a basement because it had many windows, which provided a nice view to the south, and had a glass slider that opened onto our front lawn. I had a wood stove, computer, television, fly tying and bullet making bench, gun cabinet, closets for storage, and a single bed for napping. This was a fine man-cave! We lived in this unique house until 2009.

I took pride in our landscaping. I installed our lawns myself, using a specially formulated seed mixture, which was a combination of three varieties of Kentucky blue grass, a red fescue, and a perennial rye grass. I watered and fertilized the lawns carefully, and I was pleased with the results.

Man-Cave Here

I planted the Norway spruce trees when they were five feet tall

Rear view of house and shed.
A wireless weather station is on the swing set.

My zero-turn lawn mower

I farmed some of the land.
We didn't sell vegetables anymore, we ate them and gave the rest to friends.

I enjoy smoking food, especially salmon, chicken, and turkey

In the winter, we fed deer in the driveway near the house

Making apple cider

Bonnie Marries and Has a Son, Mark

While we were living in Stratham, Bonnie moved to Boston where she went to college, worked, and met Peter Panagiotou. Bonnie and Peter married in 1997, and their marriage was blessed by the birth of a son, Mark Steven, in 1999. Peter now owns his own moving business, and Bonnie is working in the health field, specifically helping older and disabled people. They live in Dublin, Ohio.

Our home was once filled with wonderful pets. At one time we had two Golden Retrievers and five cats. When they died, we could not replace them because Peter and Mark were allergic to cats and most dogs. Mark really wanted to have a dog, but his allergy prevented both of our families from having a dog—until Bonnie discovered a special breed of dog called Coton de Tuleur. This breed of dog was non-allergenic because it had hair, not fur.

To test whether or not this breed of dog would would truly be non-allergenic, Bonnie drove her family to a breeder in Indiana to test for any allergic reactions, and there were none. We bought the only two male puppies, and gave one to Bonnie's family, and we kept the other. Mark named their dog ***"Super Ziggy,"*** and we named ours ***"Best Buddy."*** The breeder drove the dogs from Indiana to Bonnie's home in Ohio, and we flew there to get Buddy. These dogs have been, and remain, a wonderful addition to our entire family!

Bonnie, Peter and Mark

Delivery Day for Buddy and Ziggy!

The whole family had fun times in Stratham. Mark visited fairly regularly and enjoyed varied activities, from playing in the snow and garden to inspecting live lobsters. Mark has provided all of us with inimitable and wonderful memories. Mark has become an outstanding athlete, due to his innate abilities and to his father's coaching and dedication to Mark. Mark, now age fifteen, excels in hockey and baseball.

Mark, age fourteen

Grammy, Mark and
Mr. Lobster

Grammy and Mark

Mark and my giant pumpkin

Returning to a surprise party, greeted by Eddie!

Getting Roasted!

My Surprise Fiftieth Birthday Party

A surprise birthday party was planned for me. I knew about it, but never let on that I did. The plan was for my buddies to get me away for the day by taking me fishing, and then getting me back after 6:00 p.m. The fishing trip was excellent. We caught a lot of bluefish near the Maine coast, had a great time, and then headed home.

We were getting back too early, and I was paying more attention to the time than my friends. So, on the way home I suggested that we stop at nearby mutual friend's house, where we killed half an hour. We got to my house a little after six. Surprise! The house was loaded with family and friends, many of whom came from long distances. I put on a good act, and I truly was very happy for all of the attention I was getting.

I showered and changed my clothing while the guests ate, drank, and were merry. While I was getting dressed, something I that didn't know about was going on in my basement! A major roast had been planned for me, and the roasters were all getting costumed up. During the roast, an "Ode to Bernie", written by Dr. Kathleen Swallow was read by her husband, Dr. Steve Swallow. It was sort of hilarious.

Tony put on a lion costume, which was very amusing, especially since he did not like cats! Another friend, Bob Christian, dressed in drag and teased me mercilessly about my periodontal probe invention (explained later), using sexual innuendoes. I was given a red sweatshirt decorated by John's wife, Judith. She wrote, ***"Hercules"*** on the front of the shirt ***(I pretended to be Hercules as a child)*** and ***"Fifty is Nifty"*** on the back.

A striptease dancer performed. Her costume was very scanty. She had made some props about the weather and used them very suggestively on her body while she danced. Ilana's parents were present, so the plan for the dancer to "bare all" was nixed, thankfully.

When I was about to blow out the candles on my beautiful birthday cake, I paused and thought to myself about how very fortunate I was to have all these people care about me. It was a truly fabulous and memorable evening, one for which I will always be grateful, and cherish.

Bernie's surprise 50th birthday party

The person next to me is a man

More *Chance* and a Dream Fulfilled

My fondest boyhood memories are of the time, when I lived in Loch Sheldrake, near the lake. I have always wanted to try and relive those days, at least partially.

I regularly searched advertisements in the sporting newspapers from Maine and New Hampshire, looking for camps that were for sale on a lake. My purpose in seeking a camp was to get away to a quiet area that held all kinds of wildlife, had good fishing, and was in the mountains, as far north as possible, where thunderstorms and snowstorms occurred more frequently than where we lived. I doubted that this yearning for a remote camp would ever be realized.

Early in the spring of 1984, I replied to an advertisement in the Maine Sportsman, a weekly sporting newspaper. This ad described a camp on a lake, near Rangeley, Maine. Rangeley lies in the northwest mountains of Maine, and is known for its severe winter weather and great hunting and fishing.

One morning during the summer of 1984, having forgotten that I inquired about this property, by ***chance***, a patient broke an appointment, which gave me time to check the mail. An advertisement on a single sheet of white paper that was folded in half and stapled together caught my eye because it had a Rangeley post-office mark. I opened it and saw a sketch of a log cabin on a lake, with a description of a camp that seemed to have everything I could possibly want. I called my good friend John Tucker.

John and I had discussed the possibility of sharing a camp, which would allow us to have something we couldn't each have singly, because of cost. We made a date with the realtor to see the camp, with our wives, in early October. We made reservations for an overnight stay in Rangeley in its only hotel, The Rangeley Inn.

It was a five-hour ride from our area to Rangeley. We departed on a Saturday morning, and got to Rangeley in the mid-afternoon. We registered for our two rooms, and then met the realtor, Bob. We looked at a map to see exactly where the camp was located. It was situated on Little Kennebago Lake, about twenty miles north of Rangeley. This area was located in the wilderness, three miles from the Canadian border, at an elevation of almost two thousand feet, a snow lovers delight!

All four of us fell in love with the camp as soon as we saw it. It was small, with one tiny bedroom, a modest kitchen/dining room/den area, a small bathroom with a shower, plus a loft that held two single beds, and a screened in front porch overlooking the lake. It had many desirable amenities that most camps did not have: good water from a dug well, propane heat in addition to a large wood burning stove, a telephone, a septic system, a back-up generator, and a stand alone garage that had electricity. We could be totally self-sufficient here. We met the camp's owners, and the four of us bought the camp in the spring of 1985. It met all of our wishes and more.

Winter at Little Kennebago Lake Camp

During the winter, a large section of the road to camp might be impassable because of snow. It was hit or miss as to whether the road had been plowed and how far we could drive. So, getting to camp could be a problem. I always had a four-wheel drive SUV, with four snow chains available. I was very ***persistent*** in my desire to be at camp in the winter to enjoy the snowstorms. I bought a snowmobile and a dog sled. I kept them in the garage at camp. I could usually walk from the nearest plowed road to camp to get the snowmobile and dog sled. I would then ride my snowmobile, with the trailing dogsled, back to my vehicle. Then I would load the dogsled with our gear, get Ilana in back of me on my snowmobile, and drive it back to camp. We usually stayed for a week or two, and reversed the sequence of events to get back to our vehicle.

My snowmobile and dog sled

Camp in winter

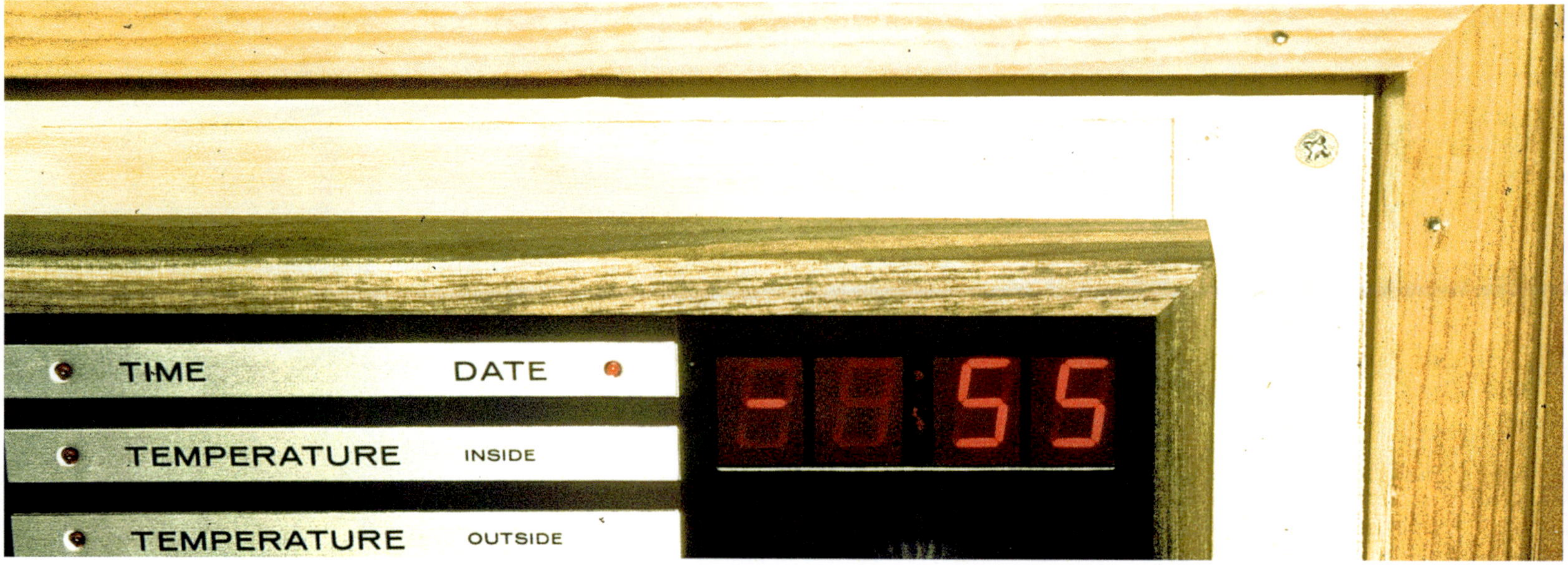

We could really chill-out here!

We both enjoyed target shooting in this snowy wilderness

Snowshoeing was great fun

I told the fish,
"I'll see you in the spring"

Ilana with her snowmobile

We enjoyed snowmobiling, and riding to Canada was fun.

I do not like heights or climbing ladders. Our camp had a flat roof at one end that needed frequent snow removal. Ilana, bless her heart, got up there and shoveled the snow off many times!

Good job Ilana!

My friend and hunting buddy, Richard Peasley, flew me over our camp one winter's day. It was an awesome flight for me in his Piper Cub! I could not only see our camp surrounded by snow, but also the ten-foot wide satellite dish I installed, so that I could receive weather information, as well as some television. Today, better reception at a fraction of the cost can be obtained with an eighteen-inch dish!

The satellite dish is next to our camp

Little Kennebago Lake

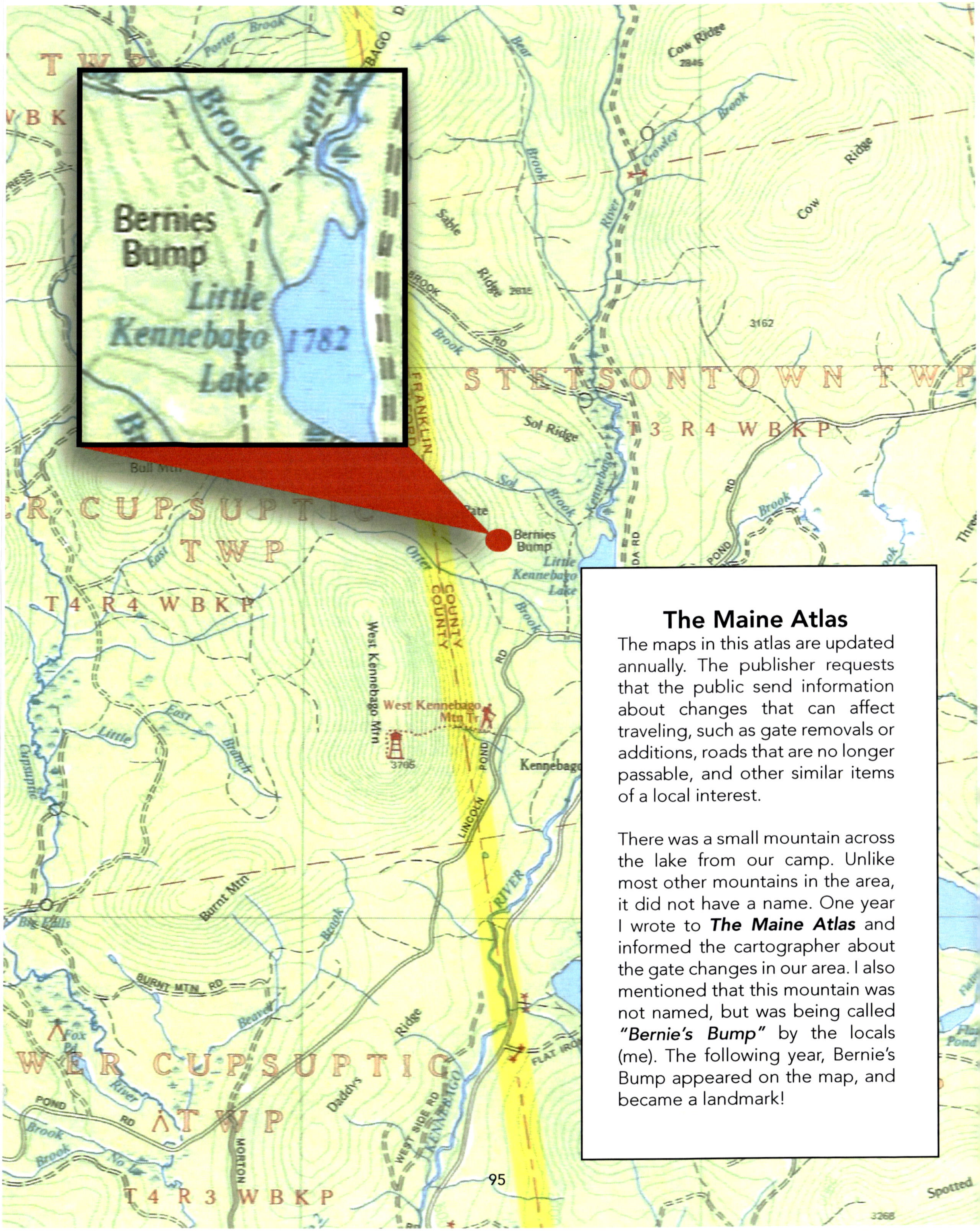

The Maine Atlas

The maps in this atlas are updated annually. The publisher requests that the public send information about changes that can affect traveling, such as gate removals or additions, roads that are no longer passable, and other similar items of a local interest.

There was a small mountain across the lake from our camp. Unlike most other mountains in the area, it did not have a name. One year I wrote to ***The Maine Atlas*** and informed the cartographer about the gate changes in our area. I also mentioned that this mountain was not named, but was being called ***"Bernie's Bump"*** by the locals (me). The following year, Bernie's Bump appeared on the map, and became a landmark!

Seen here is the website I created for PerioWise®
www.periowise.com

For in-depth information about periodontal disease I recommend going to the site of The American Academy of Periodontology: **www.perio.org**

The PerioWise® probe enables an easy and early diagnosis. The concept for using the probe is quite simple. While probing, if the dentist or hygienist can see the green mark, the gum crevice is less than three millimeters deep; then the diagnosis is "health." If the green mark is visible, but bleeding occurs, then the diagnosis is "gingivitis," and this is noted in the patient's record. If a red mark is reached, then the diagnosis is "periodontal disease." This triggers a complete and comprehensive periodontal examination, in which all probing depths are measured and recorded for all teeth.

The Patient Education Guide shows the meaning of the color-coding at various probing depths. The dentist or the hygienist, by using a mirror, can show the patient how the probing looks in the patient's mouth. The patient can then compare what they see in their mouth to the Guide, which helps the patient understand his or her own diagnosis.

I feel grateful that my invention has enabled me to contribute to the health of the public, and at the same time act as an additional source of income. These two things combined represent the riches, both tangible and intangible, described in "Acres of Diamonds."

My PerioWise® Probe

The Weather and Me

When I was six years old, I watched in awe as a hurricane lashed Flushing. I was completely fascinated by the power of Mother Nature. I had been experiencing "The Great Atlantic Hurricane," which struck full force just east of Flushing, in west-central Long Island, in 1944.

I spent the entire day running from window to window, watching trees sway in the strong wind and heavy rain, many losing large branches. It rained and blew all day. The next day I walked around the block, stepping over many downed trees and limbs. I was impressed by nature's power, never to forget how the destruction looked.

Still a child, I was becoming fascinated by the weather. I placed an indoor-outdoor thermometer next to my bedroom window. It was very important for me to always know the temperature. I was starved for weather information about upcoming weather, and I tried desperately to get any weather information I could. At 1:45 p.m. every weekday, on WNYC radio, there was a broadcast from the New York City Weather Bureau (now called the National Weather Service) detailing the weather forecast and the reasons for the forecast. Since I was in school until 3:00 p.m. I could not listen to this five-minute talk. I taught my mother to record this weather broadcast on my tape recorder. I listened to the recording immediately when I got home from school: more ***persistence***.

The chief of the New York City Weather Bureau at this time was Ernest J. Christie. He came to the Flushing Library to give a lecture. I remember sitting in awe of this man as he talked about fascinating weather events. He really did know all about the weather! My interest in weather continued to grow, rapidly.

I have always watched the skies with great curiosity. My biggest weather turn-on was snowstorms; I just went bonkers over them. I loved watching the snowflakes fall while everything turned white and became quiet. When it was snowing, I constantly checked my thermometer to see precisely what the temperature was. I learned that it is crucial that the temperature be at the freezing (melting) point, thirty-two degrees, or lower, for the snow to accumulate, unless it was snowing very hard, then thirty-three to thirty-four degrees would be cold enough to allow wet snow to accumulate.

This recording, wireless weather display, replaces the old thermometer and shows the date and time, indoor and outdoor temperature, dew point, wind speed and direction, barometeric pressure, and rainfall. I have several displays around the house so I always know what is going on outside.

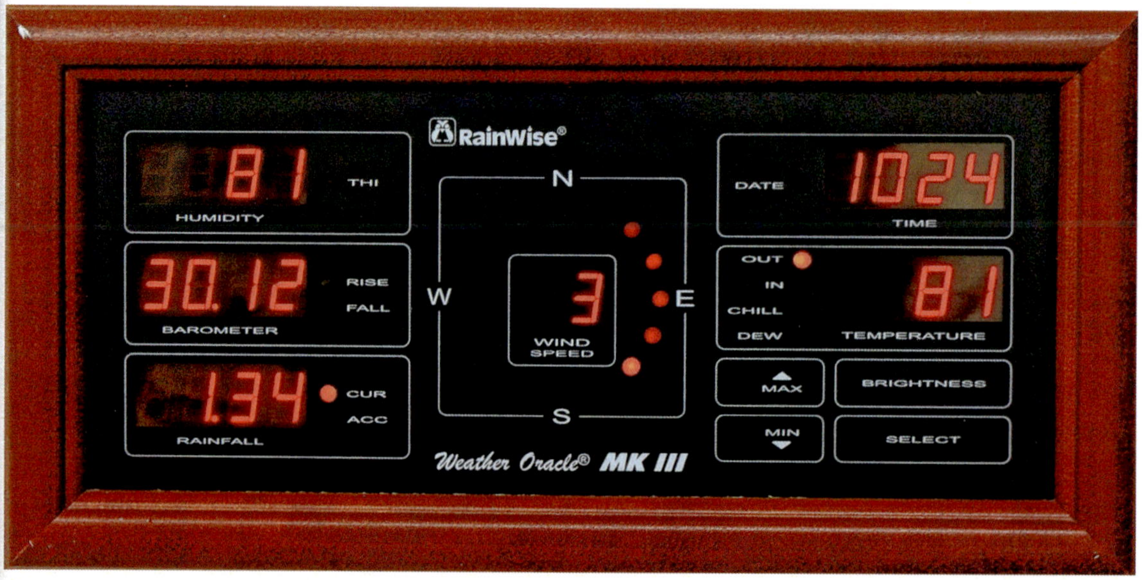

My First Great Weather Forecast

On the evening of December 25, 1947, Christmas day evening, my family was celebrating Christmas in our apartment. I was nine years old and, as always, praying for snow.

We needed more chairs, so my brother-in-law Stanley, his brother Albert, and I, walked about two blocks to their parents' apartment to get some chairs. It was a cloudless, crisp, cold, crystal-clear, bright, moonlit night, and the stars were twinkling. While we were walking, I announced that there was going to be a big snowstorm the next day. I think that my forecast was a combination of ***chance*** and wishing, which I now call a "wishcast."

To the amazement of everyone, including the Weather Bureau, my family, and especially me, The Great Blizzard of 1947 walloped New York City the next day! The storm left more than twenty-six inches of snow in Central Park, New York. Drifts exceeded ten feet; cars, buses, and even trains were stopped cold, (if you will excuse the pun), as the city came to a complete standstill. I was in weather heaven.

Historic NYC snowstorm, December 26, 1947

Photo Caption
On the morning after the storm the narrow canyon of 14th street presents an odd pattern of snow-clogged fire escapes and a marooned bus.

I loved to play in the snow. I would build forts, snow men, and have snowball fights. I had a very good and accurate throwing arm, and a good snowball fighting technique; I would make several snowballs, and throw one high up in the air, aimed to hit my opponent on its way down. My opponent would always look up to watch the snowball coming at him from above. While he was looking up, I would throw a straight, fast, snowball at him, and he had no clue the second snowball was coming. Then, bang, smash, boom, poor boy! I could do this several times, depending upon the I. Q. of my opponent.

Watch out! Junior is ready for a snowball fight!

I am not always proud of what I did with snowballs. The heat control in our apartment building was poor, and many apartments became too hot. The tenants would often open their windows to let in some cold air. When it got dark, I would go outside, and with great aim and fast legs, throw a snowball right through an open window. The occupant of the apartment usually ran to the open window, screamed out a profanity, and shouted about what just had happened. I was a bad boy, and I ran away like the wind!

My Weather Forecasting Career

While serving at Pease Air Force Base, I spent extensive amounts of time with the meteorologists at Base Operations. I became friendly with several of them and I spent hours—before and after work, lunchtime too—picking their brains and learning their methods for forecasting the weather.

I was given complete access to all of the weather forecasting equipment, including facsimile machines, weather teletypes, and radar. I became a fixture there; it was like a dream come true. Just as great as the access was for me, so were the two winters we spent at Pease, AFB.

During the two winters we lived there, snowstorm after snowstorm battered the area, shutting everything down, many times. I'm talking about one-to-two feet of snow some times!

The college courses I took in mathematics and physics, plus the weather forecasting experience I obtained while in the Air Force, enabled me to be admitted as a professional member of the American Meteorological Society in 1969, a position I still hold.

Don Kent

While at home for lunch one day, I watched an inspiring television meteorologist on channel four, NBC, Boston. His name was Don Kent. Don had energy, vitality, and a down to earth manner. I could tell instantly that he was a "weather nut" too. I wrote to him, introducing myself, and he invited me to visit him at the television station. This was the beginning of a friendship and a relationship that I will always cherish.

Don Kent was the dean of television weathermen in New England. His career began on the radio in the 1940s. He was adored by his viewers, admired by his colleagues, and was a man who, in person, was just as he appeared on television: a pleasant, vibrant, sincere, kind, and interesting person.

We got to know each other quite well. I arranged for Don to give his unique and popular New England weather talks at dental meetings, churches, and temples in our area. Don would not take money for his presentations, which were always interesting and very well attended.

I had the privilege of teaching Don how to grow vegetables. He also learned how to grow beautiful flowers, something I did not do. I always wanted to grow something I could eat!

Once Don asked me if I would like to audition for the weekend weatherman's position on channel four. I auditioned, got flustered, and did not get the job.

Don appeared on television early one morning, with his left cheek severely swollen. It was obvious to me that he had a severe dental infection. I talked with him, and then I called in a prescription for an antibiotic. Don looked and felt a lot better in two days, and then he had the problem tooth removed.

After his retirement from television, Don moved to central New Hampshire, an area he loved, where the snow really piled up. It seems that all the weathermen in New England just love snow! He took the responsibility of plowing his church's driveway and parking lot. He thrived on all kinds of gardening, and he loved making maple sugar in his sugaring off house. Someone should write a book about this wonderful man. He was always upbeat, smiling, and is sorely missed by all who knew him. Don passed away at age ninety-two, in 2010.

Weatherman Don Kent

In the early 1970s there was a national meeting for television broadcast meteorologists on Cape Cod, at the Wychmere Harbor Yacht Club in Harwich Port, Massachusetts. The meeting was very well attended. I was there with Ilana and my weather heroes from the Boston area television channels. Dinner was being served at 6:00 p.m. and I wanted to be there on time, of course.

I always watch the sky, just as I breathe, automatically. Late in the afternoon on the first day of the meeting the skies were looking ominous. I had seen thunderstorms on radar in the Boston area a few hours before, so I was alerted.

When it was time to go to dinner, I was concerned that it might rain. Being a good Boy Scout, I got my umbrella ready, gathered my wife, and we went outside and started walking toward the dinning room, which was a good distance away. We were walking with many other weathermen and their wives. All of a sudden the skies opened up, my umbrella opened up, and the rain came pouring down, but the two of us did not get wet. No one else had an umbrella!

I had the distinct pleasure to become friends with several television meteorologists in the Boston area. In addition to Don Kent, they included Bob Copeland, Harvey Leonard, and Barry Burbank. They all had something in common: they were excellent professionals, very nice people and "weather nuts!"

My Television Debut

In August of 1980 I was asked if I would like to fill in for the New Hampshire PBS television meteorologist, for three weeks, on the six o'clock evening news. I jumped at the ***chance***. I had no experience performing on live television, but I felt confidant that I could do a reasonable job because I loved talking about and forecasting the weather. The television studio was located at the University of New Hampshire, in Durham, about a half hour's drive from my house.

Ilana and I went to the television studio on Sunday, the day before my first show. I wanted to see and familiarize myself with the studio and the weather maps that I would be using. There were no computer graphics back then. I had to write all of the weather information on the maps, freehand, using water-soluble ink, so that the maps could be easily cleaned after the broadcast.

On my very first show, I had the opportunity to present the latest satellite picture of hurricane Allen, which was near Cuba. But, the timing to do this was a problem. I had to wait at home until 5:15 p.m. for the satellite picture to arrive on my facsimile machine, and I had to be at the studio by 5:45 p.m. to prepare my weather maps.

I decided to wait for the satellite picture. When it finished copying, I tore it off the facsimile machine, raced to my car, and found that there was almost no gas in it. I was frazzled, and I took Ilana's car. On the way to the studio, the skies opened up as thunderstorms arrived. I knew they were coming and had my umbrella handy. What I hadn't planned for was the railroad gates to suddenly come down and block the road because of an oncoming freight train. This happened about half way to the television studio. The freight train finally passed, and I sped to the studio. I was late; it was 6:00 p.m. when I got there!

The door to the studio was locked, and I knocked on it frantically. I was let in, and someone said, ***"Gee Bernie, we thought you chickened out!"*** The live newscast had started, and everyone was sweating because the air conditioning was broken. I quietly crept over to the weather map area, and began writing weather data on the maps, using my water-soluble marker. After a few minutes, the ink began to run because of the heat and humidity, and my writing became somewhat droopy!

I got my thirty-second warning; the red light on the camera went on, and voila! There I was on live television! After that night, things went very well. I thoroughly enjoyed my three weeks of television appearances, and my presentations improved as I became quite comfortable on camera. Ilana recorded my shows, and I still have the recordings.

Another Weather Position

I received another opportunity to forecast weather from a patient of mine, the vice president of a Fortune 500 company with headquarters near Portsmouth. Just as he was leaving the office he asked me if I would like to work for his company as a meteorologist. I thought that he was kidding and I never gave this idea another thought.

Three months later he was back for a dental visit, and he said that he was serious about the forecasting job. So, I went for an interview, and was hired. I forecast the weather for his company daily, for ten years. It was a fascinating experience, and I enjoyed the ***challenge***! This was the same person who was kind enough to let us use his company's booth for our PerioWise® dental meeting trade-show displays.

Chapter 5

1995-2013: Retirement and Beyond

Forced Retirement

In 1994 I developed severe pain in my right elbow. I could not even button my shirt or tie my necktie. After consulting with three orthopedic surgeons over a period of six months, it was determined that my pain was caused by repetitive overuse, from my practice of periodontics. The medical diagnosis was "lateral and medial epicondylitis," otherwise known as "tennis elbow." I received steroid injections and intensive physical therapy. The pain diminished, but then it came back when I worked. My doctor told me that surgury was unpredictable and not recommended because both sides of my elbow were injured. Following the advice of my doctor, the decision was made that I should work until I could not, which I did.

On Tuesday, April 25, 1995, I was about to extract an upper front tooth, place a dental implant, and perform a bone graft. When I squeezed the extraction forceps, I experienced intense pain, and I shrieked loudly. I was embarrassed and upset because everyone in my office heard me. I knew at that instant that I had to stop practicing. I finished the procedure, which I later learned from the dentist who restored the implant, was a complete success. I retired, and eventually sold my practice. I stayed busy promoting my PerioWise ® probe and giving lectures about periodontal disease, its diagnosis, and the ramifications of non-diagnosis. I also had many interests outside of dentistry to keep me very busy.

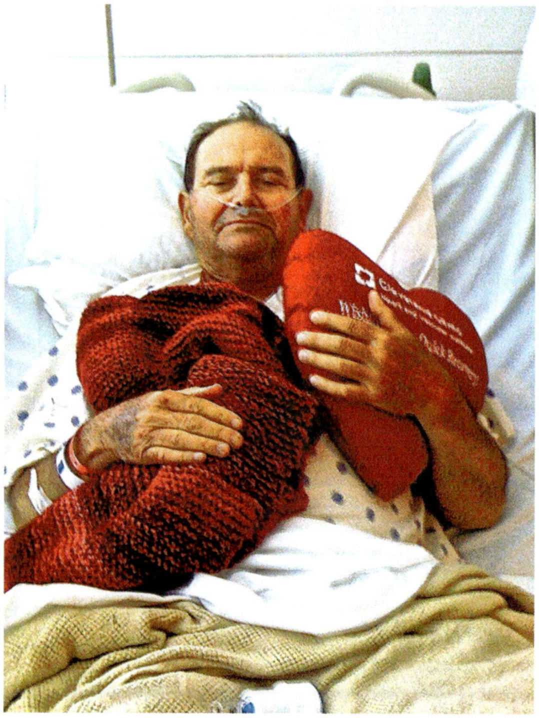

Post-op at the Cleveland Clinic

Heart Trouble

During my annual physical in 2005, my physician discovered a heart murmur. An echocardiogram revealed that my aortic valve had severe stenosis. This is a narrowing of the aortic valve opening that is a very serious condition, and life threatening over time. I had no symptoms at all.

With time, repeated echocardiograms revealed that the stenosis was getting worse. Against the recommendations of my two cardiologists, I decided, with the support of my heart surgeon, to have my aortic valve replaced.

In July of 2009 my aortic valve was replaced with a bovine valve. The surgery was performed at the Cleveland Clinic, in Cleveland, by one of the world's finest cardiothoracic surgeons, Marc Gillinov. It was definitely the correct decision, and I am fine!

Buddy helped to drive to and from Naples

Naples and Retirement

By ***chance***, my mentor, Bob Spettel, invited me to give a lecture to a group of dentists in Naples, Florida, one winter, in the the1990s. He had formed a dental study group there. That was our introduction to Naples. We liked the area very much, and in subsequent years we rented a condominium there and began spending time in Naples every winter.

Initially we could fly to Naples. However, when Buddy joined our family, we had to drive, not fly, because Buddy was just a little too big to fit in an acceptable airline dog carrier. This was a tiring, almost four-day drive. However, we did whatever it took for our kid!

We made the decision to move to Naples permanently in 2010. We love it here and we feel that this was an excellent decision. New friends and new ***challenge***s help make life good for us.

I have more time to do the things I enjoy. I continue to forecast and take delight in watching the weather, as much as ever, every day. I follow the snowstorms of which I am still in awe, using the Internet and the Weather Channel; and there is no shoveling! I enjoy sharing my life with Ilana and Buddy, making new friends, fly fishing, gardening, cooking, reading, playing tennis, exercising, swimming, following my baseball and football teams, and trying to keep up with technology, which I find a daunting task.

My Man-Cave

My new man-cave is nothing like a cave because it has skylights, very large windows and is bathed in sunlight. The view from the window where my computer sits is that of a pristine lake, frequently visited by elegant tropical birds feeding on small fish from the shoreline. The room provides me with space to pursue some of my hobbies. A long bench on one side of the room has my fly tying and bullet making equipment. The bullets are for target shooting only. One end of the room holds some of my Stan Musial memoribelia, along with a wall mounted television set and a recliner. My fishing rods are kept on ceiling mounted rod holders. The internet and computers have replaced all of the older weather information machines. There is a bed for my afternoon naps, which I seem to need more of as I get older. ***I am a very lucky and grateful person!***

Our Naples home

My Man-Cave

Weather Radar

Making Flies & Bullets

The fishing opportunities in and around Naples are spectacular! I try to fish with my friend and guide, Roan zumFelde, at least twice a month. We usually fish the bays, the near shore Gulf, and the Everglades. I also fish by myself from the Gulf beaches, from time to time.

Bonita, a fabulous fighting fish!

Choquette avocadoes

I still love to grow tomatoes, which is a major ***challenge*** here in South Florida. The sandy soil, plant diseases, insects, and humid weather create enormous problems. I ***persist*** in trying to grow them but with very limited success, so far!

I am growing a number of tropical fruit trees, including Meyer lemons, avocadoes, key limes, mangoes, bananas, and several varieties of oranges. This fun endeavor is working out well.

"Nain" banana plant

A new bunch with support

Growing the world's hottest peppers is considered a real ***challenge***, because their seeds are extremely difficult to germinate. Of course I wanted to try and grow them, and my attempt has worked out well. The peppers are far too hot to eat for ninety-nine percent of the population, including me, and they must be handled using gloves.

I give the peppers to Chef David at our country club. He likes to use them in sauces and other dishes. The world's hottest pepper is the "Trinidad Scorpion, Butch T Strain." Its potency measures over one and a half million units on the Scoville scale! This is a chemical scale used to determine the potency of hot peppers. The Habanero pepper, by comparison, which is considered to be very hot by most people, is only one third the "hotness" of Butch T!

Cooking remains a very enjoyable activity for me. One of my favorite foods to make is gravlax. Gravlax is a Scandinavian delicacy made with raw salmon, salt, sugar, and dill. I enjoy growing my own dill. The salmon is marinated for a few days in the refrigerator and then is ready to eat. It is usually served as an appetizer, with chopped eggs and onions, capers, and crackers or bread.

I also enjoy cooking a whole host of other foods ranging from my special Caesar salad to eggplant Parmesan, and barbecued chicken, using a seventy-five year-old barbecue sauce recipe, that's unsurpassed! My pickled cucumbers and tomatoes are still tasty.

Looking Back

Over the years, I have learned about life from innumerable sources. I have, and still do, spend time and energy learning from people who are experts in the field of self-improvement.

One such person who influenced my life is Dan Millman, the author of "The Peaceful Warrior." Dan's books, and his audiotape series, "Practical Wisdom," plus my residential intensive training with him in California many years ago, have influenced my life in important ways. In addition to Acres of Diamonds, Earl Nightingale has influenced my life significantly, by virtue of his excellent tape programs, "Lead the Field" and "The Strangest Secret."

Recently, by ***chance***, thanks to my world-class physician and geriatrician, Ron Garry, I have been reading and digesting an excellent book titled "Happiness is a Serious Problem" by Dennis Prager. This is a must book for anyone seeking happiness, and who can read! The book is readily available online.

Chance, persistence, challenge, fear, and my philosophy about life that: ***Much of life happens for the best and for our highest good and learning. Undesirable and bad things do happen, but occasionally they have a positive effect—given time,*** have all influenced my life in critical ways.

If my father had not by ***chance*** created a bungalow colony in Loch Sheldrake, New York, I would never have spent my wonderful boyhood years there.

I would not have become a dentist if it were not for the ***chance*** meeting of my sister with Dr. Lind.

It was by ***chance*** that I discovered Stan Musial.

It was by ***chance*** that I met Arnee, while playing ball in Loch Sheldrake. My visit to Arnee at the supermarket resulted in my first significant job, and one that I will always treasure.

The failing of my French class in college, validated my philosophy that: ***Much of life happens for the best and for our highest good and learning. Undesirable and bad things do happen, but occasionally they have a positive effect—given time.*** Forced to take French in summer school, and because of ***chance***, and my ***persistence***, I met Ilana, my wife of now fifty-three years.

The ***fear*** of not having money, and the ***challenge***s of my education, motivated me to try my best at everything I did.

It was by ***chance*** and ***persistence*** that I was chosen to be an Air Force dental intern, and was stationed at Scott Air Force base, where I met my mentor and still close friend, Bob Spettel. His teachings enabled me to seek my profession in periodontics.

It was by ***chance*** that I was stationed at Pease Air Force Base in Portsmouth, where I received weather forecasting training, and eventually located my practice.

It was by ***chance*** that my neighbor's dog got into my vegetable garden, thus enabling a wonderful and life-long friendship to develop.

It was by ***chance*** that Tony Goodwin spotted me walking by him at a dental meeting. This led to one of the finest friendships attainable. Our close relationship led to friendships with other wonderful people, their families, and many adventures, I never otherwise would have experienced. I will be forever grateful that Tony and I had our special bond.

Chance, challenge, and persistence enabled me to invent the PerioWise® Probe and Screening System. PerioWise® has helped me give something back to world, by helping to improve its health. It also has been a source of income.

I am supremely grateful for the life God has enabled me to live. I have learned what I now feel are the important things in my life. These things differ dramatically from the things that I learned from my family. Honesty, integrity, and the Golden Rule fashion my daily living.

My marriage is undoubtedly the most important aspect of my life. I love, enjoy, and protect my wonderful wife, Ilana. I could never have been successful without her devoted love for me. Ilana is truly a very exceptional person. Despite her breast cancers (a new one was just discovered), near deadly brain aneurysm, significant short-term memory loss, scalp cancer, bilateral knee replacements, and severe arthritis, she continues as if nothing is wrong, always with a smile on her face. She is a truly a remarkable person, and loved by all who know her.

Epilogue

There is a philosophical concept related to ***chance*** called synchronicity, first described in the 1920s by Carl Jung, a Swiss psychologist. It is a difficult concept to explain. It can be described as a "meaningful coincidence," comparable to ***chance*** in some ways, but different. I have experienced countless events that I consider sychronistic. Here is one example:

Ralph Chambers, who resided in the Napa Valley of California but spent time in New Hampshire, was a patient of mine. Ralph learned that I was planning a trip to the Napa Valley, and he gave me a short list of his favorite restaurants in that area.

Years later, Ilana and I vacationed in the Napa Valley. Late one evening we went to a restaurant that Mr. Chambers had recommended.

We were seated at a small table for two, way in the back, past a long bar, near the entrance to the kitchen. As soon as I sat down I was astounded, because I saw Mr. Chambers sitting at the bar, eating his dinner! There was an empty barstool next to him, which I quickly took. Disguising my voice, and not letting him see my face, I started talking to him. Eventually he turned around, recognized me, and was also astounded. Synchronicity?

I have speculated a lot about ***chance*** because it has played such an important role in my life. Science has demonstrated conclusively that all physical processes, from the behavior of the smallest sub-atomic particles to the creation of the Universe, are random, meaning that they occur by ***chance*** and behave according to the laws of physics. But, I am not convinced that science is completely correct. I feel that ***chance*** may be governed at times, in ways that science is unable to detect or explain.

My opinion, based upon my experiences and intuition, is that there is an entity that determines when ***chance*** and synchronistic events occur.

I feel that these events are not always random occurrences, but happenings controlled by a higher power, God, acting anonymously.

What do you think?

How has "***chance***" played a role in your life?

Supplement

The Supplement contains additional information about areas of my life that I have described. The areas include, My C.V, Periodontics, PerioWise®, Weather, Fishing, Gardening, and Cooking...

My Curriculum Vitae represents a summary of my formal education, qualifications and experience.

CURRICULUM VITAE

Bernard Loewenthal, B.S., D.D.S.
Diplomate American Board of Periodontology
Member American Meteorological Society

DATE/PLACE OF BIRTH: *September 10, 1938, New York City, New York*

ADDRESS: *1020 Oriole Circle, Naples, FL 34105*

TELEPHONE: *239-262-6383*

EMAIL: *cloudoc@comcast·net*

EDUCATION: *1956-1960 Queens College, New York City, B.S.*

1960-1964 New York University College of Dentistry, D.D.S.

1964-1965 United States Air Force Dental Intern, Scott AFB

1969-1970 Tufts University School of Dental Medicine, Post- Graduate Periodontology Program, Certificate

PROFESSIONAL HONORS/ AWARDS: *1964 Founder's Day Award for Outstanding Scholarship, New York University College of Dentistry*

1964 Omicron Kappa Upsilon Honorary Dental Society, Omega Chapter, New York University College of Dentistry

1964 Society for Dental Research Award, for the Advancement of Dental Research, New York University College of Dentistry

1964 New York University College of Dentistry Award for Distinguished Service to the Student Body

1964 Alpha Omega Award, New York University College of Dentistry, for Distinguished Service

1964 Mosby Scholarship Award for Scholastic Excellence

1967 Pease Air Force Base, Volunteer Dental Assistant Training Award

MILITARY SERVICE:

1964 Captain, United States Air Force, 1964-1967 (active)
Dental Intern United States Air Force

1974 Honorable Discharge, United States Air Force

POSITIONS HELD:

1963 National Institute of Health, Research Assistant in Microbiology

1966-1967 Chief, Periodontics Section, Pease Air Force Base Newington, New Hampshire

1966-1967 Chief, Preventative Dentistry Section, Pease Air Force Base Newington, New Hampshire

1968-1969 Representative to Graduate Instruction Committee, Tufts University School of Dental Medicine for Graduate and Post Graduate Students

1969-1971 Clinical Instructor in Periodontology, Tufts University School of Dental Medicine

1970-1971 Secretary, Haverhill Dental Association

1971-1972 Representative, Scientific Committee, Merrimack Valley Dental Society

1972-1973 President, Haverhill Dental Association

1972-1973 Chairman, Program Committee, Merrimack Valley Dental Society

1973-1974 President Elect, Merrimack Valley Dental Society

1976-1995 President, Great Bay Dental Study Group

1978 President, New Hampshire Society of Periodontists

1984-1990 Instructor/Lecturer in Periodontics; Institute for Advanced Dental Studies Swampscott, Massachusetts

1989-1994 Member, Public Communications Committee, American Academy of Periodontology

SOCIETY MEMBERSHIP:

American Dental Association

American Academy of Periodontology

Diplomate, American Board of Periodontology

American Academy of Oral Medicine

American Academy of Implantology

American Meteorological Society

American Academy of Osseointegration

American Association of Military Surgeons

New York University Alumni Association

Tufts University Alumni Association

Massachusetts Dental Society

New York State Dental Society

New Hampshire Dental Society

Maine Dental Society

Merrimack Valley Dental Society

Haverhill Dental Society

Alpha Omega Dental Society

PAPERS/PRESENTATIONS:

1963 "An Approach to the Diagnosis of Osteolytic Lesions", Conference on Oral Medicine, New York University College of Dentistry

1965 "Missing Teeth in a Military Population", United States Air Force Base Scott, Dental Intern Journal

1971 "Plaque Control in Dentistry", Haverhill Dental Association

1972 "Plaque Control and Preventative Dentistry", Merrimack Valley Dental Hygiene Association

1973 "The Expanding Role of the Dental Auxiliary in Preventive Dentistry", Merrimack Valley Dental Assistant's Association

1975 "Muco-Gingival Surgery", Southeast New Hampshire Dental Society

1977 "An Approach to Severe Osseous Defects", Southeast New Hampshire Dental Study Group

1981 "Modern Techniques in Weather Forecasting", Southeast New Hampshire Dental Society

1983 "Current Concepts in Periodontics", Southeast New Hampshire Dental Study Group

1985 "Predictable Periodontal-Prosthetics", American Academy of Periodontology Annual Meeting, San Francisco, California

1986 "Periodontal Prosthesis", Walter Reed Army Medical Center, Washington, DC

1986 "Practice Building Using Predictable Periodontal Prosthetics", American Academy of Periodontology Annual Meeting, Cleveland, Ohio

1988 "Integrating Implants into Predictable Periodontal Prosthetics", International Implant Symposium, Dallas, Texas

1988 "Periodontics-The Foundation of Practice Growth", New York State Ninth District Dental Society, West Point, New York

1991 "Periodontal Disease-A Growing Challenge", The Dental Assistant, Journal of The American Dental Assistants Association, May/June 1991

1991 "Implants are Here to Stay", Naples Dental Conference, Naples, Florida

1993 "Guided Tissue Regeneration-Periodontal Applications", Great Bay Dental Study Group, Portsmouth, New Hampshire

1994 "Integrating Implants into Treatment Planning", Implant Dental Study Club of New Hampshire, Portsmouth, New Hampshire

1994 "Treatment Planning Using Guided Bone Regeneration", Great Bay Dental Study Group, Portsmouth, New Hampshire

1995 "Treatment Planning Using Guided Bone Regeneration", DENTISTRY TODAY: August 1995. Vol. 14: No. 8 Pg. 60

1999 "A Patient-Centered Approach to Periodontal Disease Detection", The Journal of Practical Hygiene Volume 8 No.3 May/June 1999 39-44

INVENTION

1987 Inventor, and developer of the thrice patented, FDA, and ADA approved PerioWise® periodontal probe, currently being used worldwide, in private dental practices, and teaching institutions, and creator of the PerioWise Screening System™

METEOROLOGY

1967 to present, Professional Meteorologist and Member of the American Meteorological Society

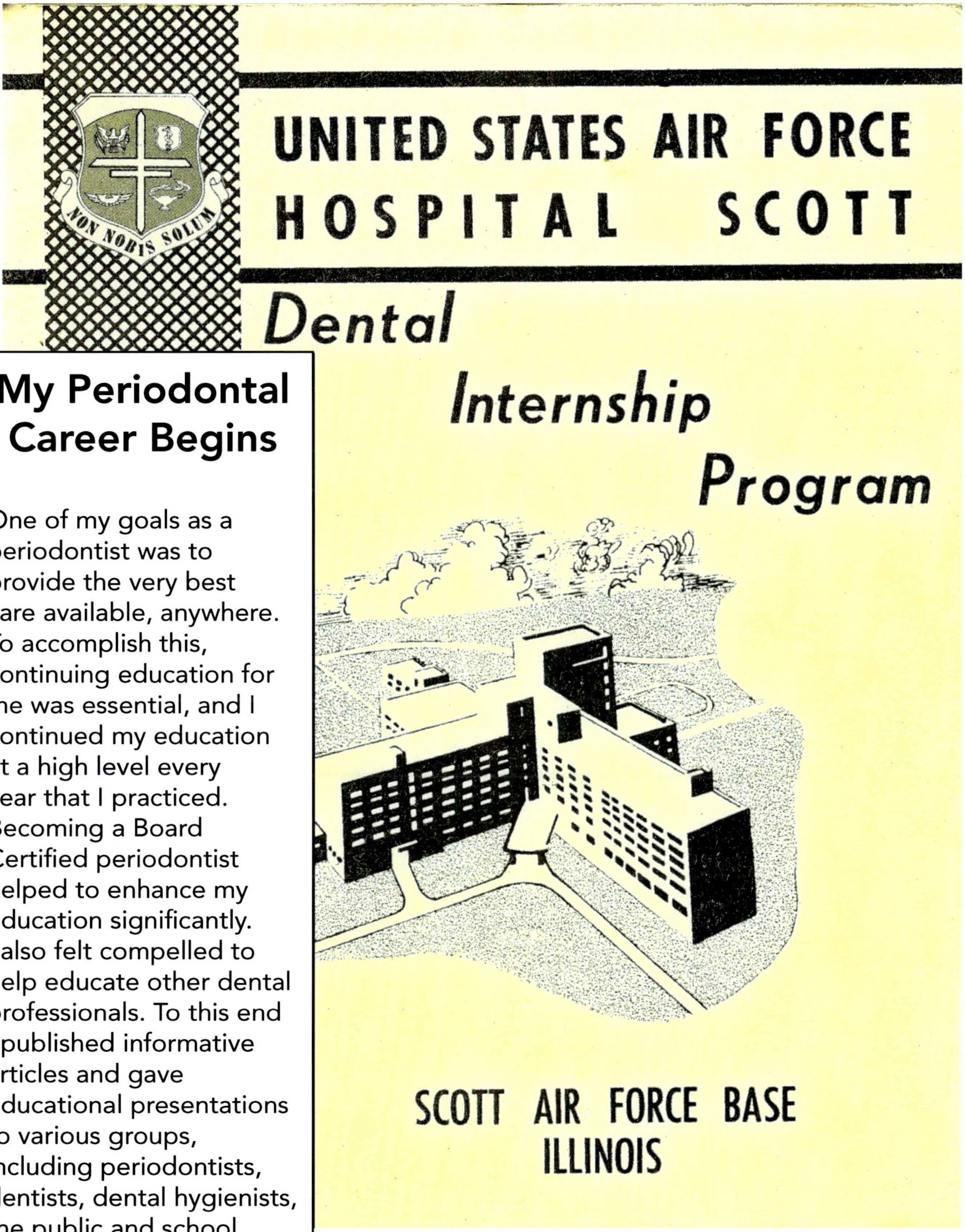

My Periodontal Career Begins

One of my goals as a periodontist was to provide the very best care available, anywhere. To accomplish this, continuing education for me was essential, and I continued my education at a high level every year that I practiced. Becoming a Board Certified periodontist helped to enhance my education significantly. I also felt compelled to help educate other dental professionals. To this end I published informative articles and gave educational presentations to various groups, including periodontists, dentists, dental hygienists, the public and school children.

GEORGETOWN UNIVERSITY
SCHOOL OF DENTISTRY
WASHINGTON, D. C. 20007

DEPARTMENT OF PERIODONTICS AND ENDODONTICS

Sept. 15, 1971

Dr. Robert L. Reeves, Secy.-Treas.
University of Southern California
School of Dentistry
925 West 34th St.
Los Angeles, California 90007

Re: Letter of Evaluation on Dr. Bernard Loewenthal

Dear Dr. Reeves:

It gives me great pleasure to submit this letter of evaluation on Dr. Bernard Loewenthal in support of his application to the American Board of Periodontology.

I have known Dr. Loewenthal both professionally and personally for six years and have had a most gratifying experience in observing his steady development into the outstanding and highly competent young periodontist that he is. I first noted his exceptional interest and ability in Periodontics when he was in the Air Force assigned to Pease Air Force Base from 1965-67. While there, he developed and directed an outstanding Periodontics and Preventive Dentistry Service as Chief of the Section, which included providing instruction and guidance to other dental officers and ancillary personnel. In 1967, he received the Dental Assistant Training Award for outstanding service at Pease AFB.

Dr. Loewenthal unsparingly gives of himself to increase his value in support of the highest ideals of this specialty. In addition to teaching Periodontics part-time at Tufts University, he is actively engaged in private practice limited to Periodontics, yet still finds time to serve on several committees and participate actively in professional organizations at the local and national levels.

Dr. Loewenthal is a very pleasant, mature and exceptionally well-motivated professional gentleman with exemplary integrity and ethical standards. His many fine personal characteristics have gained for him the respect of his colleagues and patients with whom he maintains outstanding rapport. He is the calibre of individual who will contribute much to the profession and this specialty.

Without any reservation whatsoever, I highly recommend Dr. Loewenthal to the Board for examination.

Sincerely,

Francis J. Sancha, D.D.S.

Dr. Loewenthal board diplomate

Dr. Bernard Loewenthal, periodontist, of 197 Concord St., has successfully passed the board examination of the American Board of Periodontology and has been named a diplomate.

Dr. Loewenthal received his dental degree from New York University College of Dentistry and his post-graduate training at Tufts University School of Dental Medicine. He has been the recipient of numerous awards and honors for academic excellence, research, and distinguished service at both universities.

Dr. Loewenthal served for three years on active duty in the U.S. Air Force both as an intern and as chief of periodontology, Pease Air Force Base, Newington, N.H. He is a former instructor of periodontology at Tufts University School of Dental Medicine, past president of the Haverhill Dental Society, and a member of the American Academy of Oral Medicine.

Dr. Loewenthal now practices periodontics in Portsmouth, N.H.

He has become known to Haverhill residents for his weather forecasting for the city during the winter. the study of weather has been his hobby since childhood.

DR. BERNARD LOEWENTHAL

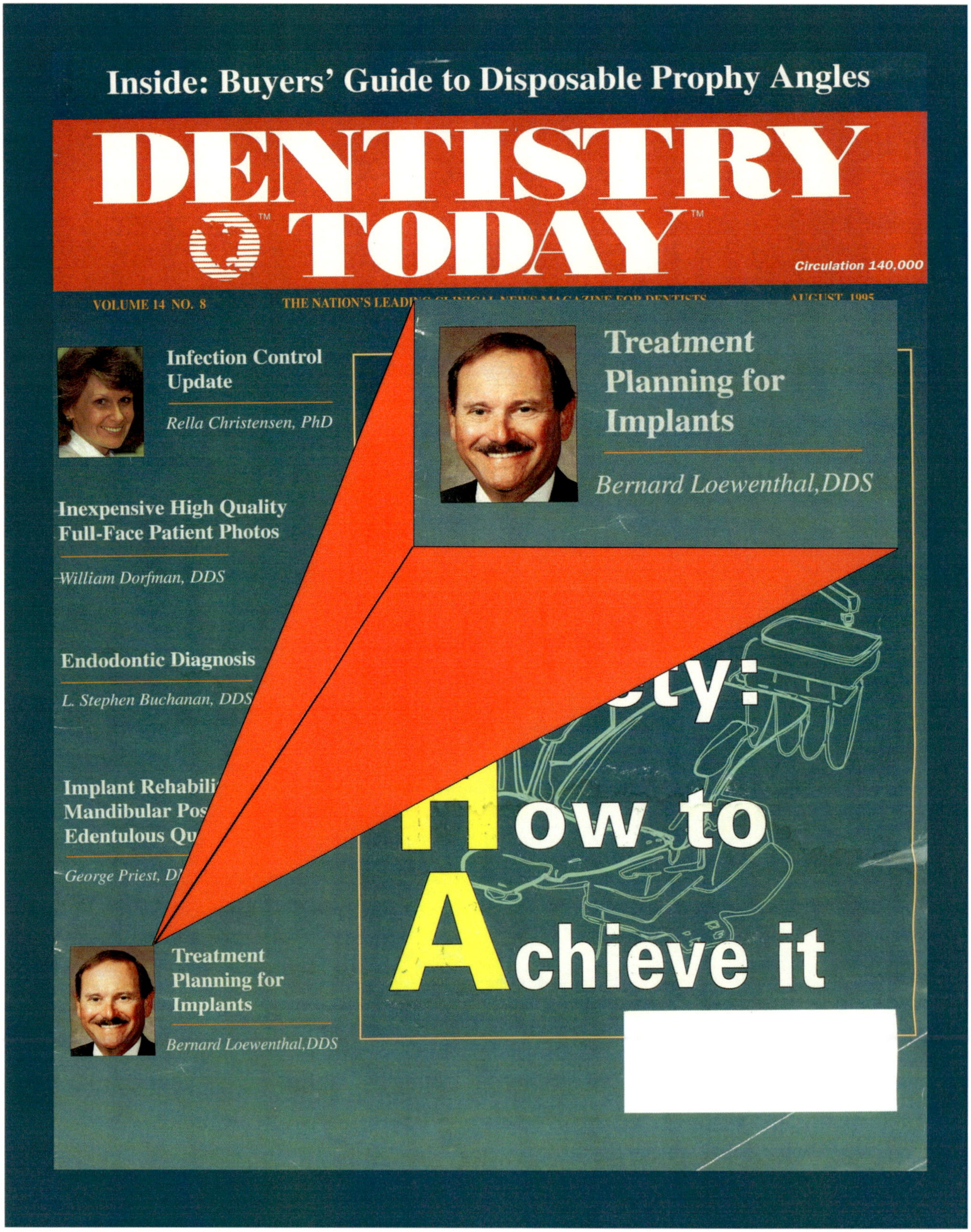
Inside: Buyers' Guide to Disposable Prophy Angles
DENTISTRY TODAY
Circulation 140,000
VOLUME 14 NO. 8
Infection Control Update
Rella Christensen, PhD
Inexpensive High Quality Full-Face Patient Photos
William Dorfman, DDS
Endodontic Diagnosis
L. Stephen Buchanan, DDS
Treatment Planning for Implants
Bernard Loewenthal, DDS
ow to
Achieve it
Treatment Planning for Implants
Bernard Loewenthal, DDS

LOCAL DENTIST SPEAKS - Dr. Bernard Lowenthal, a Portsmouth periodontist presented an all day lecture to New York's Ninth District Dental Society. During the afternoon, Dr. Loewenthal discussed the sequencing of treatment between the various members of the dental team for complicated cases requiring crown and bridge work together with periodontal care. He ended the afternoon with an in depth discussion of implantology and demonstrated, by the continued use of slides, numerous cases in which implants were used successfully to replace missing teeth and help people obtain good health, function, comfort and appearance.

Loewenthal lectures at Walter Reed Hospital

STRATHAM — Dr. Bernard Loewenthal of Stratham was recently a guest lecturer at Walter Reed Army Hospital in Washington, D.C.

He addressed Army, Navy, Air Force and civilian dentists at a week-long conference on periodontics.

His topic was "Providing Quality Care for Patients with Periodontal Problems Using Fixed Bridgework." Loewenthal discussed the importance of understanding each patient's specific needs and the sequencing of treatment between the restorative dentist and periodontist.

Loewenthal is on the faculty of The Institute for Advanced Dental Studies, Swampscott, Mass., and is the only board-certified periodontist in New Hampshire. He practices in Portsmouth.

The Hampton Union, September 25, 1985 — Page A5

Loewenthal lectures

PORTSMOUTH — Dr. Bernard Loewenthal of Stratham lectured on the topic "Predictable Periodontal Prosthetics" at the annual meeting of the American Academy of Periodontology held recently in San Francisco.

DR. BERNARD LOEWENTHAL

The bulk of his presentation dealt with the scheduling and sequencing of treatment between the restorative dentist and periodontist to obtain optimum results. Areas covered included the fabrication of provisional crown and bridgework, the achievement of periodontal health and the construction of the permanent crowns and bridges. Dr. Loewenthal used numerous slides of actual cases acquired during his years of private practice and teaching to demonstrate this approach to treatment.

Dr. Loewenthal presently practices in Portsmouth and is the only periodontist in the state who is certified by the American Board of Periodontology. He serves on the faculty of the Institute for Advanced Dental Studies and is on the staff at Portsmouth and Exeter hospitals and Hale Hospital in Haverill, Mass.

Dentist lectures colleagues

PORTSMOUTH — Dr. Bernard Loewenthal, a Portsmouth periodontist, recently presented an all-day lecture to New York's Ninth District Dental Society in West Point, N.Y.

Loewenthal used slides and handouts to illustrate his talk on the periodontal disease which affects the gum, tissue and bone supporting the teeth.

During the morning he discussed the latest concepts in diagnosing and treating the disease.

He emphasized the importance of early detection by dentists since periodontal disease frequently has no symptoms.

Loewenthal explained the importance of getting to know one's patients and understanding their particular needs, desires and concerns prior to any treatment, so that the patient's goals could be met.

He discussed various bone regeneration techniques and his patented disposable periodontal probe which will be available to dentists this winter.

During the afternoon Loewenthal discussed the sequencing of treatment between the various members of the dental team for complicated cases requiring crown and bridge work together with periodontal care.

He ended the afternoon with a discussion of implantology and demonstrated, by the continued use of slides, numerous cases in which implants were used successfully to replace missing teeth and to help people obtain good health, function, comfort and appearance.

BERNARD LOEWENTHAL
Portsmouth periodontist

Dental implants offer new chewing hope

By DOUG IRELAND
Portsmouth Bureau Chief

PORTSMOUTH — For more than two decades, merely eating a flimsy lettuce leaf or biting into a sandwich was a tremendous and often embarrassing effort for Joan Brody.

As soon as she took a big bite of food, her dentures would slip and food almost always got caught underneath them. It made eating a miserable experience, especially in public.

"It became a chore to eat out," recalled Ms. Brody, a Milton resident. "You just stayed home — it was a whole lot easier."

Ever since Ms. Brody was forced to have her severely decayed teeth removed at age 18, she has been struggling with false teeth.

But two weeks ago, all that changed.

Ms. Brody, now 41, successfully underwent three hours of surgery to receive two tooth implants — artificial replacements, identical in appearance to teeth, that are permanently screwed into her jaw.

"I think it is the best thing that ever happened in the way of dental reconstruction," Ms. Brody said in an interview only days after the operation.

Even though she didn't get a full set of implants, the two teeth serve to anchor her dentures, she said.

Already, she is a much happier person and no longer worries about her dentures slipping, sliding or irritating her mouth.

"It was impossible to get through a meal without developing pain and embarrassment," she said. "Now, that just isn't the case at all."

Before getting the implants, there were many foods she just couldn't eat because it was too much of a chore to chew. Now, she tackles everything from pizza to hotdogs.

"The difference is unbelievable. It's the most natural thing to real teeth."

Although there is nothing like the real thing, implants are rapidly establishing themselves as a preferred alternative to dentures.

According to some local dentists, the emergence of implants is making a significant difference in the lives of many people who dislike dentures.

"Implants are really revolutionizing dentistry," said periodontist Dr. Bernard Loewenthal of Portsmouth. "We can do for people now what couldn't be done before."

Though the practice of implanting false teeth is not new to dentistry, the technique was not widely practiced in the United States until about three years ago, he said.

Before the development of improved methods in Europe, many dental experts would not even consider doing implants because that type of surgery was often unsuccessful, he said.

Several months after completion of the surgery, many patients discovered their new implants would not fuse to the bone beneath the gums. Infection would sometimes result and the implants would have to be removed.

Due to modern technology, approximately 95 percent of all implants now successfully fuse to the bone, according to Loewenthal and others in the profession.

"You can't even tell it is there," he said. "The benefits outweigh the risks dramatically."

His colleagues agree, including Dr. Louis Clarizio, a local oral and maxillofacial surgeon who has performed approximately 200 implants during the past three years.

"It is definitely, definitely the healthy option," he said of the comparison between implants and traditional bridge work.

And implantation causes no more pain than a tooth extraction, he said.

Portsmouth periodontist Dr. Bernard Loewenthal demonstrates how tooth implants can be used to relieve discomfort and problems associated with dentures.
(Democrat photo — Ireland)

Yet the cost of implants can be high, with a single tooth ranging anywhere from $600 to $1,000, depending on the requirements of the surgery and the person doing the work.

And that figure does not include much of the dental attention required by the patient both before and after surgery.

The biggest obstacle faced by many people who want implants is that their insurance policy may not cover the work, said Clarizio. Because the method is relatively new in this country, most insurance companies cover it only partially or not at all.

"Financially, it's a burden," he acknowledged.

But for those patients who can afford them, they are have proven to be a real boon to denture-wearers, he said. "They have a new-found confidence in their appearance."

Dr. David Rosania, a Dover periodontist, is another advocate of implants. "I think they are definitely a major advance in terms of replacing teeth."

As far as he's concerned, implants have many advantages and only one major disadvantage — their cost.

He considers implants the next best thing to a healthy set of chompers.

Portsmouth dentist speaks at international symposium

Bernard Loewenthal, D.D.S., a Portsmouth periodontist, spoke recently at the International Dental Implant Symposium attended by nearly one thousand dentists from 15 countries worldwide.

Bernard Loewenthal

The three-day symposium brought together the leading clinicians and research authorities to exchange the latest information on dental implants. Dental implants have now been proven to be a reliable and predictable way to replace missing teeth, whether it be one tooth or all of the teeth.

Loewenthal discussed and demonstrated, with the aid of slides, the use of implants.

"We all benefited from the symposium and shared information and techniques that will help us provide excellent care to people who need teeth replaced," Loewenthal said.

Portsmouth Herald (N.H.) Thursday, June 9, 1988—9B

Portsmouth dentist lectures in Dallas

Dr. Bernard Lowenthal, D.D.S., a Portsmouth periodontist, was a featured lecturer at the International Dental Implant Symposium held this week in Dallas, Tex.

Dr. Lowenthal discussed and gave a visual demonstration concerning a variety of specialized tooth implant cases which served to restore dental imperfection sufferers to a good state of dental health, function, comfort and appearance. "We all benefited from the symposium and shared information and technique that will help us provide excellent care to people who need teeth replaced," the doctor said following the three-day session.

According to a report from the symposium, dental implants have been proven to be reliable as a replacement method for removed or missing teeth. The technique used is called osseointegration. It reportedly provides a strong union between living bone and the implant which is made of titanium, a biocompatible material readily accepted by the body.

DR. BERNARD LOWENTHAL
spoke on dental implants

INSTRUCTING - Portsmouth periodontist, **Bernie Loewenthal, D.D.S.** will be instructing a course designed for dental hygienists and dentists. For more information contact 436-7787.

FOCUS/HEALTH

PERIODONTAL DISEASE

How to recognize it

By Peter Urban
Democrat Staff Writer

Periodontist Dr. Bernard Loewenthal, demonstrates how he uses the periodontal probe.

The use of the expression "long in the tooth" to refer to advance age suggests that the shrinking of gums from the teeth is a natural process of aging.

But the assumption is false, according to local dentists who specialize in gum care. In fact, they say, keeping your gums health and your teeth intact throughout life should be commonplace.

The culprit that robs people of their natural smile, once tooth decay, now is periodontal disease – infected gums. It afflicts 90 percent of the population and causes 70 percent of all tooth loss.

Gum disease is called the "disease of neglect" because it can be prevented, corrected and controlled with proper dental care, according to Dr. Bernard Loewenthal, a periodontist practicing in Portsmouth.

A major problem is that frequently there are no early symptoms – in the same way that early cancer, diabetes and blood pressure have few noticeable symptoms, Loewenthal said.

Periodontal disease is usually a long-term chronic condition that begins before age 30 and continues until it becomes noticeable around age 40 or 50, when considerable damage already has been done.

The only way to know for sure if one is afflicted by the disease is to have a dentist check specifically for the problem.

Most dentists are trained to check for the disease, and there are three periodontists who practice in the Seacoast area: Loewenthal, Dr. Gary J. Galovic in Portsmouth, and Dr. David A. Rosania in Dover.

Gum disease is caused by accumulated bacteria, a film called plaque, which, if not removed, eventually separates the attachment between gum and teeth, explained Galovic. Plaque then moves down the root of the tooth near the bone and produces a toxin that dissolves the bone and loosens the teeth.

"It is a slow process over years and years," said Galovic. But once loosened, the teeth eventually fall out unless the condition is treated.

According to Rosania, periodontal disease is an infection and has most of the same components of other infections, it cannot be treated with antibiotics.

The bacterias that cause the disease are "native" – they normally live within most people's mouths. The problem occurs when those bacteria are given a chance to root deep between the gum and tooth.

"Millions of bacteria can fit on the tip of a toothpick. To them the space between the gum and tooth is like the Grand Canyon," Galovic said.

As plaque forms, pockets are created between the teeth and gum, allowing more room for the bacteria to grow. Those pockets, if deep enough, cannot be cleaned with proper brushing and need periodontal treatment, according to Loewenthal.

While the disease begins with few noticeable symptoms, there are early warning signs.

"It is never normal to have bleeding gums," Loewenthal said. "Healthy tissue doesn't bleed." Any time there is inflammation or bleeding, something is not right, he said.

Galovic stressed that even if bleeding and inflammation disappear, the problem is not necessarily gone. In many cases, the disease goes through active and inactive stages.

Another warning sign is bad breath or a bad taste in the moth; shifting of teeth or looseness; itching gnawing or any sensation in the gums.

Fever blisters, swelling and raw areas on the gums also can be warning signs, and pain in the gums is a problem even if it goes away.

"Half the people I see do not know they have a problem," said Rosania.

Early detection and regular, proper cleaning can save expense, pain and - ultimately – your teeth.

WEDNESDAY, JANUARY 17, 1973

Dr. Bernard Loewenthal, center, was the guest speaker at the Exchange Club of Haverhill luncheon last Thursday, at the Capt'n Chris Restaurant. William Clark, president, left, and Dr. Jack Tatirosian headed the program. Enterprise Pictures

WEDNESDAY, FEBRUARY 7, 1973

A PROCLAMATION for Children's Dental Health Month for February was signed recently at City Hall. Seated are, from left, Mayor George Katsaros, Mrs. Claudina Goss, dental hygienist. Standing, Dr. Bernard Loewenthal, president, Haverhill, dental society; Dr. William H. Sullivan, Haverhill health department advisor.

DENTAL PRESENTATION

Bernie Loewenthal, D.D.S, a Portsmouth periodontist spoke to fourth, fifth and sixth graders at the Stratham Memorial School's Enrichment Day. Dr. Loewenthal discussed the dental profession and ways to help prevent tooth loss. Dr. Loewenthal and his wife, Ilana, reside in Stratham. He has been in practice in Portsmouth for 14 years and is certified by the American Board of Periodontology. (Courtesy photo)

My Invention

"PerioWise® The Friendly Probe®"

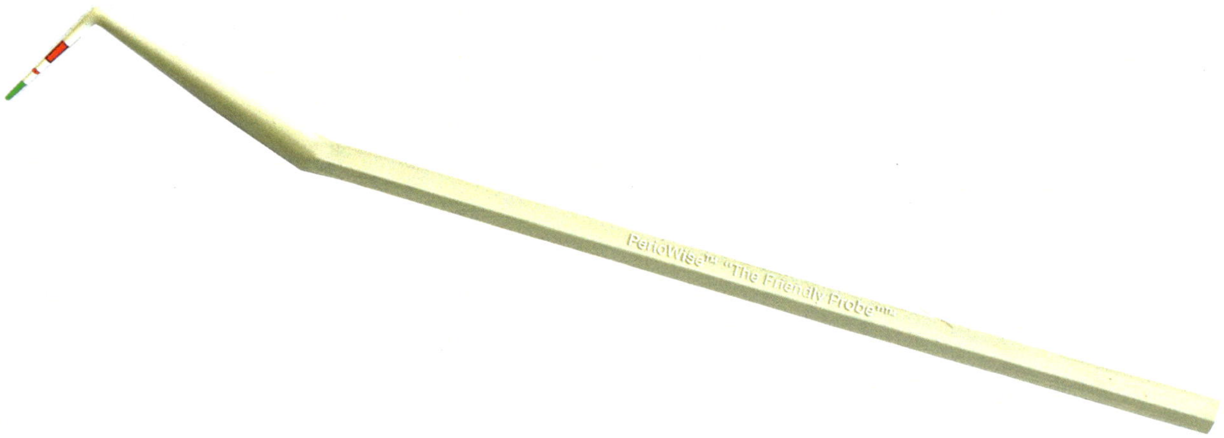

My invention, of the PerioWise® probe, and its Screening System, has become an excellent way to continue to educate all dental professionals and their patients. The probe is helping to diagnose periodontal disease earlier, more easily, and with improved patient understanding.

Just F·O·L·K·S

He Makes A Good Point

Ask anyone who knows him: Bernie Loewenthal is a probing kind of guy. A Portsmouth periodontist with a thriving practice, Loewenthal is not content to poke around other people's mouths in search of pockets and plaque. He wants his patients – and everyone else's – to do it themselves.

So in his spare time, which he and wife Alana spend vegetable gardening, weather watching (he's also a certified meteorologist) and tromping around their camp in Northern Maine, Loewenthal devised an ingenious little plastic tool that will allow gum-watchers to keep a vigilant eye on their oral hygiene. In between regular visits to the dentist, of course.

Tentatively dubbed a *Perio Test* (the name could change depending on the wisdom of marketing strategists) the tool is very similar to the stainless steel variety wielded by dentists in offices and clinics across the county. The only differences – and they're big ones – are that Loewenthal's invention is soft-tipped and disposable.

Although gum disease (one of the major causes of tooth loss in people over 30) has been around since man first discovered the pleasurable necessity of food, the condition only captured major public attention in the last decade. Often described as a problem peculiar to the mouths of Young UPwardly mobileS, gum disease is, in fact, an insidious condition that recognizes neither age nor economic barriers. It begins painlessly and ultimately progresses to gingivitis (inflammation of the gums), receding gums, bleeding gums and finally, gums that give up the ghost (in this case, teeth).

Detected early, gum disease can be checked with relatively painless dental procedures; the more advanced the condition, the more painful, limited and expensive the remedy.

Loewenthal, a periodontist whose office accomodates nearly a dozen work stations, has no desire to put himself or any other specialist out of business. Nor will he if his invention takes off in a big way.

What he hopes to do is market the probe to other professionals as a throw-away tool that doesn't require sterilization; there's no question that the Perio Test is 100 percent viral and bacterial-free. He'd like to see perio patients go home with a few disposable probes to keep them honest until their next appointment with the doctor. He also wouldn't mind selling the probe as a new product line to manufactures of dental hygiene products such as toothpaste, toothbrushes, mouthwash and dental floss.

But all this takes time says Loewenthal. There's a patent pending on the probe and more than enough nibbles from corporate giants to keep Dr. Loewenthal's invention simmering while he attends to the business at hand.

Is there a market for the probe? In this disposable society most definitely, says Loewenthal. And if it does catch on, the question remains: will Perio Test sell in Peoria? According to Dr. Loewenthal, yes, indeed. In all *probe-ability*, it'll sell very well. Peoria also had a nice little baby boom back in the 50s. Just like Portsmouth.

Helen Scheuer

The Journal of
Practical Hygiene
Improving Communications Among Dental Professionals

Volume 8 ■ Number 3 May/June 1999

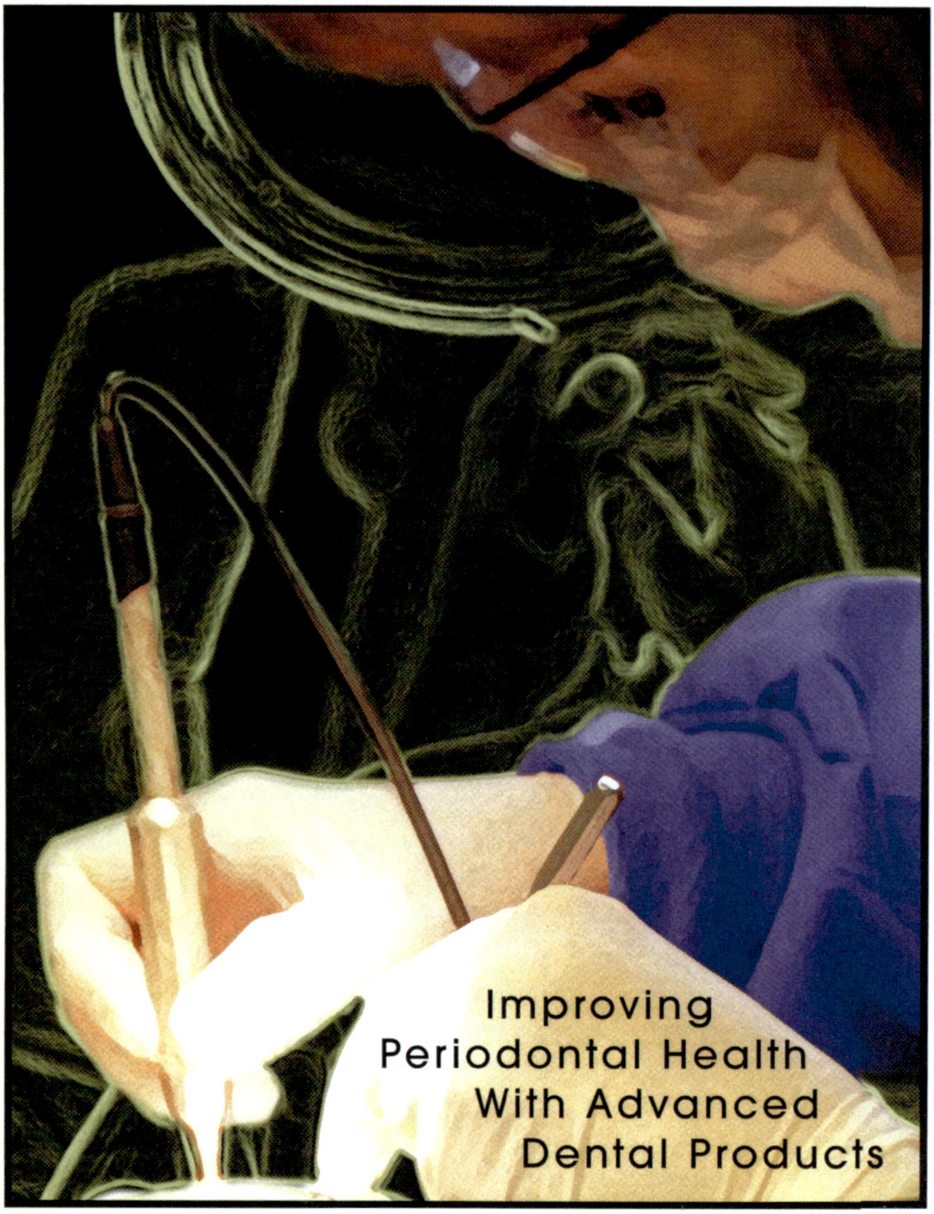

reprint**feature**

A PATIENT-CENTERED APPROACH TO PERIODONTAL DISEASE DETECTION

A Patient-Centered Approach to Periodontal Disease Detection

Bernard Loewenthal, DDS, BS

Since periodontal diseases are now considered risk factors for a number of medical problems and continue to be an important cause of tooth loss in adults, the role of the hygienist in the medical and dental communities has never been more important. This article discusses the rationale of periodontal screening systems. Considerations for integrating an organized program for detecting and treating periodontal diseases in a practice are also discussed, including factors that influence periodontal probing accuracy and the value of controlled-force electronic probes. A green/red, color-coded screening system is introduced and compared to Periodontal Screening and Recording (PSR).* The comparison includes information about the features of each system's probes, criteria for recording clinical findings, and the advantages and disadvantages of each system. It is emphasized that a screening system is not a substitute for a complete periodontal examination and charting, which should be performed periodically.

Introduction

The dental hygienist has a vital role in prevention, detection, and treatment of periodontal diseases. This role has never been more important than it is now, due to current research and findings, which indicate that periodontal diseases are a risk factor for heart disease, stroke, preterm low birthweight babies, and the regulation of blood glucose levels in diabetics.[1-5] Because of these risk factors, screening for periodontal diseases has begun to assume the same importance in the medical community as screening for hypertension and elevated blood cholesterol.

Meanwhile, periodontal diseases remain a concern in the dental community. They remain an important cause of halitosis and tooth loss in adults. This frequently results in impaired chewing and speaking, an unpleasant smile, and occlusal problems. Successful cosmetic dentistry cannot be achieved without a healthy periodontium. No restoration, regardless of its aesthetics, can appear natural while surrounded by diseased gingiva. These problems, singly or in combination, contribute to reduced self-esteem and total health. The early detection and treatment of periodontal diseases, with the aid of a clinician- and patient-friendly screening system, clearly remain opportunities to provide an important service to patients. As the population ages and lifespans increase, we can expect even higher incidence rates of periodontal diseases.[6-7] The early diagnosis and treatment of periodontal diseases, as with all diseases, would make treatment less complex, less costly, and more predictable, thereby greatly reducing its impact on the population.

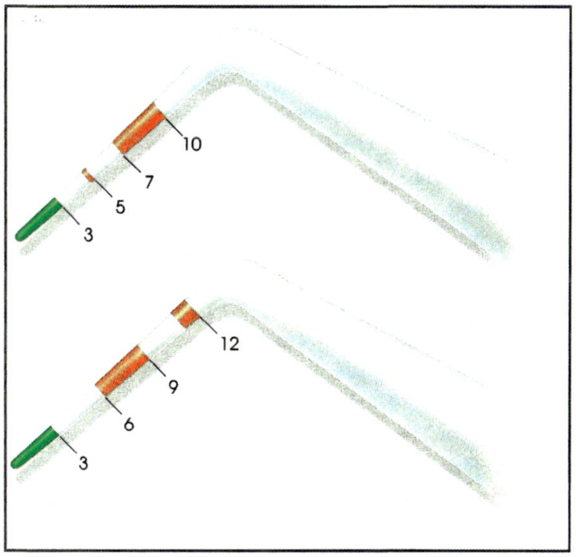

Figure 1. The color-coded probe is available in two calibrations.

Dr. Bernard Loewenthal is a board-certified periodontist, a former instructor at Tufts University School of Dental Medicine, and lecturer at The Institute for Advanced Dental Studies. He is the inventor of the PerioWise Probe and Screening System. Dr. Loewenthal can be contacted through his website www.periowise.com or at: 51 Stratham Heights Rd, Stratham, NH 03885-2547. Tel: 603-778-1234, Fax: 603-778-6422.

UNITED STATES PATENT

The United States of America

Granted on September 6, 1988

Bernard Loewenthal, B.S., D.D.S.

INVENTOR

4,768,952

DENTAL PROBE

1. A dental probe, comprising:
an elongated member having a flexible, plastic distal end with a tip thereon;
said distal end being generally cylindrical and tapered to said tip and comprising a first portion indicating a non-diseased condition and second portion indicating a diseased condition; and
said first portion disposed between the tip of said distal end and said second portion, said second portion disposed adjacent to said first portion.

The Commissioner of Patents and Trademarks has received an application for a patent for a new and useful invention. The requirements of law have been complied with, and it has been determined that a patent on the invention shall be granted under the law. Therefore, this

UNITED STATES PATENT

Grants to the person or persons having title to this patent the right to exclude others from making, using or selling the invention throughout the United States of America for the term of seventeen years from the date of this patent, subject to the payment of maintenance fees as provided by law.

PATENT AND TRADEMARK OFFICE UNITED STATES OF AMERICA

Commissioner of Patents and Trademarks

Attest

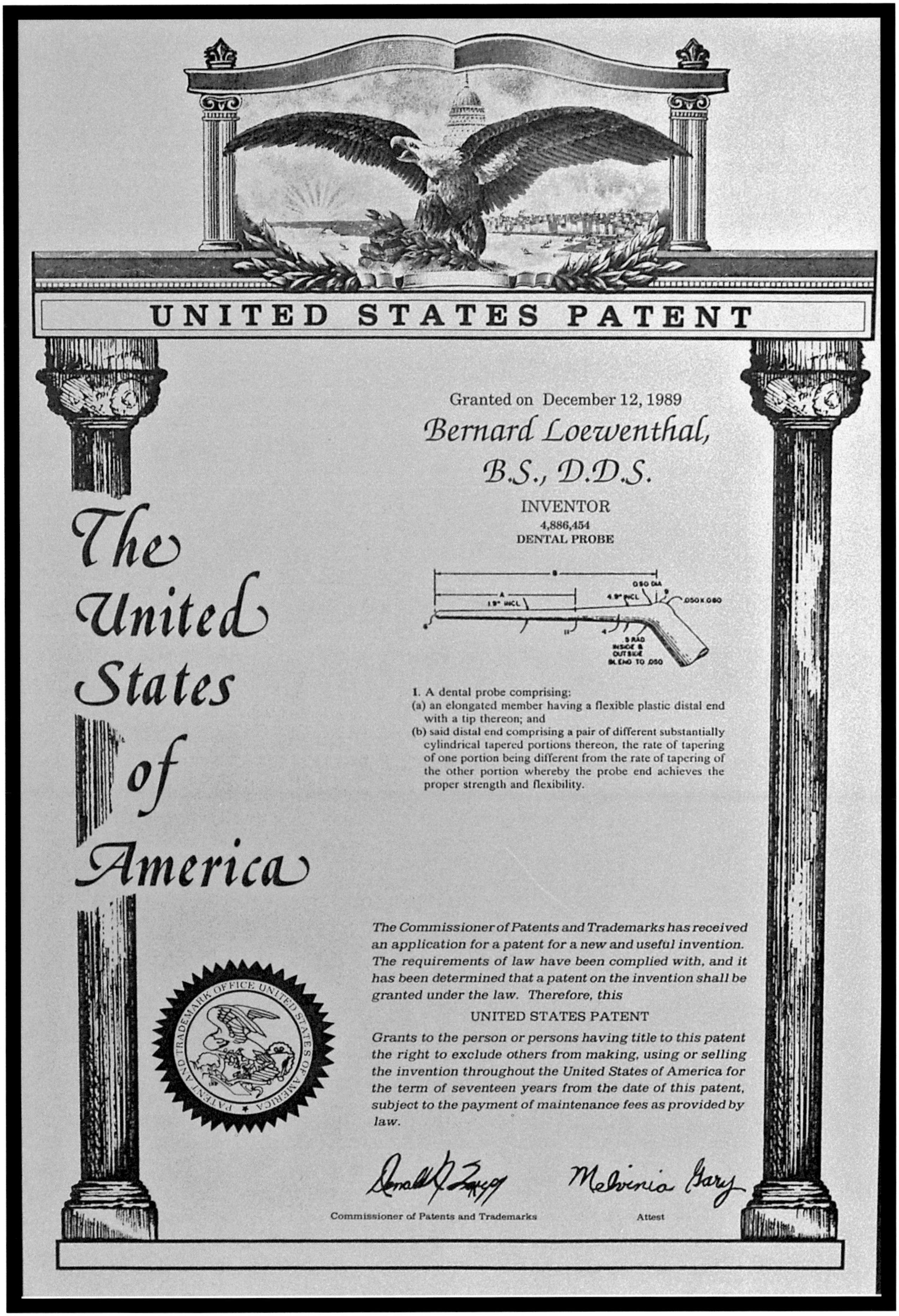

UNITED STATES PATENT

The United States of America

Granted on December 12, 1989

Bernard Loewenthal,
B.S., D.D.S.

INVENTOR

4,886,454

DENTAL PROBE

1. A dental probe comprising:
(a) an elongated member having a flexible plastic distal end with a tip thereon; and
(b) said distal end comprising a pair of different substantially cylindrical tapered portions thereon, the rate of tapering of one portion being different from the rate of tapering of the other portion whereby the probe end achieves the proper strength and flexibility.

The Commissioner of Patents and Trademarks has received an application for a patent for a new and useful invention. The requirements of law have been complied with, and it has been determined that a patent on the invention shall be granted under the law. Therefore, this

UNITED STATES PATENT

Grants to the person or persons having title to this patent the right to exclude others from making, using or selling the invention throughout the United States of America for the term of seventeen years from the date of this patent, subject to the payment of maintenance fees as provided by law.

Commissioner of Patents and Trademarks

Attest

UNITED STATES PATENT

Granted on March 17, 1992

Bernard Loewenthal, B.S., D.D.S.

INVENTOR

5,096,420

PERIODONTAL PROBE

NORMAL

The United States of America

1. A periodontal probe, comprising:
a) an elongated member having a distal end with a tip thereon; and
b) said distal end being tapered to said tip and having a plurality of condition indicating portions comprising:
(1) a first portion indicating a nondiseased condition disposed between said tip and a second portion,
(2) said second portion indicating a moderately-diseased condition disposed between said first position and a third portion,
(3) said third portion indicating a diseased condition wherein surgery is required.

The Commissioner of Patents and Trademarks has received an application for a patent for a new and useful invention. The requirements of law have been complied with, and it has been determined that a patent on the invention shall be granted under the law. Therefore, this

UNITED STATES PATENT

Grants to the person or persons having title to this patent the right to exclude others from making, using or selling the invention throughout the United States of America for the term of seventeen years from the date of this patent, subject to the payment of maintenance fees as provided by law.

PATENT AND TRADEMARK OFFICE UNITED STATES OF AMERICA

Harry F. Manbeck, Jr. — Commissioner of Patents and Trademarks

Marcia L. Campbell — Attest

Easier To Read, Gentle On Tissue.

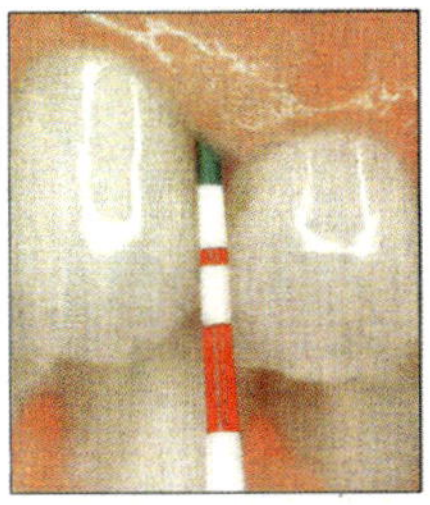

The vibrant green and red colors on the tip of PerioWise offer excellent visibility.

- Easier to read
- Safe around implants
- Slightly flexible for greater patient comfort
- Can be repeatedly autoclaved and reused

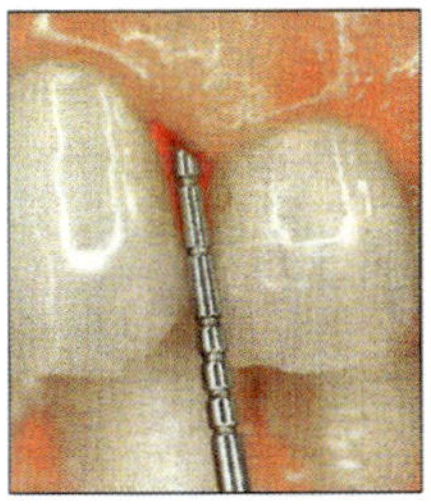

Metal probes can be difficult to read.

PerioWise® Is Safe For Use Around Implants.

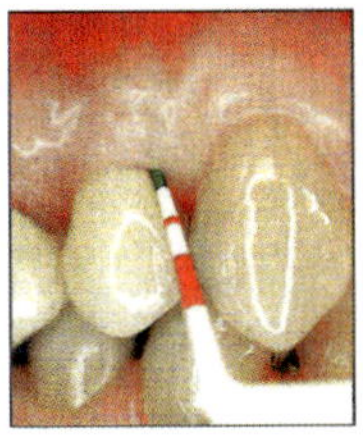

Restored implants can be difficult to identify.

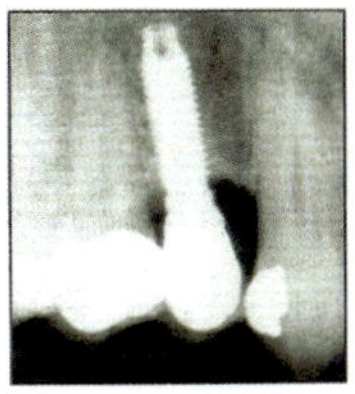

PerioWise is safe; it will NOT scratch implants.

Original (3-5-7-10mm) - (#9006102) 6-pack • (#9006101) 1-pack
NEW (3-6-9-12mm) - (#9006104) 6-pack • (#9006103) 1-pack
Each 6-pack contains a patient education guide to help improve patient compliance.

NEW! Premier® Implant Scalers

New! PREMIER® IMPLANT SCALERS are made of a revolutionary material which is hard enough to sharpen, yet safe for use on titanium implants.

Implant Scalers are available in:
2-packs (#9061401)
5-packs (#9061400)

Premier® also offers a complete selection of metal probes, including the WHO probe, to accommodate every operator's preference.

Order from an authorized dental dealer.

premier

Premier Dental Products Co.
PO Box 111, Norristown, PA 19404 USA • Tel: (800)344-8235
International Department USA: Tel: (610)277-3800 • FAX: (610)239-2394

premier

Premier Dental (Canada) Inc.
480 Hood Rd., Unit #3, Markham, Ont., L3R 9Z3 CANADA • Tel: (800)465-8455
#8690600 PPL 196 30M

New! premier PerioWise®

PLASTIC, AUTOCLAVABLE PERIODONTAL PROBES FOR EXCELLENT READABILITY, PATIENT COMFORT & ACCEPTANCE

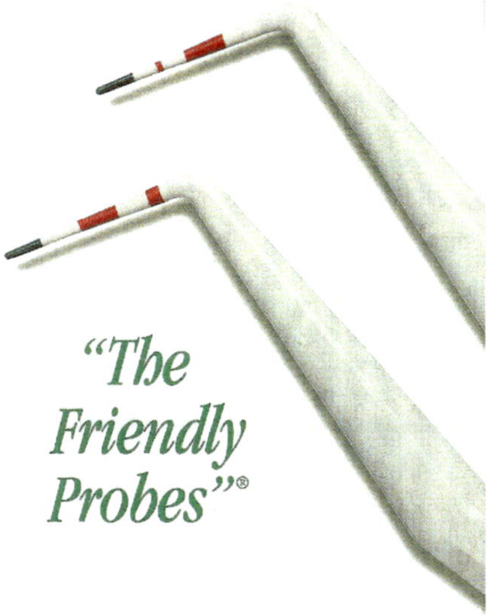

"The Friendly Probes"®

PerioWise®

Helps Improve Patient Compliance.

PerioWise® patented, multi-colored periodontal probes are extremely easy to read and gentle to tissue.[1]

Slightly flexible, with a rounded tip, PerioWise® probes offer greater patient comfort and are safe for use around implants. They can be repeatedly autoclaved and reused.

PerioWise® is ideal for a periodontal screening or a complete examination. A green mark from 0 - 3mm indicates healthy tissue; readings in the probe's red markings indicate the severity of periodontal breakdown.

NOW IT IS EASIER THAN EVER TO DIAGNOSE PERIODONTAL DISEASE, MAINTAIN PROPER RECORDS AND ENSURE OPTIMAL TREATMENT FOR YOUR PATIENTS!

PerioWise® eliminates the most frustrating part of periodontal probing - poor readability. At a glance you can quickly determine the depth of the pocket and thereby make the appropriate diagnosis.

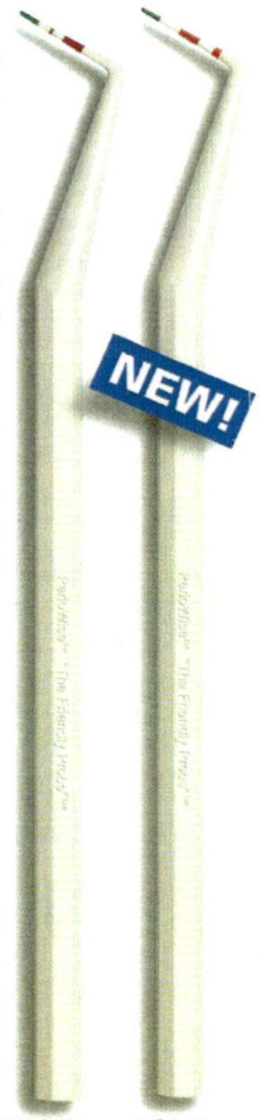

3-5-7-10mm *3-6-9-12mm*

This patient education guide is included with every six pack.

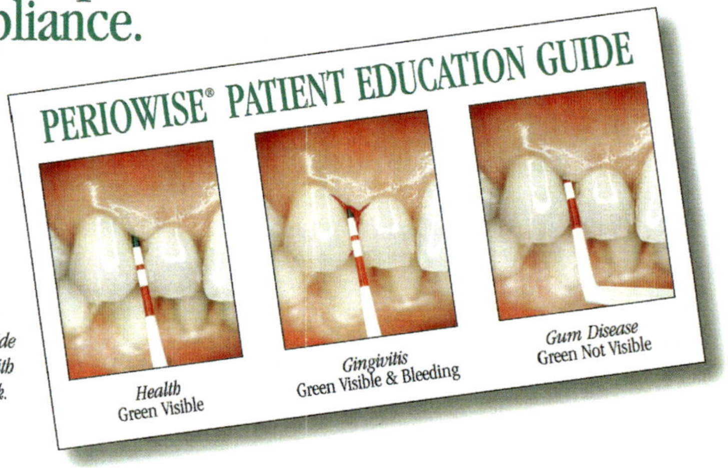

After dozens of uses, the non-toxic, FDA approved coloring on the tip of PerioWise gradually wears away. That's when it's time to reorder.

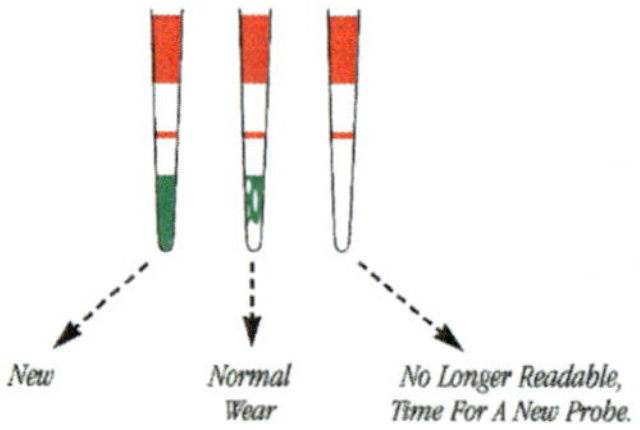

Pocket Depths
(in millimeters)

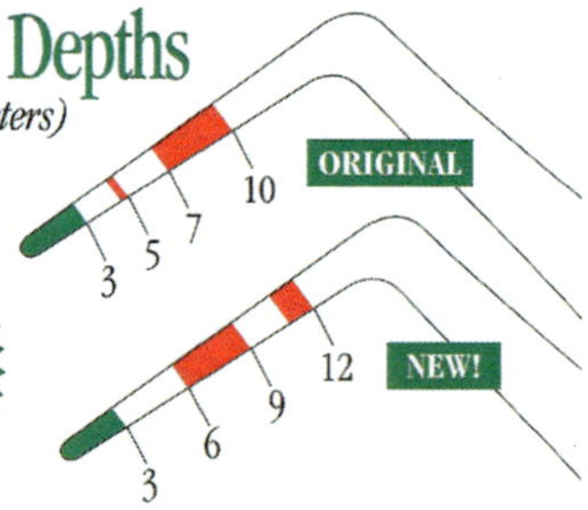

AUTOCLAVABLE CERTIFIED STERILIZABLE

PerioWise is ideal for a quick periodontal screening or a complete examination.

1. "Improved Diagnostics: Clinical Evaluation of a Color-Coded, Polymeric Periodontal Probe." CLINICAL PREV. DENT.; Vol. 14, No. 4; July/August 1992.

® Premier is a registered trademark of Premier Dental Products Co.
® PerioWise is a registered trademark of PerioWise Inc. U.S. PAT NO. 4,768,952 4,886,454 & 5,096,420
® The Friendly Probe is a trademark of PerioWise Inc.

premier

Hard work pays off for Portsmouth dentist

By DOUG IRELAND
Portsmouth Bureau Chief

PORTSMOUTH — It took a lot of work and money, but a local periodontist has succeeded in selling a dentistry tool he created to a New Jersey company that is expected to market the tool throughout the dental industry.

At a press conference Monday, Dr. Bernard Loewenthal announced he has reached an agreement with Block Drug Co. of Jersey City in an effort to maximize use of his invention, a plastic probe that measures the gap between tooth and gum that can help detect periodontal disease.

The instrument is less than six inches long, weighs only a few ounces and can be used instead if the traditional metal probe.

"It doesn't scare people as much," Loewenthal said of the probe, known as a "Perio-Test." In addition, he said it is easier to use and is disposable.

Loewenthal first unveiled his creation to the media last October. At that time, he was still negotiating with Block Drug.

In January, the two parties reached an agreement under which Block Drug has the sole right to market the probe. The firm is expected to introduce it at an American Dental Association annual meeting to be held in Washington, D.C. in October.

Block is currently working to manufacture the molds needed to produce the instruments and once these are made, they will be sold to dentists for less than 50 cents per probe.

When asked why he chose Block to market the probe, Loewenthal said he has been impressed with the company in his dealings with them.

"We feel Block would be able to do the best for us in terms of their marketing strategies," he said. "They are an honest outfit with a good reputation and integrity."

Although the probe will for now only be marketed through the dental industry, Lowenthal hopes one day they can also be sold to the general public.

Dr. Bernard Loewenthal, a Portsmouth periodontist, shows the plastic dental probe he will be marketing throughout his profession as a result of a recent agreement with Block Drug Co. of New Jersey.

(Democrat photo — Ireland)

the best for us in terms of their marketing strategies," he said. "They are an honest outfit with a good reputation and integrity."

Although the probe will for now only be marketed through the dental industry, Lowenthal hopes one day they can also be sold to the general public.

"My hope is that in five to 10 years it would become an over the counter item," he said. With this instrument, people would be able to detect periodontal disease before its effects devestate healthy gums and teeth.

Periodontal disease is the most widespread ailment in the country, according to Loewenthal, who has said it affects approximately 90 percent of the adult population.

If the disease is not detected, plaque eventually destroys the bone beneath the gums, causing teeth to often loosen and fall out or eventually require removal.

Development of this tool has occurred over nearly two years — ever since Loewenthal one day dreamed up his invention while walking down the street. The periodontist also said he spent at least $25,000 developing the instrument.

He hopes the probe can be sold to the military, hospitals and institutions and says it is best suited for use by such organizations because it is disposable and would not aid in the transmission of diseases such as acquired immune deficiency syndrome.

The produce has also received approval from the Food and Drug Administration.

Loewenthal, who has also gained notoriety as a meteorologist, has been practicing periodontal dentistry in Portsmouth for 14 years.

New Development Offers Help for Periodontal Disease Sufferers

By Thomas A. Puschock

It's not a wonder drug. Neither is it a vaccine, nor a complicated, expensive piece of the arcane analytical machinery common in large, urban medical facilities, but out of reach of most practitioners. In fact, it is a rather unassuming tool, injection molded out of about a nickel's worth of plastic and called simply *Perio-Test* by its inventor, Dr. Bernard Loenthal. What is significant, Loewenthal believes, is that *Perio-Test* will eventually have an important impact on one of the most widespread but little-known and understood epidemics in the United States today, namely periodontal disease. That impact, it is hoped, will come from an awareness of a disease which is responsible for more tooth loss in the United States than all other dental conditions combined. Although the signs of advanced gum disease are well-known — loose teeth, swollen or angry looking gums, bleeding and bad breath — the disease can also progress while showing few or no symptoms at all such as with high blood pressure. Loewenthal hopes that his tool will increase awareness of the problem among both dental practitioners and the general public, resulting in preventive measures and early detection and treatment.

Loewenthal has just licensed a major drug company to manufacture and sell the instrument to the dental profession. The first probes are expected to be available in the summer of 1988.

Loewenthal, who is the only periodontist in New Hampshire certified by the American Board of Periodontology, told *Maine DOCTOR* that he first thought of the tool about two years ago while recovering from a back operation. One of the exercises that he had to perform during his recovery was walking, and he said, "I discovered than when I walk, I think. One of the things I began thinking about during those long walks was how could I get the public involved in an understanding of periodontal disease."

As Loewenthal's ideas began to take form, they centered upon the general interest that has developed in health, fitness programs, self-diagnosis and disease prevention. Today, more than ever, people are exercising or eating in ways to keep themselves healthy and increasingly avoiding tobacco and other substances which are harmful. Added to that is an increasing interest in self-diagnosis. People now take their own blood pressures; they monitor themselves for diabetes; they test for pregnancy and even some forms of cancer. "I was trying to think of a way in a very inexpensive fashion that the public could go to the store, buy an instrument and self-examine for periodontal disease," Loewenthal said. "I thought about a periodontal probe that might be able to accomplish this."

Ports. periodontist develops new probe

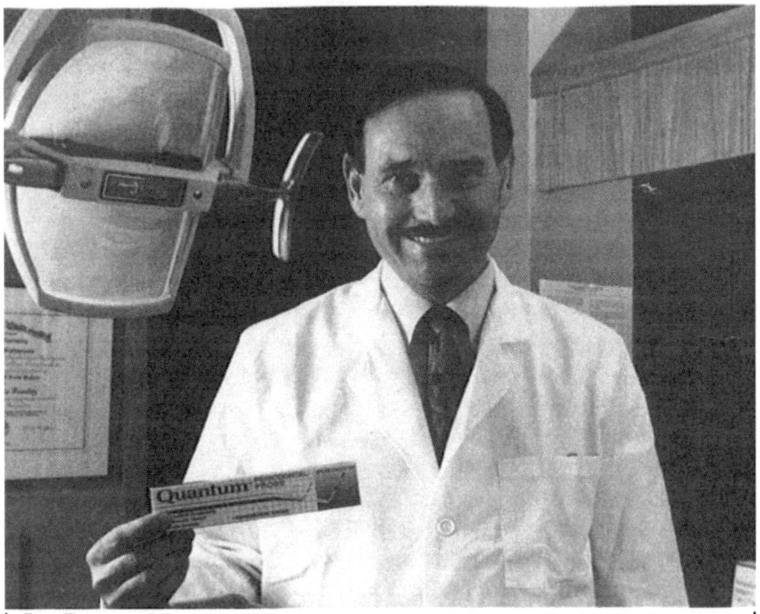

Dr. Bernard Loewenthal, a periodontist practicing in Portsmouth, has developed and patented a new product which offers dentists a more "patient friendly" instrument for diagnosing gum disease. (Courtesy photo)

PORTSMOUTH — After seven years of research and product development, a new device for detecting gum disease is now available to dentists in the northeastern United States.

Designed and patented by Dr. Bernard Loewenthal, a periodontist practicing in Portsmouth, the new Quantum perio probe offers dentists an alternative to the metal instrument traditionally used to diagnose periodontal problems.

The Quantum perio probe is being manufactured and distributed by Block Drug Corp., a leading international dental and medical supplies company. Sold directly to dental offices by consultants, Quantum's first month sales projections were exceeded during its first 10 days on the market.

Dr. Loewenthal holds several U.S. patents on the new product and has patents pending in Europe, Canada, Japan, Australia and New Zealand.

"An important and routine part of every dental checkup is a simple examination of the gums with a periodontal probe," Loewenthal explains. "Traditional metal probes can be quite uncomfortable to the patient, as well as being difficult to read. Metal probes may also damage dental implants, which more and more people are choosing in place of dentures."

According to Loewenthal, the Quantum perio probe is designed to make the detection of gum disease both easier for the dentist and more comfortable for the patient. "Quantum's patented flexible tip is color-coded for fast and accurate reading, while being gentle to sensitive gum tissue," he said.

Prior to its market introduction, Quantum was tested by the Department of Periodontology at State University of New York at Buffalo. The research findings indicated that the probe, when compared to traditional metal probes in a clinical setting, caused significantly less patient discomfort, and less bleeding of gum tissue.

Loewenthal hopes his invention will help educate the public avout gum disease and increase the detection of periodontal problems before they lead to serious gum disease.

The Quantum probe can be used with a visual teaching aid to show patients the state of their periodontal health during a routine dental examination. "Detected early enough, most periodontal problems can be treated painlessly and without surgery or major expense.

He expects the probe to be available to dentists throughout the nation by the end of the year.

Local periodontist develops special tool

Portsmouth periodontist Bernard Loewenthal has developed a plastic probe used to detect gum disease he hopes will replace the traditional metal probe used throughout his profession. (Democrat photo — Ireland)

By DOUG IRELAND
Portsmouth Bureau Chief

PORTSMOUTH — In an effort to combat gum disease, a local periodontist has developed a special, plastic tool he believes will revolutionize modern dentistry.

It is less than six inches long and weighes only a few ounces, but Bernard Loewenthal is confident it will help millions of people save their teeth from the evils of plaque.

Loewenthal, with an office at Lafayette Professional Park, has manufactured a "Perio-Test," a disposable probe used to diagnose specifically periodontal disease.

Periodontal disease is the most widespread ailment in the country, according to Loewenthal, who said it affects about 90 percent of the adult population.

Without proper dental care and regular checkups, the disease usually goes undetected, causing destruction of bone beneath the gums.

Once plaque eats away at this bone, the teeth are loosened and eventually fall out or need to be removed.

Loewenthal intends to market his invention so people will be able to purchase it as they would a tooth brush.

The small probe is used to detect the depth of pockets between gums and indicates how much bone deterioration has occurred. Its flexible, color-coded plastic tip helps pinpoint the disease without patients experiencing pain.

"It's a non-threatening instrument," Loewenthal said. "When you have a metal probe comimg at you, you tend to shy away."

Traditionally, this instrument has only been made of metal and could only be found within the dental profession. But Loewenthal plans to change that.

"I was looking for a way for the public to become aware of the fact that periodontal disease is a disease they don't very much about," he said.

If the public can be taught how to use the instrument, people will be able detect the disease before if spreads uncontrollably, Loewenthal said.

He also hopes to market the plastic instrument for roughly 40 cents, making it easy for distributors to sell to the military, hospitals and institutions.

The benefits of this tool are many, including the fact that it can be thrown away after use without risk of the spread of diseases such as acquired immune deficiency syndrome, Loewenthal said.

He has already received Food and Drug Administration approval and is trying to market the instrument with large nationwide firms.

He expects to market through dentists sometime next year, said Loewenthal who would not reveal how much it cost to develop to the product. But he did say the financial costs were "substantial."

Loewenthal has practiced periodontology out of Portsmouth for 14 years and was an instructor at Tufts University School of Dental Medicine in Boston.

He was also the chief of preventive dentistry at Pease Air Force Base for several years and is on the faculty of the Institute for Advanced Dental Studies.

Local dentist's invention approved

An invention developed by Portsmouth periodontist Bernie Loewenthal is being test marketed and has already been approved for marketing by the Federal Drug Administration. The Perio-Test is a flexible, disposable probe for diagnosing gum disease.

The traditional periodontal probe is usually made of metal. Only available to dentists for professional use, these probes penetrate between the tooth and gum to indicate the amount of bone loss due to disease.

The Perio-Test probe's flexibility lessens the discomfort of a metal probe. Because it is disposable, it can prevent cross-infection. With the concern for AIDS hepatitis and other contagious diseases, dentists can dispose of the probe or give it to their patients with no sterilization necessary.

Several national companies are considering buying rights to Perio-Test for national distribution via dentists' offices and eventually drug stores.

Bernard Loewenthal, D.D.S., whose office is located at Lafayette Professional Park in Portsmouth, has developed a new dental tool to diagnose periodontitis. The plastic **Perio-Test** is disposable and therefore can help prevent transferring contagious diseases from mouth to mouth. Having received FDA approval, Loewenthal intends to market his invention to the public.

B. Loewenthal

New dental probe easier for dentist and patient

PORTSMOUTH — After seven years of research and product development, a new device for detecting gum disease is now available to dentists in the northeastern United States.

Designed and patented by Dr. Bernard Loewenthal, a periodontist in Portsmouth, the new Quantum periodontal probe offers dentists an alternative to the metal instrument traditionally used to diagnose periodontal problems.

"An important and routine part of every dental checkup is a simple examination of the gums with a periodontal probe," explained Loewenthal. "Traditional metal probes can be quite uncomfortable to the patient, as well as being difficult to read. Metal probes may also damage dental implants, which more and more people are choosing in place of dentures."

According to Loewenthal, the Quantum periodontal probe is designed to make the detection of gum disease both easier for the dentist and much more comfortable for the patient.

"Quantum's patented flexible tip is color-coded for fast and accurate reading, while being gentle to sensitive gum tissue," he said.

The Quantum periodontal probe is being manufactured and distributed by Block Drug Corp., an international dental and medical supplies company. Sold directly to dental offices by Block Drug's dental consultants, Quantum's first month sales projections were exceeded during its first 10 days on the market. Loewenthal holds several U.S. patents on the new product and has patents pending in Europe, Canada, Japan, Australia and New Zealand.

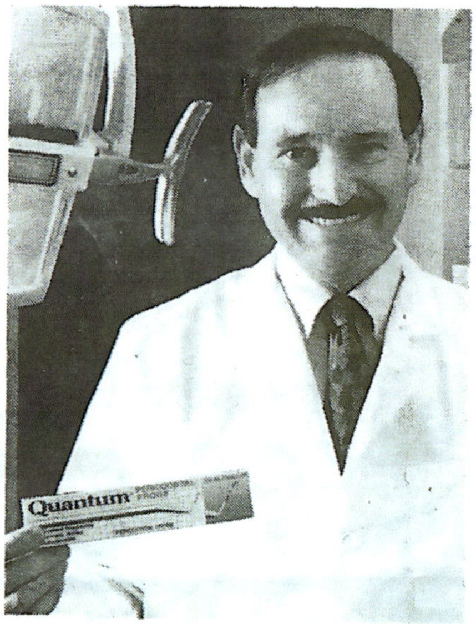

Dr. Bernard Loewenthal, Portsmouth periodontist, holds his invention to help dentists detect gum disease.

New tool detects gum disease

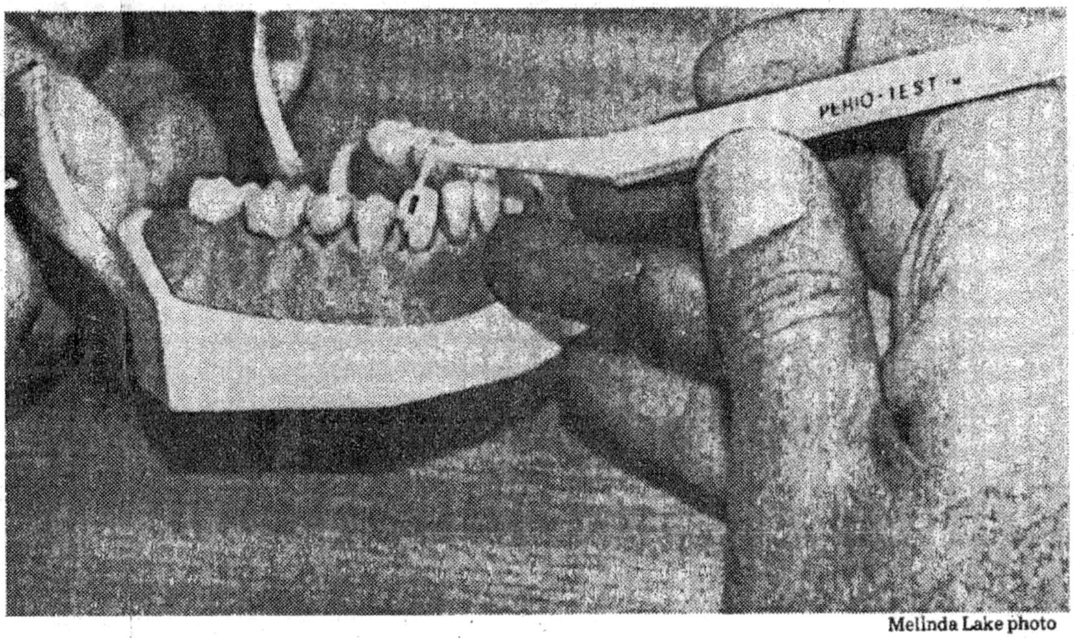

Melinda Lake photo

Dr. Bernard Loewenthal's 'Perio-Test' tool may replace metal probes used to diagnose gum diseases.

By MELINDA LAKE
York County Bureau

PORTSMOUTH, N.H. — It is an "invisible epidemic" more common than the common cold and is a disease present in nine out of 10 adult Americans, yet those affected often don't realize they have the disease.

The affliction is gum disease, with more common types being gingivitis, a superficial gum tissue inflammation, and periodontitis, involving chronic inflammation and destruction of bone around the tooth.

Untreated, gum disease causes more Americans to lose their teeth than all other factors combined.

To help bring information on the disease to as many people as possible, and to let people who have the disease know how severe their case is, Portsmouth periodontist Dr. Bernard Loewenthal has developed a "Perio-Test" tool.

Loewenthal has practiced dentistry here for 13 years, is the only periodontist in New Hampshire certified by the American Board of Periodontology, and a former chief of preventive dentistry at Pease Air Force Base in Newington.

The tool, made of plastic, may eventually replace the traditional metal probe currently used nationally by periodontists because of several innovations.

Because the Perio-Test is plastic, it is inexpensive, costing less than 50 cents apiece, Loewenthal said. That allows the probe to be disposable, preventing concerns by both dentists and patients about the spread of AIDS or other contagious diseases through a potentially poorly sterilized probe used repeatedly.

The flexible tip of the plastic probe has also received praise for being much more comfortable than the metal probe from patients in test groups around the country, he said.

Loewenthal

The traditional probe has groove markings on the tip, allowing the dentist or hygienist to see how far the disease has progressed by how far the tip slides into the gum line, but is often hard to read.

The plastic probe has colored lines instead of grooves, making it much easier to read the results and allowing the dentists or hygienists to teach their patients to test their condition on their own.

The periodontal probe is a crucial part of dental medicine, Loewenthal said, because "it is the only clinical tool which can diagnose the disease."

The probe is inserted "Three hundred and sixty degrees around the tooth" into the gum, he said, and how far the tip slides in can indicate conditions ranging from mild gingivitis to severe bone loss.

Signs of gum disease can include bleeding gums, loose teeth, swollen gums or receding gums, but often times there are no symptoms.

Perio-Test has been approved by the FDA and its trademark has also been approved, he said, with a patent pending.

Negotiations are also underway with several large drug companies interested in marketing the product.

"We expect worldwide distribution," he said.

Dental schools, military installations and prison systems are currently undertaking feasibility studies on the plastic probe, and initial feedback from dentists has been very positive, he said, with the main question being "Why hasn't someone come up with this before?" Loewenthal said.

The idea for the new probe first came to him nearly two years ago while thinking of ways to better educate the public on the problems of gum disease.

"If one thing comes out of all this, I hope it's that we can create a better awareness of this problem," Loewenthal said.

A common misconception is that the disease is only prevalent in older adults, but it can afflict anyone at any age, he said.

National Health Survey statistics show that 68 percent of teen-agers and 39 percent of children aged 6 to 11 have mild gingivitis, or the beginnings of gum disease.

Invention may ease pain of dentist visit

By Peter Parisi
THE HERALD

PORTSMOUTH, N.H. — Going to the dentist may soon become a less-painful experience, if a Portsmouth periodontist has his way.

Dr. Bernard Loewenthal has developed a dental instrument for helping detect gum disease that offers dentists an alternative to the metal instrument traditionally used to diagnose periodontal problems.

Currently being test-marketed to dentists around New England, the Quantum periodontal probe is being manufactured and distributed by Block Drug Corp., a New Jersey-based dental- and medical-supplies company.

Interviewed at his Lafayette Road offices this week, Loewenthal said the Quantum periodontal probe, which is made of plastic, was designed to make the detection of gum disease easier for the dentist and less-painful for patients. "Quantum's patented flexible tip is color-coded for fast and accurate reading, while being gentle to sensitive gum tissue," he said.

"An important and routine part of every dental checkup is a simple examination of the gums with a periodontal probe," explained Loewenthal, whose dental specialty involves the tissue and bones which support the teeth. "Traditional metal probes can be quite uncomfortable to the patient, as well as being difficult to read."

The latter consideration is important, he added with a laugh, "especially when you get to be my age."

Loewenthal, a 53-year-old graduate of the New York University College of Dentistry and the Tufts University School of Dental Medicine, said that when he first conceived the idea of making a periodontal probe out of plastic in the mid-1980s, he was told it could not be done.

Unconvinced, he sought the help of the department of plastics engineering at the University of Lowell in Massachusetts, and "in three months, I had a prototype."

He said he pitched his invention to more than 20 companies before licensing Block to manufacture and sell the device, so named because the firm held a trademark on the term "Quantum."

Prior to its market introduction, the Quantum periodontal probe was tested by the Department of Periodontology at the State University of New York at Buffalo. The research findings indicated that it caused significantly less patient discomfort and considerably less bleeding of gum tissue when compared to traditional metal probes.

It was also found to result in more consistently accurate readings, due to the simplicity and visual clarity of its red-and-green color coding system, which measures how deep the pockets around the teeth have become. Measured in millimeters, the deeper the pockets are, the more severe the periodontal problem — and the greater the risk of tooth loss unless corrective action is taken.

"Detected early enough, most periodontal problems can be treated painlessly and without surgery or major expense," said Loewenthal, who has been a dentist for 28 years and a periodontist since 1970. During a three-year Air Force hitch, he served as chief of the periodontics and preventive-dentistry sections at the former Pease Air Force Base dental clinic in 1966-67. He has been practicing in Portsmouth since 1974.

Loewenthal holds three U.S. patents on the Quantum periodontal probe: two for its flexible tip, the third for its color-coded measurement system.

Distributed by The Associated Press.

N.H. Dentist's Invention Hits The Market

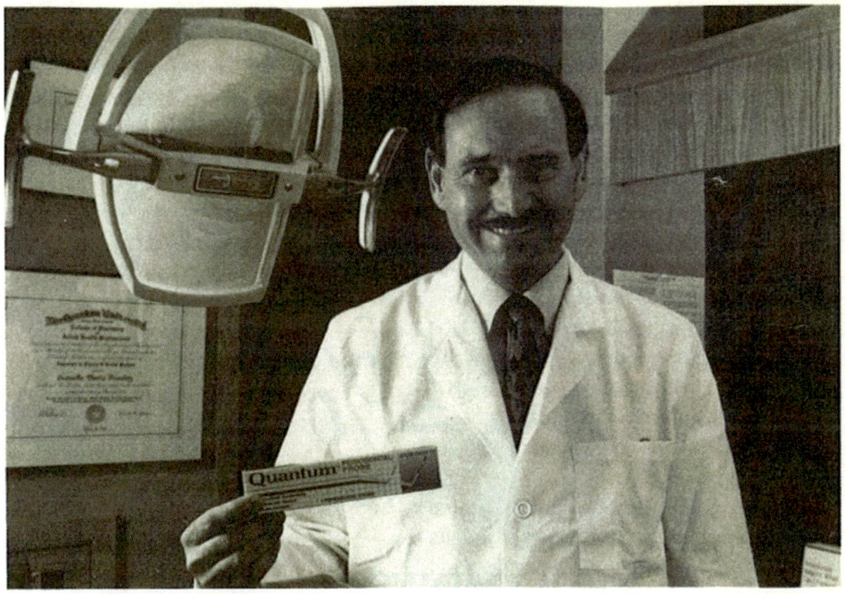

Dr. Loewenthal displays his hot-selling new invention

After seven years of research and product development, a new device for detecting gum disease is now available to dentists. Designed and patented by Dr. Bernard Loewenthal, a periodontist practicing in Portsmouth, New Hampshire, the new Quantum™ perio probe offers dentists an alternative to the metal instrument traditionally used to diagnose periodontal problems.

The Quantum™ perio probe is manufactured and distributed by Block Drug Corporation, a leading international dental and medical supplies company. Sold directly to dental offices by Block Drug's dental consultants, Quantum™'s first month sales projections were exceeded during its first ten days on the market. Dr. Loewenthal holds several U.S. patents on the new product and has patents pending in Europe, Canada, Japan, Australia, and New Zealand.

"An important and routine part of every dental checkup is a simple examination of the gums with a periodontal probe," explains Dr. Loewenthal. "Traditional metal probes can be quite uncomfortable to the patient, as well as being difficult to read. Metal probes may also damage dental implants, which more and more people are choosing in place of dentures."

According to Dr. Loewenthal, the Quantum™ perio probe is designed to make the detection of gum disease both easier for the dentist and much more comfortable for the patient. "Quantum™'s patented flexible tip is color coded for fast and accurate reading, while being gentle to sensitive gum tissue."

Prior to its market introduction, Quantum™ was tested by the Department of Periodontology at the State University of New York at Buffalo. The research findings indicated that Quantum™, when compared to traditional metal probes in a clinical setting, causes significantly less patient discomfort, and significantly less bleeding of gum tissue. Quantum™ also provides consistently accurate readings, due to the simplicity and visual clarity of its color coding system.

> ***Dr. Loewenthal hopes that his invention will help educate the public about gum disease and increase the early detection of periodontal problems.***

Dr. Loewenthal hopes that his invention will help educate the public about gum disease and increase the early detection of periodontal problems. "Recent public surveys conducted by Teledyne Water Pik and Warner-Lambert (in conjunction with the American Dental Association) revealed that Americans have very little idea what gum disease is and how to prevent it," he states. "Although three out of four Americans can expect to have some form of gum disease in their lifetime, and 74 percent of those surveyed have a major symptom of the disease (bleeding gums), 76 percent of all Americans believe they will not get the disease."

The Quantum™ perio probe can be used with a visual teaching aid to show patients the state of their periodontal health during a routine dental examination, explains Dr. Loewenthal. "Detected early enough, most periodontal problems can be treated painlessly and without surgery or major expense."

Dr. Loewenthal expects the Quantum™ perio probe to be available to dentists throughout the nation by the end of 1992. ■

Rebecca Gould / Portsmouth

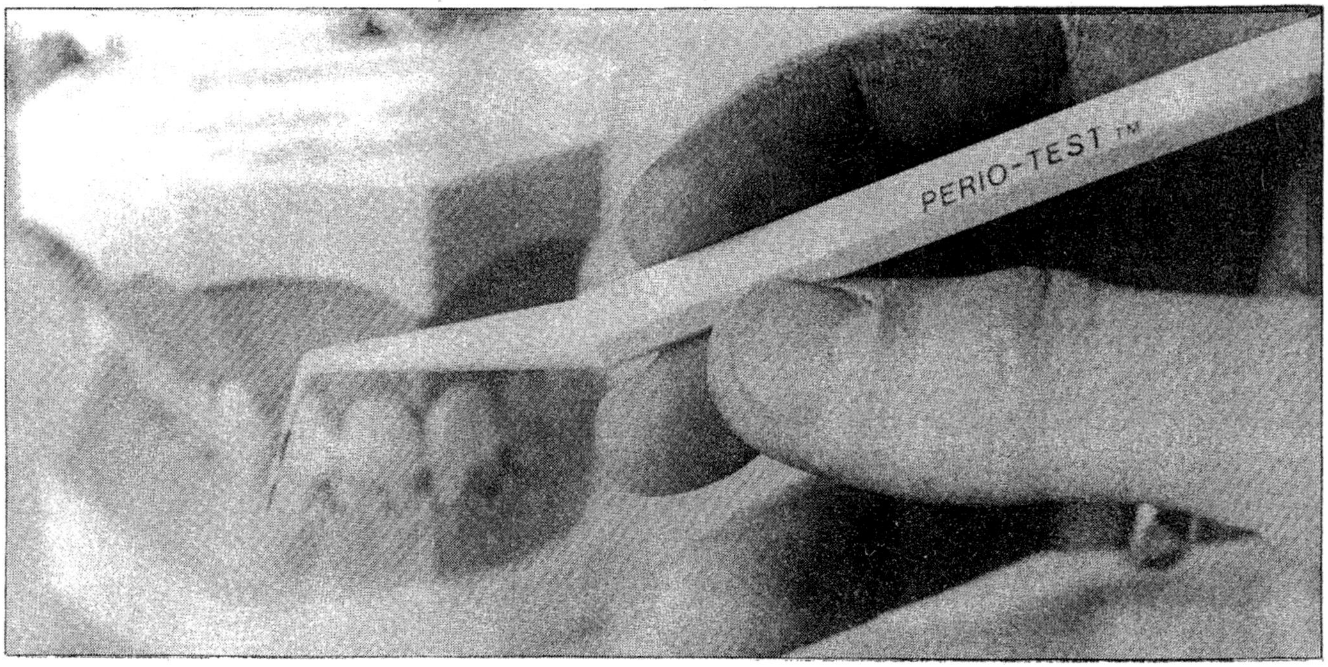

Press photo by Gregg Matthews

PROBING: Perio Test, devloped by Dr. Bernard Loewenthal, is more flexible and less painful than the conventional metal dental tools. It also helps detect gum disease in the preliminary stages.

Home dental care takes a step beyond floss and toothpaste

By HEATHER McCONNELL
PRESS STAFF WRITER

PORTSMOUTH — A local dentist has developed an instrument to diagnose gum disease, and reduce the chance of cross infections, such as AIDS, sometimes transferred by unsanitary tools.

Dr. Bernard Loewenthal simply refined the idea of the metal probe used by dentists by designing a plastic disposable one. It is the same length as a toothbrush with a curved and pointed end.

"Perio Test" is more flexible and less painful than the metal version and is designed for self-examination, after a dentist has used it on the patient.

"The instrument is kinder than the conventional metal," said Loewenthal, who now only uses plastic probes on his patients.

Although it has not yet been approved by the Food and Drug Administration as a home testing device, the probe acts as preventative medicine, much like dental floss or brushing regularly. While the tool should not replace regular dentist visits, it could alert patients to the early stages of gum disease.

Loewenthal spent 18 months developing the tool, paying all expenses himself. He estimates the eventual market price to be less than 50 cents, although he is currently giving the probes to his clients free of charge. Loewenthal has received approval from the FDA to begin marketing the probe.

Dr. Bernard Loewenthal
Perio Test inventer

"I wish I had applied for a grant but I didn't," said Loewenthal. Other area dentists have also used the instrument with patients according to Loewenthal and been pleased with the results.

Periodontitis, or gum disease, can lead to the destruction of bone supporting teeth and eventually, loss of teeth. According to the American Academy of Periodontology and the American Dental Association, the disease is present in nine out of ten adults.

Seventy percent of tooth loss after age 40 is due to periodontitis. Sixty-eight percent of children and teenagers are estimated to have either periodontitis, or gingivitis, a milder form of gum disease according to the AAP and ADA.

"We think dentists will find the new plastic probe to be much more comfortable for their patients than the traditional metal probe.

"Our goal is to help prevent gum disease through use of the give-away probe while creating national awareness of this relentless disease," said Loewenthal.

Loewenthal, whose office is on 278 Lafayette Road, is the only dentist in New Hampshire certified by the American Board of Periodontology.

Dentist Markets Gum Decay Probe

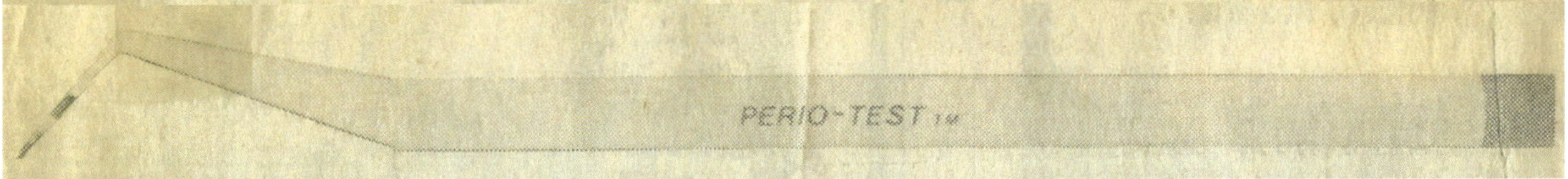

By JOHN HART
Sunday News Correspondent

PORTSMOUTH — A Port City dentist has developed a disposable plastic dental probe for diagnosing periodontal disease and gingivitis, which affect about 90 percent of the population.

Dr. Bernard Loewenthal said Friday that his "Perio-Test Dental Probe" has been approved for marketing by the U.S. Food and Drug Administration and is being test marketed now. He declined to identify the company involved in the testing.

Loewenthal expects that within a year the throwaway probe will be used by dentists worldwide.

The next step will be marketing the probe across drug store counters "...so the consumers can take it home and (do) self diagnosis."

The Perio-Test Dental Probe is color-coded with a calibrated tip for "painless" diagnosing of periodontal disease.

Loewenthal listed several advantages of the new periodontal plastic probe over the conventional metal probe.

For example, the conventional probe is inflexible. The Perio-Test Probe is designed to allow fexibility when probing pockets in the gums of a patient's mouth.

The plastic probe can bend and considerably lessen the discomfort caused by the metal probe, according to Loewenthal.

In the past year, the majority of his patients reported that when he used both new and old probes in their examinations, they felt less or no pain with the plastic probe.

Loewenthal stressed that the new probe can significantly increase dentist's awareness of periodontal disease, which he said is prevalent in about 90 percent of the adult population.

The disease is basically an inflammatory disease of the gums which spreads to and destroys the supporting bone of the teeth, Loewenthal explained.

Over time, periodontal disease causes teeth to abscess or loosen and either fall out or have to be removed by a dentist, he added.

The periodontal probe is the only significant clinical tool used for checking a person's periodontal disease status, said Loewenthal.

Until now, the probe has only been available to dentists for professional use.

The Perio-Test Dental Probe is color-coded with a calibrated tip for "painless" diagnosing of periodontal disease. Loewenthal listed several advantages of the new periodontal plastic probe over the conventional metal probe.

DR. BERNARD LOEWENTHAL

Perio-Test's unique disposable nature can also prevent "cross-infection," he continued.

With the emphasis on preventing the spread of AIDs, hepatitis, and other contagious diseases, dentists can either dispose of the probe or give it to the patients.

"We think dentists will find the new plastic probe to be much more comfortable for their patients than the traditional metal probe," said the doctor.

"Our goal is to help prevent gum disease through the use of this throwaway probe while creating a national awareness of this relentless disease," Loewenthal said.

Loewenthal has spent an average of 20 hours a week for the past 18 months in research and development of his Perio-Test Dental Probe.

He is currently promoting the disposable probe as a breakthrough for the dental profession in terms of preventing cross-infection.

According to Loewenthal, dental schools, military installations and prison systems are currently undertaking feasibility studies on the probe.

Loewenthal is a graduate of the New York University School of Dentistry and is certified by the American Board of Periodontology. Since 1974, he has operated a dental office in Portsmouth.

Dentist markets new tool

PORTSMOUTH — A new rubber-tipped plastic probe, designed by the only dentist in the state who is licensed to practice periodontics, may soon be marketed nationwide to help the public diagnose the most widespread disease in the country: gum disease.

At a recent press conference Dr. Bernard Loewenthal, D.D.S. P.A., unveiled his Perio-test tool, aimed at allowing people at home to possibly discover if they have periodontitis before suffering discomfort.

"Over 90 percent of the population has this disease and many don't know it," said Loewenthal.

The disease is generated by sugary foods and plaque buildup.

"It's worse than the common cold. This tool allows people in the home, in the age of self-care, to find out for themselves what condition their gums are in."

If periodontal disease goes untreated, the teeth can eventually fall out when the gums no longer provide support.

The condition often does not include pain and discovery may be too late.

Gingivitis which occurs in the early stages, includes inflamed gums, can be treated with a cleaning, harder brushing and flossing. Indicators of trouble include bleeding gums, loose teeth, teeth that seperate or spread apart, swollen or receeding gums.

Loewenthal said the color, composition, tri-colored tip, and feedback from testing at the Walter Reed Army Hospital have made the Perio-test a well-received item already. A patent is pending.

"It doesn't look as scary as a steel tool does," said Loewenthal. "The colored tip allows us to better measure the distance under the gum and it won't hurt or possibly pierce the gum tissue wall."

Random testing on patients in his office led hygenists to record many comments such as, "It didn't hurt."

The tool has already received Federal Drug Administration approval for marketing and Loewenthal is talking with approximately 15 companies regarding possible distribution and cost.

Made out of plastic, the Perio-test would also be useful in the armed service where using it as a throw-away item would save sterilizing costs and would reduce the risk of transmitting AIDS.

BERNARD LOEWENTHAL
Invents diagnostic tool

"I think it would be more cost-effective as a disposable," Loewenthal said.

It was estimated that the Perio-tool could be produced for under 50 cents.

Its low production price per unit also makes it feasible for a dentist to use it as a give-away item.

"It's dishwasher safe and it could be rinsed off and placed right next to the toothbrushes," noted Loewenthal. "The potential for this is enormous."

With the idea secured a year-and-a-half ago, it took Loewenthal a long time to find a plastics company that could and did figure out how to manufacture the tool.

"It did seem at first like it would be easy to manufacture it," agreed Loewenthal, "but we found out there is an awful lot more to it."

The angles and tapered tip complicated the problem.

Loewenthal estimated he has put in 10 to 20 hours per week of his own effort and "a substantial" amount of money.

He said another plastic dentist tool used for scaling or cleaning teeth was not well endorsed from other practioners because it didn't clean well enough.

He advised anyone concerned about this silent disease to make an appointment with a dentist for an examination so that corrective action can be taken if needed.

B. Loewenthal

Bernard Loewenthal, D.D.S., of Portsmouth has developed **Perio-Test,** a flexible, periodontal probe with a color-coded, calibrated tip for diagnosing periodontal disease and gingivitis. The periodontal probe is the only significant clinical tool used for checking a person's periodontal disease status. The conventional probe is inflexible and usually made of metal. Lines on the probe indicate the depth that the probe penetrates between tooth and gum. A deep insertion indicates a problem that has a direct correlation between the depth of insertion and the amount of bone loss. The new probe is also disposable, which helps prevent cross-infection. Eventually, the Perio-Test will be marketed to the general public.

Portsmouth dentist sells company rights to probe

PORTSMOUTH — The exclusive worldwide rights to a plastic periodontal probe have been sold to the Block Drug Company by Portsmouth dentist Bernard Loewenthal.

The trademark "Perio-Test" also has officially been registered with the U.S. Patent and Trademark Office with a patent pending.

Block Drug, an international company headquartered in New Jersey, plans to begin national marketing to the dental profession. According to Dr. Loewenthal, the flexible, color-coded plastic probe will be introduced at the American Dental Association's national conference in Washington, D.C., this coming October.

Dr. Loewenthal, who spent nearly two years developing the probe, said he'd invested "well over" $25,000, and that didn't include the time he'd invested in it. The idea for the probe came to him while he was out walking, recuperating from a back operation.

Not only did Block Drug do the test marketing of the probe, now that it has bought the rights for it, its marketing of the new tool will include sending out literature on it to the approximately 125,000 dentists throughout the country.

Dr. Loewenthal, who indicated he was impressed with Block Drug's aggressive marketing strategy, noted that the company had given back to him what he'd put into developing the probe. Once there's a patent applied to the product, he will receive a royalty based on the company's net sales.

Periodontal disease remains the leading cause of tooth loss in the U.S. and is prevalent in approximately 90 percent of the adult population.

"Block is now working with my plastics engineer to manufacture the molds needed to produce the instruments," Dr. Loewenthal said. The company will sell directly to the dental profession, and it would be several years before it might possibly be an over-the-counter item for home use.

The periodontal probe is the only significant clinical tool used for checking a person's periodontal disease status. The conventional probe is inflexible and usually made of metal.

DR. BERNARD LOEWENTHAL

The "Perio-Test" probe is designed to allow flexibility when probing. It can bend and considerably lessen the discomfort felt by a metal probe. Its color coding allows easy-to-read findings. It also is disposable, which can help prevent cross-infection.

Weather

The weather has been a wonderful and integral part of my life, long before and after my career as a periodontist. I enjoy watching and forecasting the weather daily as much as almost anything else in my life, except for being with my family! My weather adventures were of interest to a wide variety of people, some of who wrote about the weather and me. Our local newspaper published winter weather alerts ***on its front page*** based on my forecasts. It was good, free, PR!

An article published by the American Dental Association.

New England Dentist Doubles As Weatherman for Community

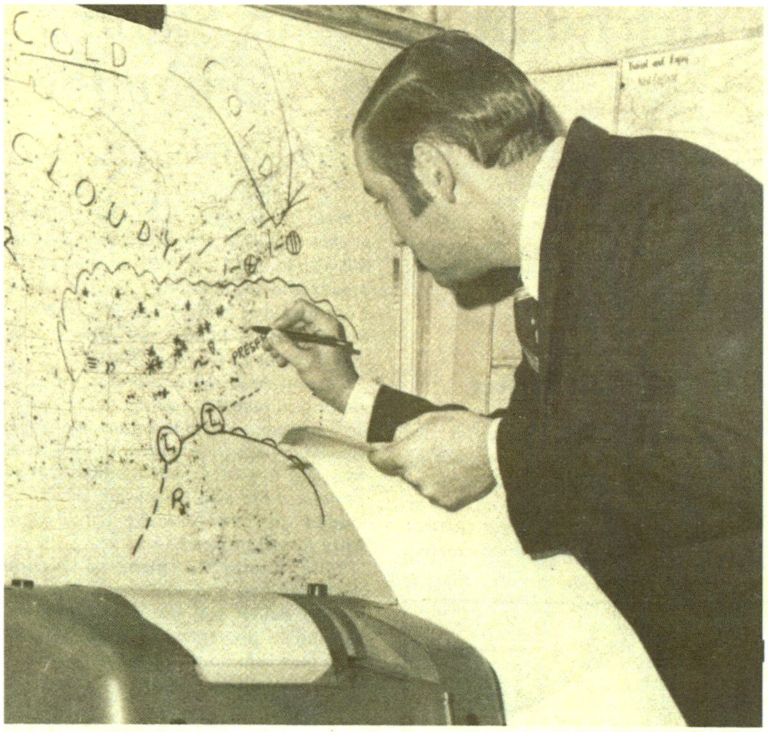

Meteorologist-dentist Bernard Loewenthal charts a weather map

Haverhill, Mass—Periodontal disease is not caused by a high pressure system over the New England coast, nor is a rainy day caused by a lack of toothbrushing. But a dentist here has combined dentistry and meteorology.

Bernard Loewenthal, 33, a periodontist and part-time clinical instructor in periodontics at Tufts University School of Dental Medicine, has been the weather adviser here for more than three years.

He provides day-to-day weather information strictly on a public service basis —to police and highway officials and to the schools. Three years ago Dr. Loewenthal had a special radio show which had listeners call in weather questions to him.

Recently he combined his dental practice with weather forecasting by posting the daily weather bulletins on a blackboard in the office.

"When I was a boy I always wanted to be a dentist, but my hobby was meteorology," said Dr. Loewenthal. While serving as a dentist in the Air Force he received enough additional training in meteorology to become a professional.

When contacted by the ADA NEWS, Dr. Loewenthal quickly gave the Chicago weather report—and was correct. "It is snowing in Chicago with cold weather, and it will get colder tonight."

He said it is impossible for anyone to give an accurate long-range weather prediction, "even with computers."

"The five-day forecast even leaves a lot to be desired," he said. "There are so many factors (such as wind patterns) which can change the picture quite rapidly.

"When you get right down to it, the meteorologist must make a decision.

BERNARD LOEWENTHAL

Sometimes there is a lot of luck involved, but I think also that some weathermen have a sixth sense about it. At any rate, ultimately, he cannot hedge."

Bernie Loewenthal weathers the highs and lows of a dual career

by Clare Kittredge

In offices softened with the earth tones of wood, wicker, cork and copper, Dr. Bernie Loewenthal will explore the microscopic world of your teeth. One of four Seacoast periodontists, he employs a staff of nine to keep track of a thick file of patients from six to 86.

If you read the vellum pinned to the bulletin board of his Portsmouth waiting room, you will also learn something about the monumental world of weather. "Storminess on the horizon," reads the headline printed in brown ink. Further details on cloud patterns, precipitation, temperature and winds follow, with the next day's outlook and sketch of major causes like "jet-stream patterns" and "high pressure systems." Teeth and weather are an unlikely pair, perhaps, but Bernie Loewenthal combines both. A periodontist first, he is also a full-fledged weatherman, and passionate about his field.

Both have drawn him since childhood. "As a little boy growing up in New York City in the '40s, I can remember pressing my nose to the window to watch a hurricane," he says. "I remember climbing over fallen trees outside and being moved by the power of wind and rain." Come summer in the Catskills, he says he remembers watching the clouds build up in the Northwest and roll down the mountains. Once, as an experiment, he poured water on hot pavement and made his own cloud.

Likewise, early on, he was exposed to the mysteries of human dentition. "My sister was a dental assistant," he says. "I used to watch what dentists did. It was fascinating and complicated, and they seemed to enjoy what they were doing." Later, he found that dentistry broke down into myriad specialties, and that he could choose one that called for a high degree of expertise.

"As time went on, I had to decide between meteorology and dentistry. For a number of reasons, I decided to do both. Actually," he observes in a low-key precise voice, "what I have is a dual career."

This didn't happen overnight. Basic science, he studied in New York City at Queens College in the late '50s. During the '60s, he went to dental school at New York University, worked in both weather and dentistry during a stint in the Air Force, and studied periodontology at Tufts School of Dental Medicine.

In 1968, he was officially recognized by the American Meteorological Society and became a professional meteorologist. "That's important," he says, "because otherwise, you can't forecast the weather for the public." That year, he moved to Haverhill and became city weather forecaster. For 10 years, he says, he advised the Public Works Department on when to haul out their snow-removal equipment and when not to, saving thousands of dollars.

Loewenthal has a lot of other professional affiliations, but none as hard-earned as his certification by the American Board of Periodontology. He is the only New Hampshire periodontist to be certified by this board. Getting this, he says, took four years of college, four years of dental school, another three years of "perio" training and then, once he was eligible to take the exam, three to five more years experience in the field.

But both professions excite him. His Stratham home is his weather operations base. Carefully positioned to give unobstructed views of south and west, and open to all the weather that pours into New England from all parts of the country, his home houses a weather room equipped with ultra-sensitive tools.

Maggie Harrison

Dr. Bernie Loewenthal has a dual career. Besides being a periodontist, he is a professional meteorologist with The Signal Corp. as one of his clients.

At the same time, he was still going to Tufts, where he taught periodontology part time after his residency. In 1970, he opened a practice in Haverhill and four years later, he moved to Portsmouth. Today, he is on the faculty of the Institute for Advanced Dental Studies, a Swampscott, Mass.-based institution that helps dentists from all over the world keep up with the profession after school.

A high-speed data terminal plugged into Weather Services International, a Bedford, Mass., computer, gives him weather information on the rest of the world. A facsimile machine, a duplicate of which sits

Loewenthal

in his office, is hooked directly by phone to the National Weather Services and produces weather maps and computer charts showing weather patterns over the next 12 to 84 hours. A "Dial" radar allows him to contact any radar in the country.

Several years ago, a patient who worked for the Signal Corp. in Hampton suggested he predict the weather for Signal, and Loewenthal became Signal's official weatherman. Unless there's a storm brewing, he usually rises around 6 a.m. to prepare the forecast. "On stormy nights, I stay up all night. I don't go to sleep," he explains. "It's too exciting. It's how I get my kicks."

Maggie Harrison

Loewenthal's wife, Alana Mirkin, is part-time receptionist in the Portsmouth office.

Around 7:30 a.m., he reads the forecast over the phone to Signal. Copies of it are then distributed to company employees who use the information to plan travel, entertainment and leisure activities. The forecast is also useful, he says, because the corporation flies executives in from all over the world.

To be good at forecasting, Loewenthal says it helps to be local. "It takes experience in one area (where you constantly see changes in the weather), to be an accurate forecaster," he says. "You also have to have deep love for the weather, because if you love what you do, and you're involved with it all the time, you do it well. And I *love* the weather."

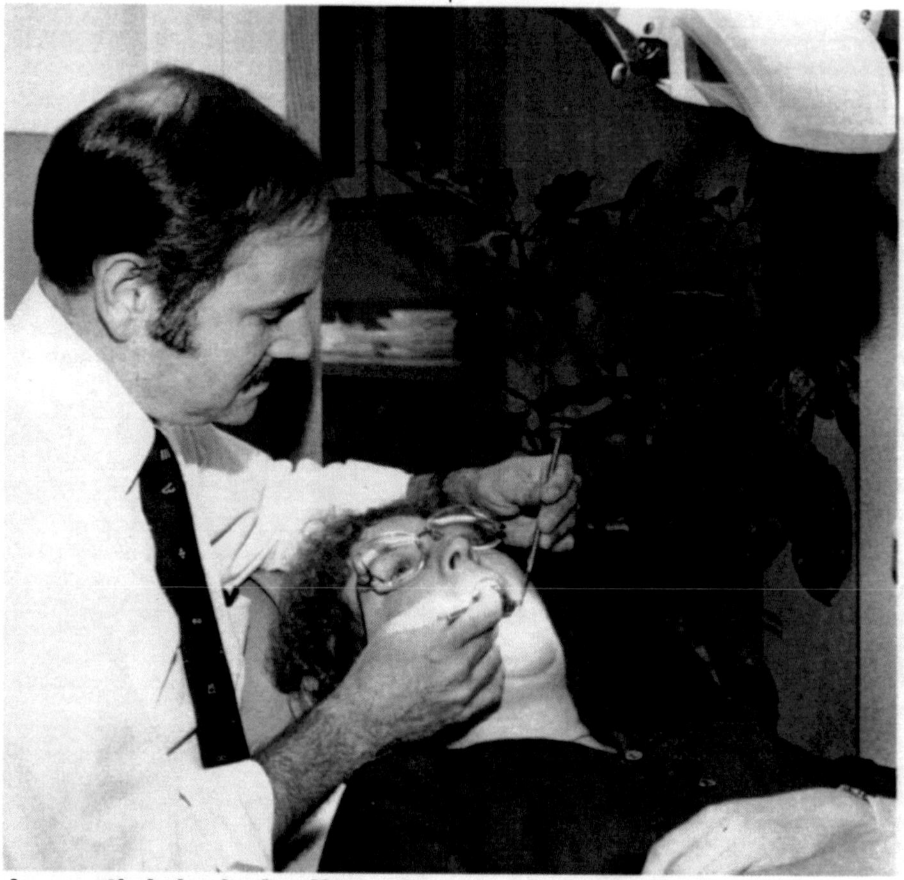

Loewenthal checks Jan Knauss' teeth. One of his most valued affiliations is his certification by the American Board of Periodontology.

From the snowstorms that close down businesses and make ski areas thrive to lightning, tornadoes, hurricanes and larger phenomena like acid rain and the greenhouse effect, he says the weather affects everyone. "We are weather-dependent in every way. People love to talk about the weather because it affects us all so drastically. Weather is monumental, awesome."

Weather is also a great icebreaker at the office where Loewenthal delves with equal intensity into people's teeth. His job, he believes, is to keep teeth firmly anchored where they belong, in people's mouths, embedded in healthy bone and gums.

Periodontal disease, he says, is rampant. "The reason people are losing their teeth now is because of gum disease. Ninety percent of the people we know have it. It's as common as the common cold." Today, he says, a more health-orientated public wants to fight against it. "Today, people want to achieve greater levels of health. You hear a lot about jogging, dieting, aerobics— the field of periodontics fits into that. If people lose their dentition, they can't eat their food. They can't taste it. It doesn't fit with their self-image."

The problem, he says, is complex. "A case can be slight or severe. It can involve one or several teeth." Whatever the case, bleeding gums, he says, are a sign of trouble. "The only time bleeding is normal is during menstruation."

The cause, he says, is bacteria, and solutions range from conservative to drastic depending on the case. "The solution is to create an environment in which the teeth are clean. This does not always involve surgery," he adds.

"Ninety percent of the time, periodontal disease can be treated and people can keep their teeth. The key is early detection." Currently, Loewenthal speaks to local dental study groups, gives presentations in classrooms and on television, and works with referring dentists in the area. He also gives one-time consultations to people who are worried about the condition of their teeth and gums.

Although it's not immediately obvious, there is a connection, he says, between teeth and the weather. "With both, you're at the mercy of mother nature. Just as every new patient is a challenge, every new day is a challenge— it's unending, infinite."

The difference, he says, is that however good a forecaster may be at predicting the moods of the weather, forecasting, unlike periodontics, is not only hard science. "Forecasting is a science, but it's also an art— there are still many things about it we don't understand." •

Haverhill Dentist Subs As City Weatherman

By MERRILL B. WHITING
. . . staff reporter

Haverhill is unfortunate from the standpoint of winter's wintry blasts of sleet, cold and snow, but fortunate because it is one of few communities with its own weatherman, Dr. Bernard Loewenthal, 197 Concord St.

Never a day goes by that the sunroom of his home doesn't resound with the ticking of the teletype machine, the "high-pitched tone indicator" signaling a weather map transmission over the facsimile machine, or the scratching of a felt-tip pen over a weather map, drawing the surface temperature-dew point-barometric readings for nearby potential storms.

All the reasoning in the world wouldn't necessarily answer why Dr. Loewenthal, whose profession is that of dentistry (periodontist), completes his day's work to run home to his weather equipment, and devote hours to it, finishing in time to go to bed. The best explanation Dr. Loewenthal has is — "Because I love it, and feel it is worthwhile to the community's needs."

He has been a dentist-meteorologist since 1968, having started with maps and a teletype, and "graduating" this season (1973-74) to the rental of a facsimile machine, with continent-wide weather maps and weather indications even of a global nature.

The map, shown in the accompanying picture, is from the facsimile machine, which transmits over Western Union wires linked to a central office in Lawrence.

120 Maps Daily

The machine produces as many as 120 maps daily, but Dr. Loewenthal uses about half that number, or those he considers necessary for this area.

His predictions since 1968 have become more widely reported and respected, since most of them are "on the money, accuracy-wise," according to Meteorologist Don Kent, of WBZ Radio and Television.

Kent said during a talk last year at Groveland Congregational Church that the Haverhill dentist's forecasts are better than his own, for this immediate area.

Low pressure (storms) with the mixing of high pressure areas, which usually signal fair weather, are the major components to an average weather map, Dr. Loewenthal says. However, in New England, he added, the complexity of forecasting is enhanced by ocean water temperature and moisture import from the Atlantic, to say nothing of the fact Haverhill is directly in the west-to-east path of most storms.

"There are nights when I feel I can take it easy because there are no storms in sight," he said, "then a couple hours later I find something in the midwest has changed the pattern for more bad weather on the way."

He believes a weatherman who enjoys adventure should forecast in New England.

He telephones his forecasts in daily to the mayors office in City Hall, and, when conditions warrant, to school headquarters. He also sends emergency data to the Department of Public Works (DPW), which finds his service invaluable during the winter.

Only Winter Forecasts

Dr. Loewenthal only forecasts in the winter, since rental costs of machines prohibits a year-round operation.

He doesn't get paid for the service and, in fact, takes money out of his pocket to help pay rental fees for the facsimile machine, a highly-sophisticated and expensive device.

"Even with all the sophistication of the industry in the world at your fingertips, the forecast remains a human product of decision, coupled with an element of knowing the machinery of weather," the doctor said.

And, he'll be the first to agree, the most important factor of all in forecasting is to relate the information to the reader or listener in a concise, understandable manner.

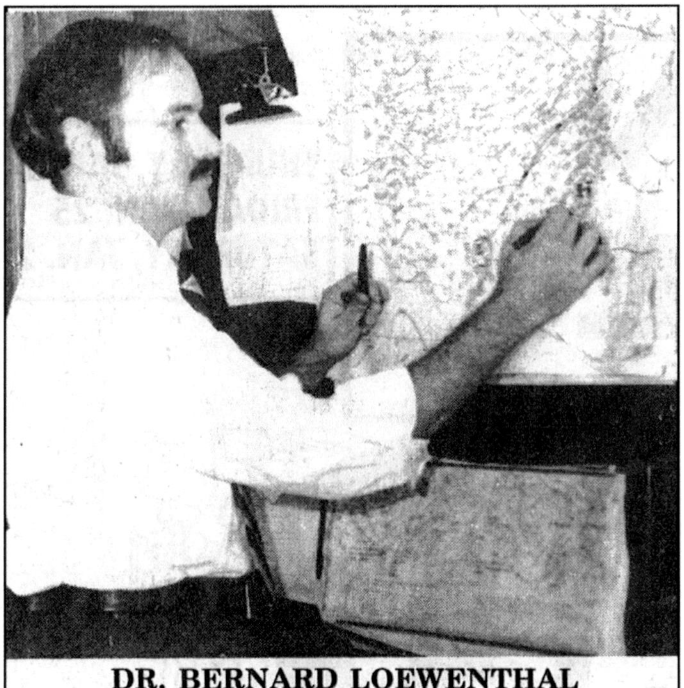

DR. BERNARD LOEWENTHAL
. . . marking weather map

Snow Forecast Accurately

Dr. Bernard Lowenthal, Haverhill dentist who also provides the highway department, police and school department with daily weather forecasts, has been "on the money" on each of his reports dealing with snow. Yesterday morning he predicted four-to-eight inches, and then at 4:45 yesterday afternoon updated his forecast to six to 12 inches, ending his message with, "It looks like a White Christmas."

Loewenthal: a man for all seasons

Undaunted, young Loewenthal continued his interest in weather, and for a time it was a toss-up between meteorology or dentistry. Finally, he decided; 'Why not both?'

In his Stratham home, Loewenthal has meteorological accoutrements one would find in a TV newsroom.

By Herb Philbrick
Staff Reporter

STRATHAM — Although Dr. Bernard Loewenthal of Stratham is highly skilled in two professions, both of them calling for exceptional ability, neither one of them can be found in the classified section of the telephone directory.

As a consequence, you can let your fingers walk all over the yellow pages and you will search in vain to find Loewenthal listed under (a), periodontology or (b), meteorology. . . although, in both fields, he is acknowledged by his peers to be an expert.

Loewenthal's interest in these uncommon occupations — uncommon, apparently, insofar as the telephone company is concerned — stems back to when he was not more than 4 or 5 years old. Conversing with him, one quickly finds that he has lost none of his youthful enthusiasm for either field of endeavor.

His stature in profession "a" — to which the doctor devotes four days and several evenings a week — was reached by virtue of four years of college training in basic science and biochemistry at Queens College in New York. That was followed by four years of dental study at NYU; another three years of specialized study in periodontology at Tufts School of Dental Medicine; then by a period of time as a U.S. Air Force dentist; topped off with 10 years of practice in Haverhill, Mass., before setting up his present practice in Portsmouth.

Today, with the assistance of his wife, Ilana, he oversees a staff of nine at his office in Lafayette Professional Park. He is a member of the faculty at the Institute for Advanced Dental Studies, a Swampscott, Mass., institution established to assist dentists worldwide to stay abreast with a host of new techniques; and, fully accredited by the American Board of Periodontology.

Loewenthal is also the inventor of a special diagnostic dental tool, patented under the name "Perio-Test," now being test marketed by a leading international firm.

The implement is expected to be mass produced and distributed, probably under another trade name, by 1991.

Second Profession

By way of contrast with the art of periodontology, one of the very latest sciences known to man, Loewenthal's second full-fledged profession is one of mankind's oldest: the art — or science, if you will — of meteorology, which dates back at least 2,500 years and probably before that.

We do know that Aristotle published a treatise on the subject of meteorology, more commonly known as weather watching, at around 350 years before Christ.

Aristotle called his work "Meteorogica." And although many generations of "weather-watchers" have come and gone since that time, for nearly 2,000 years the "science" of predicting weather changed very little.

The first, and very slight advance, occurred in 1607 when Galileo invented the thermometer. Another tiny leap forward was made in 1643, with the invention of the barometer.

Weather forecasting as we know it today, however, is less than 150 years old. Not until 1845, with the practical application of the telegraph, did it become possible to establish a communication system capable of communicating weather information quickly from one place to another.

The next advance came between 1900 and 1920, with the development of radio. But the "great leap forward" came when, on Feb. 20, 1945, for the first time, and using war-time radar, technicians tracked a shower seven miles off the English coast. Now one could not only "see" a storm in the distance, but could also accurately track its speed, direction, and amount of precipitation.

Today, modern radar sites dot the entire country, each gathering data about 50 miles in radius, encompassing 7,850 square miles. Each modern radar scanner accomplishes what would otherwise require several hundred rain gauges.

'Thing in the Heaven'

At a very early age, not more than 4 or 5 years old, "Bernie" Loewenthal became intrigued, as did Aristotle, with "meteorologia" — Greek for "thing in the heaven above." Thunderstorms fascinated him.

He recalls — also at around 4 or 5 years old — hearing that clouds were made from evaporating and condensing water. Thus informed, on a very warm day he poured a glass of water onto the hot pavement in front of his home. The water did indeed evaporate, as he had been told. Much to his dismay, no cloud was formed.

Undaunted, young Loewenthal continued his interest in weather, and for a time it was a toss-up between meteorology or dentistry. Finally, he decided; "Why not both?"

Thus, today, in addition to his four-and-a-half days and a few evenings practicing or teaching periodontology, the doctor spends another four or five evenings — and Sunday and holidays, and early mornings, and late nights — as a full-fledged weatherman, certified as a professional by the American Meteorological Society.

A visit at the Stratham Heights home of Ilana and Bernie, as he prefers to be called by his friends, is an experience in itself. The dwelling is designed specifically to maximize their ability to keep a sharp eye on the weather, and the Loewenthals spent more than a year looking for exactly the best place to build.

They finally found the ideal spot, at the peak of Brumley Hill, featuring unobstructed views clear to the horizon to the south and the west. Windows and skylights are strategically placed to allow a maximum of the outdoors to come in, while blocking wind, rain, snow and cold. Loewenthal can recline in his big easy chair and by simply turning his head a bit, can observe the weather in virtually every direction, including through the roof.

In the home's interior, in what would normally be a den, is the "weather room," featuring sophisticated, state-of-the-art wall-to-wall meteorological equipment on par with any television newsroom in New England.

Direct telephone links to the National Weather Service, Weather Services International and other sources provide constant data to either a sophisticated facsimile machine, a computer screen, or both.

Maps are produced, illustrating present, past, or future weather conditions.

A large "dish" in Loewenthal's back yard tracks and gathers information from a weather satellite high over the earth. A push of a button, and a photograph of cloud formations over New England is produced.

On one wall, a large digital readout panel reveals minute-by-minute changes in the weather over Stratham. A keyboard-code produces on one computer screen present weather conditions from any city in the United States; dew point, humidity, temperature, sky conditions, the height and type of clouds, wind speeds and directions aloft and at ground level, visibility, and more.

What is the weather going to be like in Albany, N.Y., tomorrow? The information appears in seconds, followed, also in seconds, by data from Fairbanks, Alaska, and Tallahassee, Fla.

Practical use

If all of this seems to be fun and games — which it is — there is also a more immediate and practical use to all of this gadgetry. Loewenthal admits that in very stormy weather he often stays up all night. "It's too exciting to sleep," he declares. Ilana agrees, explaining that this is

See SEASONS, Page 21

especially true when violent thunder storms rage over the Seacoast area. Because of the openess of the skylights and the sliding glass windows, every room in the house becomes filled with the brilliant, radiant flash and flare that only lightning bolts can produce.

It is on the practical side, however, that Loewenthal's weather-predicting ability comes into play.

While practicing dentistry in Haverhill, Loewenthal was also retained as the town's weather forecaster. By advising the Public Works Department when not to haul out its snow removal equipment, thousands of dollars were saved.

As a consulting meteorologist for large business firms, Loewenthal can advise executives when to travel, and when to cancel. Is the weather next weekend favorable to play golf with a valued client? Or how about a planned company cookout? With snow clouds gathering, should the employees continue to work to closing time or should they be sent home early? Will our yacht find clear sailing from Portsmouth to Bermuda? Is it safe for our company president to fly out of Logan next morning, or will he be wasting valuable time socked in and waiting for the weather to clear? The weather is fine here, but what about the city I am headed for?

For top business firms and executives, such information produced by Loewenthal can be very valuable indeed.

That is why he is up and about every morning at 6 o'clock, checking data which has come in during the night on "auto-pilot" and then supplementing it with the very latest information from nearly everywhere. By 7:30 a.m. his weather forecast is ready, either to be telephoned, telefaxed, or transmitted by computer communications.

His last chore before leaving the house: printing out the weather forecast with a large marker on bulletin-size paper for posting on the wall of his Portsmouth waiting room.

"It's a great ice-breaker," Loewenthal says. "And when patients start talking about the weather, they forget to be nervous."

N.E. Weather Not Changing In Opinion Of Expert

By DR. BERNARD LOEWENTHAL
. . . city's weather forecaster

DR. BERNARD LOEWENTHAL

Is New England weather changing? I have been asked this question by some people who think it is and that winters are warmer.

From where I stand, the answer to this question is a resounding no. But personal opinion does not hold much water as a recent survey has shown. The responses to this question, "Is New England weather changing?" were a definite yes. But half of the people thought that the weather was changing one way while the other half thought it was changing the opposite way. It is apparent that we need some cold, hard facts.

Since climate is the composite of numerous weather events, what should be a simple answer to this question becomes a complex one. This is because we measure weather occurences in many different ways, such as precipitation, temperature, humidity, wind, pressure, cloudiness, sunshine, and now air pollution. In turn, each of these categories is further broken down into many subdivisions. For example, precipitation is measured as rain, freezing rain, drizzle, freezing drizzle, snow, sleet, hail, and on and on. The end result is a tremendous accumulation of statistical information dating back over 100 years which can become very confusing. We all also know what can be done with statistics. So, rather than cite along list of numbers and records, my point can be made with two good examples.

How often have you heard, "Winters sure aren't cold and snowy like they used to be when we were kids"? Well, let's lay that one to rest right now. Here goes. Three of our five greatest snow storms in the last century have occurred in the last 15 years with the granddaddy in February 1969 (about 30 inches). The decade of the 1960's was one of the snowiest on record. A recent study on snowfall amounts published in a meteorological journal showed conclusively that there is no trend in yearly snowfall amounts nor is there evidence of snowfall cycles. So much for winter.

Dearth Of Hurricanes

Some people also are under the impression that our summer weather is changing. Fewer hurricanes and severe local storms is the basis for their viewpoint. Admittedly, there has been a dearth of hurricanes in recent years here in New England, but as in the past, this too will change — just wait. In terms of severe local storms, one need only look back a year or so to the devastating tornadoes that occurred in Stockbridge, and as nearby as Chelmsford. The fact is that during last year, the record was set for the highest number of tornadoes here in the United States.

It is not realistic to separate New England's weather from that of the rest of the world, though we tend to do so. There is little or no evidence that global weather is changing and New England is certainly no exception. Climatic changes even of small magnitude take many centuries and it is folly to think that two winters with below normal snowfall constitute a trend or climatic change.

Mother Nature has a way of balancing things. Very often while we are in a winter warm spell, other parts of the country are in the deep freeze with snow. The reverse is also true. Our "normals" for the elements of weather are merely averages of all that has been recorded in the past, including the extremes. It is not usual to have a "normal" day. Though we had record heat recently, I am now looking out at temperatures below 20 degrees and the threat of snow.

To be sure, our weather is changeable. Changing, I don't think so.

HAVERHILL, MASS., WEDNESDAY, JANUARY 9, 1974 15 CENTS

Area Gets First Major Snowstorm

The winter's first major snowstorm, which started at daybreak, will have deposited four-to-eight inches of snow before ending this evening, according to early estimates.

The storm began shortly before 7 this morning with temperatures hovering around 10 degrees.

Dr. Bernard Loewenthal, city weather forecaster, said he issued a heavy snow warning to city and school officials at 5 this morning, after reports a deepening storm over Ohio was bringing snow into New ngland well in advance of the storm's center.

Loewenthal said the possibility was also good for a coastal storm (secondary) development, which would bring warmer temperatures to the region, possibly turning snow to rain in coastal sections.

School sessions were not canceled.

Motorists Warned

Motorists were warned to drive with extra caution as snow accumulated rapidly, covering highways within two hours after its initial start.

City highway crews were pressed into operation by mid-morning to sand and salt roads, and plows were readied for the expected depth of four to eight inches.

Skiing and snowmobile enthusiasts were happy to see snow finally arrive.

Northern ski areas will benefit from the storm, with up to 10 inches forecast for Vermont.

Three-to-five inches was forecast for northern sections of New England and New Hampshire and Maine.

Loewenthal said the storm, which was moving at a rapid rate should end by early tonight, but warned of increased storm activity through the week with cloudiness again coming into the area late Thursday.

New Snowstorm Grips Area

PARKING METERS in Washington Square were nearly covered as snow began falling at 5 a.m. (Whiting Photo)

6-To-10 Inches Being Forecast

A snowstorm that began at 5 this morning is expected to leave six-to-10 inches, according to Dr. Bernard Loewenthal, who forecasts weather for the city.

Earl F. Smith, Haverhill weather observer, reported three inches had already fallen by 7:30 this morning.

Dr. Loewenthal said we could expect six-to-10 inches of "heavy, wet stuff that has a small chance of turning to rain."

Dr. Loewenthal predicted the storm will abate during the day but resume and finally end during the middle of the night.

This would give the city more than two feet of snow in the eight-day period beginning last Saturday when 17.1 inches fell. Another three inches fell during Wednesday night.

Roads became slippery early this morning but police reported no accidents.

The National Weather Service predicted four-to-six inches, possibly changing to rain then back to snow, in coastal areas. Temperatures today and tomorrow are expected to be in the 30s according to the weather service.

City officials have issued repeated warnings to motorists to gets their cars off streets or they will be towed. More than 240 autos have been towed since the Saturday storm because they blocked snow removal operations.

Late Winter Snowstorm Belts Area

It was back to snow shovels, abandoned cars and closed schools and stores today as Greater Haverhill began clearing operations of a late winter snowstorm.

A total of 10.5 inches fell by 9:30 this morning, according to Earl F. Smith, weather observer, with several more inches accumulating before the storm tapered off late in the morning.

The storm proved less damaging than previous ones with few skidding accidents reported and hardly any disruption of power service. All area schools were closed.

But snow plows again had to contend with hundreds of parked cars on streets.

Public Works Supt. Donald G. Ethier said hired plows were called out at 1:30 a.m. and city trucks were on the roads at 7 a.m., their usual starting time. Sanding trucks were out by 8 last night, however, and streets were in fairly good shape until midnight when the storm intensified and accumulations mounted.

Interstate 495 was not cleared until early morning hours and traffic along the highway was at a crawl by 9 last night.

The storm began shortly after noon in the area and was forecast as dumping up to four inches of snow.

Major Factor

Dr. Bernard Loewenthal, city forecaster, said, however, that the late winter storm would be "tricky" with the snow-rain dividing line being the major factor in the amount of accumulation.

He said the storm was coastal and slowed during the night, grew and intensified. He noted that Bedford reported rain this morning and that Logan International Airport had rain since 5 a.m.

But Haverhill was expected to get only wet snow, he said.

Police reported only two skidding accidents last night involving two and three cars, respectively. A two-car accident was reported at 6 p.m. at Kenoza Ave. and Lakewood Ter. and a three-car mishap at 7:30 p.m. at Chestnut St. and Ginty Blvd.

Police said they received more than 200 calls after 5:45 a.m. inquiring about school and work closings.

The department started towing operations this morning to clear streets for plows. A car on Nichols St. was towed last night but not because of the storm.

Massachusetts Electric Co. reported no power disruptions except a minor outage in Salisbury. There was no storm damage to equipment.

GETTING READY — Highway Department employes Jean A. Dodier, left, and Albert C. Hardy, put chains on truck in anticipation of a snow storm tomorrow. (Chase photo)

After Season's Coldest Morning

Heavy Snow Watch For Area Tomorrow

A heavy snow watch has been posted for the Haverhill area Wednesday, in the wake of the coldest temperatures of the season this morning.

Dr. Bernard Loewenthal, Haverhill weather forecaster, said the "watch" will be changed to a "warning" if east to northeast winds develop. The storm is expected to start at dawn. Temperatures are expected to be in the 20s tomorrow.

Haverhill's temperature this morning plunged to two above zero, coldest here in more than a year.

Earl F. Smith, weather observer, said the reading was the lowest in Haverhill since Jan. 18, 1974, when it was eight below.

Dr. Loewenthal said tomorrow's storm will be influenced by cold air, transported into the area since last week on northwest winds.

The record temperature for this date, Feb. 4, is six below, set in 1971.

EARLY MORNING DRIVERS found their autos ice-covered today and some like these, took precautions to prevent further icing. (Burbank photo)

Early Morning Driving Perilous

Storm Ices Highways

A combined ice and sleet storm brought hazardous driving and walking conditions to Haverhill last night and today and caused cancellation of mail deliveries this morning.

The freezing rain started as snow about 10:30 last night and turned to freezing rain an hour later, according to Dr. Bernard Loewenthal, city weather forecaster.

It was the secmmajor ice storm here this winter, the other being Dec. 17.

Earl F. Smith, Haverhill weather observer, said today's storm as of 7:30 a.m. left a quarter-of-an-inch accumulation of ice and sleet.

The storm came on the heels of Haverhill's coldest temperature reading (—8) Friday morning since Feb. 2, 1971. Smith said it was four degrees away from a date (Jan. 18) record of —12 in 1957.

Some side streets had not been sanded at 9:30 a.m. and it was impossible for drivers to reach main roads. Ty side streets not sanded included some on which businesses are located and employes were ice-bound.

Road conditions began to improve later and sand and salt crews moved in with five automatic sanders and two shovel crews, according to Wallace Woodall, Department of Public Works employe.

Mail trucks from Waltham did not make predawn delivery of incoming mail because of slippery road conditions.

Assistant Postmaster Joseph O'Brien said it was the first cancellation of routine mail deliveries since the 1971-72 winter season.

Dr. Loewenthal said overnight temperatures were in the low to middle 20s, rising to the low 30s before clearing this morning.

The forecast is for clearing skies today with temperatures dipping to the low 20s, with cloudiness again on the increase tomorrow and snow or rain late Sunday, Dr. Loewenthal said.

He said a new storm formed off Cape Cod this morning which increased hazards until thawing temperatures set in.

Up To Foot Of Snow Due

The city alerted its snow-fighting crews today in the wake of forecasts of heavy snow tonight and tomorrow, perhaps one foot or more.

Mayor George K. Katsaros said equipment is on standby and ready to go.

Dr. Bernard Lowenthal, the city's weather forecaster, issued a heavy snow warning tonight and all day tomorrow, with only a "slight" chance the snow will change to rain.

Dr. Lowenthal predicted winds of 30-40 miles an hour tomorrow. He said the storm has a "potential of a foot or more of snow."

Early Spring Due Tomorrow

Haverhill will go from "the dead of winter to the middle of spring" tomorrow, according to Dr. Bernard Loewenthal, city forecaster.

Dr. Loewenthal is predicting a "beautiful spring day" to give area residents a chance to dig out from the snowstorm which left more than a foot of snow.

"It's the first day of spring, weather - wise," according to the doctor, even if we get snowstorms in April.

Snow Due Tonight

City weather forecaster, Dr. Bernard Loewenthal, today issued a travelers' warning for tonight, and estimated the city will get two to four inches of snow.

The prediction came in the wake of early-morning freezing rain which coated city streets and sidewalks with ice, making travel perilous.

There were no skidding accidents reported to police, but pedestrian travel was particularly hazardous until temperatures climbed to freezing.

Dr. Loewenthal said falling temperatures later would turn drizzle to snow, with winds increasing.

He made a preliminary estimate of two to four inches of snow tonight, and said tomorrow and tomorrow night will be much colder.

'Tricky' Storm Alert Given

Greater Haverhill was alerted today to a "tricky" late winter storm, which could mean more than four inches of snow.

Dr. Bernard Loewenthal, forecaster for the city, said a "light to moderate" northeaster is possible tonight and tomorrow, with a "tricky" dividing line between rain and snow the deciding factor.

If Haverhill is on the snow side of the line, he said, "we could get two to four inches, or a little more."

Dr. Loewenthal predicted snow showers this afternoon, snow tonight, possibly changing to sleet or rain, and snow or rain tomorrow, ending in the afternoon.

Temperatures will hover in the low 30s.

Snow And Sleet Warning Given

Travelers' warnings for late today and tonight have been issued by Dr. Bernard Loewenthal, city weather forecaster. caster.

Dr. Loewenthal said a mixture of snow and sleet is expected, changing to freezing rain and sleet after a few hours.

There will be a gradual change to all rain tonight, he said, with rain continuing tomorrow morning.

Wet Snow Due Tonight

Today's heavy rain was expected to turn to wet snow by tonight, according to Dr. Bernard Loewenthal, city forecaster.

Dr. Loewenthal said winds would gust to 25-35 miles per hour, with the possibility of "some slushy accumulation of snow" by tomorrow morning.

Snow And Rain Forecast

The Haverhill area can expect snow tomorrow, but it will likely turn to rain after a period of slippery road conditions.

Dr. Bernard Loewenthal, city forecaster, said snow will develop tomorrow, changing to sleet and freezing rain before turning to all rain late in the day or at night.

He said foggy weather is expected Sunday, with periods of rain.

3 To 5 Inch Fall Of Snow Forecast

Highway crews were called out by police at 1 p.m. as a "borderline" storm which began before noon intensified.

The call for sand indicated roads were slippery in many parts of the city. Fire department officials ordered that chains be put on trucks.

Forecasters were unsure whether this area would get snow or rain but police said Dr. Bernard Loewenthal, weather observer, predicted three to five inches of snow.

Up To Four Inches Of Snow Forecast

The Haverhill area was expected to get up to four more inches of snow today and tonight.

Dr. Bernard Loewenthal, city forecaster, revised an earlier forecast of rain and snow mixed, saying the storm is now expected to remain all snow.

Dr. Loewenthal's latest forecast calls for two to four inches of snow, with driving conditions expected to be tricky.

Another Northeaster Due Tonight

Dr. Bernard Loewenthal, who forecasts weather for the city, said "another soaking Northeaster" is expected tonight, with heavy rain, strong winds, a chance of thunder and perhaps some wet snow.

The new storm, Dr. Loewenthal said, should end by late Thursday.

And More Today

Area Got Eight-Inch Snowfall

The season's first major snowstorm swept through the area yesterday, dumping eight inches of dry, easy-to-move snow here.

Public Works Director Armand E. Provost Jr. called out all available public and private equipment. The storm was fought with sand, salt and plows.

More snow was expected today, but forecasters say it will change to sleet and freezing rain, then probably all rain tomorrow.

The storm made driving conditions hazardous, with most streets slippery and visibility limited.

School sessions in many areas were shortened, and night meetings, for the most part, were postponed. Some business firms and factories sent employes home early.

Despite conditions, only four two-car skidding accidents were reported in the city by police, and there were no injuries. Police said 130 vehicles were tagged for violating on-street parking ordinances.

On-street parking hampered plowing operations in some areas, according to Highway Supt. Donald G. Ethier. He said, however, that the new system allowing residents to call special snow-removal numbers made it possible to handle complaints easier and quicker.

One problem developed when gasoline tanks at the Primrose St. garage went dry, but Ethier said gasoline was borrowed from the park department's Kenoza Ave. tanks. Gasoline was delivered to Primrose St. this morning.

Ethier said a decision would be make later on whether to pick up snow in downtown areas tonight, depending on weather conditions. Church areas were cleaned out today.

About 40 pieces of equipment were used to fight the storm.

Earl F. Smith, Haverhill weather observer, said the eight-inch storm was the heaviest here since Jan. 29, 1973, when the city got 8½ inches.

3-To-6 Inches More Possible

The city might get another three to six inches of snow from a storm which moved into the area early today, according to r. Bernard Loewenthal, city weather forecaster.

In an advisory issued this morning, Dr. Loewenthal said snow will continue through the day with temperatures between 15 and 20 degrees. Snow will probably change to freezing rainlate today and will continue into Friday.

This could cause "very hazardous" driving conditions on all surfaces, he warned.

Temperatures tonight will be in the 20's, possibly rising to near 32 degrees by Friday.

Heavy Weekend Snow Forecast

Heavy snow warnings have been posted for the Haverhill area for tonight and Sunday.

Dr. Bernard Loewenthal, Haverhill weather forecaster, said the potential for a heavy snowstorm will come on the heels of a storm which is expected to dump two to four inches today and early tonight, with temperatures dipping to the 20s tonight. An even heavier fall could occur tonight and Sunday.

Two-Day Snowfall Forecast For Area

The Haverhill area can expect a couple of days of occasional snow, according to Dr. Bernard Loewenthal, city forecaster.

He said today's precipitation will produce "an inch or two of dry, light, fluffy snow," with light snow or freezing drizzle tonight.

Dr. Loewenthal said tomorrow will be continued cloudy, with a chance of snow, possible mixed with freezing rain.

Storm Warning Given

The Haverhill area can expect some tricky driving conditions tonight, according to Dr. Bernard Loewenthal, city forecaster.

Dr. Loewenthal issued a hazardous driving warning for late today and tonight, with precipitation starting as light snow in the afternoon.

He said the snow is expected to turn to sleet and freezing rain tonight, causing icy driving conditions after a possible accumulation of one to three inches of snow.

By tomorrow, the precipitation will be all rain, Dr. Loewenthal predicted.

Temperatures rose slowly today after a low of 15 degrees this morning, second coldest of the season.

Winter Arrives On Stormy Note

A winter weather warning was issued today, the first day of winter, by Dr. Bernard Loewenthal, city weather forecaster.

Dr. Loewenthal said a complex weather pattern has enveloped the area, and it may well last into the weekend.

He predicted occasional light snow today and tonight, with a chance of heavier snow, sleet or freezing rain developing during the night and continuing Friday. The storm could change to all rain tomorrow, Dr. Loewenthal said.

Meanwhile, motorists were urged to use caution and to park off-street.

Light Snowfall Forecast For Area

A light snowfall was forecast for the Haverhill area through this evening, while six to eight inches were generally forecast for southern New England.

Dr. Bernard Loewenthal, city forecaster, said "a slight change of the storm's projected course could put us in a heavy snow belt."

He said the path of the storm posed a "tricky situation."

The National Weather Service (NWS) expected many northern New England ski areas would miss the storm entirely.

Tuesday's storm produced an inch of snow, according to Earl F. Smith, Haverhill weather observer, bringing Haverhill's snowfall for the month to 12½ inches.

With 4-To-6 Inch Snowfall

Northeaster Is Forecast

The area's first northeaster in two years could be on its way, with four to six inches of snow likely beginning late tonight, according to Dr. Bernard Loewenthal, Haverhill weather forecaster.

There is the possibility of more than four to six inches, Dr. Loewenthal said, if a second coastal storm forms off New England.

He said there is a slight chance of freezing rain and sleet tomorrow afternoon, before the storm ends. He explained the snow area would depend a great deal on the path of the storm.

He said the storm's path also holds the possibility for coastal flooding in low land areas tomorrow, the second day this year for astronomical high tides caused by alignment of the earth positioned between the sun and moon.

Temperatures of 15 to 20 degrees today are expected to rise slowly tomorrow but still remain below freezing on 15-to-20-mile-an-hour east to northeast winds, Dr. Loewenthal said.

Temperatures this morning were in the single numbers. A reading of nine degrees was reported by Earl F. Smith, Haverhill weather observer.

Another Northeast Storm Forecast

Forecasts of another northeast storm for Greater Haverhill have prompted city officials to warn that cars will be towed away if they interfere with snow-removal work as they did last weekend.

Dr. Bernard Loewenthal, who forecasts weather for city departments, gave a "preliminary heavy snow warning" for tomorrow.

He said most signs indicate the storm will be "important." Dr. Loewenthal predicted snow tomorrow, becoming heavy, but did not at this time forecast any specific amount.

Mayor George K. Katsaros and Public Works Commissioner Thomas A. Sotera this morning warned illegal parkers.

More than 240 were towed after the last storm, and even more would have been affected if tow trucks were available.

Katsaros promised "wholesale towing" if cars are not off the streets for snow-fighting work.

Heavy Snowstorm Forecast For Area

Dr. Bernard Loewenthal, Haverhill dentist, who provides weather observations for the city, today predicted a heavy snowstorm.

His forecast calls for eight to 12 inches or more of snow, beginning at midday and continuing into Thursday.

Winds from the northeast are expected to range between 30 and 50 miles an hour with temperatures ranging between 28 and 32 degrees.

Other forecasters, including UPI, call for six to 12 inches of snow, with a possibility that precipitation along the coast will be mostly rain.

Public Works Commissioner Thomas A. Sotera alerted all available city and private crews, but added he expected to be short-handed.

Sotera warned he will use his snow emergency powers, and will order vehicles towed away if they interfere with snow-removal operations.

Fishing

I find fishing a marvelous way to forget about life's problems and be in the moment. I am able to focus on the ***challenge*** of catching fish and nothing else. Over time I decided to practice "catch and release", so I no longer, except on a rare occasion, keep any fish. Flyfishing has become my passion because I find it more fun and ***challenging*** than other types of fishing.

The Challenge of Catching Bonefish with a Fly Rod!

A Handsome Redfish

Labrador has the world's largest Brook Trout!

Catching one of these makes me smile!

Labrador Trout are Sweet Enough to Kiss!

Ilana and a Large Mouth Bass

Ilana's Maine Brook Trout, regular size by the way.

Bernie with a nice size Florida Redfish

Bernie and Ilana with a Jack Crevalle

Bernie and and another Jack Crevalle

Grandson Mark and his Florida Gag Grouper

Bernie and a Smallish Snook

Say Hello to My Redfish Friend!

Bernie and a Florida Redfish

A Florida baby Tarpon with friend & guide Roan z

Atlantic Salmon

Striped Bass

Another Striper!

A Codfish

Ilana and Bluefish on Cape Cod

Two Big Mouths

Gardening Fun

I enjoy growing a wide variety of vegetables. Gardening is somewhat of a ***challenging*** hobby, and perhaps that is one reason I like it. I also get a feeling of self-reliance, knowing that I can grow food. I grew giant pumpkins because it was a ***challenge***, and fun.

A Fine Harvest

Hey Bernie, How does your garden grow?

My Big Cabbage!

Eggplants

My Passion is Tomatoes

Bernie picking Sour Cherries

My Garden

Zucchini Plants
on black plastic for weed and moisture control

Purple Cauliflower

Chinese Chestnuts

A laboratory test conducted in March 2011 measured a specimen of Scorpions at 1,463,700 Scoville heat units, officially ranking it the hottest pepper in the world at that time. The Scorpions are so hot that, in order to harvest the peppers, cultivators have to wear chemical masks and body suits. They have also reported feelings of numbness in their hands for more than two days afterwards.

Young Butch T Scorpion -Plants World's Hottest Pepper - Started from Seeds

Hot pepper harvest!

How to Grow a Giant Pumpkin

Step 1

Step 2

05 18 2002
Step 3

940 MOMBERT
FROZEN YOGURT
NONFAT
ORGANIC
05 19 2002
Step 4

Step 5

Step 6

Step 7

Step 8

Step 9

Results of Fertilization!

Shading the Pumpkin to Prevent Sun Damage

Step 10

When fully grown this pumpkin was about 100lbs. shy of the world's record!

Having Fun Cooking!

A Collection of Some of My Favorite Easy Recipes

I enjoy cooking just because it's fun and of course I like eating my favorite foods. I don't consider myself a gourmet chef at all. I savor many of my favorite recipes, they are simple and easy to make. Here are some examples.

GARDEN BOUNTY INSPIRES

By Dorothy Patten

Bernie Loewenthal wears many hats...all creatively and with expertise.

His patients know him as Dr. Loewenthal, dentist with a specialty in periodontics and a Portsmouth, N.H. practice... in weather circles (which is everywhere) he is well-known as a professional meteorologist who has the knack and knowledge for accurately calling the forecasts...his neighbors know him as an avid gardener with bountiful harvests...his family and friends know him as an interesting and talented cook.

The past week has been a fascinating one for weather-watchers, particular Dr. Loewenthal, who has banks of weather machines which produce hourly reports and detailed maps. As it happened, during both of the twin storms which hit here Friday and Monday, I was at the Loewenthal weather laboratory in his Concord St. home, watching the complex facsimile machine produce its computerized weather maps which are changed hourly by the National Weather Circuit. His two teletypes give country-wide as well as "local loop" weather information from Logan Airport compiled from radar reports.

Weather-watching was not the purpose of the visit, but the excitement of seeing, graphically, how the monstrous storms were building and progressing was an added bonus.

Dr. Bernard Loewenthal prepares a Caesar's Salad with a "different" touch.

Farmer and cook

I'm going to talk about Dr. Loewenthal, the farmer and cook. He plants a 10,000 square foot garden adjacent to his home each summer, and says his interest in cookery followed quite naturally. He's not a gourmet cook, he says, but enjoys devising meals and adapting recipes using the bountiful produce from the garden.

The Loewenthals have installed special refrigerators and freezers in their basement to preserve the products of their garden for winter use. When tomatoes are ripe, Dr. Loewenthal and his wife, Ilana work for hours, preparing gallons of basic tomato sauce, which they freeze for later use in may recipes. While basil and onions are added, the sauce is "not quite complete" so it can be varied depending on the future recipe used.

"This tomato sauce has unlimited usefulness, and has literally hundred of different applications, depending on personal preference," said Dr. Loewenthal. "It is good on any pasta and is frequently combined with meat dishes, such as meat balls, meatloaf, sausage and chicken and seafoods. It can be partially cooked and frozen and then varied by adding different spices and hers, such as hot pepper."

He said summer is a great time to make tomato sauce, when the juicy, plump, fresh, home-grown tomatoes are abundant. "The better the quality of the tomato, the better of the sauce is apt to be," he said. "Italian plum tomatoes are probably the best ones to use. Fresh basil also complements tomatoes nicely."

(Dr. Loewenthal said the best way to peel tomatoes is to dip them in boiling water for 20-30 seconds, then plunge them into cold water. The skin will then slip off easily.)

Bernie's Tomato Sauce

- 12-18 tomatoes, or enough to make 8 cups of tomato puree
- 4 cups chopped onion
- 2-3 cloves of garlic, finely minced
- 6 tablespoons tomato paste
- 1/2 cup chopped fresh Italian parsley
- 4 tablespoons olive oil

4-6 sprigs of fresh basil, chopped, or 2 teaspoons dried basil
- 1/2 teaspoon dried thyme
- 1 cup red burgundy wine
- 1/2-2/4 pound inexpensive beef, defatted (shin bone is best)

DR. LOEWENTHAL'S HEARTY COOKERY

Salt and freshly ground pepper to taste

Use medium large heavy bottom saucepan. Cook the onion and garlic in the olive oil until the onion is wilted. The peeled tomatoes can be pureed in an electric blender. Seeds may be removed if desired by straining.

Pour the tomato puree and all remaining ingredients into the saucepan and bring to a boil. Simmer gently at least 1-2 hours. Adjust to taste. The sauce can be frozen at this point for later use, or it can continue to simmer with the addition of perhaps meatballs and sausage.

Water will have to be added to thin the mixture occasionally. Serve hot on your favorite pasta.

One of the Loewenthal favorites for a company dinner is Mixed Seafood Fra Diavolo, which combines the special spices of tomato sauce with white wine and delectable seafoods.

Mixed Seafood Fra Diavolo

• 2 live lobsters, about 11/2 pound each
• 12 Littleneck clams or 8 oz. can of clams
• 1/2 pound medium uncooked shrimp
• 1/2 pound sea scallops
• 6 tablespoons olive oil – salt and freshly ground pepper to taste
• 3 tablespoons finely chopped garlic
• 1/2 cup finely chopped shallots
• 1/2 cup dry white wine
• hot red pepper flakes to taste
• 1-2 bay leaves
• 1 teaspoon oregano (optional)
* 3 cups tomato sauce, previously made as described

Kill each lobster and break off the tail from the body. Cut the tail into thirds with the shell on, and cut the main body into four to six pieces. Crack the claws.

In a large skillet, heat the oil and add all the lobster, stirring frequently. Sprinkle with salt and pepper. When the lobster pieces have turned bright red all over, sprinkle on the garlic and shallots. Add the wine and cook until the wine has evaporated.

Now, add previously prepared tomato sauce, plus bay leaves and hot red pepper flakes to taste. Oregano is optional. Simmer the mixture about 15 minutes. Add the clams and scallops followed by the shrimp 10 minutes later. Cook until the clams open (about another 10 minutes). Serve piping hot on linguine.

Soups are a specialty of the Loewenthal house. Onion soup is a favorite of Dr. and Mrs. Loewenthal, and is frequently made using garden onions. Here is his version: it takes about four hours from start to the eating, and serves six to eight.

Onion Soup

• 3 pounds or 10 cups of thinly sliced onions
• 3 tablespoons butter
• 1 tablespoon olive oil
• 11/2 teaspoons salt
• 1/2 teaspoon sugar
• 3 tablespoons flour
• 2 quarts boiling beef bouillon
• 1/2 cup dry white vermouth
• 1/4 teaspoon ground fresh pepper
• 1-2 cups grated Gruyere or Swiss cheese
• French break, 6-8 slices cut 1 inch thick
• 2/3 cloves garlic

Cook the onions with the butter and oil slowly in a heavy covered saucepan for 20 minutes. Uncover, raise heat to moderate, and stir in slat and sugar. Cook for about 50-60 minutes or until onions are a deep yellow. Stir frequently, being careful not to burn. Sprinkle on flour, stirring vigorously for two minutes.

Remove from heat and add boiling bouillon, then vermouth, salt and pepper. Simmer partially covered for 2-3 hours skimming every half hour. Set aside until ready to heat and serve.

Bake slices of bread at 350 degrees for 20 minutes, or until dry and slightly toasted. Rub gently with garlic clove.

Place bread in soup bowl, cover with hot soup and sprinkle with cheese individually.

An alternate method is to put boiling soup into fireproof individual tureens, float the toast and cover with thinly sliced cheese and a dab of butter. Bake for 20 minutes and serve at once.

Making sauerkraut is an annual tradition for the Loewenthals, who use up the products of their cabbage patch for this delicious accompaniment to any meal.

Sauerkraut

• 10 to 30 pounds of cabbage, depending on quantity desired
• pure, granulated salt (not table salt)
• 2-3 heavy duty, clear, watertight plastic bags.

Remove outer leaves and undesirable portions from firm, mature heads of cabbage; wash and drain. Using a shredder, sharp knife or food processor, cut cabbage into shreds about the thickness of a dime.

In a large container thoroughly mix exactly three tablespoons of salt with every five pounds of shredded cabbage. Exact measurements are very important says Dr. Loewenthal. Let stand for five minutes and then pack firmly into plastic bucket. Tamp down until juice comes to the top. Repeat the shredding, salting and packing as many times as desired.

To cover the cabbage, put one plastic bag inside another and place on top of cabbage. Fill inner bag with enough water to weight down the cabbage so that it is covered with brine. Leave at 65-70 degrees (room temperature) for four to six weeks, tasting each week until the desired taste is reached. When done, the sauerkraut should be white to light yellow in color, crisp and tangy. (Now that's real sauerkraut!)

When done, it can be refrigerated, which stops the fermentation or it can be canned.

A very special soup is Vichyssoise (pronounced veeshee-swahze), and Bernie Loewenthal's recipe will serve six.

Vichyssoise

• 5 leeks, white parts sliced
• 1 medium onion, sliced
• 5-6 medium potatoes, peeled and sliced
• 1 quart chicken broth
• 1 tablespoon salt
• 1-11/2 cups heavy cream
• 1/2 teaspoon white pepper
• 3-4 tablespoons mince chives

Simmer the vegetables in the broth for about 50 minutes, or until very tender. Puree in an electric blender until very smooth. Stir in the cream slowly. Add salt and white pepper to taste, over-salting slightly. Chill soup well; serve in chilled cups garnished with minced chives.

Barbecue Secret Is In The Sauce

By DOROTHY PATTEN

As nearly everyone knows, men, if they put their minds to it, are usually more clever in the culinary arts department than their mates. One of those who puts his mind to it is multi-talented Dr. Bernard Loewenthal, 197 Concord St.

His attractive wife Ilana agrees his cooking is imaginative, spicy and colorful. When the Loewenthals plan a dinner party at home, it is a team effort and the making of the meal is half the fun.

Dr. Loewenthal long ago added cookery to his special interests (which include weather forecasting . . . he is the city's weather advisor.) He has polished up his skills some since the fried toast-and-egg days of his teens, and one of his favorites is a barbacue sauce he devised.

The secret to successful barbecuing he says, is to marinate the meat or chicken for several hours or overnight in the sauce prior to cooking.

"I think this is important," he added. "The flavors really go through completely. When basting with the sauce during the cooking, I use a spoon, not a brush."

His recipe given here is for one batch. This can be doubled or quadrupled, and frozen for future use.

Barbecue Sauce

¼ cup vegetable oil
¾ cup chopped onion

DR. BERNARD LOEWENTHAL enjoys cooking as a hobby and shares his recipe for Spanish Gazpacho.

In a salad bowl, toss shrimp and dressing with macaroni mixture, saving a few shrimp for garnish. With egg slicer, slice each egg nearly through and arrange around edge of salad with olives between. Top with reserved shrimp.

¾ cup ketchup
¾ cup water
⅓ cup lemon juice
3 tablespoons sugar
3 tablespoons Worcestershire sauce
2 tablespoons deli-style mustard
2 teaspoons salt
½ teaspoon pepper

Cook chopped onion in oil until soft; add remaining ingredients and simmer for about 15 minutes.

* * *

The Loewenthals this summer discovered the delight of serving (and eating) Gazpacho, that spicy, cold Spanish soup. Dr. Loewenthal experimented until he perfected the recipe for the tangy soup base, which is served from a large bowl in the center of the table.

Guests add their choice of condiments to "customize" their portions according to their own tastes.

The condiments, diced or chopped, are served in a large divided dish, and can include diced cucumbers, chopped onion, diced tomatoes and green peppers and croutons.

For the soup:

GAZPACHO

½ cup diced green pepper
½ cup chopped onion
1 clove garlic
½ cup diced cucumber
⅓ cup vinegar
3 tablespoon olive oil
⅛ teaspoon freshly ground pepper
1 can tomato soup
1 can water

Put ingredients into blender and blend well. Chill.

* * *

A good dish for a buffet dinner, summer or winter, is Dr. Loewenthal's shrimp and macaroni salad. No bland dish, this. Its high flavor is achieved with a blend of several ingredients, which have a chance to mingle when the salad is put together early in the day.

Shrimp and Macaroni Salad

Macaroni to equal four pounds of potatoes.
5 eggs
1 pound small shrimp
3 tablespoons Italian dressing
1 cup mayonnaise
¼ cup prepared mustard
2 tablespoons lemon juice
1 tablespoon instant minced onion
¼ teaspoon pepper
1 teaspoon salt
1 cup celery slices cut diagonally
pitted ripe olives
¼ cup mayonnaise
2 tablespoons chili sauce

Early in the day: cook macaroni. Hard boil the eggs, shell and refrigerate. Cook shrimp, cool, and toss with Italian dressing, chili sauce, and ¼ cup mayonnaise; refrigerate.

In a small bowl, combine one cup mayonnaise, mustard, lemon juice, onion, pepper, and salt. With a fork, toss with macaroni and celery. Refrigerate at least one hour.

Recipe for:

BERNIE'S BAR-B-QUE SAUCE

Ingredients

Single recipe	Quadruple recipe
1/4 cup canola oil	1 cup
3/4 cup chopped Onion	3 cups
3/4 cup ketchup	3 cups
3/4 cup water	1 1/4 cups
1/3 cup lemon juice	3/4 cup
3 tbsp. sugar	3/4 cup
3 tbsp. Worcestershire Sauce	1/4 cup
2 tbsp. deli mustard	8 tbsp.
2 tbsp. table salt	8 tbsp.

Method: Cook onion in oil until soft. Add remaining ingredients. Simmer ~30 minutes. Marinate chicken in sauce 1 hour, in fridge.

Grill chicken VERY slowly with medium, then low heat. Start with skin side down on grill, baste chicken frequently, & turn every 15 minutes for even cooking.

BBQ, Serve—and Enjoy!

Sauce freezes VERY well.

Recipe for:

BERNIE'S SPICY CHINESE STYLE CHICKEN

Ingredients

3 lb. chicken • 3-5 scallions, shredded • 1-2 cups steamed rice

For sauce

4 tbsp. honey • 4 tbsp. sesame seed paste • 1 tbsp. hot pepper oil
5 tbsp. Soy sauce • 6 cloves garlic, finely chopped

Method: Steam chicken for about 35 minutes or until done.
Cut up chicken into small pieces.

Mix all sauce ingredients together and pour over chicken on serving plate, and place shredded scallions around chicken. Have cooked rice in a separate bowl.

Serve—-& enjoy!

BERNIE'S IMPROVED CAESAR SALAD

Recipe for:

The author of this delicious dressing wishes it understood that the proportions of the ingredients can be proportionally re-proportioned according to the individual taste. In fact, it is one of the strengths of the concoction that some variation is possible without compromising the result. Accordingly, the directions are in a semi-narrative form so that the essence of the preparation can be captured rather than having just a measure and mix list. This is for four servings.

First, a wooden bowl. Well seasoned and cherished is best. Although if you don't have one yet it's a good time to get one, and save it for these salads.

Secondly, in your cherished bowl place the juice from 1-2 lemons. Take a couple fresh peeled cloves of garlic, grate them with a rasp grater, and place garlic in lemon juice, let stand for 10 minutes. The purpose of this is to make the garlic milder. Place a few anchovies, or a teaspoon of anchovy paste in the bowl, and grind them well into the lemon/garlic mixture.

Now add ten or so turns of your pepper mill and 1/4 cup or of extra light tasting olive oil, and 1/4 cup vegetable oil.

Then add 1/2 teaspoon dry mustard, 6-8 drops of Tabasco Sauce, 1 tablespoon+ Worcestershire Sauce, add about 1/4 cup of good red wine vinegar and stir in 1/2 cup grated parmesan cheese vigorously. Now stir in two tablespoons Egg Beaters, mix well.

Stir and let sit until ready. An hour or so is good to let the flavors marry into a blissful union.

When ready, just before serving, stir well again, and add the cold crisp lettuce (Romaine probably), some grated Parmesan cheese, croutons and anchovies if desired. Toss well, lightly and lovingly a bit more, and put on salad plates.

Sprinkle on a bit more Parmesan and -- Serve---and Enjoy!

Edited by Tony Goodwin

Recipe for: BERNIE'S YUMMY SHRIMP AND PASTA SALAD

Ingredients

1 lb. pasta—elbows or shells preferable · 8 eggs · 11/2 lbs. medium shrimp
11/2 cups mayonnaise · 1/4 cup Dijon mustard · 1/4 cup lemon juice
1 large onion coarsely chopped · 1/2 tsp. ground pepper
1/2 tbsp. table salt · 1-2 diced celery stalks
2 cans large black olives, each olive cut in half
1 bunch of scallions, chopped

Method: Cook pasta early in the day per directions. Hard boil the eggs, shell them, slice into thick pieces. Cook shrimp being careful not to overcook, when cooled, cut each in half lengthwise, & add to pasta. Add halved black olives, & chopped scallions to pasta

Marinade:
In a small bowl carefully combine mayo, mustard, lemon juice, pepper & salt. Mix into pasta very thoroughly.

Serve—and enjoy!

Recipe for:

BERNIE'S CLAM/FISH CHOWDER

Ingredients

Butter or salt pork • Finely sliced bacon • 2-4 envelopes freeze dried clam broth
2-4 cups water • 1-2 large potatoes, peeled, diced bite size • 1 bay leaf
1 1/2- 2 cups half & half • 1 cup whole milk
Salt to taste (use lots of salt when sautéing onions, as water, cream, etc. dilute the salt)
FISH—many choices, be creative—cod, haddock, scallops, shrimp, clams, anything you like
chopped parsley • ground thyme • pepper
Use 3 qt. heavy bottom saucepan

Method: Use butter or salt pork. (cook enough salt pork to yield 2 tbsp. fat, remove pork). Fry bacon and cut into small pieces. Sauté onions, add salt. Add clam broth (dry), then add water to dissolve the broth. After bringing almost to a boil, add potatoes. Cook until potatoes almost done, (fork test), then add bacon.

Add cream & milk, LOWER HEAT, DO NOT ALLOW SOUP TO BOIL!

Add all fish, cook slowly until fish is cooked adequately.

Add parsley, thyme, and pepper to taste.

Serve—and enjoy!

BERNIE'S MUSSELS

Recipe for:

Ingredients

3-4 dozen mussels • 4 oz. chopped onions • 2 oz. chopped garlic
14 oz. canned tomatoes with juice • fresh basil • 1/2 cup lemon juice

Lemon Butter Sauce

1/4 cup butter • 2 tbsp. minced onions • 1/3 cup lemon juice
2 tbsp. minced garlic • 2 tbsp. dry white wine • kosher salt
white pepper • 2 tbsp. cold butter

Method:

For mussels: 1. Coat hot skillet with melted butter,
2. Add onions, garlic, tomatoes, cook until mussels open.

For lemon butter sauce: 1. Melt butter over low heat, remove, let solids settle, then skim clear butter from top.
2. Sauté garlic in 2 tbsp. melted clarified butter 3. Stir in lemon juice & white wine, season with salt & pepper 4. Simmer 2-3 minutes to reduce liquid 5. Remove from heat & swirl in cold butter until smooth & butter melted. Pour sauce over opened mussels.

Serve---and enjoy!

Recipe for: **BERNIE'S ORIENTAL NOODLE SOUP**

Ingredients

3 oz. bean thread noodles or 8oz. angel hair pasta
32 oz. of chicken broth • 2 tbsp. veg. oil • 1/2 lb. shrimp
6 green onions (scallions) cut into 2" lengths & shredded, use all of green part
5 tbsp. peeled and shredded fresh ginger
6 large leaves Bok Choy, X cut into 1" pieces lengthwise
2 tbsp. soy sauce • 1 tbsp. sesame oil • 1 cup water chestnuts • fresh ground pepper

Method: If using cello noodles, place in bowl & cover with boiling water. When ready, place in soup. If using fresh noodles, or pasta, place in boiling soup, giving just enough time to cook.

Meanwhile, heat vegetable oil in wok over high heat. Add shrimp, scallions, ginger, & stir-fry these ingredients. Add Bok Choy and stir-fry.

To soup---add remaining scallions, ginger, soy sauce, sesame oil, water chestnuts, and pepper. Then add all of stir-fry ingredients to soup.

Adapted from a recipe by Buzzy Price.

Serve---and enjoy!

Recipe for:

BERNIE'S GRAVLAX RECIPE
A Scandinavian Delicacy

Ingredients

Two large salmon fillets · 1/2 cup kosher salt · 1/2 cup sugar · 1 tbsp. coarsely ground black pepper

Method: In a bowl, mix the salt, sugar and pepper together. Then rub this mixture liberally onto both salmon fillet's flesh sides.

Line the bottom of a deep glass casserole with lots and lots of dill. Place one salmon fillet skin side down on the dill. Sprinkle the fillet with a little more sugar/salt mixture, and cover fillet with lots and lots of dill. Place the second fillet on this dill covering skin side up, so that the meat on the fillets are facing each other. Cover the second fillet with dill and then place a board or another glass casserole with weight atop the whole thing. Put in fridge for three to five days, but turn the fillets over every day to distribute all the juices evenly.

Serve----and Enjoy! Gravlax freezes very well.

Step 1

Step 2

Step 3

Step 4

Step 5

Step 6

Recipe for:

BERNIE'S EGGPLANT PARMESAN

Ingredients

3-4 medium eggplants • 3-4 eggs • kosher salt • parsley • pepper
grated Parmesan cheese • 4 cups shredded, skim milk mozzarella cheese
2-3 cups white flour, mixed with pepper, garlic powder, and dry oregano
1-2 cups light olive oil for sautéing • 32 oz. your favorite Italian tomato or pizza sauce

Method: The treatment of the eggplant itself is crucial. Getting the water out of the eggplant is the first key step. Peel (optional) the eggplant and create 1/4 inch thick slices. Place the slices in a large colander and sprinkle kosher salt thoroughly on each slice. Let the slices stand for at least an hour, water will drain from the colander. Then DRY each slice THROUGHLY using paper towels and hand pressure.

Prepare the "egg mixture" for dipping the eggplant before sautéing. Add a little water, plus parsley, salt, and pepper to the eggs and beat them thoroughly.

The next step is dipping each slice in flour mixture, (much better than breadcrumbs), and then the egg mixture. Then gently sauté each eggplant slice using medium heat, in light olive oil, until soft, turning frequently, [Studies show that eggplant treated in the above manner retains far less oil than if not treated with salt and dried].

After sautéing, put the slices on paper towels to blot off any excess oil. Then, starting with sauce on the bottom, layer the eggplant slices in a baking dish, alternating each layer with your favorite Italian tomato or pizza sauce, grated mozzarella cheese, and a sprinkling of Parmesan cheese. Bake for about one hour at 350 degrees.

Serve----and enjoy!

Bernie & Ilana Loewenthal

I sincerely hope you enjoyed reading my story and found it interesting and entertaining.

All the best,

Bernard Loewenthal, Jr.

Bernard Loewenthal, Jr.
1020 Oriole Circle
Naples Florida, 34105
Email: cloudoc@comcast.net

September 10, 2013, my 75th Birthday

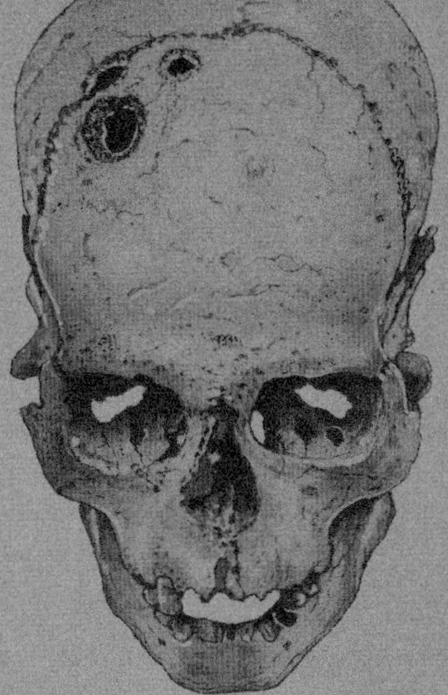

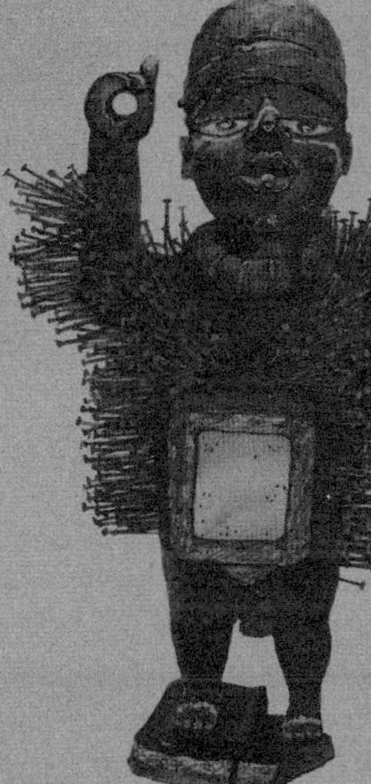
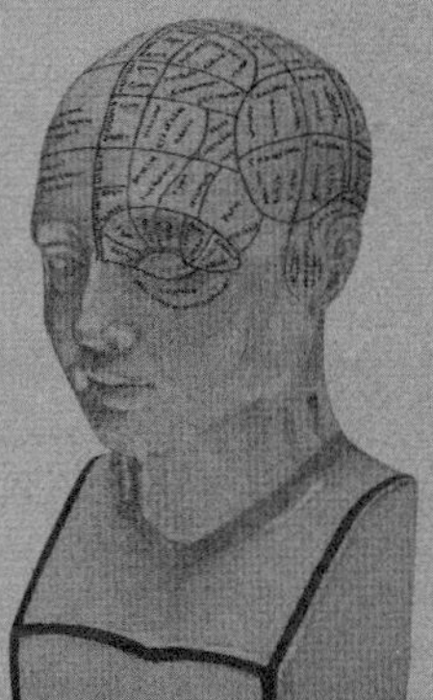

EXPLORONS L'HISTOIRE

L'HISTOIRE DE LA MÉDECINE

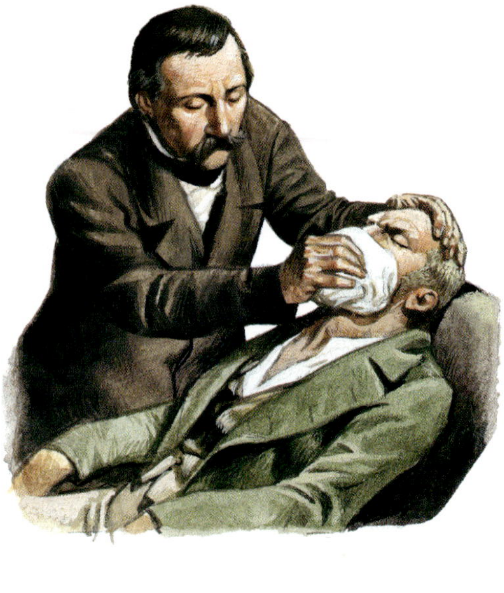

• EXPLORONS L'HISTOIRE •

L'HISTOIRE DE LA MÉDECINE

La médecine à travers les âges
et autour du monde

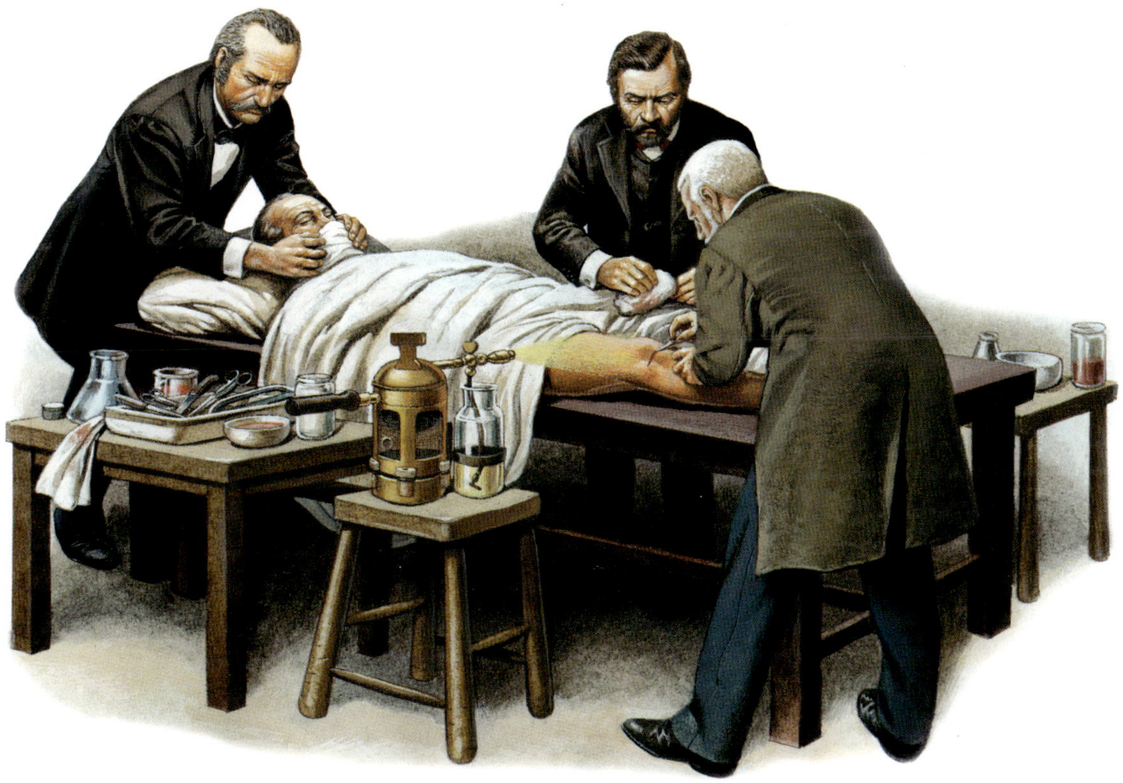

• BRIAN WARD •

GAMMA • ÉCOLE ACTIVE

London SE1 8HA
Titre original : *The Story of Medecine.*

Traduit par Dominique Guinet.
Dépôt légal : 1er trimestre 2001.
Bibliothèque nationale.
ISBN 2-7130-1913-3

Exclusivité au Canada :
Éditions École Active
2244, rue de Rouen, Montréal,
Qué. H2K 1L5.
Dépôts légaux : 1er trimestre 2001.
Bibliothèque nationale du Québec,
Bibliothèque nationale du Canada.
ISBN 2-89069-648-0

Loi n° 49-956 du 16 juillet 1949
sur les publications destinées à la
jeunesse.

Imprimé à Singapour.

L'éditeur remercie les artistes suivants
qui ont contribué à la réalisation de ce livre.
Vanessa Card; Terry Gabbey (AFA); Sally Holmes; Richard Hook (Linden Artists); John James (Temple Rogers); Shane Marsh (LindenArtists); Peter Sarson; Rob Sheffield; Guy Smith (Mainline Design); Mike White (Temple Rogers); Janos Marffy; Roger Gorringe (Illustration Ltd.); Ch'en Ling; Terry Riley Studio; Peter Gregory; Mike Saunders; Helen Parsley (JM & A Associates); Alison Winfield; Andy Beckett (Illustration Ltd.);
Clive Spong (Linden Artists).
Maps: Steve Sweet & Stuart Squires (SGA).

Crédits photographiques
Page 9 (hg) Mary Evans Picture Library; 10 (br) Mary Evans Picture Library; 11 (bc) Buddy Mays/ CORBIS; 22 (bc) Mary Evans Picture Library; 23 (hg) Mary Evans Picture Library; 24 (cd) Ann Ronan Picture Library; 25 (hd) Bettmann/ CORBIS; 27 (hd) The Bridgeman Art Library, (cg) Bettmann/ CORBIS; 30 (cd) Bettmann/ CORBIS; 31 (bg) CORBIS; 34 (bg) Mary Evans Picture Library; 36 (hg) Mary Evans Picture Library; 37 (bg) Hulton-Deutsch Collection/ CORBIS; 38 (c) Bettmann/ CORBIS; 40 (hg) CORBIS (bg) Hulton-Deutsch Collection/ CORBIS; 41 (hd) CORBIS; 42 (cd) Bettmann/ CORBIS; 43 (hd) Bettmann/ CORBIS; 45 (bg) CORBIS, (bc) Bettmann/ CORBIS; 46 (bc) Ann Ronan Picture Library; 47 (hg) Nathan Benn/ CORBIS; 48 (bg) Bettmann/ CORBIS; 49 (hd) Bettmann/ CORBIS; 51 (hd) Mary Evans Picture Library; 53 (cd) Lisa M McGeady/ CORBIS, (c) Lynda Richardson, (bg) photo courtesy of the British School of Shiatsu-Do (London); 55 (cd) AFP/ CORBIS; 57 (bg) Roger Ressmeyer/ CORBIS; 58 (hd) Ann Ronan Picture Library, (bg) CORBIS; 60 (c) Hank Morgan/ Science Photo Library.
Toutes les autres photographies proviennent de
Dover Publications et Miles Kelly Archives.

SOMMAIRE

Introduction
6

L'aube de la médecine
8

Les chamans
et le surnaturel
10

La médecine ayurvédique
12

La médecine chinoise
14

Hippocrate
et les Grecs
16

La médecine romaine
18

Le monde arabe
20

L'héritage de Galien
22

Les découvertes
de la Renaissance
24

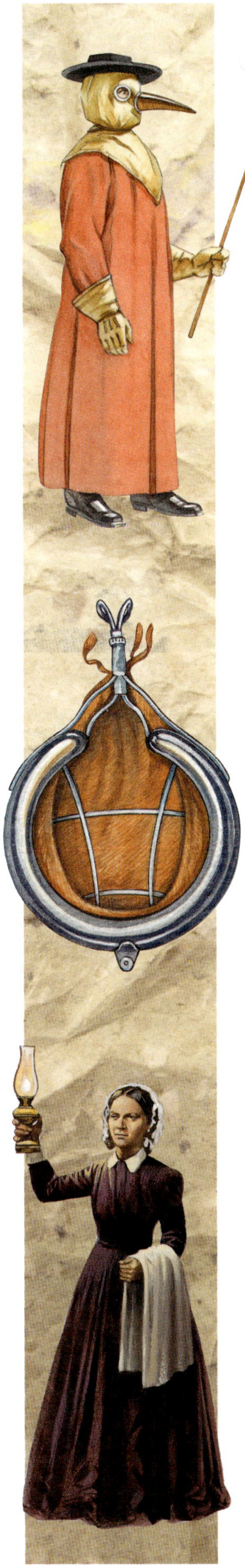

Peste et grands fléaux 26

Établir un diagnostic 28

L'aube de la chirurgie 30

Stérile et indolore 32

Les charlatans 34

La santé publique 36

Les micro-organismes 38

L'immunisation 40

Tueurs de microbes 42

Les pionnières de la médecine 44

Reconstruire le corps 46

Soigner l'esprit 48

Plantes et médicaments 50

Les médecines alternatives 52

Les médecines naturelles 54

Les technologies modernes 56

Les images du corps 58

Regard vers l'avenir 60

Glossaire 62

Index 64

Introduction

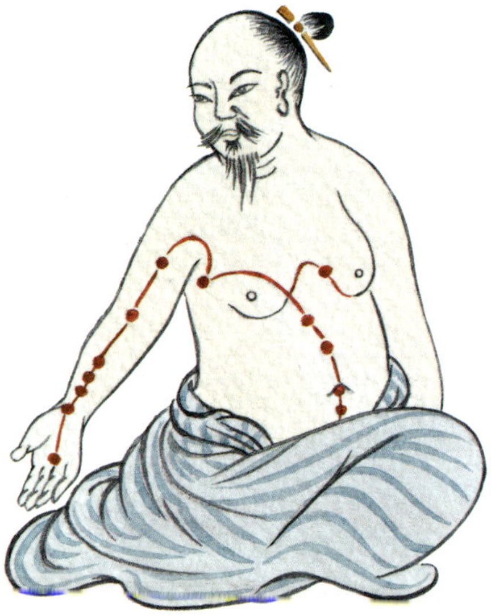

▲ LA MÉDECINE CHINOISE
La médecine chinoise s'est développée sur une base entièrement différente de celle de la médecine occidentale qui repose exclusivement sur la science. Elle traite le corps dans son ensemble en restaurant l'équilibre des forces qui y circulent. Cette médecine, ainsi que d'autres formes de médecine traditionnelle, suscite à l'heure actuelle un regain d'intérêt.

QU'EST-CE QUE LA MÉDECINE ? ET QU'EST-CE QUE LA SANTÉ ? LES RÉPONSES à ces questions peuvent varier selon les cultures et les époques. Dans la tradition médicale occidentale moderne, l'objectif principal est de combattre la maladie, puis de maintenir les gens en bonne santé. Dans ses débuts, la médecine occidentale reposait sur un mélange confus de prières, de remèdes populaires et de théories issues des civilisations antiques. Les véritables progrès de la médecine apparurent au XIXe siècle, c'est seulement à cette époque récente que la médecine parvint à réduire les taux élevés de mortalité liée aux infections. La médecine orientale partit du principe différent selon lequel le corps doit être traité dans son ensemble afin d'être maintenu en bonne santé et protégé de la maladie. Aujourd'hui, la médecine occidentale commence à considérer le corps comme un tout qui doit être maintenu en bonne santé.

Il y a maladie lorsque le corps ne fonctionne pas normalement. La notion de bonne santé est plus complexe à définir. Une personne âgée de 70 ans ou plus peut se sentir en parfaite santé alors qu'une personne plus jeune peut mal vivre les douleurs et les essoufflements souvent liés au vieillissement. Les symptômes de la vieillesse sont presque considérés

▼ AU FER ROUGE
Au fur et à mesure de l'évolution des connaissances et de la technologie, certaines pratiques médicales sont devenues obsolètes et ont été abandonnées au profit de méthodes plus efficaces. Pendant des siècles, le fer chauffé au rouge était utilisé pour refermer ou cautériser les vaisseaux sanguins et empêcher l'hémorragie après une opération.

▼ DATES CLÉS

L'ANTIQUITÉ

2700 av. J.-C. Le légendaire Shennong apporte aux hommes la connaissance des plantes médicinales.

2600 av. J.-C. Imhotep décrit la médecine de l'Égypte ancienne.

v. **2000** av. J.-C. Date légendaire de l'écriture du Neijing.

v. **1700** av. J.-C. Le code d'Hammourabi établit des lois pour les médecins.

Hammourabi roi de Babylone

1550 av. J.-C. Le papyrus d'Ebers consigne les pratiques médicales égyptiennes.

1200 av. J.-C. Asclépios établit des dispensaires en Grèce.

460 av. J.-C. Naissance d'Hippocrate, fondateur de la médecine grecque.

Hippocrate

v. **300** av. J.-C. Fondation de l'école de médecine à Alexandrie.

40 - v. **90** apr. J.-C. Dioscoride écrit un manuel sur la médecine par les plantes.

129 - **216** apr. J.-C. Galien développe les anciens écrits grecs et initie les études de médecine expérimentale.

LE MOYEN ÂGE

832 apr. J.-C. Les textes médicaux non islamiques sont traduits à Bagdad.

800 apr. J.-C. Rhazès prépare son compendium médical.

v. **1000** apr. J.-C. Avicenne écrit le *Canon de médecine*.

1100 - **1300** Des écoles de médecine sont fondées un peu partout en Europe.

1215 Le Pape décrète que tous les médecins doivent être agréés par l'Église.

v. **1200** - **1300** Mise en place d'organisations médicales professionnelles.

1258 Les textes médicaux conservés par les Arabes retournent à l'Ouest.

Paracelse

LA RENAISSANCE

1527 Paracelse établit les bases d'études des traitements chimiques des maladies.

1543 Vésale publie des illustrations précises de l'anatomie humaine.

1628 William Harvey publie sa théorie sur la circulation du sang.

1665 Le roi Charles II et la cour royale fuient Londres pendant la Grande Peste.

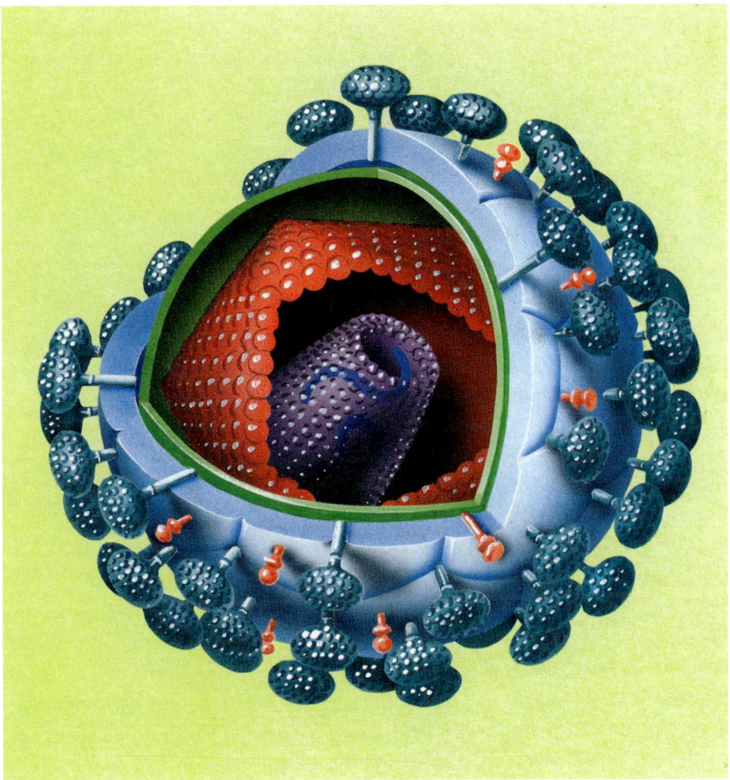

▲ LE VIRUS VIH
La compréhension de la structure des virus comme celui du sida, a montré comment ils s'attaquent au système immunitaire. Les recherches peuvent révéler leur point faible, afin de trouver des médicaments pour les détruire.

comme une maladie dans certaines sociétés occidentales, où les gens vivent plus longtemps. Aujourd'hui, grâce à la médecine moderne, il est possible de rester actif jusqu'à un âge fort avancé, alors qu'autrefois une maladie cardiaque ou de l'arthrite était un handicap. Cependant, dans certains pays en voie de développement, où la malnutrition et les infections sont courantes, une espérance de vie de 40 ans est, dans ce contexte, considérée comme bonne.

Les maladies mortelles, qui habituellement emportaient la moitié des enfants d'une famille, sont aujourd'hui contrôlées par les médicaments et les vaccinations dans les pays occidentaux. Pourtant, de nouvelles affections comme le SIDA sont apparues et ne sont pas encore sous contrôle. Certains, parmi les anciens microbes connus, ont trouvé le moyen de lutter contre les antibiotiques et menacent une fois de plus la santé. La seule réelle conquête sur la maladie a été l'éradication de la variole.

La médecine a fait des pas gigantesques dans d'autres domaines. Les médecins possèdent la technologie qui leur permet d'examiner presque chaque partie du corps. Les scientifiques commencent à comprendre les réactions chimiques complexes qui régissent le corps. La chirurgie, pratiquée depuis des siècles, a fait de grands pas dans les techniques de transplantation d'organes et d'organes artificiels.

LES TEMPS MODERNES

1673 Van Leeuwenhoek fabrique le premier microscope et découvre les microbes.

1714 Gabriel Fahrenheit invente le thermomètre au mercure.

1796 Edward Jenner vaccine contre la variole.

1819 René Laennec introduit le premier stéthoscope.

Le stéthoscope de Laennec

1847 Ignac Semmelweis démontre que des mains non lavées peuvent transmettre une infection.

1853 La reine Victoria utilise le chloroforme comme anesthésiant en accouchant.

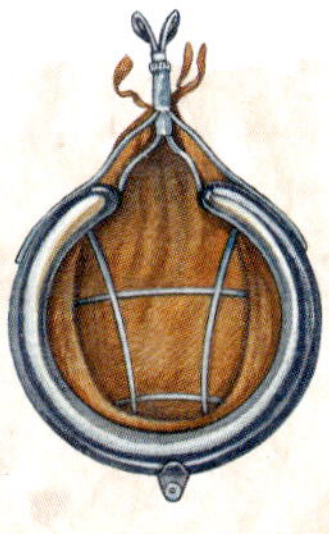

Masque de chloroforme

1854 John Snow démontre que le choléra s'attrape en buvant de l'eau contaminée.

1865 Joseph Lister pratique la première opération en utilisant un antiseptique, le phénol.

1878 Louis Pasteur présente sa théorie de l'infection bactérienne.

1882 Robert Koch découvre le bacille de la tuberculose.

1885 Louis Pasteur teste avec succès son vaccin contre la rage.

1895 Wilhelm Röntgen découvre les rayons X.

1898 Marie Curie découvre la radioactivité du radium.

Marie Curie

1901 - 1902 Les groupes sanguins sont décrits par Karl Landsteiner, ce qui permet la transfusion.

1902 L'ablation de l'appendice infecté devient une pratique courante grâce à Frederic Treves.

1928 Alexander Fleming découvre le premier antibiotique, la pénicilline, qui permet de lutter contre les maladies bactériennes.

1953 James Watson et Francis Crick découvrent la structure de l'ADN.

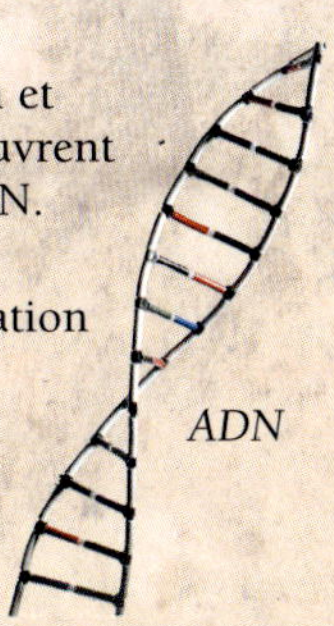

ADN

1954 La transplantation du rein est réalisée pour la première fois avec succès.

1955 Jonas Salk introduit le premier vaccin contre la polio.

1961 La thalidomide, un sédatif, est retirée du marché après avoir causé des malformations congénitales.

1964 Christiaan Barnard pratique la première transplantation du cœur.

1974 Le dernier cas naturel de variole est enregistré.

1983 Le virus VIH est identifié en France et aux États-Unis.

L'aube de la médecine

▲ LES OUTILS DE TRÉPANATION
Les hommes de l'âge de pierre se servaient d'un foret pour percer un trou dans le crâne. Il s'agissait d'un bâton muni à son extrémité d'un morceau de silex taillé. Un arc permettait de faire tourner le bâton.

LES PREMIERS RESTES HUMAINS témoignent de tentatives médicales, dont les plus spectaculaires restent les trépanations, c'est-à-dire le forage ou le découpage net de trous dans le crâne. De telles pratiques visaient sans doute à faire sortir une maladie du corps. Des crânes trépanés ont été découverts en Europe et en Amérique du Sud. Sur certains d'entre eux, le trou s'est refermé, ce qui prouve que le patient a survécu quelque temps à l'opération. D'autres encore portent les traces de plusieurs trépanations pratiquées à différentes occasions.

La médecine par les plantes a probablement aussi de tout temps été en usage. Les grands singes, comme les chimpanzés, la pratiquent parfois lorsqu'ils mâchent des plantes aux vertus médicinales qui ne font pas partie de leur régime habituel.

Bien que les hommes préhistoriques aient sans doute souffert de nombreuses maladies, ils n'ont probablement pas été touchés par des infections à propagation rapide qui, plus tard, ont provoqué les épidémies. Ils vivaient en petits groupes et n'étaient donc pas suffisamment nombreux pour permettre aux maladies de s'étendre rapidement.

Vers 3000 av. J.-C., les hommes ont commencé à vivre dans de grandes cités comme Babylone. C'est dans ce contexte qu'ont pu se développer les grandes épidémies. Vers 1700 av. J.-C., les médecins babyloniens ont dû se conformer à un certain nombre de lois, transcrites dans le Code d'Hammourabi. L'une des pratiques du code consistait à sacrifier des animaux et à examiner leurs organes, pour dire si le patient allait mourir ou non.

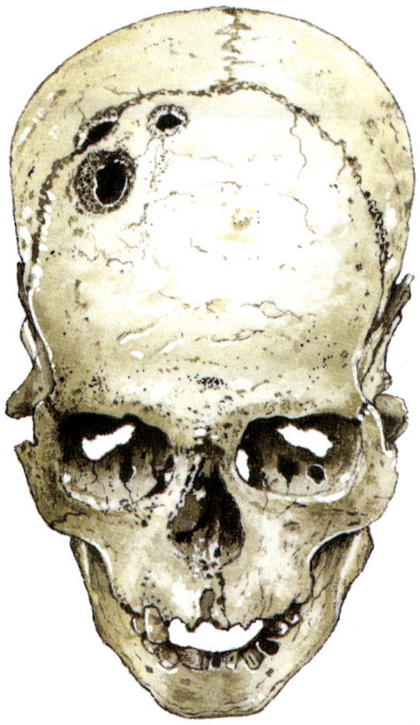

▶ DES TROUS DANS LA TÊTE
Ce crâne a été découvert à Jéricho et date de 2000 av. J.-C. Il possède trois trous de trépanation soigneusement exécutés, ainsi qu'un trou cicatrisé. Ils sont ronds, ce qui montre qu'ils ont dû être forés. Sur d'autres crânes, on a trouvé des orifices carrés, découpés au couteau.

LA MÉSOPOTAMIE ET L'ÉGYPTE

Le plus vieux texte de médecine existant est le papyrus d'Ebers qui provient d'Égypte. Il date d'environ 1550 av. J.-C. Ce rouleau de papyrus fait 20 m de long et décrit de nombreuses maladies et leurs remèdes. 700 médicaments et 800 préparations médicales y sont répertoriés, dont un traitement contre les morsures de crocodile. Le papyrus d'Ebers donne des instructions pour combiner ces médicaments afin d'en faire des onguents, des cataplasmes, des cachets et des inhalations. On y trouve également les descriptions d'amulettes les unes destinées à protéger, les autres à jeter des sorts.

▼ LE PREMIER MÉDECIN
Imhotep était un prêtre d'Égypte ancienne qui vécut il y a 4 500 ans. Il a laissé les descriptions détaillées de nombreuses maladies et traitements. Après sa mort, on l'a érigé en dieu.

◀ INSTRUMENTS DE CHIRURGIE
Ces couteaux de bronze et de cuivre proviennent de Mésopotamie. Ils ont dû servir à extraire les organes des corps défunts.

▶ LE CODE DE CONDUITE
Hammourabi, roi de Babylone, a édicté 17 lois destinées aux médecins dans son Code qui regroupait toutes les lois. On y trouvait des peines à infliger aux médecins dont les traitements étaient sans effet.

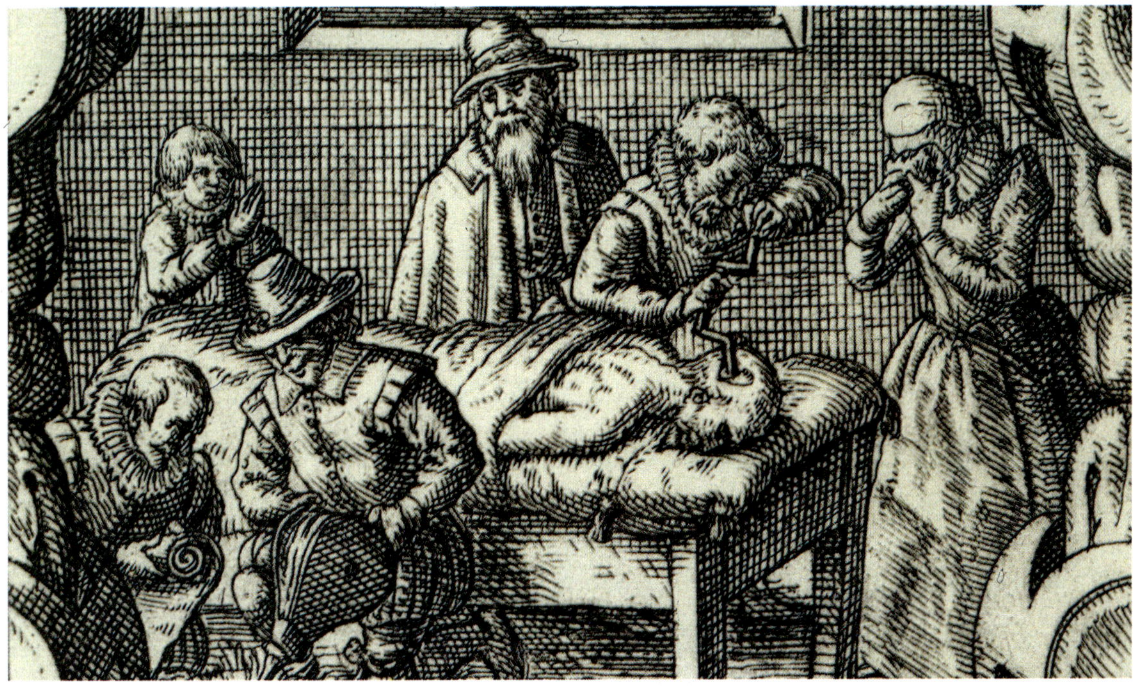

◀ ÉVOLUTION DE LA TRÉPANATION
Cette illustration du XVIe siècle représente un médecin trépanant un patient. Autrefois, cette pratique avait pour objectif de libérer le cerveau des esprits qui l'habitaient. La trépanation est une opération particulièrement dangereuse, car elle présente le risque de mettre les bactéries en contact avec le cerveau.

▼ LA MÉDECINE DES ANIMAUX
Les animaux, comme ce bébé gorille, recherchent des plantes médicinales pour se soigner. Même les carnivores, comme les chats, mâchent parfois des feuilles et des brins d'herbe.

Les Égyptiens anciens ont laissé des témoignages précis décrivant toute une panoplie de pratiques médicales et de médicaments. Le plus célèbre des médecins égyptiens est Imhotep, également grand prêtre, architecte et astrologue. Les médecins avaient recours à la chirurgie pour réduire les fractures et recoudre les plaies. Cependant, ils s'intéressaient peu à l'anatomie interne. Ceci est très étonnant, car leur intérêt pour la momification des corps après la mort leur a sans doute apporté des connaissances dans ce domaine. La médecine égyptienne reposait essentiellement sur les traitements par les plantes.

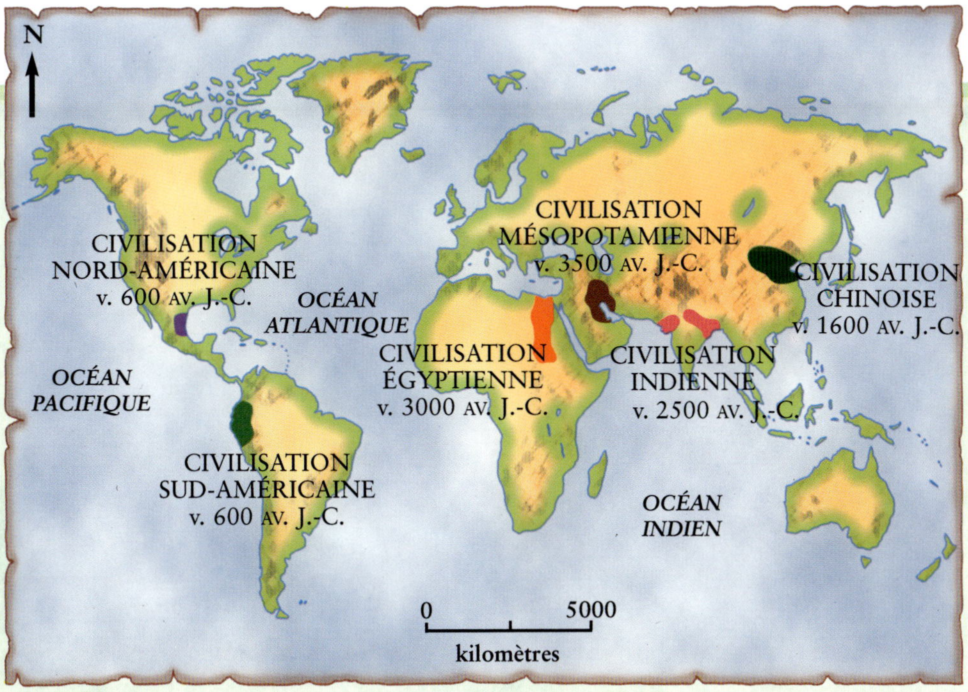

▲ LES DÉBUTS DE LA MÉDECINE
La médecine était pratiquée par les civilisations répertoriées ci-dessus, mais il est presque sûr qu'elle était connue dans toutes les civilisations anciennes.

Dates clés

- 10 000-2000 av. J.-C. Preuve des pratiques médicales en Égypte.
- 5000 av. J.-C. Le crâne trépané d'Ensisheim en France est la preuve de trépanation la plus ancienne.
- v. 2686-2613 av. J.-C. Vie du médecin égyptien Imhotep.
- 1792-1750 av. J.-C. Hammourabi règne à Babylone.
- 1550 av. J.-C. Écriture du papyrus d'Ebers en Égypte.
- 650 av. J.-C. Les tablettes d'argile de Mésopotamie décrivent des remèdes à base de plantes.

Les chamans et le surnaturel

À L'ÉPOQUE OÙ LES GENS SE regroupaient en petites communautés apparut le chaman, un individu capable de combiner la fonction de guérisseur et celle de communiquer avec les dieux et les esprits. Sur certaines peintures rupestres de France réalisées il y a environ 17 000 ans, on peut voir des hommes revêtus de masques d'animaux pratiquant des danses rituelles. Les chamans existent encore dans de nombreuses cultures à travers le monde. On les rencontre dans les régions arctiques, notamment en Sibérie, parmi les Indiens d'Amérique du Nord et du Sud, au sud-est de l'Asie et dans les îles du Pacifique. En Afrique occidentale, on parle d'« hommes médecine » ou de sorciers pour désigner les chamans. Leur rôle est, entre autre, de soigner avec des drogues accompagnées de prières, et parfois de jeter un mauvais sort à un ennemi. Selon la croyance populaire, les chamans auraient le pouvoir de provoquer des maladies, d'assurer la fertilité, et de

▲ POUPÉE ASHANTI
Les chamans soignent par la magie. Ils représentent souvent leurs patients par des poupées.

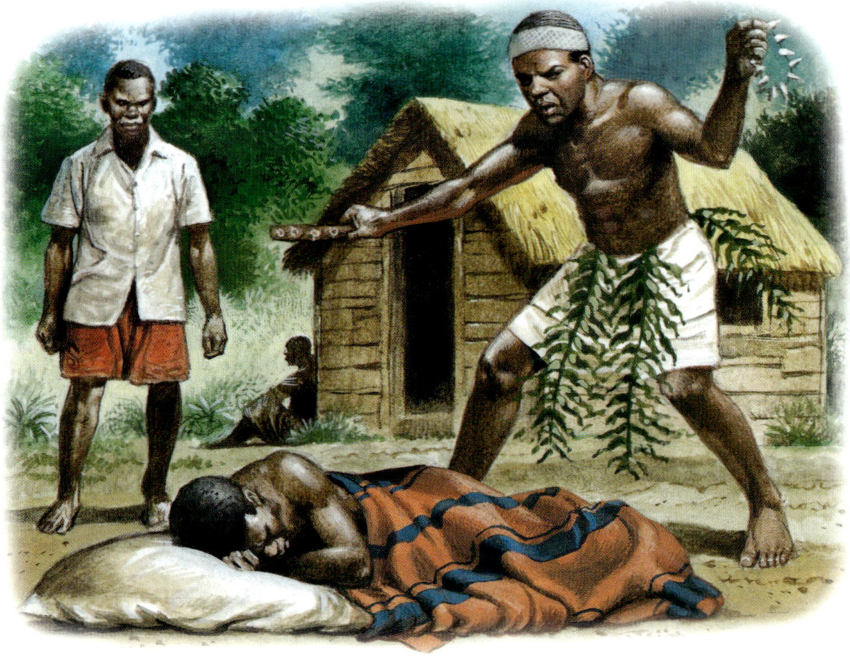

▶ RITUEL DE GUÉRISON CHAMAN
Lors du rituel de guérison, comme cette cérémonie au Cameroun en Afrique de l'Ouest, le chaman danse autour du patient et chante des prières aux esprits.

LA MÉDECINE AMÉRINDIENNE
Tous les Amérindiens avaient des chamans. Ceux du peuple des Ojibwa formaient des sociétés secrètes et se spécialisaient même dans des domaines médicaux particuliers, comme la médecine par les plantes. La maladie était souvent considérée comme une punition infligée à ceux qui s'étaient mal conduits. Pour soigner, les Navajo s'adressaient aux esprits par des chants, des danses, des prières ou par des peintures de sable. Les bull-roarers étaient des morceaux de bois plats attachés à un cordon qui produisaient un vrombissement lorsqu'ils tournoyaient à vive allure. On s'en servait pour invoquer le vent ou la pluie et chasser les mauvais esprits.

◀ COLLIER MAGIQUE
Cette amulette magique a été portée par un sorcier apache. Elle est faite de perles de verre et de dents humaines.

▶ LE SORCIER
300 peuples amérindiens différents se côtoyaient, chacun avec ses propres coutumes. Ce sorcier vient du peuple des Pieds-Noirs qui vivaient sur les plaines du nord-ouest des États-Unis.

protéger contre la maladie grâce à des onguents, des talismans et des fétiches. On attribue aux chamans le pouvoir de parler avec les dieux, les esprits et les morts. Ils sollicitent souvent des faveurs particulières auprès des esprits, comme une bonne récolte.

Le chaman joue en général le rôle de guide spirituel. Le chamanisme n'est pas organisé comme les grandes religions du monde. Il rassemble tout un éventail de croyances populaires et de mythes. Le chaman est capable d'entrer en transe. Il semble alors déconnecté du monde qui l'entoure. Il parvient à cet état second sous l'action de drogues, de danses et de musique.

Dans la plupart des cultures où existent les chamans, la maladie est attribuée à l'abandon du corps par l'âme. Par la transe, le chaman communique avec l'âme qui a probablement été volée par sorcellerie ou magie, et il la convainc de réintégrer le corps. C'est un long procédé, rendu souvent dangereux par l'utilisation de drogues.

On pense parfois qu'une maladie est liée à la présence d'un objet déposé par magie à l'intérieur d'un malade. Le chaman aspire alors fortement à l'endroit douloureux et recrache ensuite des morceaux de bois ou des cailloux, prétendus responsables de la maladie. Pour soigner, les chamans se servent d'instruments et de fétiches variés, de masques et d'autres parures rituelles.

◀ FÉTICHE BAHUNGANA
Un fétiche est un objet censé posséder des pouvoirs magiques. Celui-ci porte un sac de médecine comme en utilise le chaman.

▶ FÉTICHE YOMBE
Ce fétiche vient de la tribu yombe de la République du Congo. Il peut servir à soigner ou jeter un sort lorsqu'on enfonce des clous dans l'image lors d'un rituel magique. Les clous sont enfoncés dans la partie du corps qui doit être touchée.

▼ LE COHOSH NOIR
Les Amérindiens utilisaient les racines de cohosh noir comme analgésique. Cette plante a aujourd'hui été adoptée par les herboristes occidentaux.

▶ PEINTURE DE SABLE
Les Navajo se servaient de grains de sable colorés pour créer des images magiques appelées peintures de sable. Certaines d'entre elles étaient assez grandes pour permettre au malade de s'asseoir au milieu.

Dates clés

- 15 000 av. J.-C. Peintures rupestres représentant des danses rituelles.
- v. 3000 av. J.-C. Un cheval d'ambre montre comment les amulettes étaient utilisées pour chasser la maladie.
- 1492 apr. J.-C. Christophe Colomb « découvre » l'Amérique.
- 1520 Cabeza de Vaca observe des sorciers soignant les maladies en soufflant sur les patients.
- 1800 La tradition des sorciers disparaît quand les Européens exterminent les Amérindiens.

La médecine ayurvédique

LES *VÉDAS* SONT UNE SÉRIE de textes hindous écrits en Inde entre 1200 et 900 av. J.-C. Dans les parties des *Védas* relatives à la religion, il existe des explications concernant le fonctionnement du corps, et des descriptions détaillées de maladies. Les traitements recommandés dans les *Védas* comprenaient des remèdes à base de plantes, mais aussi des prières et des rituels magiques destinés à exorciser les démons. La médecine védique a été pratiquée jusqu'en 1000 av. J.-C. environ.

Après 1000 av. J.-C., l'Inde a connu l'émergence d'une nouvelle école de médecine, encore basée sur les *Védas*, mais influencée par d'autres principes comme ceux du bouddhisme. Il s'agit de la médecine ayurvédique (connaissance de la vie), dont les principes sont contenus dans deux livres de référence, la *Caraka-samhita* et la *Sushruta-samhita*, écrits par deux médecins, Caraka et Sushruta. D'après ces derniers, les désirs compromettent l'équilibre du corps, et ceux-ci doivent donc être satisfaits avec modération.

Les hindous croyaient que le corps était construit à partir de trois « humeurs », l'air, le flegme et la bile. Pour qu'une personne soit en bonne santé, ces humeurs devaient s'équilibrer. On évoque également la production de sept tissus corporels : la nourriture, le sang, la chair, la graisse, les os, la moelle et la semence. Un traitement ayurvédique se devait de rétablir l'équilibre des humeurs en combinant prières, médecine par les plantes, régime et parfois intervention chirurgicale.

Les médecins indiens faisaient de très bons diagnostics (identification d'une maladie). Pour soigner les malades,

▲ LE FEU ET LA FIÈVRE
Agni était le dieu du feu. En cas de fièvre, on l'invoquait par la prière.

▶ LA POSITION DU LOTUS
La méditation et l'exercice physique ont une grande importance dans la médecine indienne. La position du lotus est pratiquée dans le yoga pendant la méditation. Le yoga permet d'atteindre un état d'illumination spirituelle, et maintient l'équilibre entre les trois humeurs.

CHIRURGIE INDIENNE

Les chirurgiens hindous développèrent les premières formes de la chirurgie plastique. Ils étaient capables de refaire intégralement un nez. L'amputation du nez était en effet une punition courante. Ils pratiquaient des greffes de peau en prélevant des morceaux de peau sur d'autres parties du corps et en les fixant sur les zones endommagées. Ils plaçaient des tubes à l'intérieur des narines pour permettre au patient de respirer jusqu'à la cicatrisation des plaies. Les chirurgiens occidentaux furent très surpris par cette technique.

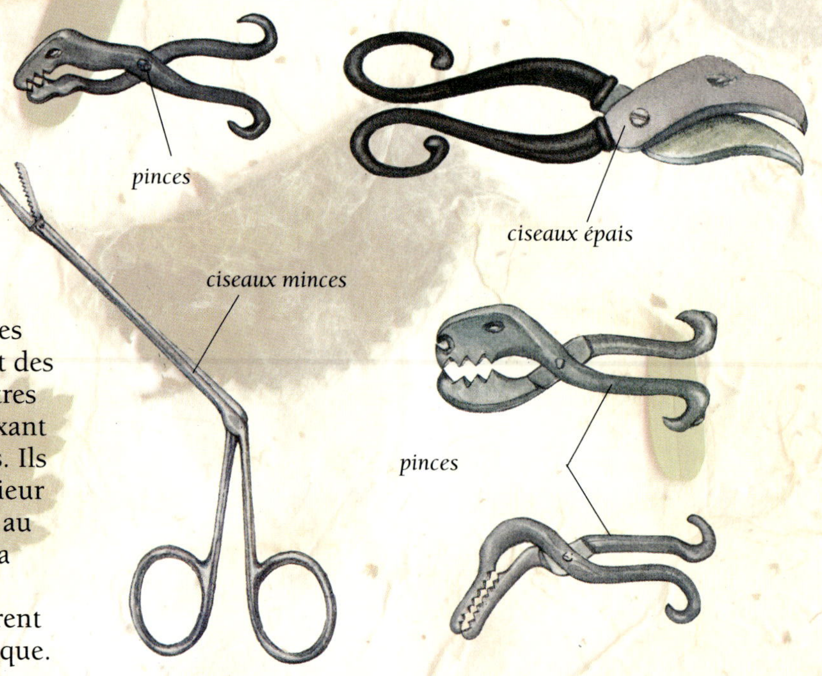

◀ INSTRUMENTS DE CHIRURGIE
Les médecins ayurvédiques mirent au point des techniques chirurgicales sophistiquées. Pour opérer, ils utilisaient des instruments d'acier, comme ceux-ci datant d'environ 1100 apr. J.-C. L'acier ne s'oxyde pas, ce qui rend ces instruments beaucoup plus hygiéniques.

ils pouvaient choisir parmi un large éventail de plantes médicinales, et aussi parmi des préparations à base de parties d'animaux ou de minéraux. L'hygiène revêtait une importance particulière aux yeux des chirurgiens ayurvédiques. Les médecins insistaient sur l'importance de se laver régulièrement le corps et les dents.

Les chirurgiens hindous étaient particulièrement avancés. Ils savaient opérer les tumeurs et les cataractes, réduire les fractures, recoudre les plaies, pratiquer des césariennes et des amputations. Ils étaient aussi capables d'enlever les calculs rénaux. Grâce à une bonne hygiène, les chirurgiens de l'Inde de 800 av. J.-C. avaient chez leurs patients un taux de survie supérieur à celui des Européens jusqu'au XIXe siècle.

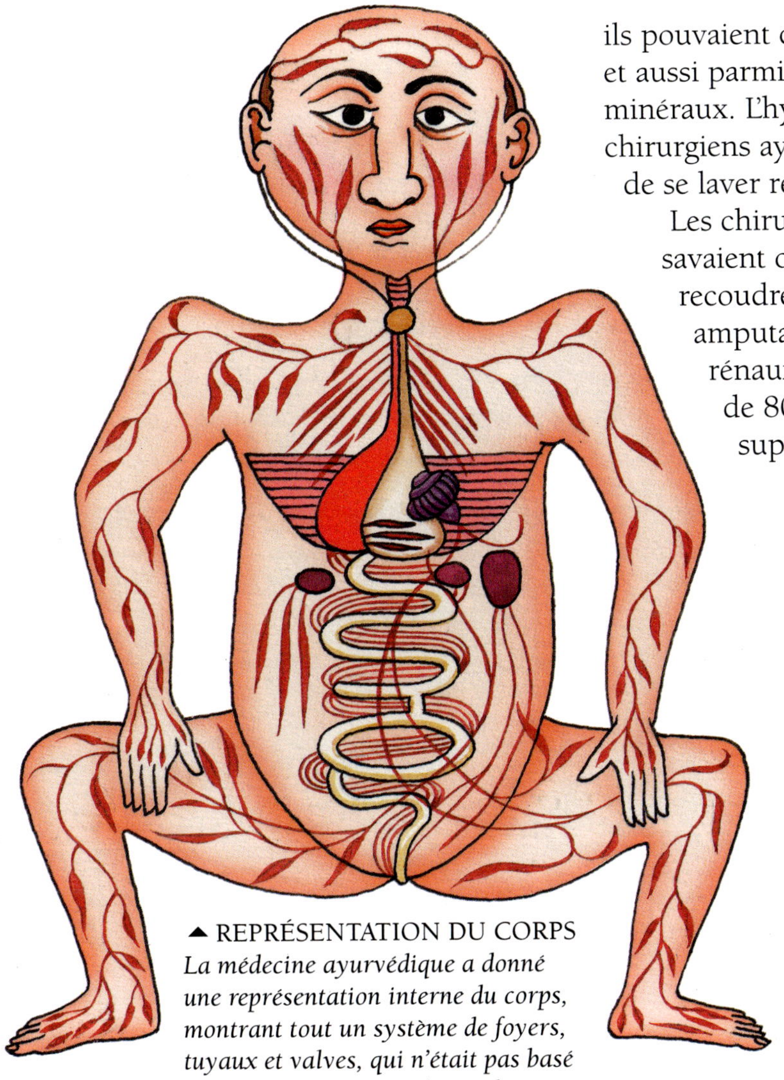

▲ REPRÉSENTATION DU CORPS
La médecine ayurvédique a donné une représentation interne du corps, montrant tout un système de foyers, tuyaux et valves, qui n'était pas basé sur la réalité, puisque leur religion interdisait aux hindous d'ouvrir un cadavre humain.

▲ LE SEIGNEUR BRAHMA PRÉSIDE À LA COUR
C'est Brahma, l'un des trois dieux régnant de la trinité hindouiste, qui aurait développé la médecine ayurvédique. Les Védas *sont un recueil contenant aussi bien des enseignements religieux et philosophiques que des notions médicales.*

▼ FOURMIS-MÉDECINS
Les plaies étaient recousues par des fourmis féroces qui en maintenaient les bords avec leurs mandibules.

▶ LA RÉFECTION D'UN NEZ
Ce sont les médecins ayurvédiques qui mirent au point les techniques de la chirurgie plastique. Ils savaient qu'il était essentiel de garder un pont de tissu vivant dans le rabat de peau qu'ils utilisaient pour reconstruire le nez. Grâce à lui, le tissu greffé continuait d'être irrigué et ne mourait pas.

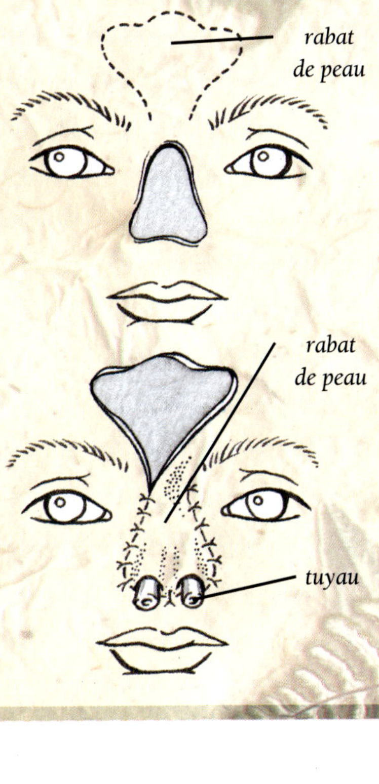

Dates clés

- 1200 - 900 av. J.-C. Les *Védas*.
- 200 av. J.-C. Premières descriptions des techniques du yoga dans les *Yoga-sutras*.
- 100 apr. J.-C. La version finale du *Caraka-samhita* est écrite.
- 600 La version finale du *Sushruta-samhita* est écrite.
- 1000 L'islam propose de nouvelles pratiques médicales.
- 1500 Les Européens apportent les idées médicales de l'Occident.
- 1793 Des médecins britanniques s'intéressent à la chirurgie

La médecine chinoise

▲ LE YIN ET LE YANG
Le symbole du yin et du yang représente la loi des opposés, si importante en médecine chinoise. Le yin est sombre, froid et passif. Son opposé, le yang, est lumineux, chaud et actif. La médecine chinoise cherche à rétablir l'équilibre entre ces opposés.

La médecine chinoise s'est développée pendant des siècles, presque sans aucune influence extérieure. Le *Neijing* est un ouvrage médical ancien. Selon la légende, il est attribué à l'empereur Huangdi. Il est probable qu'il ait été rédigé entre le Vᵉ siècle av. J.-C. et le VIIᵉ siècle apr. J.-C. et a servi de référence à la plus grande partie de la littérature médicale chinoise.

La médecine chinoise est essentiellement basée sur le concept du yin et du yang, c'est à dire d'états opposés. Le yin est féminin, terrestre, sombre, froid, passif. Le yang est masculin, céleste, lumineux, chaud, actif. D'après le *Neijing*, le yin et le yang gouvernent le corps, considéré comme un minuscule pays. Ce pays possède aussi un système de communication de douze rivières calquées sur les grands fleuves de Chine. Ces rivières sont ramifiées en minuscules canaux où coulent le sang et l'énergie vitale (Qi).

Ces lignes relient les organes entre eux. Par exemple, les reins sont connectés à l'oreille, le poumon au nez et le cœur à la langue. Le corps est en bonne santé lorsque la circulation dans ces canaux est fluide. Des points situés le long de ces lignes peuvent servir à influencer le flux de Qi.

La médecine chinoise repose largement sur ces lignes et leur influence sur le corps. L'acupuncture était souvent utilisée pour soigner les malades : des aiguilles étaient alors piquées sur certains points du corps parmi les centaines situés

▶ HUANGDI
L'empereur Huangdi aurait vécu, selon la légende, autour du IIIᵉ millénaire av. J.-C. Il serait l'auteur du grand ouvrage médical chinois, le Neijing, *qui est à la base de toute la médecine chinoise.*

RESTAURER L'ÉQUILIBRE

Le médecin chinois n'était payé que si son patient recouvrait la santé. Ainsi, si une personne tombait malade, il était très important de rétablir chez elle l'équilibre du Qi et d'autres éléments de son corps. Un mélange d'exercices physiques et mentaux, régime diététique et autres moyens, était prescrit pour parvenir à ce résultat. Des médicaments chinois étaient fabriqués à partir d'ingrédients investis de propriétés particulières.

▶ MÉDECIN ET PATIENT
La pratique de la médecine chinoise traditionnelle nécessite une longue discussion entre patient et médecin, qui traite le corps comme un tout, et non pas la partie malade seulement.

◀ DENTS D'ANIMAUX PRÉHISTORIQUES
Les « dents de dragon » sont de nos jours encore réduites en poudre et largement utilisées en médecine chinoise. Bien entendu, les dragons n'existent pas. Les énormes dents prélevées sur les restes exhumés des animaux préhistoriques sont souvent utilisées par les pharmaciens, mais aussi les dents de nombreux animaux dont, celles des grands singes (gigantopithèques) disparus.

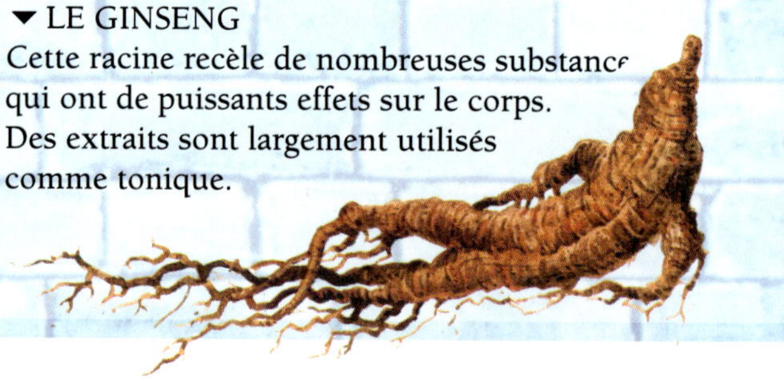

▼ LE GINSENG
Cette racine recèle de nombreuses substances qui ont de puissants effets sur le corps. Des extraits sont largement utilisés comme tonique.

◀ UNE PAGE DU NEIJING
Le Neijing *explique comment les forces du yin et du yang interagissent et influencent le flux de Qi. D'après cet ouvrage, le corps humain est constitué de cinq éléments de base : le bois, le feu, la terre, le métal, et l'eau.*

▶ SHENNONG
Cet empereur légendaire aurait découvert la pharmacopée chinoise. Dans un ouvrage datant d'au moins 2 000 ans, le Shennong Bencao Jing, *il décrit 365 substances médicinales différentes.*

le long des « méridiens » véhiculant l'énergie vitale. Ceci stimulait le flux de Qi et le patient recouvrait la santé. Parfois, dans un but similaire, on faisait brûler des cônes d'herbes sèches sur la peau, au niveau de ces points. L'acupuncture est pratiquée depuis plus de 4 500 ans. Elle tient une place importante en médecine chinoise et est maintenant pratiquée en Occident.

La médecine chinoise a largement recours aux remèdes à base de substances naturelles, dont beaucoup ont été introduites en médecine occidentale. C'est le cas de l'huile de castor, du camphre, de l'huile de chaulmoogra comme traitement contre la lèpre, et du fer pour soigner l'anémie. Le ginseng est un tonique chinois très connu.

Les Chinois anciens ont inventé la vaccination comme traitement contre la variole. Ils injectaient chez des gens bien portants une faible quantité de pus provenant d'un bouton de variole. Ils recevaient ainsi une forme atténuée de la maladie et devenaient résistants à l'infection. Les Chinois ont abandonné cette technique qui a été oubliée. Les Européens n'ont découvert la vaccination qu'au XVIIIe siècle.

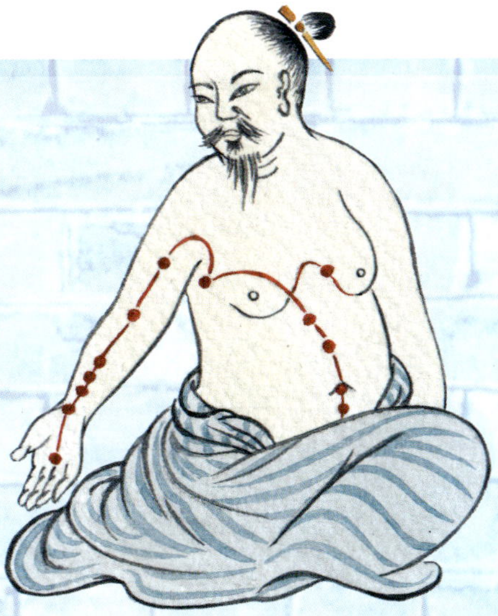

▲ LES MÉRIDIENS DE QI
Des aiguilles d'acupuncture sont piquées dans la peau sur les points situés le long de lignes appelées méridiens. Le point où l'acupuncteur enfonce l'aiguille peut être très éloigné de la partie du corps à soigner.

◀ LES AIGUILLES D'ACUPUNCTURE
Les acupuncteurs (personnes pratiquant l'acupuncture) utilisent de très longues aiguilles qu'ils peuvent enfoncer à plusieurs centimètres sous la peau. Puis, ils manipulent ou tournent l'aiguille pour rétablir le flux de Qi. L'acupuncteur moderne fait parfois passer un courant électrique à travers l'aiguille.

Dates clés

- 2700 av. J.-C. Vie du légendaire empereur Shennong qui découvrit la phytothérapie.
- 2698-2598 av. J.-C. Règne de Huangdi, fondateur légendaire de la médecine chinoise.
- 200 av. J.-C. Le *Neijing* est écrit.
- 280 apr. J.-C. Wang Shu-he rédige le *Maying* en 10 volumes (traité classique sur les pouls).
- 1601 Yang Ji-Zhou écrit le *Zhen-Jiu Da-Cheng* en 10 volumes, qui décrit l'acupuncture.
- 1600 Les premières descriptions des pratiques médicales chinoises parviennent en Occident.

Hippocrate et les Grecs

▲ LE CADUCÉE
Le symbole du physicien grec Asclépios qui vécut vers 1200 av. J.-C. était un serpent enroulé autour d'une baguette de bois. Aujourd'hui encore, le caducée est le symbole des professions médicales dans de nombreux pays partout dans le monde.

LE MÉDECIN GREC ASCLÉPIOS vécut vers 1200 av. J.-C. Selon la légende, il soignait avec tant de succès qu'on en fit un dieu. Les malades venaient dormir dans les temples où il exerçait. Ils croyaient qu'Asclépios les guérirait dans la nuit. Le traitement consistait en un régime et des bains d'eau minérale, mais l'essentiel reposait sur des prières et des rituels magiques. Cependant, dès 400 av. J.-C., les philosophes grecs cherchèrent une approche plus pratique de la maladie.

Grâce aux conquêtes d'Alexandre le Grand, les Grecs anciens étaient en contact étroit avec le Moyen-Orient et l'Asie. En Inde, ils rencontrèrent sans doute les croyances védiques. Ceci expliquerait pourquoi les philosophes grecs croyaient eux aussi que l'Univers était constitué de quatre éléments, l'air, la terre, le feu et l'eau. Cette croyance fut à l'origine de celle selon laquelle

▲ LES QUATRE HUMEURS
Cette illustration médiévale représente les quatre humeurs dont on pensait que le corps était constitué : le sang, le flegme, la bile jaune ou la colère, et la bile noire ou la mélancolie. Il fallait maintenir l'équilibre entre les quatre.

SOIGNER
Hippocrate et ses confrères médecins pensaient que leur rôle était d'aider le corps à se soigner. Ils avaient peu recours aux médicaments, sauf à l'opium utilisé pour soulager la douleur. Ils possédaient des notions de chirurgie, mais la pratiquaient peu. Les Grecs ont laissé des descriptions détaillées de trépanations. Les écrits d'Hippocrate font état d'une méthode pour remettre en place une épaule démise, méthode encore utilisée aujourd'hui et toujours connue sous le nom de méthode d'Hippocrate.

▶ LA MANDRAGORE
La racine de mandragore était investie de puissantes propriétés magiques, car elle présente quelques similitudes avec la forme du corps humain. La mandragore est en réalité une plante très toxique.

▼ LE MÉDECIN
Les médecins grecs se déplaçaient pour rendre visite à leurs patients. Ils étaient très au point pour l'examen des patients et précis dans leur diagnostic, mais ils avaient peu de médicaments à leur disposition.

▲ LA SAIGNÉE
Sur ce vase grec datant d'environ 470 av. J.-C., on voit un médecin se préparant à saigner un patient en ouvrant une veine. Le sang était sans doute recueilli dans la jarre suspendue au mur derrière eux.

◀ LE PÈRE DE LA MÉDECINE
Hippocrate était le plus grand médecin de la Grèce antique et son influence perdure jusqu'à nos jours. Il aurait écrit plus de 70 livres sur la médecine et la chirurgie. Le serment d'Hippocrate exposait les responsabilités auxquelles étaient tenus les médecins, selon Hippocrate, vis-à-vis de leurs patients et de la société.

▶ TABLETTE VOTIVE
Il n'était pas rare de dédier une tablette aux dieux en remerciement pour une guérison. Celle-ci est destinée à Asclépios, probablement pour le remercier d'avoir soigné des varices, représentées sur la jambe que tient le dieu.

le corps est lui aussi constitué de quatre humeurs.

Hippocrate, le père de la médecine occidentale, soutenait cette théorie. Il naquit à Cos vers 460 av. J.-C. Selon Hippocrate, les maladies avaient des causes naturelles. Il croyait à l'importance du diagnostic et encourageait les médecins à mettre par écrit le maximum de détails sur l'évolution d'une maladie. Il pensait que le corps se soignait seul, et que la guérison pouvait être accélérée par un régime, de l'exercice physique et du repos, qui aidaient à rétablir l'équilibre des humeurs. Si la maladie ne régressait pas, on évacuait les humeurs en pratiquant des saignées ou en faisant transpirer le malade. Ces traitements donnaient souvent un résultat, même si le raisonnement qui le sous-tendait était faux. C'est probablement la raison pour laquelle la théorie des humeurs, ainsi que les traitements d'Hippocrate ont survécu jusqu'au XIXe siècle en médecine occidentale.

▶ LA DIFFUSION DE LA MÉDECINE GRECQUE
Les idées des Grecs anciens ont été diffusées tout autour de la Méditerranée, jusqu'au Moyen-Orient et en Égypte. De la même manière, les remèdes et les traitements à base de plantes de ces régions ont été intégrés dans la médecine grecque. Plus tard, les Romains ont à leur tour adopté les méthodes médicales et chirurgicales grecques.

Dates clés

- 1200 av. J.-C. Asclépios crée des dispensaires. Il est ensuite vénéré comme un dieu.
- 490-430 av. J.-C. Vie d'Empédocle qui décrivit les quatre humeurs.
- 460-377 av. J.-C. Vie d'Hippocrate.
- 429 av. J.-C. Création d'une école de médecine à Cyrène.
- 356-323 av. J.-C. Vie d'Alexandre le Grand dont l'Empire s'étendait jusqu'en Inde.
- v. 300 av. J.-C. Création de la célèbre école de médecine d'Alexandrie.
- v. 100 av. J.-C. Les médecins grecs exportent leur savoir à Rome.

La médecine romaine

▲ CELSE
Vers 25 av. J.-C., le Romain Celse rédigea son imposante encyclopédie. L'un des volumes, De medicina, *regroupait toutes les connaissances en médecine.*

La célèbre école grecque d'Alexandrie demeura le grand centre d'enseignement médical, même après la conquête de la Grèce par les Romains. Asclépiade de Bithynie (la Turquie actuelle) vécut de 124 à 40 av. J.-C. Il introduisit à Rome les idées grecques sur la médecine. Il ne croyait ni au pouvoir guérisseur de la nature, ni à la théorie selon laquelle les humeurs étaient à l'origine des maladies. Il recommandait des traitements comme les cataplasmes, les massages, les régimes et beaucoup d'air frais. Asclépiade fut également le premier à soigner les maladies mentales. Il prescrivait la musique, la thérapie par le travail et l'exercice physique, combinés à la consommation de vin aux effets calmants.

Un Romain, Cornelius Celsus (ou Celse), rédigea une histoire détaillée de la médecine vers 25 av. J.-C. Les médecins se sont servis de cet ouvrage jusqu'en 1400. Pendant les deux premiers siècles apr. J.-C., de nombreux médecins grecs se sont installés à Rome.

▼ LES VENTOUSES
Les Romains et les Grecs extrayaient les humeurs malignes du corps par des ventouses. Une compresse était enflammée et placée dans une cloche de verre que l'on pressait contre la peau, contre une blessure ouverte ou une incision chirurgicale. L'oxygène était brûlé et le vide se créait dans la ventouse, provoquant une succion qui aspirait les « humeurs malignes ».

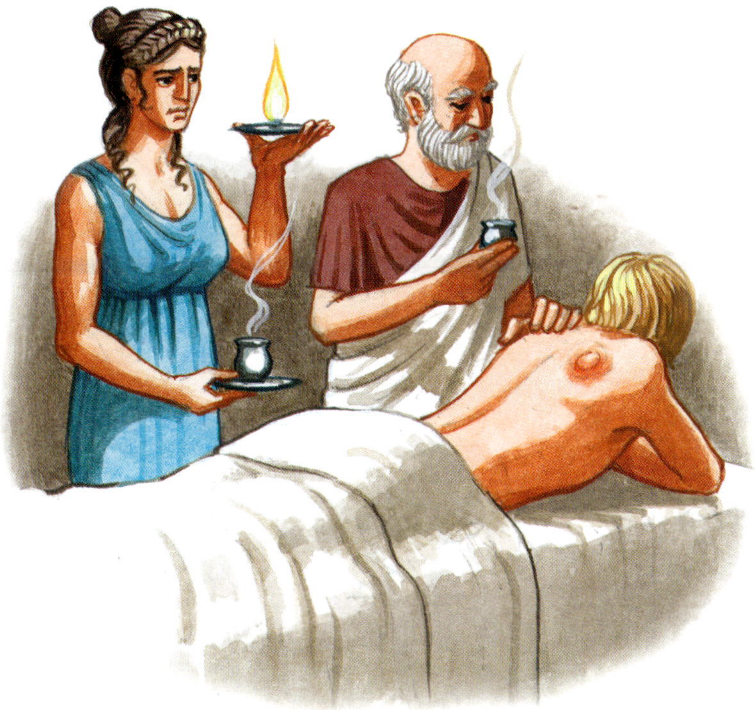

LES ENSEIGNEMENTS DES COMBATS

D'après Galien, beaucoup de maladies étaient la conséquence d'un excès de sang qui se dégradait quelque part dans le corps, et devait donc être évacué par des saignées. Les patients étaient parfois saignés jusqu'à l'évanouissement. Comme les autres enseignements de Galien, cette pratique persista jusqu'au XIXe siècle et provoqua de nombreuses morts inutiles.

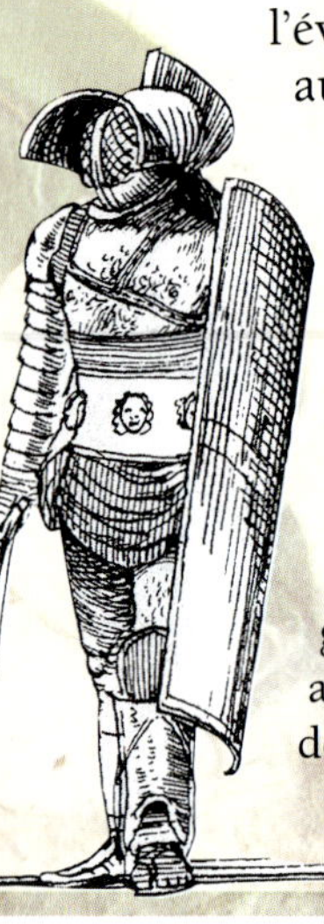

◀ GLADIATEUR ROMAIN
Avant de s'installer à Rome, Galien était le médecin des gladiateurs d'Alexandrie. Il dut acquérir une solide expérience de l'anatomie et de la chirurgie en les soignant.

▲ MÉDECINE DE GUERRE
L'armée romaine était la seule à utiliser des médecins sur le champ de bataille. Ils y montaient des hôpitaux de terrain.

▶ CROCHET CHIRURGICAL
Les chirurgiens romains utilisaient un crochet de bronze pour écarter les tissus lors d'une opération. Le crochet maintenait les vaisseaux sanguins et les muscles, ce qui permettait au médecin de mieux voir la zone à opérer.

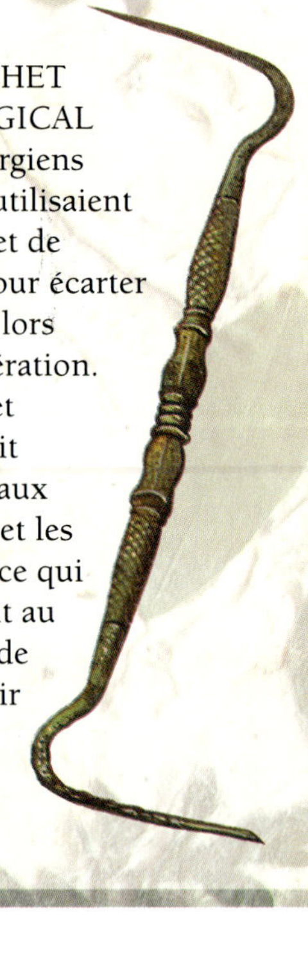

◀ LES THERMES
Les Romains prenaient grand soin de leur corps. Ils passaient de longues heures dans les eaux chaudes ou froides des bains publics ou à se faire masser. Ceci leur permettait d'éviter les infections.

▼ L'AQUEDUC ROMAIN
L'approvisionnement en eau potable fut une mesure de santé publique importante introduite par les Romains. Les aqueducs acheminaient l'eau depuis des sources éloignées de plusieurs kilomètres.

Claudius Galien est arrivé à Rome en 162 av. J.-C. où il est devenu le médecin de cinq empereurs romains différents. Il développa la théorie concernant les humeurs mais, contrairement aux Grecs, il croyait en l'expérimentation. Comme la dissection humaine n'était pas autorisée, Galien apprit l'anatomie en disséquant des singes et d'autres animaux. C'est pourquoi beaucoup de ses suppositions se sont révélées fausses par la suite. Galien montra que le sang circulait grâce aux battements du cœur, mais il ne mit pas en évidence cette circulation à travers le corps. Il écrivit au moins 350 livres sur la médecine, dont certains décrivent des opérations d'une complexité extrême.

Ses ouvrages inspiraient un tel respect que, pendant des siècles, ils ne furent pas remis en cause. Même ses erreurs furent largement acceptées jusqu'au XVIe siècle où les médecins se remirent à expérimenter.

Alors que l'influence de la Grèce comptait pour une large part dans les progrès médicaux réalisés à Rome, les Romains progressèrent de manière significative dans le domaine de la santé publique, ce qui réduisit les maladies infectieuses. L'eau potable était acheminée dans les villes, et des thermes furent construits. Il existait un système d'évacuation des déchets. Des cliniques et des hôpitaux furent fondés et des médecins militaires accompagnaient les armées pour soigner les blessures de guerre des soldats.

▲ UN SCALPEL PLIANT
Les Romains se servaient de scalpels comme celui-ci lors d'opérations chirurgicales. On pouvait le replier lorsqu'on ne l'utilisait pas.

▼ UN HÔPITAL MILITAIRE
Cette maquette représente un hôpital militaire, ou *valetudinarium*. Les Romains avaient développé un système sophistiqué de soins pour leurs soldats.

Dates clés

- 53 av. J.-C. - 7 apr. J.-C. Vie de Cornelius Celsus (ou Celse), auteur de *De medicina*.
- 40-90 apr. J.-C. Vie du chirurgien militaire de Néron, Dioscoride, qui décrivit environ 600 plantes et plus de 1000 médicaments dans son livre, *De materia medica*.
- 77 apr. J.-C. L'*Historia Naturalis* de Pline l'Ancien décrit la chirurgie et les plantes médicinales.
- v. 100 apr. J.-C. Soranus rédige des textes sur le contrôle des naissances et sur la grossesse.
- 129 - 216 apr. J.-C. Vie de Galien qui s'appuie sur les écrits grecs.

Le monde arabe

▲ CISEAUX CHIRURGICAUX
L'usage des ciseaux s'est développé, car ils sont plus précis que les scalpels.

▶ AVICENNE
Avicenne était un médecin perse. Son livre, le Canon de la Médecine, *servit de référence à travers le Moyen-Orient et l'Europe, pendant des siècles.*

SOUS L'EMPIRE BYZANTIN (300 av. J.-C.-1453), les ouvrages des médecins grecs et romains furent rassemblés. Certains parurent dans des langues parlées aux confins de l'Empire, comme le perse et le syrien. Cependant, l'Empire arabe gagnait en puissance et en influence. Les Arabes favorisèrent d'abord leurs remèdes traditionnels, mais à mesure que la religion islamique se propageait, beaucoup de traitements traditionnels disparurent. Les médecins se tournèrent vers les idées de la Grèce antique et traduisirent les textes grecs en arabe. Ainsi, le savoir de la Grèce antique se diffusa dans tout l'Empire arabe, en Europe et autour de la Méditerranée.

De grands centres d'études apparurent à Bagdad, au Caire, à Damas, au Moyen-Orient, et à Tolède, Cordoue et Séville, dans ce qui est maintenant l'Espagne. Les scientifiques et les médecins arabes publièrent des copies des premiers ouvrages médicaux. Certains d'entre eux furent même traduits en latin et utilisés dans les écoles de médecine européennes du XIIIe siècle.

Les médecins arabes apportèrent peu de connaissances nouvelles, mais firent des descriptions détaillées de maladies et de leur diagnostic. La chirurgie pâtit pendant les premières années de l'interdiction de disséquer, et l'on connaissait donc peu de choses sur l'anatomie. Cependant, un chirurgien arabe de Cordoue écrivit un texte sur les techniques chirurgicales, et d'autres développèrent des méthodes pour opérer les yeux. Les Arabes s'intéressaient à l'alchimie. Leurs expériences dans ce domaine leur firent découvrir de nombreux remèdes par hasard.

LES MÉDECINS PIONNIERS

Les médecins n'étaient pas tous arabes ni musulmans. Beaucoup étaient perses, juifs ou chrétiens. Rhazès, un Perse, écrivit un imposant compendium médical. Maimonide, un médecin juif né au XIIe siècle, exerça sous le règne du roi saraceni Saladin. Ses nombreux ouvrages étaient fondés sur la médecine grecque.

◀ RHAZÈS
Le médecin perse Rhazès naquit vers 865 apr. J.-C. Il écrivit plus de 200 livres traitant de sujets très divers. On l'admirait pour les soins qu'il administrait gratuitement aux pauvres.

▲ LA CHIRURGIE DE L'ŒIL
La cataracte est une opacité du cristallin de l'œil et peut, à long terme, conduire à la cécité. Les chirurgiens arabes inventèrent une technique pour déplacer le cristallin opacifié et l'ôter du champ de vision, restaurant ainsi partiellement la vue.

Les alchimistes mirent également au point des techniques pour purifier les produits, techniques encore en vigueur aujourd'hui. Les apothicaires arabes compilèrent de longues listes de remèdes par les plantes- pour certains plus de 3000 -, recueillis dans les pays qu'ils avaient conquis. Le soin dont firent preuve les Arabes à consigner l'information fait la véritable valeur de leurs écrits. Ces grands ouvrages étaient laborieusement recopiés et diffusés dans tout l'Empire arabe.

◀ LES MÉDICAMENTS
Les apothicaires perses et arabes mirent au point de nombreuses préparations de médicaments.

▼ PILON ET MORTIER
Le moyen le plus simple pour préparer un médicament à base de plantes était d'en écraser les ingrédients à l'aide d'un pilon et d'un mortier. On obtenait une poudre qui, mélangée à de l'eau, serait bue ou transformée en pâte ou onguent. Le pilon et les mortiers sont encore utilisés de nos jours.

▼ LA MÉDECINE DE L'EMPIRE ARABE
L'Empire arabe s'étendit largement autour de la Méditerranée et au Moyen-Orient et adopta les remèdes traditionnels des régions qu'il avait conquises. Les érudits arabes conservèrent certaines traditions grecques et romaines et consignèrent leurs nouvelles découvertes médicales.

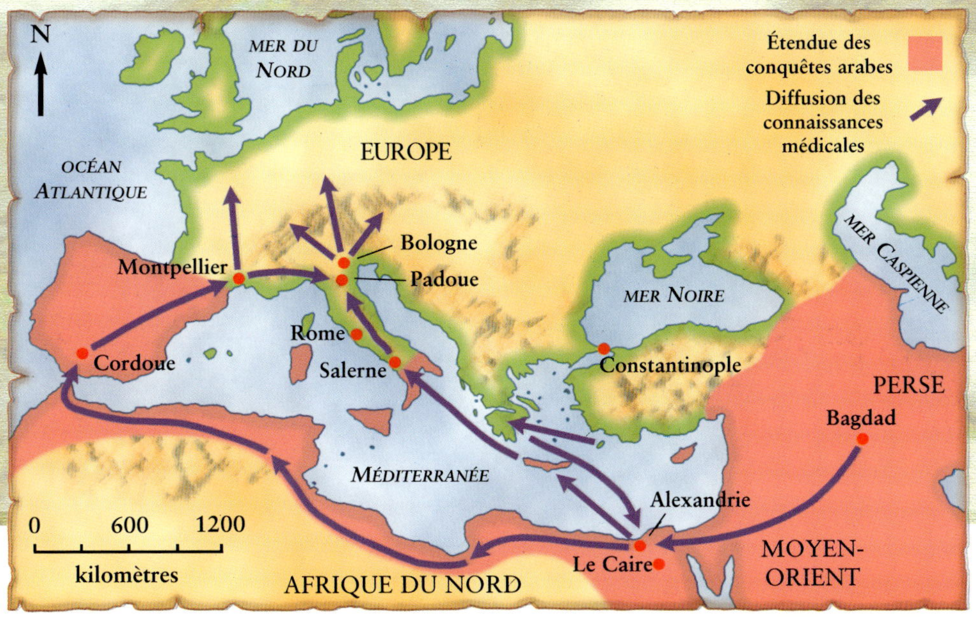

Dates clés

- 620 apr. J.-C. Mahomet fonde l'Islam.
- 832 Bagdad devient un centre d'enseignement.
- 850 Le savant musulman al-Tabari compile les écrits médicaux de Grèce et de Rome.
- v. 865 - 928 Vie de Rhazès.
- 980 - 1037 Vie d'Avicenne.
- 1174 Maimonide est nommé physicien de la cour de Saladin.
- 1236 Les Arabes quittent Cordoue.
- 1258 Les Mongols mettent Bagdad à sac. Les informations médicales détenues par les Arabes commencent à gagner l'Ouest.

L'héritage de Galien

▲ EXAMEN D'URINE
Au cours des XIIIe et XIVe siècles, il existait peu de moyens pour diagnostiquer une maladie. L'une des méthodes consistait à examiner l'urine du patient, sa couleur, sa clarté et même son goût.

Quand l'empereur Constantin instaura le christianisme comme religion officielle de l'Empire romain, la médecine grecque et l'enseignement de Galien furent supplantés par les croyances religieuses. La maladie était considérée comme une punition infligée par Dieu à ceux qui avaient commis des péchés. Les remèdes recommandés étaient souvent la prière et les pèlerinages vers des reliques sacrées. Ainsi le culte des saints guérisseurs devint une pratique régulière.

On associa les saints chrétiens à différentes maladies. Saint Christophe était invoqué en cas d'épilepsie ; Saint Roch était le saint patron des victimes de la peste ; on avait recours à Sainte Apolline lorsqu'on souffrait des dents et Sainte Marguerite protégeait les femmes pendant l'accouchement.

Tertius operuz Galeni Tomus.

Hypocr. Galenus Auicen.

Librorum principis medicoru Galeni, quos nuper insignes viri feli cissimis tralationibus illustrarunt Tomus, exquisitissima cura re cognitus: Una cum indice re

▶ LES GÉNIES DE LA MÉDECINE
Dans cette édition des œuvres de Galien publiée en 1528, ce dernier est représenté avec Hippocrate à gauche, et Avicenne à droite.

Cependant, les malades pouvaient recevoir des soins dans de nombreux monastères. Des hôpitaux furent fondés à travers l'Europe, souvent à proximité des lieux de pèlerinage. Des établissements spéciaux furent construits pour les lépreux qui, considérés comme malpropres, étaient traités avec beaucoup de répugnance.

La connaissance médicale progressa au XIe siècle grâce au travail d'un petit groupe de médecins exerçant à Salerne, en Italie. Ils fondèrent une école médicale influente et remirent au goût du jour d'anciennes

FAUSSES CROYANCES

Tout au long du Moyen Âge, les pratiques médicales se fondèrent sur la superstition. Les herbiers étaient des livres répertoriant les propriétés médicinales supposées des plantes. Quelques-unes d'entre elles produisaient le résultat escompté, mais la plupart restaient sans effet. On recommandait les saignées, l'utilisation des sangsues et les lavements. Faire vomir le patient était pratique courante.

◀ LA PULMONAIRE
Beaucoup de plantes étaient utilisées en médecine en fonction de leur apparence. On pensait ainsi que les feuilles de pulmonaire, ressemblant à des poumons, étaient un bon remède contre les maladies du poumon.

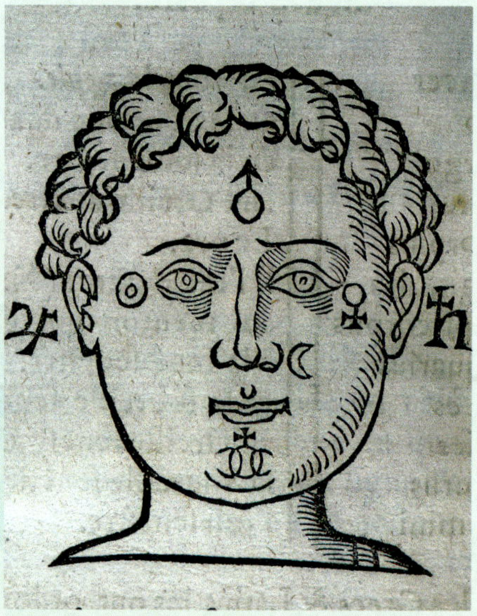

◀ L'ASTROLOGIE
L'astrologie était censée indiquer le lien entre les parties du corps, les planètes et les signes du zodiaque. Voici un schéma représentant l'influence des planètes sur la tête.

▶ PURGE
On faisait vomir le malade à l'aide de puissants médicaments pour débarrasser son corps de ses poisons.

pratiques, en particulier celles de Galien. Les médecins considéraient comme exacts les enseignements de Galien même si certains avaient été modifiés ou omis dans la traduction, et si d'autres étaient complètement erronés. Régime et médicaments, dont beaucoup étaient importés d'Orient, étaient les principaux traitements administrés par les médecins.

La chirurgie devint une branche séparée de la médecine. Elle était pratiquée par des chirurgiens - barbiers qui prodiguaient un vaste éventail de services. Ils coupaient les cheveux, arrachaient les dents, pratiquaient des lavements et des saignées. Une technique grecque, au moins, fut abandonnée. Hippocrate avait recommandé de laisser les plaies ouvertes pour favoriser la cicatrisation. Un chirurgien français, Henri de Mondeville, qui vécut de 1260 à 1320 ne partageait pas cet avis. Il préconisait de fermer la blessure le plus rapidement possible et de la maintenir au sec et couverte afin d'éviter toute infection. Grâce à lui, de nombreux membres furent sauvés et des vies épargnées.

▲ LES SANGSUES
Les médecins utilisaient souvent des sangsues d'eau douce pour aspirer le sang. On a récemment réintroduit l'utilisation de ces animaux en médecine pour réduire les hématomes.

▼ CAUTÉRISER AU FER ROUGE
Pour arrêter le sang, les médecins médiévaux avaient l'habitude d'appliquer un fer chauffé au rouge pour coaguler le sang. Ce procédé était particulièrement douloureux et beaucoup de blessures s'infectaient.

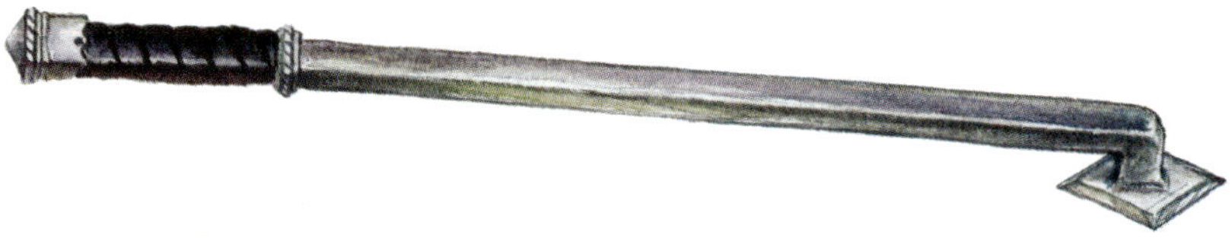

▼ SENTEUR
Au Moyen Âge, les gens pensaient que les mauvaises odeurs propageaient la maladie. Beaucoup, pour chasser les odeurs nauséabondes, portaient sur eux un diffuseur de parfum telle une orange piquée de clous de girofle.

▲ LES YEUX MIRACULEUX
Lucie de Syracuse devint la sainte patronne des maladies oculaires. La légende veut qu'elle se soit arraché les yeux, mais que ceux-ci aient repoussé.

Dates clés

- 1100 - 1300 Des écoles de médecine et des hôpitaux sont fondés à travers l'Europe.
- 1100 Trotula rejoint l'école de médecine de Salerne. Elle écrit la première œuvre complète sur la santé des femmes.
- 1200 - 1300 Les médecins et les chirurgiens se regroupent en corporations.
- 1215 Le Pape Innocent III décrète que les médecins doivent recevoir l'approbation de l'Église et interdit les lépreux dans les églises.
- 1260 - 1320 Henri de Mondeville préconise de refermer les plaies.

Les découvertes de la Renaissance

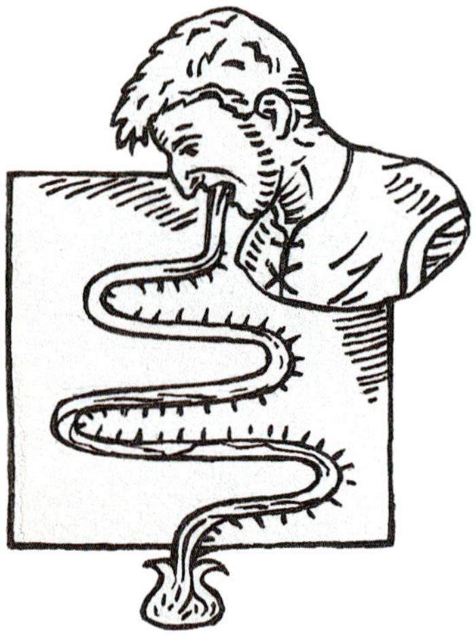

▲ LE THERMOMÈTRE
Contrairement au thermomètre moderne, ce thermomètre au mercure du XVe siècle devait rester dans la bouche du patient plus de 25 mn.

PENDANT LA RENAISSANCE, du XVe au XVIIe siècle, les scientifiques et les médecins remirent en question les écrits des anciens Grecs. Ils rejetaient la tradition et se tournaient vers la découverte et la recherche.

Les scientifiques commencèrent à disséquer le corps humain et furent sidérés de voir que leurs découvertes ne correspondaient pas aux descriptions de Galien. De leurs nouvelles connaissances résultèrent de grands progrès en chirurgie.

Le travail du médecin flamand André Vésale révolutionna profondément la compréhension de

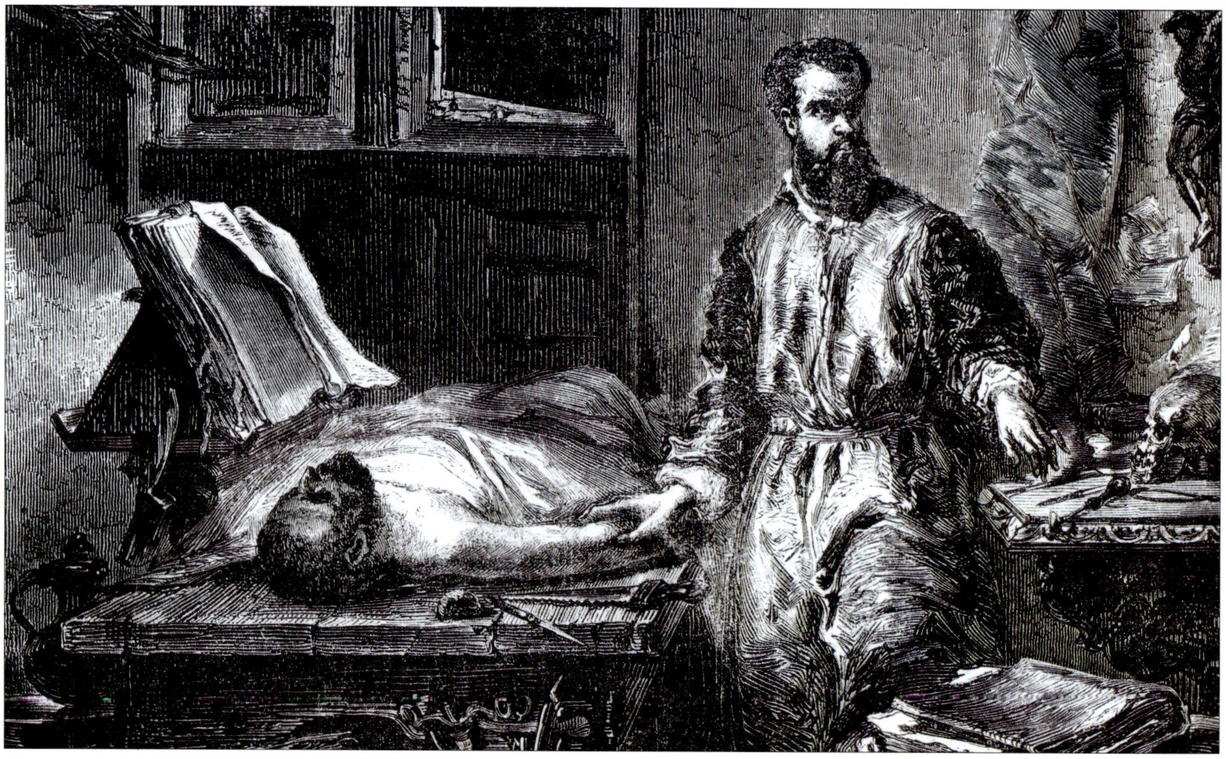

▶ VÉSALE
Cette gravure d'Édouard Hamman fut réalisée au XIXe siècle. Elle montre Vésale disséquant des corps humains afin de réaliser des dessins d'anatomie extrêmement détaillés.

LES RÉVOLUTIONS MÉDICALES

On avait adhéré aux idées d'Hippocrate et de Galien pendant si longtemps, sans les mettre en doute, qu'il fut difficile de les abandonner. Beaucoup de médecins traditionnels rejetèrent les nouvelles idées. Malgré l'opposition, les scientifiques et les médecins progressistes persévérèrent et firent des découvertes qui révolutionnèrent leur temps.

▲ WILLIAM HARVEY
Harvey fut le premier à prouver que le cœur propulsait le sang à travers le corps, en identifiant la direction du flux sanguin. Il fit même la démonstration de sa théorie au roi Charles Ier d'Angleterre.

▶ PARACELSE
Paracelse était un médecin suisse. L'alchimie, à laquelle il croyait, bien qu'elle ne fût pas bien considérée à l'époque, lui permit de découvrir de nouveaux médicaments.

▼ MARCELLO MALPIGHI
Le biologiste et médecin italien Malpighi compléta partiellement la théorie de la circulation sanguine. Il découvrit les vaisseaux capillaires qui relient les artères aux veines, ce qu'Harvey n'avait pas réussi à voir.

l'anatomie et de la physiologie. En 1543, il publia des planches détaillées sur la dissection du corps humain. L'un de ses successeurs, Hieronymus Fabricius étudia la fonction des valves dans les veines et en conclut qu'elles permettaient au sang de circuler dans une seule direction. Mais, comme Galien, il ne réalisa pas que le sang circulait à travers le corps. C'est l'un de ses étudiants, un Anglais nommé William Harvey, qui démontra la circulation du sang. Cependant, même ce dernier ne mit pas en place le maillon final, car il ne comprit pas que le sang passait des artères aux veines.

Les médecins prenant conscience que beaucoup des anciens manuscrits étaient inexacts, collectèrent de nouvelles propriétés de plantes médicinales dans des livres appelés herbiers. Ceci leur permit de découvrir un grand nombre de plantes et médicaments inconnus auparavant en Europe occidentale. C'est ainsi que la racine de rhubarbe (décrite pour la première fois dans un herbier chinois plus de 4 000 ans auparavant) commença à être utilisée comme purgatif. Les explorateurs du Nouveau Monde, les Espagnols et les Portugais en particulier, rapportèrent de leurs voyages de nouvelles plantes aux propriétés thérapeutiques étonnantes. Pendant ce temps, les voyageurs d'Extrême-Orient, rapportaient eux aussi, de leurs expéditions de nouveaux remèdes.

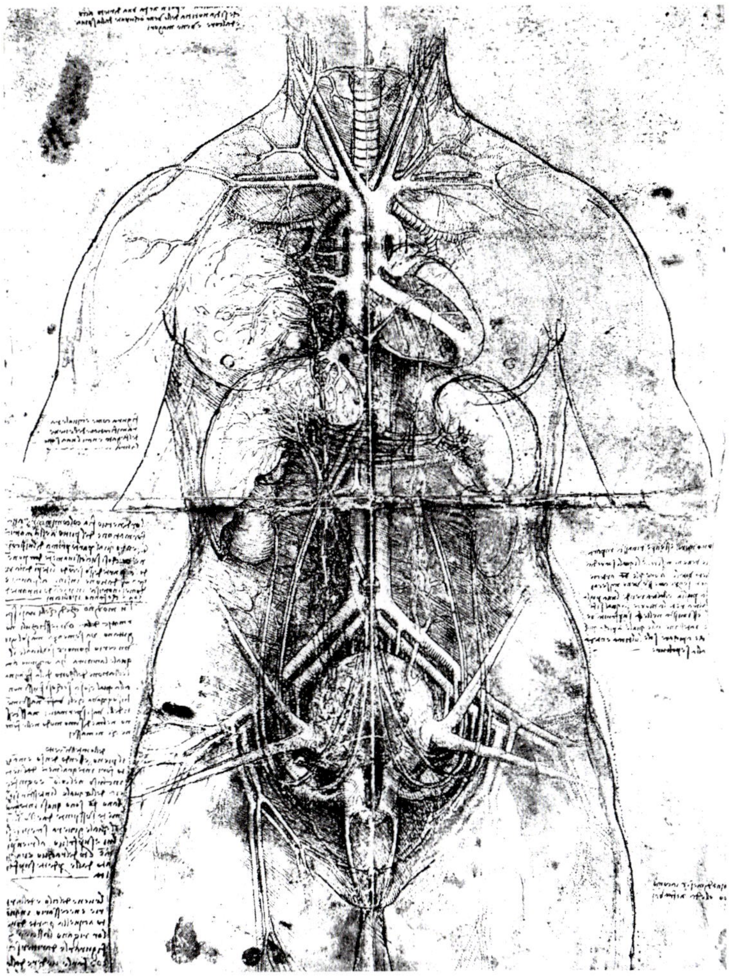

▲ LES PRINCIPAUX ORGANES DU CORPS
Les planches d'anatomie de Léonard de Vinci étaient sans aucun doute des œuvres d'art. Cependant, elles étaient souvent inexactes, car davantage basées sur des présomptions que des dissections détaillées, le maître n'en pratiquant pas lui-même.

▲ AMBROISE PARÉ
Paré, un médecin militaire français, remarqua que la cautérisation des plaies entraînait souvent la mort du patient. Il mit au point une technique plus douce pour ligaturer des vaisseaux sanguins sectionnés, ce qui fit progresser les soins en chirurgie.

▼ GIROLAMO FRACASTORO
Cet Italien émit l'idée selon laquelle l'infection pouvait se transmettre d'une personne à l'autre par contact physique ou par l'air. Il devina que cette contamination était sans doute causée par de minuscules organismes vivants qu'il appela « graines ». Sa théorie fut largement discréditée.

Dates clés

- 1482 Le Pape Sixte IV autorise la dissection des criminels exécutés.
- 1527 Paracelse brûle les livres d'Avicenne et de Galien.
- 1537 Ambroise Paré développe son concept du traitement des blessures.
- 1546 Fracastoro publie sa théorie des microbes et de la maladie.
- 1628 William Harvey publie sa théorie de la circulation sanguine.
- 1661 Marcello Malpighi publie sa théorie sur la circulation du sang à travers les poumons.

Établir un diagnostic

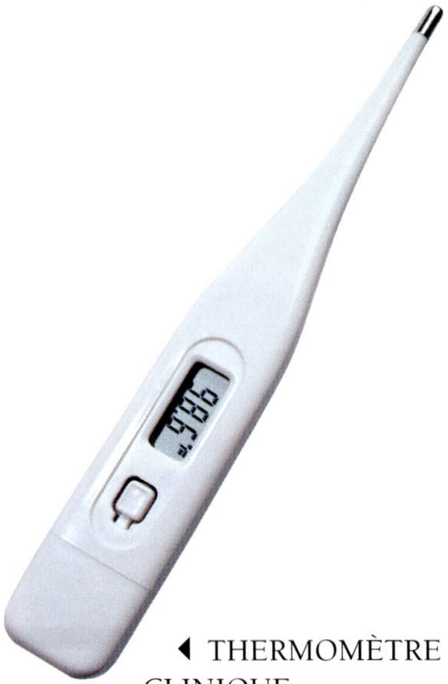

◀ THERMOMÈTRE CLINIQUE
Le thermomètre numérique est rapide, facile d'utilisation et particulièrement précis. Il ne contient pas de mercure toxique, comme les thermomètres traditionnels qui, en outre, étaient fragiles.

Le diagnostic est l'identification d'une maladie par ses symptômes. Il y a peu de temps encore, les tests permettant aux médecins d'identifier une maladie étaient rares. À la place, les médecins parlaient avec leurs patients, les examinaient et observaient leur comportement.

En Grèce, au temps d'Hippocrate, la réputation d'un médecin reposait sur sa capacité à prédire avec le maximum d'exactitude l'évolution de la maladie de son patient, et dire si ce dernier guérirait ou mourrait. Ainsi, les médecins grecs se servaient de tous leurs sens pour faire leur diagnostic. Le toucher, le goût, la vue, l'ouïe et l'odorat pouvaient servir à déceler de précieux indices. Ces principes s'appliquent encore aux médecins modernes.

À l'époque de Galien, le diagnostic reposait aussi sur la prise du pouls, qu'on qualifiait de rapide ou normal.

▶ L'UTILISATION DU STÉTHOSCOPE
Le stéthoscope inventé par Laennec en 1819 était rigide et peu pratique, contrairement au stéthoscope moderne muni d'un tube de caoutchouc souple.

LES INSTRUMENTS

Le diagnostic a progressé avec l'invention d'instruments permettant au médecin de percevoir ce qui se passe à l'intérieur du corps. Toute une série de nouvelles observations furent ainsi rendues possibles. De meilleures mesures du rythme cardiaque, de la tension et de la température contribuèrent à un diagnostic plus précis.

◀ LE PREMIER STÉTHOSCOPE
En 1819, le médecin français René Laennec utilisa le premier stéthoscope, un instrument de bois, long de 23 cm qui amplifiait les sons produits dans la poitrine.

▼ LE STÉTHOSCOPE AUJOURD'HUI
Le stéthoscope moderne est un instrument très simple et très léger. Il permet aux médecins d'écouter les sons produits par les poumons et le cœur.

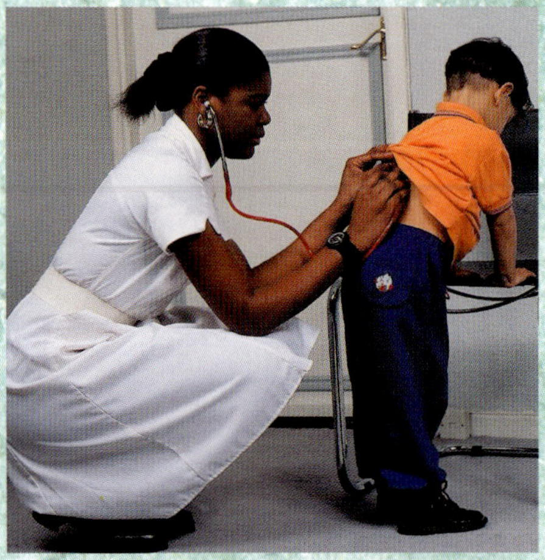

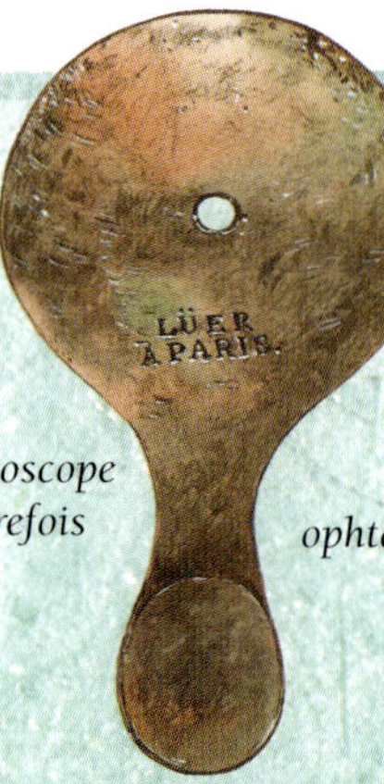

ophtalmoscope d'autrefois

ophtalmoscope moderne

▲ L'ESPION DE L'ŒIL
Les médecins utilisent des ophtalmoscopes pour examiner l'œil d'un patient. Les premiers n'étaient que de puissantes loupes améliorées. L'instrument moderne a de fortes lentilles et des lumières qui permettent au médecin de voir le fond de l'œil.

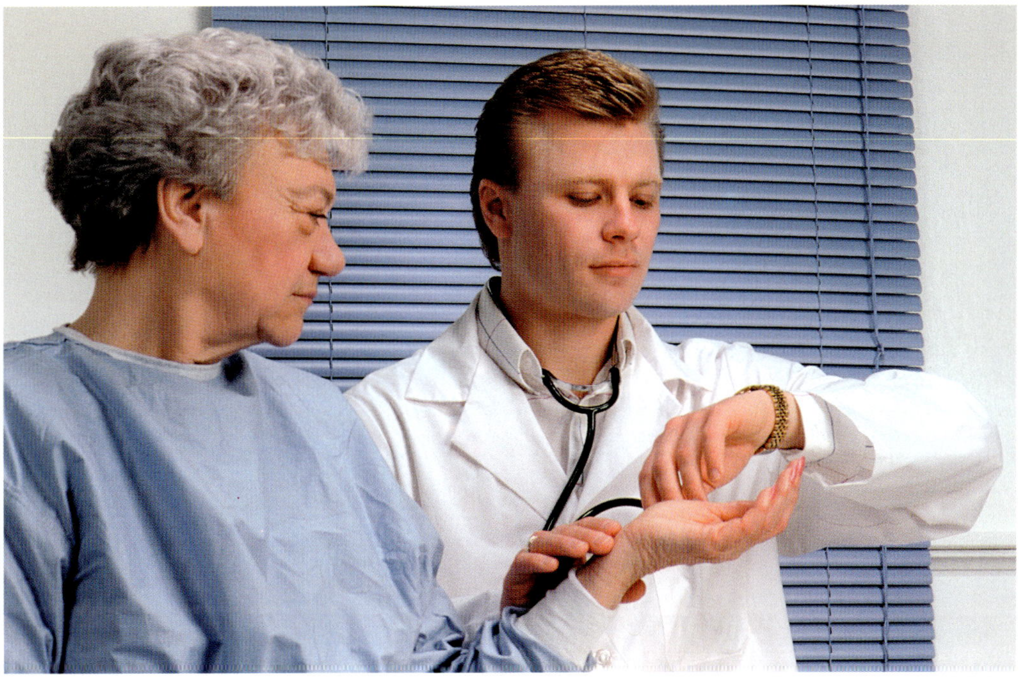

Dans le monde arabe, le diagnostic comprenait un examen minutieux des parties malades, de la tension et de l'urine.

Dans la majeure partie de l'Europe, le diagnostic était plutôt sommaire, car la maladie était considérée comme un châtiment de Dieu. Ce dernier ne pouvant être remis en cause, il n'était possible de traiter la maladie que par des prières.

Il fallut attendre le XVIIIe siècle pour que de réels progrès soient faits dans l'art du diagnostic. En 1761, un médecin viennois, Léopold Auenbrugger, remarqua que le fait d'appuyer fortement sur la poitrine d'un patient produisait des sons qui prouvaient une maladie du poumon. Cette technique fut difficilement acceptée, mais elle est encore en usage aujourd'hui. La plupart des médecins ne pratiquaient cependant pas d'examens physiques et établissaient leur diagnostic en interrogeant leur patient. L'auscultation (l'écoute des bruits produits par les organes) n'a progressé qu'avec l'invention du stéthoscope en 1816. Cela permit aux médecins d'entendre clairement les battements du cœur et de diagnostiquer différentes maladies cardiaques.

L'examen de l'urine était une méthode courante pour diagnostiquer toutes sortes de maladies. Sa couleur, son odeur et même son goût étaient censés révéler l'état de santé du patient. Les analyses d'urine sont encore utilisées aujourd'hui dans certaines formes de diagnostic, par exemple, pour déceler un diabète ou une grossesse.

▲ LE POULS
Pendre le pouls d'une personne renseigne le médecin sur le rythme cardiaque. Les artères situées au niveau du poignet sont très proches de la surface de la peau, et à chaque battement, l'artère se gonfle légèrement.

▲ SOUS PRESSION
Le sphygmomanomètre mesure la pression artérielle. Le médecin enfile, sur le bras du patient, une manche qui est gonflée pour suspendre le flux dans les artères. La manche est alors doucement dégonflée et l'instrument mesure la pression artérielle.

▼ LA CHIMIE DU SANG
On se sert d'analyses de sang pour mesurer les changements survenant dans la composition chimique du sang. Celles-ci peuvent indiquer qu'une personne souffre d'une infection, de diabète ou d'autres troubles hormonaux.

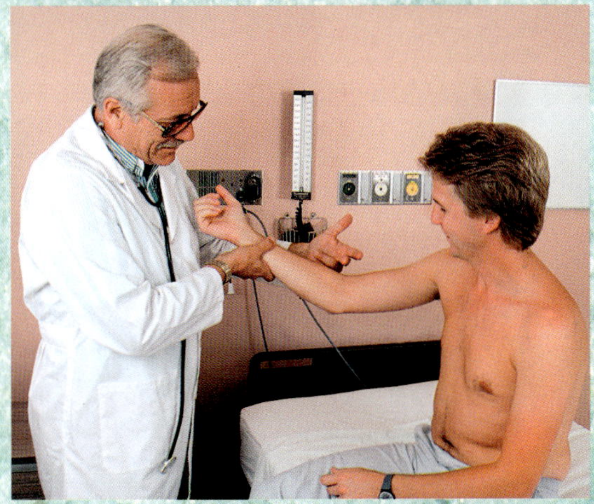

Dates clés

- 1714 Gabriel Fahrenheit invente le thermomètre au mercure.
- 1761 Léopold Auenbrugger publie ses découvertes sur les sons provenant de la poitrine.
- 1816 René Laennec utilise le premier stéthoscope.
- 1851 Hermann von Helmholtz invente l'ophtalmoscope.
- 1868 Carl Wunderlich généralise l'utilisation du thermomètre.
- 1895 Wilhelm Röntgen découvre les rayons X.
- 1896 Scipione Riva-Rocci invente le sphygmomanomètre.

L'aube de la chirurgie

▲ JOHN HUNTER
Né en Écosse en 1728, John Hunter joua un rôle important dans la chirurgie moderne. Grâce à lui, les gens se mirent à considérer la chirurgie comme une discipline médicale à part entière. Il rassembla une collection de spécimens médicaux qui se trouve aujourd'hui à Glasgow.

La chirurgie est probablement la plus ancienne pratique médicale. Sur des squelettes préhistoriques, on retrouve des traces de réductions de fractures sur les os et des marques de trépanation. Certaines civilisations anciennes pratiquaient des opérations chirurgicales très sophistiquées, notamment sur les yeux et les intestins. Cependant, l'art de la chirurgie fut presque perdu au Moyen Âge. Dans la plupart des écoles de médecine européennes, cette discipline n'était pas enseignée. Elle était laissée aux bons soins des barbiers qui l'utilisaient en général en dernier recours.

Pendant la Renaissance, on essaya de faire progresser la chirurgie. Cependant, la plupart des patients mouraient d'infections dues au manque d'hygiène. En 1547, le chirurgien français Ambroise

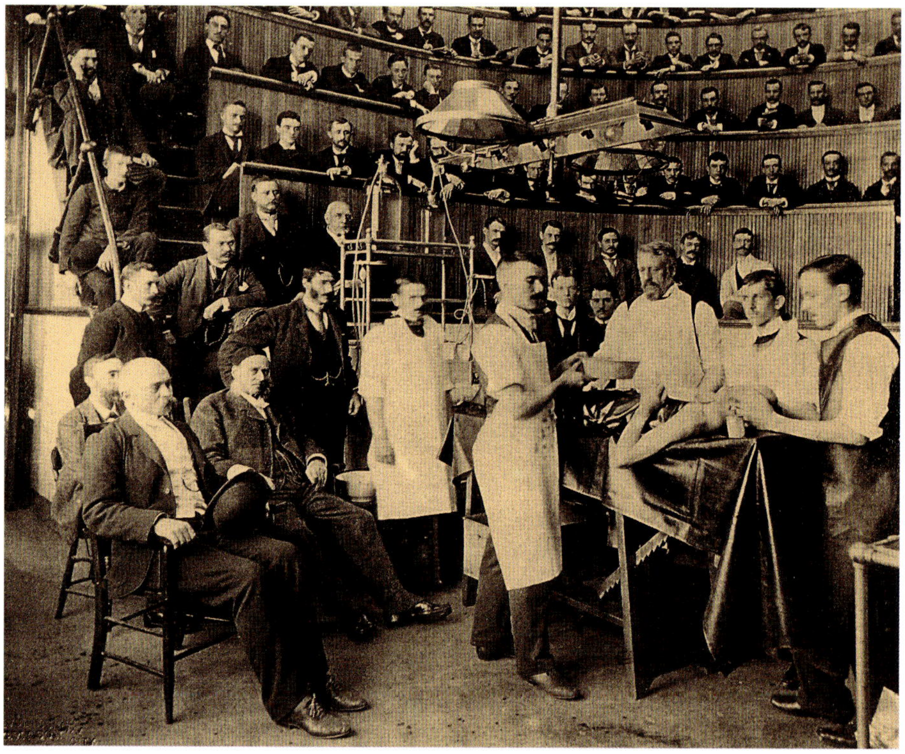

▶ CHIRURGIE DANS UN AMPHITHÉÂTRE
Sur cette photo, qui date de 1898, une opération est pratiquée à l'hôpital Bellevue de New York. Des confrères chirurgiens et des étudiants en médecine y assistent afin d'apprendre les dernières techniques chirurgicales.

LES PREMIERS ACTES DE CHIRURGIE
On pratiquait déjà la chirurgie en Mésopotamie 2000 ans av. J.-C. Au 1er siècle av. J.-C., les chirurgiens indiens étaient particulièrement qualifiés et laissèrent des descriptions détaillées d'opérations délicates. Dans la Chine ancienne, on pratiquait peu d'opérations chirurgicales. Les Grecs anciens et les Romains pratiquaient une chirurgie évoluée. Leur science se répandit dans l'Empire arabe avant de retourner en Europe bien plus tard.

▼ HUA TUO
En Chine ancienne, on n'encourageait pas la pratique chirurgicale. Le seul témoignage dans ce domaine est celui de Hua Tuo, opérant le bras du général Guan Yun. Hua Tuo est connu pour les césariennes qu'il pratiquait. Il fut aussi le premier à utiliser le chanvre indien comme analgésique.

◀ LES SAIGNÉES
La saignée était l'un des actes chirurgicaux les plus courants et les plus anciens. Plus tard, elle fut pratiquée par les barbiers. Elle servait à soigner presque toutes les maladies. Lorsque, les patients étaient déjà très malades, le fait de perdre du sang les affaiblissait à tel point qu'ils finissaient par mourir.

Paré abandonna la cautérisation traditionnelle au fer rouge, particulièrement douloureuse. Il découvrit qu'il était possible de stopper l'hémorragie en ligaturant les vaisseaux. Mais il fallut encore attendre deux siècles avant que d'autres progrès soient réalisés.

Au XVIIIe siècle, une meilleure connaissance de l'anatomie rendit bénignes les opérations destinées à ôter les tumeurs et les calculs rénaux. Les amputations étaient pratiquées en moins de cinq minutes pour minimiser la douleur et le choc chez les patients. On les calmait à l'aide d'opium ou d'alcool, et ils étaient fermement maintenus par des assistants. Cependant, nombreux étaient encore ceux qui mouraient à la suite d'infections causées par l'opération.

À partir de 1760, le chirurgien britannique John Hunter transforma la chirurgie, de boucherie d'amateurs qu'elle était, en profession scientifique. Il donna des conférences et produisit de nombreux écrits. Hunter était un expert de la dissection.

Une fois que la douleur et l'infection purent être contrôlées, la chirurgie comporta moins de risques. Des opérations bénignes devinrent pratique courante. Dès le XVIe siècle, on savait reconnaître une appendicite, mais l'ablation de l'appendice était considérée comme très dangereuse. Puis, en 1902, Frederic Treves draina un abcès de l'appendice sur le Prince de Galles, juste avant qu'il soit couronné sous le nom d'Édouard VIII. Treves fut fait chevalier et, à partir de ce moment-là, l'opération de l'appendicite devient très à la mode.

▼ OPÉRATION DE L'ŒIL

La chirurgie moderne nécessite des instruments extrêmement précis. Ce chirurgien de l'œil utilise un scalpel muni d'une minuscule lame de diamant particulièrement tranchante. Le médecin regarde l'œil à travers une loupe puissante.

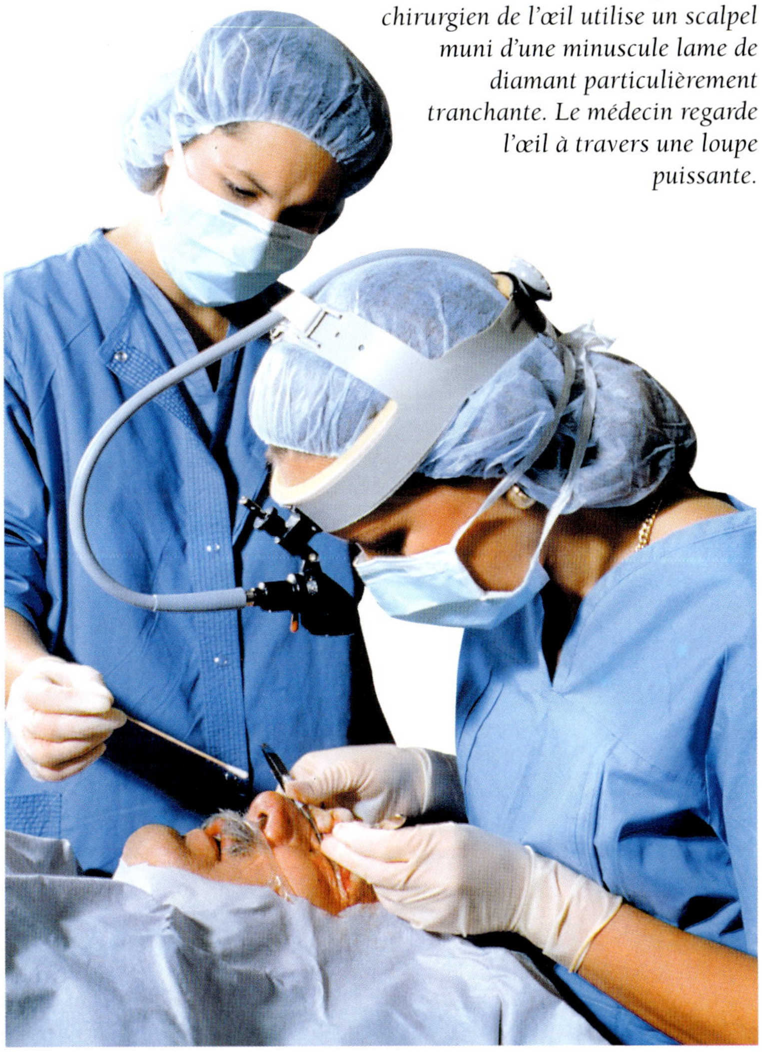

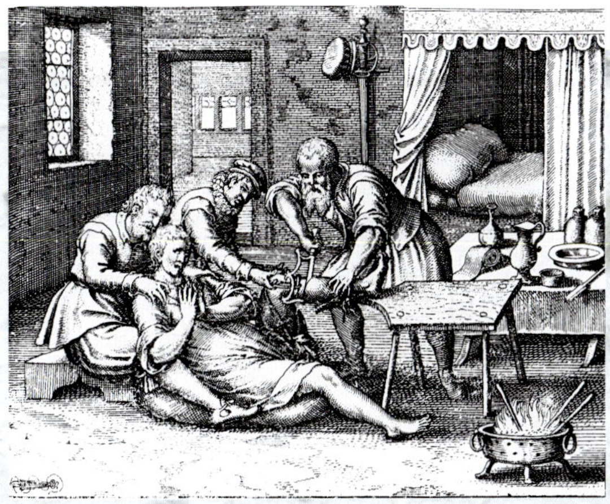

▲ L'AMPUTATION

Les amputations étaient des actes brutaux. Elles devaient être pratiquées avec rapidité pour éviter que le patient meure des suites de l'hémorragie ou du choc. Sur cette gravure de 1618, les fers à cautériser chauffent dans le brasero, prêts à être appliqués sur la plaie.

▼ LE GARROT

Le tourniquet fut inventé pour stopper l'hémorragie après une amputation. On attachait solidement la sangle autour du membre au-dessus de l'endroit à couper. Puis on serrait la vis pour comprimer les artères et arrêter le flux sanguin.

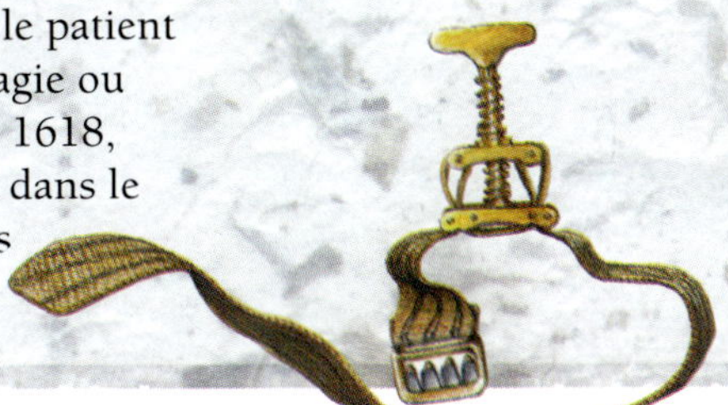

▲ UNE SCIE

Des scies de charpentier furent d'abord utilisées pour les amputations. Plus tard, on mit au point des scies spéciales.

Dates clés

- 600 av. J.-C. Le *Sushruta-samhita* décrit plus de 120 instruments de chirurgie en acier.
- 1728–1793 Vie de John Hunter qui révolutionne l'enseignement et la pratique de la chirurgie.
- 1793 Le chirurgien militaire français Dominique-Jean Larrey met au point le premier service d'ambulances.
- 1809 L'Américain Ephraïm McDowell fut à l'origine de la chirurgie gynécologique en enlevant une tumeur d'un ovaire.
- 1902 Frederic Treves soigne l'appendicite du Prince de Galles.

Stérile et indolore

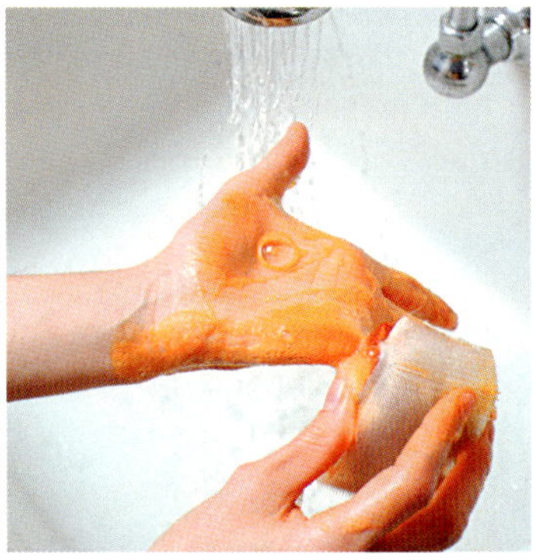

▲ L'HYGIÈNE
Se laver les mains est encore le moyen le plus sûr de limiter la transmission de l'infection à l'hôpital, mais aussi à la maison.

▶ IGNAC SEMMELWEIS
Semmelweis constata que le manque d'hygiène était la cause de nombreuses morts parmi ses patients. C'est pourquoi il astreignit son équipe à une hygiène rigoureuse. Son attitude fut jugée outrageante et il fut contraint de quitter son hôpital de Vienne.

LA CHIRURGIE AU XVIIe SIÈCLE ÉTAIT une activité très dangereuse. La notion d'hygiène n'existait pas. Les chirurgiens travaillaient avec des vêtements ordinaires, maculés de sang. Ils utilisaient les mêmes instruments, sans les nettoyer entre chaque opération. La « fièvre de l'accouchement » tuait de nombreuses femmes dans les quelques jours qui suivaient l'accouchement. Un médecin hongrois, Ignac Semmelweis, remarqua que les patients avaient plus de risques de souffrir d'une infection s'ils avaient été auscultés par des étudiants en médecine qui avaient auparavant pratiqué des dissections. C'est pourquoi Semmelweis imposa des règles d'hygiène très strictes dans son hôpital, ce qui fit chuter le taux de mortalité.

À cette époque, personne ne savait que la maladie se transmettait par les microbes. C'est seulement en 1860 que Louis Pasteur découvrit la nature bactérienne de l'infection. Le chirurgien britannique Joseph Lister fit une autre découverte décisive. Il avait constaté que beaucoup de gens mouraient des suites de fractures osseuses ouvertes. Il observa que si l'os s'était cassé sans déchirer la peau, les risques qu'une infection se déclare étaient faibles. Par contre, si un fragment d'os trouait la peau et était ainsi exposé à l'air, souvent une infection se déclarait, ce qui conduisait la plupart du temps à l'amputation ou la mort.

Lorsque Lister prit connaissance des travaux de Pasteur, il réalisa que le problème n'était pas lié à l'air, mais aux bactéries contaminant la plaie. Lister avait entendu dire qu'on pouvait utiliser le phénol pour nettoyer les égouts. Il essaya donc de badigeonner les plaies de phénol dilué. Son expérience connut un résultat spectaculaire. Sa découverte fut d'abord rejetée par le corps médical, mais lorsque elle fut enfin acceptée, les opérations de routine purent être

ENDORMIR LA DOULEUR

Les anesthésiants ont une longue histoire. En Grèce antique, on soulageait la douleur à l'aide de drogues. Au XIXe siècle, l'opium était utilisé comme soporifique. L'alcool servait également en chirurgie à décontracter le patient. L'éther et l'oxyde nitreux furent les premiers anesthésiants modernes. Ils étaient tous deux inhalés. Peu de temps après, on découvrit le chloroforme. Après une certaine résistance initiale, ces trois anesthésiants furent largement utilisés.

▼ WILLIAM MORTON
Morton, un dentiste américain, expérimenta les effets de l'éther comme anesthésiant. En 1846, il anesthésia un patient pour le chirurgien John Collins Warren.

▼ LE CHLOROFORME
Pour endormir au chloroforme, on imbibait de produit un masque de tissu muni d'une armature de fer et on recouvrait le nez et la bouche du patient afin qu'il en inhale les vapeurs.

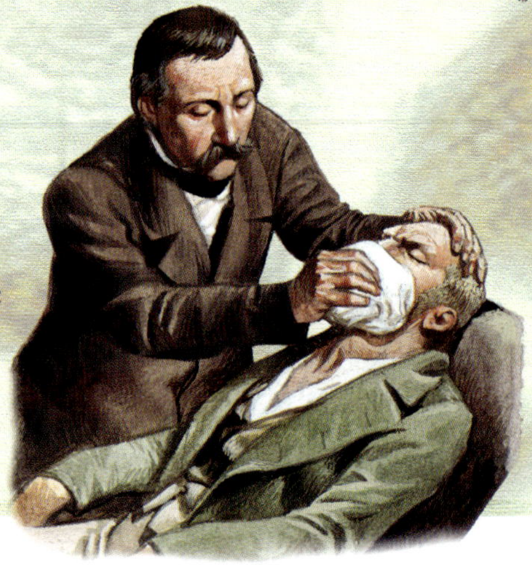

▲ PREMIÈRE ERREUR
En 1848, Hannah Greener fut la première personne à mourir des effets nocifs du chloroforme lors d'une opération bénigne destinée à enlever un ongle d'orteil.

pratiquées presque sans risque pour le patient. L'asepsie, la prévention contre l'infection, était un moyen plus sûr que de laisser l'infection s'installer et tenter ensuite de la traiter avec des antiseptiques. Ainsi, pour protéger les plaies des bactéries, les chirurgiens stérilisèrent leurs instruments et portèrent des masques et des blouses.

Peu de temps après la découverte de l'asepsie, des médecins trouvèrent une méthode pour soulager la souffrance en utilisant des anesthésiants. En 1846, le dentiste William Morton montra que l'éther pouvait endormir la douleur pendant l'opération. John Warren fit la même expérience avec l'oxyde nitreux, un gaz hilarant. John Snow se servit du chloroforme pour aider la Reine Victoria à accoucher du Prince Léopold. Depuis lors, l'usage de ce produit s'étendit.

▲ LE PULVÉRISATEUR
Joseph Lister inventa le pulvérisateur de phénol. Il diffusait, dans la salle d'opération, un fin brouillard de phénol qui tuait les bactéries. Le taux de mortalité tomba de 50 à 5 chez les patients de Lister.

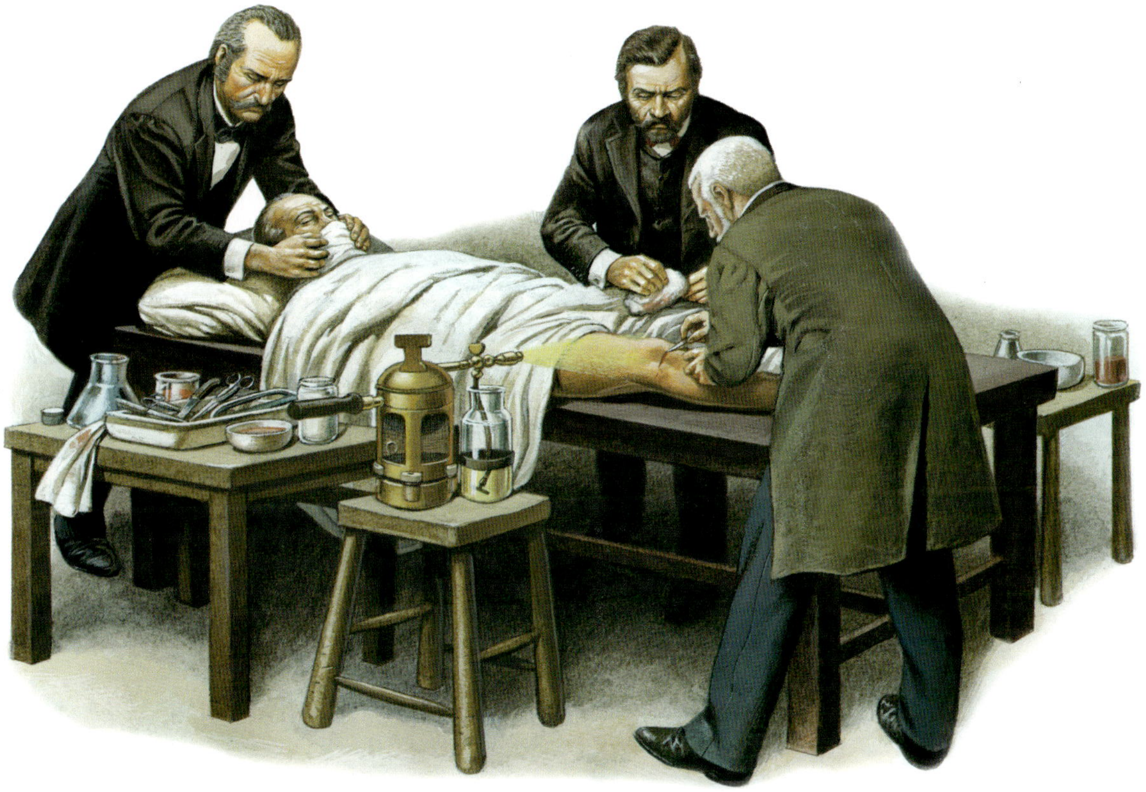

◀ SOUS LE BISTOURI
À partir de 1860, les opérations eurent lieu dans des conditions aseptiques. Un pulvérisateur de phénol diffusait un brouillard antibactérien dans la salle. La chirurgie devint aussi plus confortable pour le patient. Un masque de chloroforme le maintenait en état d'inconscience pendant l'opération.

▶ L'ANESTHÉSISTE MODERNE
Pour anesthésier, on utilise aujourd'hui un mélange de gaz. L'anesthésie ralentit toutes les fonctions du corps. C'est pourquoi pendant l'opération le patient doit être surveillé par l'anesthésiste, à droite sur la photo.

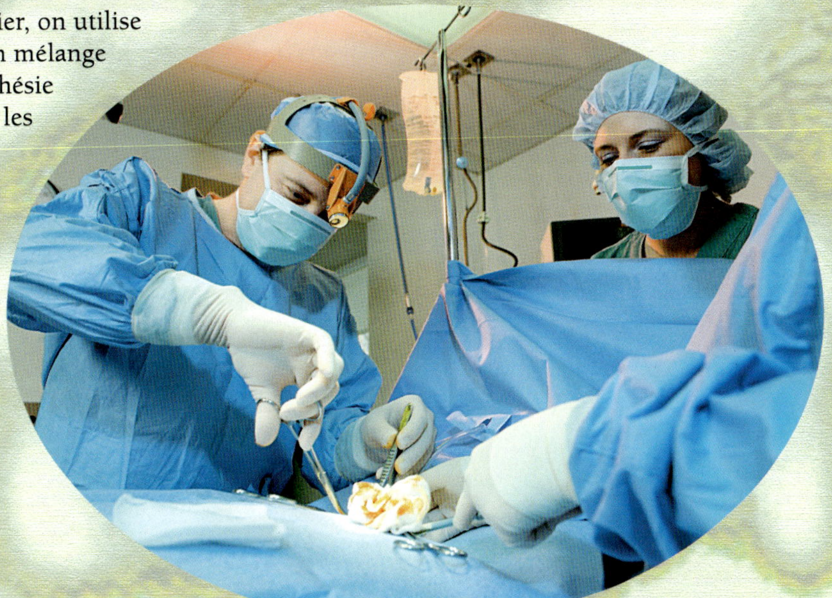

Dates clés

- 1800 Humphrey Davy déclare que l'oxyde nitreux peut conduire à l'état d'inconscience.
- 1831 Découverte du chloroforme.
- 1844 Horace Wells anesthésie un patient avec de l'oxyde nitreux.
- 1846 William Morton anesthésie un patient avec de l'éther.
- 1847 Ignac Semmelweis oblige son personnel à se laver les mains.
- 1865 Joseph Lister utilise son pulvérisateur de vapeur de phénol.
- 1884 La cocaïne sert d'anesthésiant et d'analgésique local.
- 1886 La chirurgie aseptique.

Les charlatans

▲ LA MARQUE KOLA
Cette affiche fait la promotion d'un stimulant contenant de la cocaïne. Certains remèdes étaient inoffensifs. D'autres, comme la marque Kola, étaient constitués d'ingrédients dangereux et créant une accoutumance.

Il nous est facile de considérer les médecins du passé comme des charlatans qui escroquaient leurs patients en leur vendant de faux médicaments. C'était probablement le cas pour certains d'entre eux, mais leurs pratiques étranges sont à replacer dans le contexte des connaissances scientifiques de l'époque. Il aurait, par exemple, été impossible de convaincre Hippocrate ou Galien de l'existence des bactéries, parce qu'on ne peut les voir qu'à travers un microscope. La plupart des pratiques médicales se révélaient impuissantes à soigner la maladie.

▶ DES REMÈDES MIRACLES
Tous les moyens étaient bons pour attirer l'attention sur la marchandise présentée par les charlatans. Certains portaient des vêtements accrocheurs et tous haranguaient la foule de leurs boniments.

Les médecins étaient contraints de prendre des mesures désespérées pour soigner leurs patients. Parfois, les gens guérissaient naturellement ; mais quand le traitement d'un médecin avait des effets, il était considéré comme miraculeux.

La prière et l'utilisation de reliques sacrées sont peut-être des remèdes de charlatans, mais ces pratiques sont utilisées de nos jours, tout comme l'imposition des mains et d'autres formes de thérapie basées sur le spirituel.

En Grande-Bretagne, la médecine miracle connut un essor considérable au XVIIIe siècle. Des médicaments exotiques étaient vendus au coin des rues et dans les foires. Au XIXe siècle, la population prit conscience que des escrocs exploitaient les malades en leur vendant des médicaments inefficaces. Des associations médicales virent le jour ; elles écartaient les escrocs et régulaient les pratiques des médecins membres.

FAUX ESPOIRS

À mesure que la médecine progressait, des traitements prescrits par de respectables médecins furent abandonnés, car considérés comme de l'escroquerie. Par exemple, les cures thermales très en vogue en Europe occidentale vers 1900 sont aujourd'hui tombées en désuétude, et de nombreux médecins ne croient pas à leurs vertus. Elles restent cependant très populaires en Europe de l'Est.

◀ CORSET ÉLECTRIQUE
Aux XVIIIe et XIXe siècles, on attribuait des pouvoirs curatifs à l'électricité. C'est ainsi qu'on faisait passer des courants électriques dans diverses parties du corps pour soigner tous types de maux.

▼ BAINS DE BOUE
Les bains de boue chaude sont une pratique largement répandue pour soigner des maladies comme l'arthrite, notamment en Europe de l'Est.

▲ FRANZ MESMER
Le médecin allemand Franz Mesmer a fondé la théorie du magnétisme animal. En 1778, ses expériences sur le baquet, autour duquel se groupaient ses malades, le rendirent célèbre. Mesmer finit par être accusé d'escroquerie.

◀ LES PILULES MORISON
Au début du XIXe siècle, les pilules Morison connurent un immense succès commercial dans toute l'Europe et les États-Unis. Elles étaient censées soigner toutes sortes de maladies. En réalité, c'était un mélange de laxatifs puissants. Cette illustration de l'époque rit des gens qui croyaient à ces remèdes miracles. Elle sous-entend que l'homme a avalé tellement de pilules Morison qu'elles ont pris racine dans son estomac et que de l'herbe a germé sur sa peau.

Peu à peu, des lois empêchant la vente de produits miracles furent édictées. Le remède miracle de Lydia Pinkham, inventé en 1873, était très populaire, peut-être parce qu'il contenait de l'alcool. Il fut vendu pour soigner tous types de maux.

Aux États-Unis, les charlatans commercialisaient des traitements contre le cancer à des prix prohibitifs. Les cancéreux désespérés étaient prêts à payer n'importe quel prix pour guérir. De telles pratiques sont encore d'actualité. Depuis 1970, beaucoup de malades souffrant de cancers graves se sont rendus au Mexique pour y acheter un prétendu médicament, appelé laetrile, qui en réalité est toxique.
Des commerçants peu scrupuleux vendent aujourd'hui des pilules douteuses aux gens contaminés par le virus du sida.

◀ FRANZ GALL
Le médecin allemand Franz Gall inventa le concept de phrénologie. Il s'agissait d'une forme de diagnostic basé sur l'examen du crâne. Gall affirmait que la forme du crâne révélait les fonctions intellectuelles. Il « lisait » le crâne en palpant les bosses. La phrénologie survécut pendant de nombreuses années, mais est aujourd'hui complètement abandonnée.

▼ LA PHRÉNOLOGIE
On a tracé sur cette tête de porcelaine les régions identifiées par Franz Gall. Chaque zone est censée traduire un aspect de la personnalité ou du comportement de la personne.

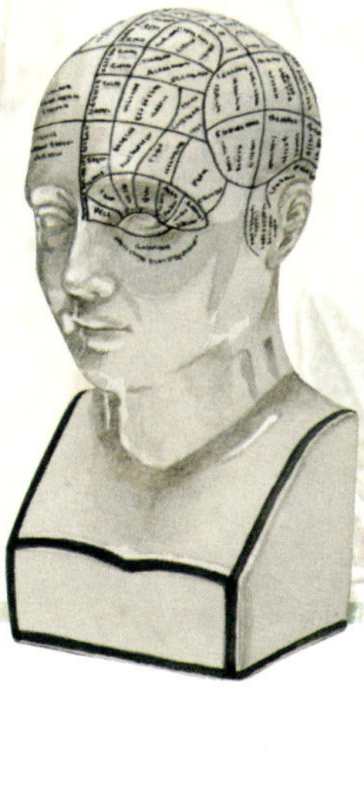

Dates clés

- 1775 Franz Mesmer invente sa théorie du magnétisme animal.
- 1780 James Graham ouvre son Temple de la Santé à Londres.
- 1810 Franz Gall développe son concept de la phrénologie.
- 1970 Commercialisation du laetrile comme traitement contre le cancer.
- 1991 La Société américaine contre le Cancer déclare le laetrile toxique, mais celui-ci demeure en vente, notamment sur l'Internet.

La santé publique

▲ LE CHOLÉRA
Cette peinture du début du XIXe siècle représente le choléra sous la forme d'un spectre fauchant ses victimes. Plus de 7 000 Londoniens moururent d'une épidémie de choléra en 1832.

La santé publique n'est pas une idée nouvelle. Les Romains comprirent l'utilité d'un approvisionnement en eau potable et érigèrent de longs aqueducs pour conduire l'eau dans le centre des grandes villes, avec des fontaines et des bains publics. Ils construisirent également des réseaux d'égouts pour évacuer les eaux usées de leurs villes.

Les écrits de Chine et d'Inde anciennes préconisaient alimentation équilibrée et hygiène rigoureuse pour se maintenir en bonne santé. Mais ces conseils furent oubliés dans l'Europe médiévale. L'Église n'encourageait pas la toilette, considérant que se laver était un plaisir corporel. La notion d'hygiène n'existait pas. On jetait les eaux usées et les ordures directement dans la rue. Les épidémies de peste, de lèpre, de tuberculose, de typhoïde et de choléra qui ravagèrent l'Europe à cette époque ne sont pas une coïncidence. Les gens pensaient que ces maladies se propageaient par des miasmes, des odeurs dangereuses de matières putrides. Cette croyance encouragea probablement l'établissement de décharges. La théorie de l'infection par les miasmes perdura jusqu'au XIXe siècle, jusqu'à ce que l'origine bactérienne des maladies soit finalement prouvée.

Pendant des siècles, les eaux de la Tamise avaient servi d'égouts et d'approvisionnement en eau potable. Un fonctionnaire, nommé John Chadwick, publia en 1842 un rapport qui faisait état des causes probables de maladies dans les quartiers les plus pauvres de Londres et proposait des solutions pratiques telles que l'approvisionnement des maisons en eau courante potable et des systèmes d'évacuation des eaux usées.

Peu de temps après l'établissement de ce rapport, lors d'une terrible épidémie de choléra en 1854, la preuve fut faite des risques provenant de l'eau contaminée. John Snow, un médecin londonien, remarqua que de nombreux cas de choléra provenaient d'une petite zone non loin de Broad Street. L'enquête montra que tous les habitants tiraient leur eau de la même pompe publique. Snow enleva le bras de la pompe, et l'épidémie fut enrayée en quelques jours. Malgré cet épisode, la profession médicale mit quelques années à reconnaître que le choléra n'était pas transmis par un air vicié, mais par la consommation d'eau contaminée par les égouts.

DES SOLUTIONS HYGIÉNIQUES

Les toilettes à chasse et l'eau courante potable dans les maisons restèrent des exceptions jusqu'au XIXe siècle. À la fin du XIXe siècle, les autorités publiques commencèrent à démolir les quartiers insalubres pour les remplacer par des habitations plus saines. Au début du XXe siècle, la santé des enfants s'améliora. L'école nourrissait les plus démunis et des visites médicales permettaient de détecter rapidement les maladies.

▸ LES EAUX USÉES
Le médecin britannique John Snow enraya l'épidémie de choléra de Londres en 1854. Il préconisa ensuite des améliorations dans le système des égouts.

▸ LES TOILETTES
Les toilettes à chasse d'eau, comme celles-ci datant de 1880, étaient un grand progrès dans le domaine de la santé publique. Les premières toilettes étaient souvent décorées avec raffinement.

▲ UN ÉVIER AMÉRICAIN (1888)
La cuisine du XIXe siècle n'était pas toujours très hygiénique. L'eau courante chaude était un luxe rare. La propreté dépendait du nombre de serviteurs qui frottaient les plans de travail et les sols qui étaient souvent des nids à microbes.

▶ L'HYGIÈNE DANS LES VILLES
Au XIXᵉ siècle, les pauvres vivaient dans des conditions misérables. Ils s'entassaient dans des maisons sans sanitaires. De telles conditions de vie étaient un terrain idéal pour le développement des maladies.

▼ LES ÉGOUTS
Les épidémies répétées finirent par conduire à la construction de réseaux d'égouts comme celui-ci, creusé à Londres en 1862. Les gros collecteurs aboutissaient à des déversoirs, beaucoup plus loin, sur la Tamise.

▲ LE ROYAL VICTORIA HOSPITAL, À MONTRÉAL
De nombreux hôpitaux comme celui-ci furent construits au XIXᵉ siècle. Cependant, comme il existait peu de traitements médicaux efficaces, beaucoup de patients entraient à l'hôpital pour y mourir.

Dates clés

- 312 av. J.-C. Les Étrusques construisent le premier aqueduc.
- 300 apr. J.-C. Des toilettes à deux places en forme de temple sont en usage en Grèce.
- v. 1590 John Harrington invente des toilettes à chasse d'eau.
- 1770 - 1915 Développement des toilettes modernes.
- 1854 John Snow montre que l'eau polluée est la cause du choléra.
- v. 1880 La plupart des grandes villes anglaises possèdent des équipements de traitements des eaux usées, conformément à la Loi sur la Santé publique de 1875.

Les micro-organismes

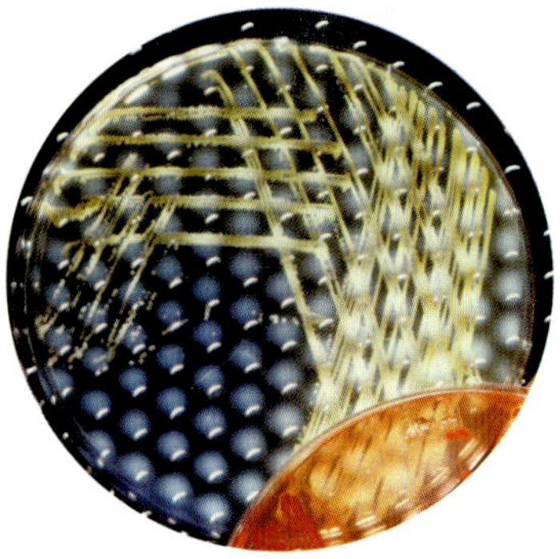

▲ LES CULTURES DE BACTÉRIES
Les chercheurs cultivent des bactéries sur de la gélose dans des boîtes de Petri, boîtes de verre ou de plastique, de forme cylindrique très aplatie.

À L'ÉPOQUE DE LA Renaissance, la population supposait que la maladie se transmettait au contact d'une personne contaminée, mais personne ne savait pourquoi. Au début du XVIIIe siècle, le scientifique hollandais Antonie Van Leeuwenhoek décrivit de minuscules structures qu'il observa au microscope en examinant des liquides organiques.

Deux cents ans plus tard, le scientifique français Louis Pasteur prouva que les microbes sont à l'origine des maladies infectieuses. Il démontra tout d'abord qu'ils faisaient tourner le lait et fermenter le vin. Il découvrit également que la chaleur détruisait ces microbes. Cette technique, appelée pasteurisation, est encore employée de nos jours pour conserver le lait. Pasteur démontra aussi que la maladie charbonneuse des moutons est due à une bactérie. En 1879, il découvrit le principe des vaccinations préventives et mit au point les vaccins contre le charbon et la rage.

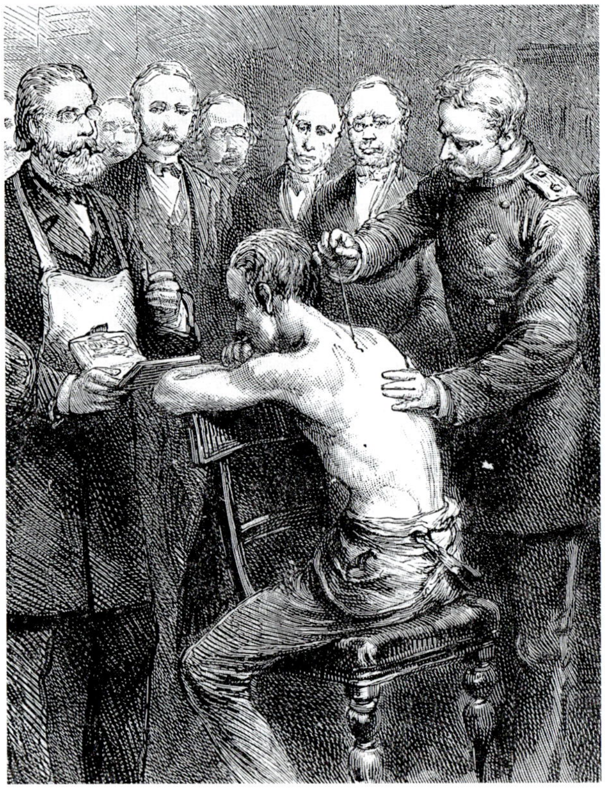

Cependant, il ne réussit pas à identifier l'organisme responsable de la rage, car il s'agit d'un virus visible seulement à l'aide d'un microscope électronique puissant.

Koch, un médecin allemand de la même époque, établit les règles pour prouver

◀ ROBERT KOCH
La réputation de Koch est liée à sa victoire sur la diphtérie. Il examine ici un patient atteint de tuberculose. Koch réussit à identifier la bactérie responsable de la tuberculose, mais il ne parvint pas à mettre au point un vaccin.

SUR LA PISTE

La colonisation de régions chaudes mit les Européens en contact avec des maladies tropicales contre lesquelles ils n'avaient pas d'immunité naturelle. Le paludisme, la fièvre jaune et d'autres maladies tropicales véhiculées par les piqûres d'insectes provoquaient de longues maladies et parfois la mort. Ce n'est qu'en 1897 que l'on réalisa qu'une piqûre de moustique pouvait transmettre le paludisme. En quelques années, les médecins découvrirent que les piqûres d'insectes étaient aussi à l'origine de la maladie du sommeil, de la peste et de la fièvre jaune.

▶ LE PREMIER MICROSCOPE
Van Leeuwenhoek était un spécialiste de la fabrication des lentilles. Il fabriqua le premier microscope en 1671. Il conserva jalousement sa technique de fabrication des lentilles.

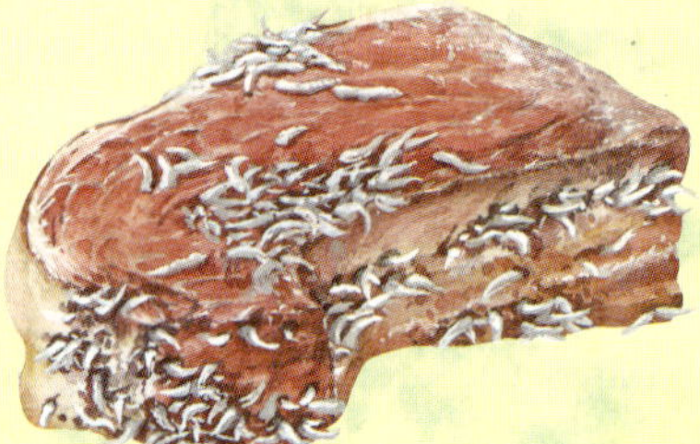

▲ LES ASTICOTS
En 1699, Francesco Redi montra que les asticots n'apparaissaient pas sur la viande que l'on avait protégée des mouches. Auparavant, les gens pensaient que les asticots apparaissaient spontanément sur les matières qui pourrissaient.

▼ RUDOLF VIRCHOW
Virchow démontra que la maladie n'apparaissait pas spontanément à partir d'humeurs, mais que « toutes les cellules proviennent de cellules », en d'autres termes, que les bactéries produisent de nouvelles bactéries.

qu'un microbe particulier est à l'origine de chaque maladie infectieuse. Ces règles sont encore suivies aujourd'hui. Le microbe devait être mis en évidence dans des cultures biologiques ou sur des animaux de laboratoire. On devait aussi le trouver au moment où la maladie était transmise à un autre animal. Ces règles permirent à Koch de prouver qu'une bactérie est la cause de la tuberculose. Il voyagea en Égypte et en Inde pour étudier le choléra et démontra que cette maladie est aussi causée par une bactérie qui vit dans l'intestin humain et se transmet par les eaux polluées. En 1883, il avait prouvé scientifiquement ce que John Snow avait découvert auparavant sur les causes du choléra. Koch découvrit aussi les micro-organismes responsables de la diphtérie, de la typhoïde, de la lèpre et de nombreuses autres infections.

◄ LOUIS PASTEUR
Les expériences de Pasteur démontrèrent que les microbes étaient responsables de la fermentation et des maladies infectieuses.

▼ UNE EXPÉRIENCE
Pasteur prouva par cette expérience l'existence des microbes. Il chauffa un bouillon de culture dans une fiole. Ce procédé tua les microbes. Il scella la fiole pour empêcher d'autres microbes de rentrer. Le bouillon ne se gâta pas jusqu'à ce qu'il ouvre la fiole et permette aux germes de l'air de pénétrer dans le récipient.

▼ LE MOUSTIQUE
En 1897, Ronald Ross découvrit des parasites du paludisme dans un moustique anophèle. Ceci acheva de prouver la relation entre ces insectes et la maladie mortelle.

▲ LE VIRUS VIH
La découverte du virus VIH en 1983 expliqua la mystérieuse apparition du SIDA. Le virus VIH attaque et affaiblit le système immunitaire. Le corps ne peut alors se défendre contre les attaques des autres organismes.

Dates clés

- 1673 Antonie Van Leeuwenhoek observa au microscope des formes de vie minuscules.
- 1858 R. Virchow déclare : « toute cellule provient de cellules ».
- 1878 Louis Pasteur présente sa théorie des germes infectieux à l'Académie de médecine.
- 1882 Robert Koch isole le bacille de la tuberculose.
- 1883 Robert Koch isole la bactérie du choléra.
- 1897 Ronald Ross explique le rôle du moustique dans le paludisme.
- 1983 Découverte du virus VIH.

L'immunisation

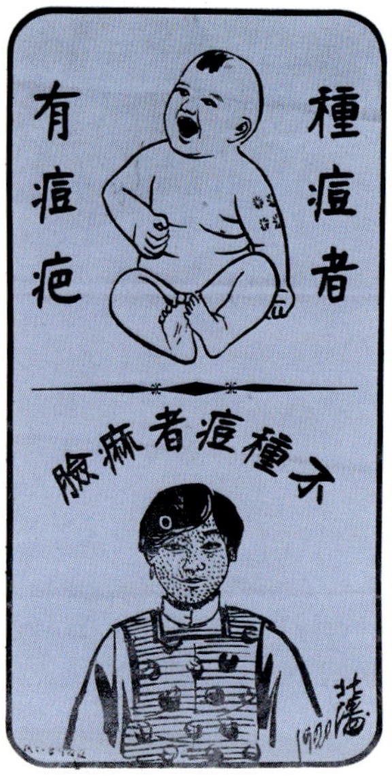

▲ LA FIN DE LA VARIOLE
On réussit à éradiquer la variole en lançant une très grande campagne de vaccination expliquant la nécessité de faire vacciner les gens. Cet exemple vient de Chine.

L'HISTOIRE DE LA vaccination est aussi en grande partie celle de la variole. Cette maladie virale tua ou défigura des gens dans le monde entier. Dans les colonies américaines, elle éradiqua les civilisations inca et aztèque.

En 1717, Lady Mary Wortley Montagu, l'épouse de l'ambassadeur de Grande-Bretagne à Constantinople, rapporta que les Turcs utilisaient une méthode traditionnelle pour se prémunir contre la variole. Ils prélevaient du pus sur des boutons de variole et grattaient la peau d'une autre personne pour l'y faire pénétrer. Ce procédé produisait une légère infection qui ne laissait pas de cicatrice. Le plus important était que la personne semblait alors immunisée contre des infections ultérieures. Lady Montagu eut suffisamment confiance dans cette méthode pour l'essayer sur son propre enfant. Ce procédé fut bientôt en usage dans toute l'Europe.

L'étape suivante se fit avec le médecin britannique Edward Jenner qui avait entendu dire que les vachères qui avaient contracté la vaccine de leurs vaches semblaient résistantes à la variole. La vaccine n'était pas une maladie grave. En 1796, Jenner inocula le virus de la vaccine à un jeune garçon. Six semaines plus tard, il le mit en contact avec le virus de la variole, mais le garçon ne développa pas la maladie. Cette technique se généralisa et dans les années 1970, la variole avait complètement disparu.

◀ EDWARD JENNER
Cette statue commémore la première vaccination expérimentale de Jenner sur James Phelps avec la vaccine. Elle protégea le garçon contre la variole.

LA PRÉVENTION

Les virus, tels celui de la grippe ou le VIH, changent très rapidement de forme et modifient l'organisation des protéines de leur surface. L'organisme a alors du mal à construire une immunité efficace, car la maladie évolue sans arrêt. D'autres maladies, comme la polio ou la rougeole, restent sensiblement stables. La vaccination offre donc au corps une immunité forte et permanente.

▶ LE VACCIN CONTRE LA RAGE
Louis Pasteur produisit le vaccin contre la rage en cultivant le virus dans des cerveaux de lapins. Il fallait ensuite faire sécher la cervelle et la moelle épinière pendant deux semaines, ce qui affaiblissait suffisamment le virus pour qu'il puisse être injecté chez l'homme.

▲ VICTIME DE LA POLIO
En 1921, Franklin Roosevelt attrapa la poliomyélite à l'âge de 40 ans. Elle le laissa infirme des jambes, ce qui ne l'empêcha pas de devenir président des États-Unis.

▸ LA VACCINE
Une fois que les gens eurent pris connaissance de l'importance de la découverte de Jenner, ils se précipitèrent pour se faire inoculer la vaccine afin d'être protégés contre la variole. Ce dessin humoristique de l'époque montre la peur que provoquait cette injection de la vaccine de la vache.

Le corps s'immunise en créant ses propres défenses contre l'agression d'un microbe, que ce soit une bactérie, un virus ou un parasite. Le système immunitaire utilise les globules blancs du sang qui reconnaissent les cellules de notre corps. Lorsqu'ils rencontrent des microbes venus de l'extérieur, ils les attaquent, car ils ne les reconnaissent pas. Ils produisent des substances appelées anticorps qui détruisent les microbes, dont les restes sont ensuite digérés par d'autres globules blancs. C'est ainsi que disparaît l'infection. Les globules blancs gardent en mémoire le type d'anticorps utilisé pour éliminer un microbe. Si ce type de microbe pénètre à nouveau dans l'organisme, les globules blancs produisent alors l'anticorps approprié avec une telle rapidité que l'infection ne peut se développer.

La vaccination crée une immunisation selon le même processus. Le vaccin contient des microbes atténués ou tués qui, en provoquant une version sans danger d'une maladie, permettent à l'organisme de fabriquer les anticorps qui lui serviront de protection s'il est exposé plus tard aux formes dangereuses du microbe, du moins s'il s'agit exactement du même microbe que celui utilisé dans le vaccin.

▸ SERINGUE À USAGE UNIQUE
Les seringues modernes sont jetables, ce qui diminue le risque d'infection.

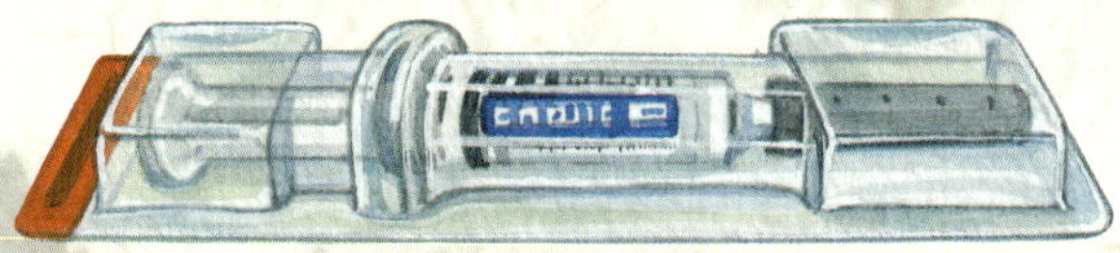

▸ PISTOLET À VACCIN
Pour les programmes de vaccination de masse, on utilise parfois un pistolet. Il injecte le vaccin sous la peau à très haute pression sans avoir recours à une aiguille. Ces pistolets sont aujourd'hui remplacés par les seringues jetables à dose unique.

▾ CAMPAGNE DE VACCINATION
La vaccination est fondamentale dans les pays en voie de développement où l'accès à la santé est limité. Les ONG et les gouvernements organisent des programmes de vaccination.

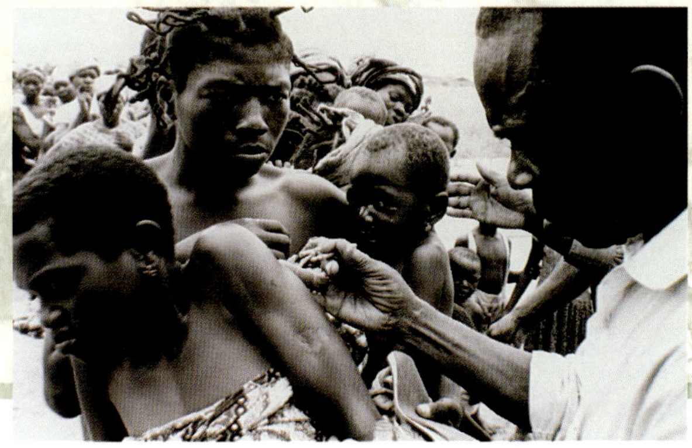

Dates clés

- 1717 Lady Wortley Montagu fait état de la méthode traditionnelle turque d'inoculation pour se prémunir contre la variole.
- 1796 Edward Jenner inocule la vaccine chez un jeune garçon et démontre qu'il est dorénavant immunisé contre la variole.
- 1885 Pasteur teste son vaccin contre la rage.
- 1955 Jonas Salk introduit le vaccin contre la polio.
- 1974 La variole est éradiquée.

Tueurs de microbes

Howard Florey

▲ ▼ LES PRIMÉS
Howard Florey et Ernst Chain découvrirent un moyen de produire la pénicilline en grande quantité et reçurent le prix Nobel.

Ernst Chain

ALORS QUE PAR LA VACCINATION on pouvait se protéger contre de nombreuses maladies, on savait traiter très peu d'infections. La première fut le paludisme qu'on soignait avec de la quinine, extraite de l'écorce d'un arbre d'Amérique du Sud, le quinquina. Le mercure était utilisé comme remède contre la syphilis, mais il se révéla très toxique par la suite. Un nouveau médicament synthétique, le Salvarsan, fut élaboré par Paul Ehrlich en 1910. Puis, en 1932, le scientifique Gerhard Domagk créa le Prontosil, capable d'attaquer le streptocoque, une bactérie à l'origine de multiples infections, comme celle de la méningite.

À partir du Prontosil, on fabriqua une série de médicaments antibactériens, les sulfamides qui empêchent la multiplication des bactéries. Ainsi les défenses immunitaires du corps disposent de suffisamment de temps pour détruire les bactéries. Cependant, les sulfamides n'étaient pas toujours efficaces et avaient des effets secondaires désagréables. On continua donc à rechercher de nouveaux médicaments.

Alexander Fleming, un médecin britannique, travaillait sur les staphylocoques, des bactéries à l'origine des furoncles, et les cultivait sur des lamelles

▼ ALEXANDER FLEMING
Fleming découvrit par hasard la pénicilline, mais il ne réalisa pas immédiatement l'importance de sa découverte. Il fallut attendre encore dix ans pour que Florey et Chain trouvent un moyen de la produire en grande quantité.

DES MÉDICAMENTS QUI SAUVENT LA VIE

Les antibiotiques sont utilisés pour lutter contre toutes sortes d'infections. On en administre également au bétail et à la volaille pour prévenir les maladies et pour accélérer leur croissance. Cependant, à force d'être exposées aux antibiotiques, certaines bactéries sont devenues résistantes. Les médecins évitent d'en prescrire pour des infections mineures afin que les bactéries ne s'y habituent pas.

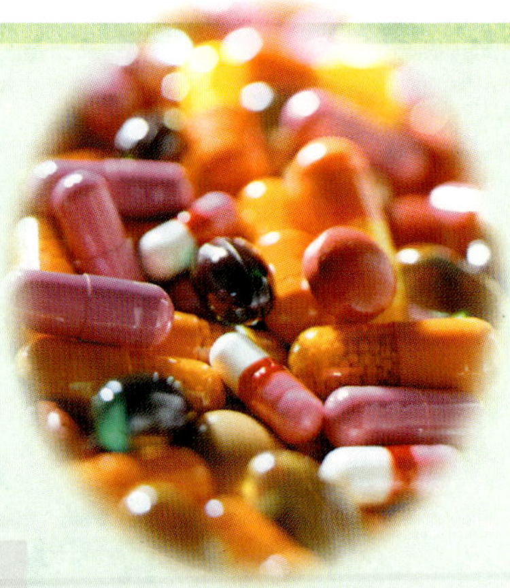

◄ LES ANTIBIOTIQUES
La plupart des antibiotiques sont administrés sous forme de gélules remplies de poudre que l'on avale. Cependant, certains sont injectés.

◄ LA 2E GUERRE
Lorsque la guerre éclata, les gouvernements prévoyèrent de grands risques d'infections dues au nombre de soldats blessés. Ils investirent alors beaucoup pour produire suffisamment de pénicilline.

▼ ATTAQUES ANTIBIOTIQUES
Les antibiotiques s'attaquent à la membrane cellulaire d'une bactérie.

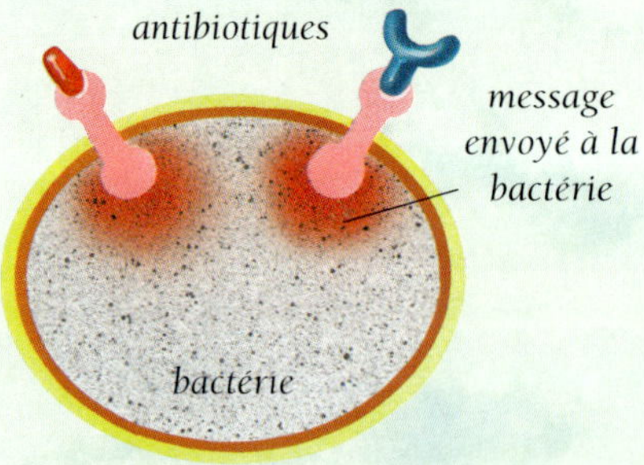

▸ PAUL EHRLICH
Au début du XXᵉ siècle, Ehrlich produisit et testa plus de 600 composés de l'arsenic pour trouver un remède contre la syphilis. L'une de ces substances, le Salvarsan, s'avéra très efficace. C'était le premier médicament à avoir un effet antibactérien.

de gélose. En 1928, alors qu'il rentrait de vacances, il remarqua que de la moisissure se développait sur l'une des lamelles qu'il avait jetées, et que les colonies de staphylocoques autour de la moisissure étaient mortes. Fleming identifia cette moisissure et découvrit qu'elle produisait un antibiotique, la pénicilline. Il ne prit pas conscience immédiatement de l'importance de la pénicilline mais, dix ans plus tard, des chercheurs d'Oxford exploitèrent le rapport de Fleming. Ils effectuèrent de nombreuses expériences qui mirent en lumière la remarquable efficacité de la pénicilline contre les bactéries.

Le nouveau médicament connut un tel succès que la demande fut massive et immédiate. Deux scientifiques, Howard Florey et Ernst Chain mirent au point des méthodes de production industrielle de la pénicilline. Ce médicament servit à traiter les blessures de guerre durant la Deuxième Guerre mondiale. L'unique problème était qu'il ne tuait pas tous les types de bactéries.

Aujourd'hui, des recherches ont lieu dans le monde entier, depuis le fond des océans jusqu'aux forêts tropicales, dans le but de trouver des organismes naturels capables de produire de nouveaux antibiotiques. Lorsque des chercheurs découvrent un antibiotique naturel, ils essaient d'en identifier les molécules actives afin de les recréer artificiellement. La plupart des antibiotiques empêchent les bactéries de construire de bonnes membranes cellulaires lorsqu'elles se divisent. Sans membrane complète, les bactéries meurent. En général, les antibiotiques n'abîment pas les cellules humaines parce qu'elles n'ont pas de membrane rigide.

▴ SELMAN WAKSMAN
Ce scientifique américain inventa le mot « antibiotique » en 1941. Après la découverte de la pénicilline, il rechercha d'autres antibiotiques dans les microbes du sol. En 1943, il découvrit la streptomycine, le premier remède contre la tuberculose.

▾ LES ALIMENTS ET LES ANTIBIOTIQUES
On ajoute souvent des antibiotiques dans la nourriture des animaux pour les faire grossir et les empêcher de tomber malades. Cependant, cette pratique s'est révélée un véritable désastre, car elle a favorisé l'apparition de bactéries résistantes aux effets des antibiotiques. Ainsi, certains sont aujourd'hui presque inutiles.

Dates clés

- 1910 Paul Ehrlich découvre le Salvarsan.
- 1928 Alexander Fleming découvre la pénicilline.
- 1935 Gerhard Domagk développe le Prontosil.
- 1939 H. Florey et E. Chain mettent au point la production industrielle de la pénicilline.
- 1943 Selman Waksman découvre la streptomycine, le premier remède efficace contre la tuberculose.
- 1945 Fleming, Florey et Chain reçoivent ensemble le prix Nobel pour la fabrication de la pénicilline.

Les pionnières de la médecine

Les femmes ont toujours joué un rôle en médecine, bien qu'elles aient souvent été écartées par les hommes jusque dans les années 1950. L'accouchement était un événement dont les hommes étaient habituellement exclus. Les sages-femmes surveillaient les grossesses et se transmettaient leur savoir de mère en fille, ce qui explique qu'il reste peu de traces écrites de leur travail. Les médecins reconnaissaient rarement l'importance des sages-femmes.

Il y eut au Moyen Âge quelques célèbres guérisseuses. L'une d'entre elles, Trotula, exerçait à Salerne dans les années 1000. Elle écrivit un livre intitulé *Les souffrances des femmes* qui fut utilisé comme texte médical pendant les sept siècles qui suivirent.

Hildegarde, une guérisseuse allemande, vécut à peu près au même moment que Trotula. Elle combina les

▲ FLORENCE NIGHTINGALE
Les soldats reconnaissants pendant la guerre de Crimée surnommèrent Florence Nightingale « la Dame à la lampe ». Dans les années 1850, elle fut pionnière dans le domaine de l'hygiène infirmière.

▶ L'HÔPITAL DE SCUTARI
Florence Nightingale et son équipe d'infirmières apportèrent des techniques de soins très strictes. Avant leur arrivée, l'hôpital de terrain de Scutari, en Turquie, connaissait une mortalité très élevée. De retour en Angleterre, elle se servit de son expérience pour améliorer les soins.

LE COMBAT DES FEMMES

La pratique de la médecine était fermée aux femmes. L'Église, mais aussi les hommes médecins s'y opposaient. C'est seulement en 1849 qu'Elizabeth Blackwell obtint son diplôme de médecin. Au début du XXᵉ siècle, les suffragettes se battirent pour les droits des femmes. Marie Stopes en Grande-Bretagne et Margaret Sanger aux États-Unis luttèrent pour le contrôle des naissances. Ceci libéra les femmes de leur charge de familles nombreuses et améliora leur santé et celle des enfants.

◀ SE DÉGUISER
Mary Walker était chirurgienne pendant la guerre de Sécession aux États-Unis (1861-65). Pour se soustraire à la méfiance des hommes, elle se déguisa en homme.

▲ ELIZABETH BLACKWELL
Beaucoup d'écoles de médecine refusèrent Elizabeth Blackwell, avant qu'elle finisse par obtenir son diplôme de médecin aux États-Unis en 1849. L'idée d'une femme médecin scandalisait la profession médicale.

▶ MARIE CURIE
Les femmes étaient exclues de tous les domaines scientifiques. Marie Curie fit exception à la règle. Elle découvrit le radium avec son mari Pierre en 1898. Grâce à leurs recherches sur la radioactivité, un traitement contre le cancer fut découvert.

▶ INFIRMIÈRES MILITAIRES
Pendant la Deuxième Guerre mondiale, les forces armées possédaient un système performant pour soigner les blessés. Des hôpitaux de terrain mobiles et des services d'ambulances furent établis. Le personnel était constitué de femmes, jugées trop délicates pour les devoirs militaires.

textes religieux et médicaux avec l'histoire naturelle. Elle donna en particulier des descriptions détaillées de remèdes à base de plantes médicinales. Elle était respectée par les rois et les papes.

Dans les hôpitaux du Moyen Âge et de la Renaissance, la plupart des soins étaient administrés par des religieuses rattachées à divers ordres. Lorsque de grands hôpitaux furent construits au XIXe siècle, le rôle des religieuses diminua. Elles furent remplacées par des femmes de la classe ouvrière qui n'avaient reçu aucune formation, ce qui explique le niveau très bas des soins de l'époque.

La première école laïque d'infirmières fut construite en Allemagne en 1842. Les étudiantes recevaient un enseignement sur trois ans. Florence Nightingale y suivit brièvement des cours en 1851. Elle continua son cursus à Paris et devint infirmière en chef au King's College Hospital. En 1854, elle fut envoyée auprès des troupes pendant la guerre de Crimée (1853-56). Les conditions de l'hôpital de terrain étaient déplorables, mais en améliorant l'hygiène, Florence Nightingale réduisit le taux de mortalité de 40 à 2 %. Après la guerre, elle ouvrit une école d'infirmières à l'hôpital St Thomas à Londres.

Il fallut longtemps, et bien des efforts de la part de nombreuses pionnières, pour faire évoluer l'attitude des hommes vis-à-vis des femmes dans la profession médicale. L'une de ces pionnières, le Dr Elizabeth Blackwell, avait suivi une formation à New York malgré l'opposition de ses condisciples. En 1869, elle revint en Angleterre et participa à la fondation d'une école de médecine pour femmes à Londres (London School of Medecine for Women). Malgré tout, la médecine demeura une profession dominée par les hommes jusque dans les années 1950.

▲ MARGARET SANGER
Margaret Sanger travaillait aux États-Unis comme infirmière dans les quartiers insalubres. Elle fut envoyée un mois en prison après avoir ouvert la première clinique pratiquant le contrôle des naissances en 1916.

▼ MARIE STOPES
En 1921, Marie Stopes ouvrit la première clinique britannique de contrôle des naissances. Elle offrait des consultations et des contraceptifs gratuits, et recommandait une planification familiale.

Dates clés

- 1849 Elisabeth Blackwell obtient son diplôme de médecin aux États-Unis.
- 1854 Florence Nightingale arrive à l'hôpital de terrain de Scutari.
- 1898 Marie Curie découvre la radioactivité du radium.
- 1911 Marie Curie reçoit un second prix Nobel pour son travail.
- 1916 Margaret Sanger ouvre la première clinique de contrôle des naissances aux États-Unis.
- 1921 Marie Stopes ouvre la première clinique de contrôle des naissances en Grande-Bretagne.

Reconstruire le corps

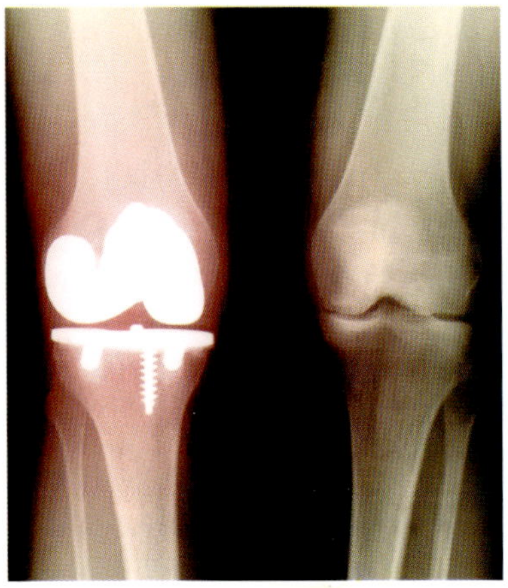

▲ ARTICULATIONS ARTIFICIELLES
Les articulations s'usent avec l'âge, souvent à cause de l'arthrose. Cette radiographie montre le remplacement d'une articulation du genou, faite en plastique et en métal. De nombreuses autres articulations peuvent être remplacées de la même manière.

Les prothèses sont des parties du corps artificielles. Elles existent depuis des millénaires, mais se sont considérablement améliorées au cours du XXe siècle. Les membres artificiels se sont allégés et ont un aspect plus naturel. Ils peuvent aujourd'hui être connectés au système nerveux et permettent donc les mêmes mouvements que les parties réelles du corps.

En cas de fracture d'un membre, l'os est maintenu dans la bonne position grâce à une attelle ou un plâtre jusqu'à ce qu'il se ressoude. Si l'os est sérieusement brisé, des plaques de métal vissées dessus lui donnent une meilleure tenue. L'os est parfois remplacé par une matière comme le corail. De nouvelles cellules osseuses se développent dans le corail et le remplacent par de l'os vivant.

Des valves du cœur endommagées par la maladie peuvent être remplacées par des valves mécaniques en plastique ou en métal. Un stimulateur cardiaque électronique est implanté dans le corps pour provoquer la contraction du cœur quand celle-ci ne s'effectue pas normalement.

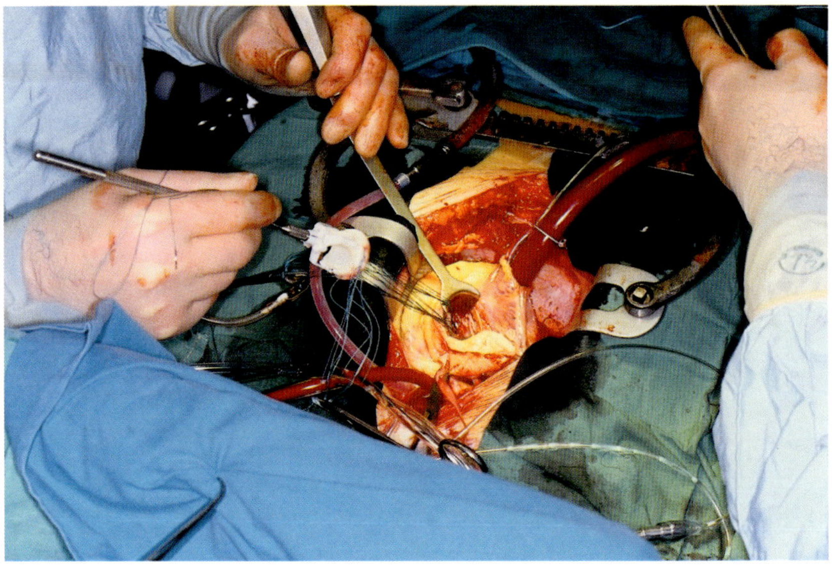

▶ TRANSPLANTATION CARDIAQUE
Remplacer le cœur nécessite une opération compliquée qui suppose d'avoir à sa disposition un cœur de rechange compatible avec les tissus du receveur. Il doit être prélevé sur un donneur mort dans un accident.

LES PREMIERS JOURS

Le premier exemple de prothèse était sans doute la branche d'arbre. Elle servait de simple béquille pour une personne qui s'était cassé la jambe. Avec l'apparition de la chirurgie, l'amputation des membres devint pratique courante, bien qu'entraînant la mort de nombreux patients. On fixait des membres et des mains de remplacement en bois aux survivants. Parfois, on mettait de simples crochets à la place des mains.

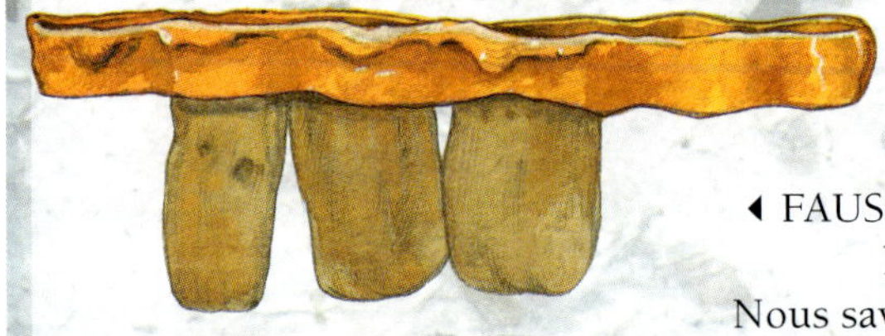

◀ FAUSSES DENTS ROMAINES
Nous savons que les fausses dents sont utilisées depuis l'Égypte antique. Les Romains fabriquaient des bridges en or qui supportaient de fausses dents de métal ou d'ivoire. Les dentistes romains connaissaient aussi diverses recettes pour garder les dents saines.

▲ GREFFE DU NEZ
Au XVIIIe siècle, les médecins occidentaux furent très étonnés de constater que les chirurgiens indiens pratiquaient des opérations de chirurgie plastique compliquées. Ce nez sectionné a été refait puis recouvert par une greffe de peau.

▼ JAMBE DE BOIS
Ce pirate malchanceux a perdu une jambe et une main. Il a pu continuer à vivre avec une jambe de bois et un crochet en guise de main. Les membres artificiels sont aujourd'hui plus esthétiques et plus confortables ; ils sont en plastique léger et articulés.

▲ VALVE CARDIAQUE ARTIFICIELLE
Des valves cardiaques qui fuient peuvent nuire à la santé ou entraîner la mort. C'est pourquoi il faut les remplacer par les substituts artificiels. Ce sont de simples valves en métal et en plastique, des matières qui ne pourront être attaquées par le système immunitaire.

Les greffes constituent un autre moyen de reconstruire le corps. Les premières tentatives eurent lieu au XVIIe siècle, mais ce n'est qu'au XIXe siècle qu'elles ne présentèrent plus de risques, car la connaissance des groupes sanguins était alors établie.

Les transplantations provenant d'une autre personne sont délicates parce que le système immunitaire attaque immédiatement tout organe étranger. Des médicaments très puissants sont requis pour empêcher le rejet. C'est pourquoi, dans le cas d'une transfusion sanguine, le groupe sanguin du donneur doit être compatible avec celui du receveur. Le second problème est de trouver des organes disponibles. Certains sont prélevés chez les personnes qui étaient en bonne santé avant de mourir dans des accidents. Mais il y a toujours une pénurie d'organes.

La recherche actuelle s'intéresse aux moyens de créer de nouveaux organes entiers à partir des propres tissus du patient, afin qu'ils ne soient pas rejetés. Une autre possibilité très controversée consisterait à utiliser les organes d'animaux, comme les porcs.

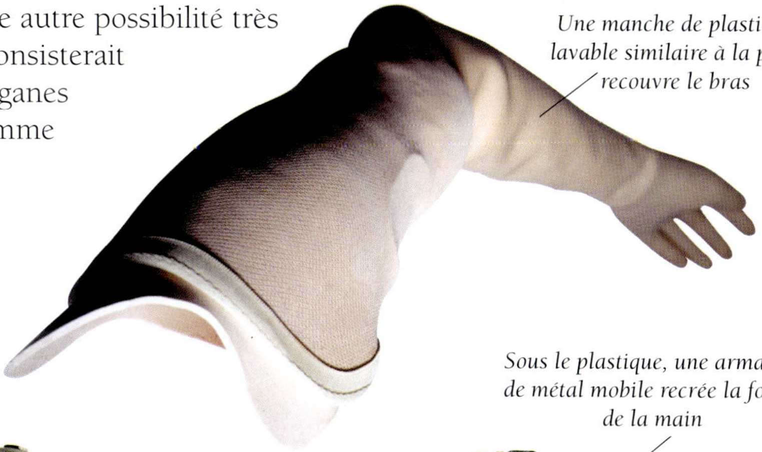

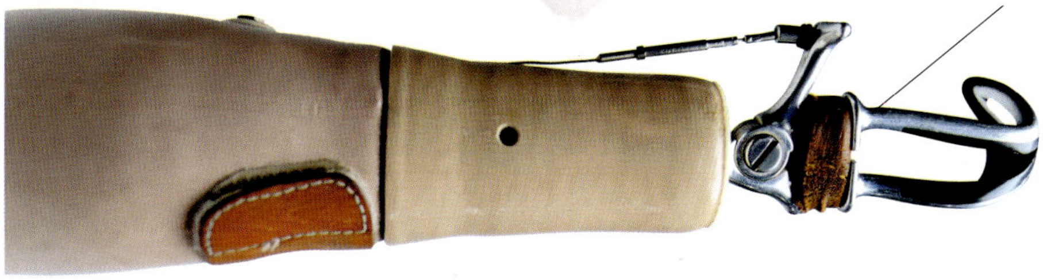

▶ PROTHÈSE DE BRAS
Des bras artificiels ne permettent que des mouvements limités. Des crochets ou des doigts sont reliés aux muscles restants. De nouvelles recherches se penchent sur la manière de rendre le mouvement plus naturel, en connectant la prothèse aux nerfs du bras.

▲ GROUPES SANGUINS
Karl Landsteiner identifia les groupes sanguins en 1901. Il les appela O, A, B, et AB. Il fut dorénavant possible de transfuser les patients avec le sang d'un donneur compatible avec le leur.

▶ REIN ARTIFICIEL
Les seuls traitements pour le dysfonctionnement des reins sont la transplantation ou la dialyse régulière par rein artificiel. La première tentative de dialyse eut lieu avec des chiens en 1914 et avec l'homme trente ans plus tard.

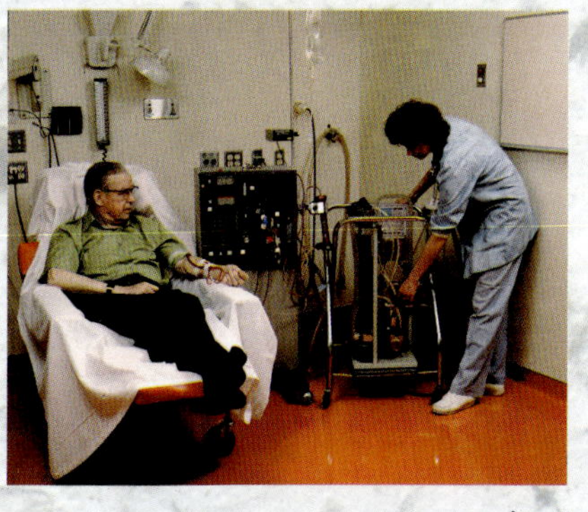

Charles Best

Frederick Banting

◀ TRAITEMENT DU DIABÈTE
En 1921, Charles Best et Frederick Banting sauvèrent la vie d'un chien diabétique avec de l'insuline prélevée dans le pancréas d'un autre animal. Ceci conduisit à l'utilisation actuelle de l'insuline produite artificiellement pour traiter les diabètes.

Dates clés

- 2500 av. J.-C. Les Égyptiens utilisent de fausses dents.
- 1901 Karl Landsteiner identifie les groupes sanguins.
- 1921 Banting et Best se servent de l'insuline pour traiter le diabète des chiens.
- 1950 Production de l'insuline synthétique.
- 1954 Succès de la première transplantation de rein.
- 1960 Installation du premier stimulateur cardiaque.
- 1963 Première greffe du poumon.
- 1964 Christiaan Barnard pratique la première transplantation cardiaque.

Soigner l'esprit

APRÈS AVOIR ÉTÉ NÉGLIGÉS pendant des siècles, les asiles psychiatriques se développèrent au XVe siècle. Leur principale fonction était de maintenir les aliénés à l'écart de la société. Les internés vivaient dans des conditions atroces. Beaucoup étaient enchaînés, et leur rendre visite constituait une forme d'attraction.

Il fallut attendre le XIXe siècle pour que la situation s'améliore. Philippe Pinel, un psychiatre parisien, fit cesser la pratique des chaînes dans les asiles où il travaillait. Un élève de Pinel, Jean Esquirol, mit en place des communautés où les patients vivaient en groupe avec leur médecin. Au lieu d'être traités comme des bêtes, ils étaient considérés comme des individus ayant besoin d'aide. Ce traitement améliorait parfois suffisamment leur état pour qu'ils puissent être réintégrés dans la société.

▲ CAMISOLE DE FORCE
On se servait de camisoles de force pour entraver les patients violents.

▶ L'ASILE DE FOUS
Les asiles psychiatriques étaient des lieux de souffrance. Les patients y étaient enchaînés et souvent battus.

LES FORMES DE THÉRAPIES MODERNES

La psychothérapie marqua un tournant face aux idées traditionnelles concernant la cause et le traitement de la maladie mentale. Les psychiatres commencèrent à s'intéresser aux problèmes émotionnels qui semblaient être à l'origine de la maladie, et à les explorer avec leurs patients afin de les éclairer sur leur état.

▲ UNE THÉRAPIE PAR L'ART
Les hôpitaux psychiatriques modernes encouragent les patients à peindre. Dans leurs peintures, ils expriment des émotions dont ils ne peuvent parler aux médecins.

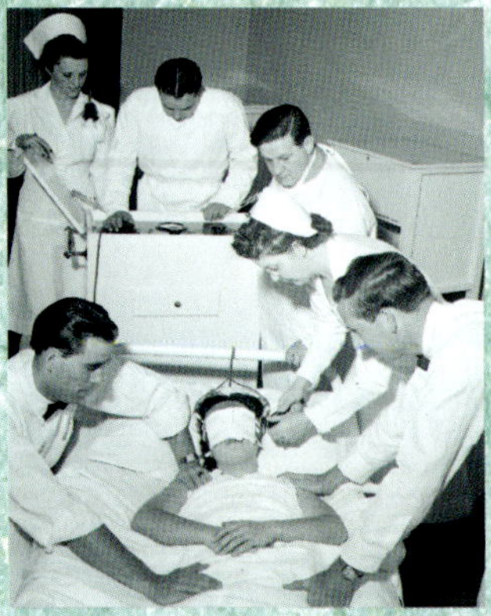

▶ LES ÉLECTROCHOCS
Les électrochocs furent beaucoup utilisés de 1950 à 1960 pour soigner les dépressions graves. Les médecins font passer un bref courant électrique dans le cerveau qui provoque une convulsion et soulage parfois la dépression. Cela peut aussi entraîner des pertes de mémoire.

▼ DANS UN FAUTEUIL
Lors d'un examen par un psychiatre, il est très important que le patient se sente détendu. C'est pourquoi les psychiatres proposent des fauteuils confortables ou même des divans aux patients.

Mais tous les traitements n'évoluèrent pas dans ce sens. Beaucoup de psychiatres continuèrent à enchaîner leurs patients, à les battre ou à leur faire subir des traitements de choc en les plongeant dans des bains d'eau froide. Cependant, les conditions de vie dans la plupart des asiles s'améliorèrent sensiblement.

Au milieu du XIXe siècle, Jean Martin Charcot, fonda l'école de neurologie de la Salpêtrière à Paris. À la fin du XIXe siècle, le médecin allemand Emil Kraepelin fit une classification des maladies mentales les plus graves et étudia plus particulièrement la schizophrénie.

▲ LIBÉRER LES MALADES MENTAUX
Philippe Pinel fut le premier médecin à mettre en place un traitement plus humain pour les malades mentaux. Il exigea que les chaînes et les entraves leur fussent ôtées dans les hôpitaux français où il travaillait.

À partir de 1880, Sigmund Freud développa la psychanalyse. Pour Freud, la personnalité se forme à partir du refoulement dans l'inconscient de situations vécues dans l'enfance. Carl Jung continua à développer les idées de Freud. Certaines méthodes de Freud ou de Jung, qui visent à la prise de conscience par le patient de situations refoulées, sont encore en usage aujourd'hui.

▶ SIGMUND FREUD
La grande innovation de Freud fut d'essayer de comprendre les causes de la maladie mentale. Il encouragea ses patients à parler de leurs expériences passées. Un tel procédé nécessite beaucoup de temps.

Au XXe siècle, l'usage des médicaments bouleversa la médecine psychiatrique. À partir du moment où l'on comprit que le cerveau subit des modifications chimiques, on commença à donner des médicaments aux malades afin de rétablir cette chimie du cerveau. Les médicaments entraînent cependant des effets secondaires, comme celui de l'accoutumance, et les médecins continuent à chercher de nouvelles solutions.

▲ QU'EST-CE QUE C'EST ?
Le psychiatre suisse Hermann Rorschach imagina son test de la tache d'encre en 1918. Il demandait au patient à quoi la tache lui faisait penser. Les réponses qu'il recevait l'aidaient à découvrir ce qui préoccupait le malade.

▼ LES TRAITEMENTS CHIMIQUES
Le Prozac est l'un des nouveaux médicaments destinés à rétablir l'équilibre chimique du cerveau. Les scientifiques recherchent des traitements qui permettraient de recouvrer une santé mentale normale tout en évitant les effets secondaires. On utilise des médicaments pour traiter les cas de dépression et de schizophrénie.

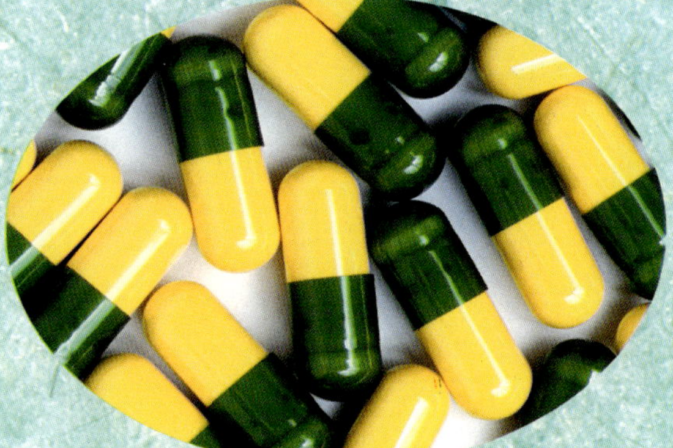

Dates clés

- 1793 Philippe Pinel libère les malades mentaux de leurs chaînes.
- 1856 - 1939 Vie de Sigmund Freud, père de la psychanalyse.
- 1943 La découverte accidentelle du LSD conduit à la fabrication de médicaments pour traiter des maladies telles que l'anxiété et la schizophrénie.
- 1950 - 60 On utilise largement les électrochocs pour soigner les dépressions graves.
- 1990 Le Prozac et d'autres médicaments proches servent à soigner la dépression.

Plantes et médicaments

▲ LA DIGITALE
La digitale contient la digitaline, un produit utilisé dans le traitement des troubles cardiaques.

▶ APOTHICAIRE
L'apothicaire médiéval diagnostiquait les maladies et fabriquait des remèdes à base de plantes et autres produits.

DEPUIS LA PRÉHISTOIRE, LES hommes utilisent des plantes pour se soigner. Certaines ont été découvertes dans les sépultures les plus anciennes. Quelques-unes étaient employées pour leurs propriétés médicales évidentes, d'autres pour des raisons magiques ou spirituelles.

Une grande partie de la population mondiale dépendrait encore des plantes médicinales, bien que la médecine occidentale actuelle ne repose que sur quelques remèdes à base de plantes. Nombre de ces remèdes sont d'ailleurs identiques à ceux mentionnés dans les écrits de l'Antiquité. Les préparations à base de plantes de Galien et d'autres médecins grecs furent reprises par les Arabes. Elles continuèrent à être en usage au

PRENDRE DES MÉDICAMENTS

La plupart des médicaments se prennent par voie orale sous forme de cachet ou de sirop, mais peuvent revêtir d'autres formes. L'asthme peut être traité en inhalant une poudre qui va droit dans les poumons. Les piqûres servent à administrer très rapidement de grandes quantités de produit. Certaines substances injectées par piqûre sont conçues pour être absorbées très lentement par les tissus afin d'avoir un effet prolongé.

▼ L'INDUSTRIE PHARMACEUTIQUE
L'industrie pharmaceutique moderne utilise des lignes de production de haute technologie pour préparer des médicaments à grande échelle.

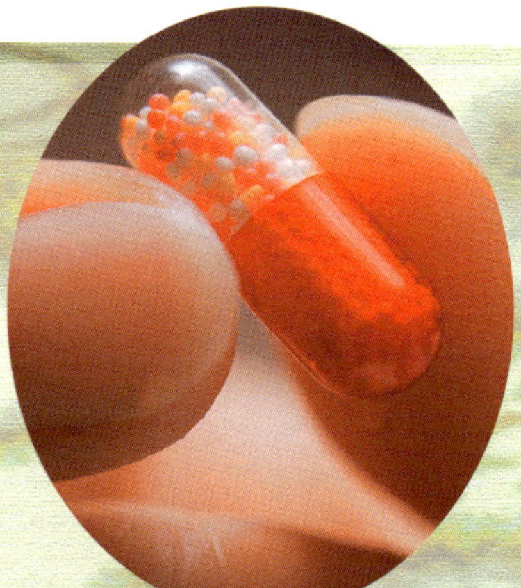

▲ GÉLULES À DIFFUSION LENTE
Certains produits sont évacués rapidement par l'organisme. Il faudrait que les malades prennent des doses répétées tout au long de la journée pour maintenir suffisamment de produit dans la circulation sanguine. Les gélules à diffusion lente libèrent graduellement le médicament.

Moyen Âge. Dans bien des monastères et des boutiques d'apothicaires, on cultivait des plantes médicinales. Les explorateurs de la Renaissance rapportèrent de nouvelles plantes provenant des terres récemment découvertes. Certains herbiers écrits au XVIIe siècle qui contiennent une profusion d'observations détaillées, sont encore imprimés aujourd'hui.

Au cours du temps, de nombreuses plantes répertoriées dans les anciens herbiers sont passées de mode, mais les remèdes les plus efficaces subsistent. L'écorce de quinquina contenant la quinine fut introduite dans la médecine occidentale au XVIIe siècle comme traitement contre le paludisme. La digitale est utilisée depuis 1785 pour soigner l'hydropisie, et les médecins constatèrent qu'elle pouvait servir de précieux remède contre certaines maladies cardiaques.

À moins de subir une préparation particulière, un grand nombre de plantes sont extrêmement toxiques. La colchicine par exemple, extraite de la fleur de colchique, peut être mortelle. Mais elle sert aussi de traitement contre la goutte. Après la découverte par les alchimistes de la technique de la distillation, l'extraction de la partie active des plantes médicinales devint vite une science. Cette méthode consiste à faire bouillir un liquide jusqu'à évaporation de l'eau afin qu'il ne reste plus que le concentré, l'extrait.

Ces techniques de purification sont à l'origine de l'industrie pharmaceutique moderne. Beaucoup de médicaments actuels sont des versions synthétiques d'extraits de plantes. Des recherches se poursuivent dans le monde entier pour identifier des remèdes traditionnels et enquêter sur leurs molécules actives.

◀ ÉCORCE DE SAULE
On utilisait des extraits d'écorce de saule pour soulager la douleur. Ce n'est qu'en 1852 qu'une version du produit actif fut synthétisée et commercialisée sous le nom d'aspirine.

Cy commence la declaració des proprietes du romarin. la fleur du romarĩ liee en drap ꝛ boullie en eaue iusques au degastemẽt de la moytie ꝺ leaue beue vault a toutes maladies dedens le corps. Jtẽ la fleur boullie auec vin blanc qui en laue sa face garde destre pogreyre. ꝛ de choir les soucis. Jtez se tu portes sur toy des fueillez de romarin elles te ferõt ioyeux ꝛ liez. Jtẽ se tu frotes tes dãs du charbon fait du boiz de romarin ꝛ mis en poudre. ꝛ mise en vng drapel si il ya aucuns vers ilz mourrõs. Jtez laue tes pies en fueilles en vinagre ꝛ tu les auras sains ꝛ sans ex

◀ LE JARDIN DE LA SANTÉ
Le Hortus Sanitaris *(Jardin de la Santé) est un herbier écrit en Allemagne au XVe siècle. Il établit une liste des remèdes utilisés par les apothicaires, et des propriétés qui leur étaient attribuées. La plupart des informations proviennent de l'époque d'Hippocrate.*

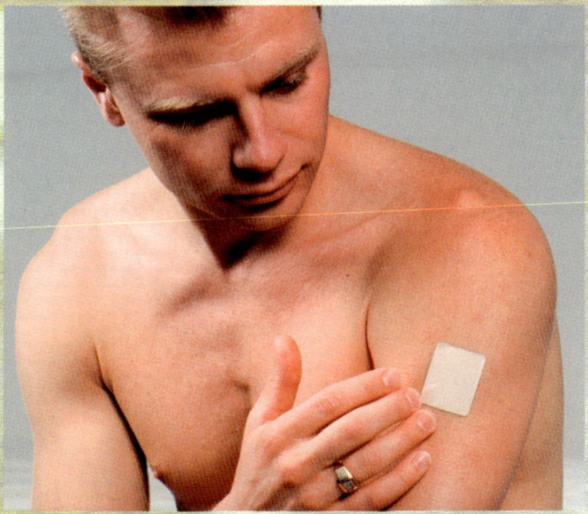

▲ LE TIMBRE NICOTINE
Certains produits sont absorbés à travers la peau. C'est le cas du timbre (ou patch) qui libère de petites quantités de nicotine dans le sang pour aider les fumeurs à se désaccoutumer de la cigarette.

▼ L'INHALATEUR
Les médicaments contre l'asthme sont en général pulvérisés directement dans les poumons. Ceci réduit les effets secondaires des produits dans les autres parties du corps.

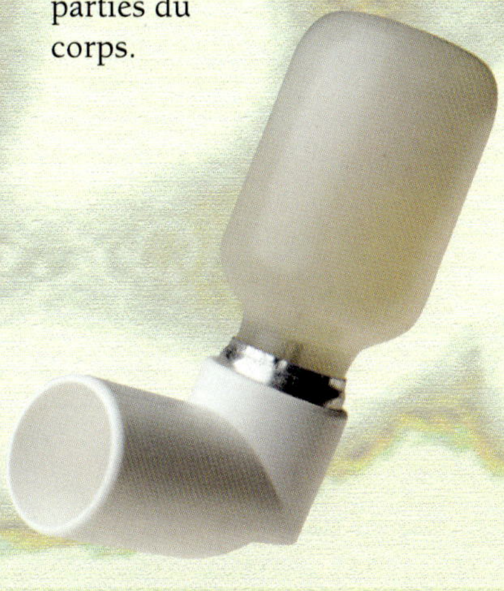

Dates clés

- 1852 L'aspirine est synthétisée.
- 1903 Introduction des sédatifs (calmants) à base de barbituriques. Ils contiennent de l'acide barbiturique contenu dans le lichen *Usnea barbata*.
- 1930 La cortisone est isolée, ce qui permet le développement des stéroïdes modernes.
- 1935 Les sulfamides antibactériens sont développés.
- 1961 Le sédatif de la thalidomide est retiré après avoir causé de terribles dommages chez les fœtus.
- 1980 L'AZT est utilisé comme traitement contre le SIDA.

Les médecines alternatives

CERTAINES PERSONNES rejettent complètement la médecine moderne. Les scientistes chrétiens par exemple pensent que toute maladie peut se soigner par la prière et la foi. Les Témoins de Jéhovah ne refusent que quelques aspects de la médecine conventionnelle, comme les transfusions.

Mais tout le monde ne se détourne pas des traitements traditionnels pour des raisons religieuses. Certains pensent que la médecine traditionnelle ne peut résoudre leur problème de santé et cherchent donc une alternative.

Les années 1990 ont vu se développer un intérêt accru pour les alternatives à la médecine traditionnelle. Il existe une différence entre les thérapies alternatives, où le malade rejette la médecine conventionnelle et cherche d'autres formes de thérapie, et une médecine parallèle, dans laquelle le patient suit une thérapie en

▲ LA CAMOMILLE
La camomille est utilisée en homéopathie pour soulager la douleur. Les homéopathes utilisent de faibles quantités de médicaments qui produisent les mêmes symptômes que ceux qu'ils veulent soigner.

▶ LA MOXIBUSTION
Une forme d'acupuncture s'appelle la moxibustion. Des cônes d'herbes sont brûlés sur la peau aux points des méridiens décrits dans la médecine chinoise.

LES MANIPULATIONS

Il existe en Europe occidentale une forte tendance qui pousse les gens à s'orienter vers les thérapies non conventionnelles. Les malades qui se sentent exclus de leur traitement peuvent aujourd'hui choisir et être partie prenante de leur thérapie. Les gens qui souffrent de maux de dos continuels hésitent à utiliser de puissants analgésiques à cause de leurs désagréables effets secondaires, comme la somnolence. L'ostéopathie, la chiropractie et les massages constituent des alternatives.

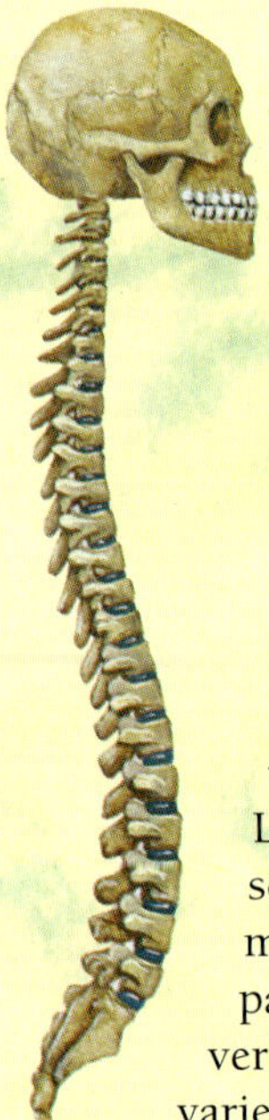

◀ LA COLONNE VERTÉBRALE
L'ostéopathie et la chiropractie sont deux thérapies basées sur la manipulation du corps, et plus particulièrement de la colonne vertébrale. Bien que les méthodes varient, ces manipulations soulagent souvent des maux de dos.

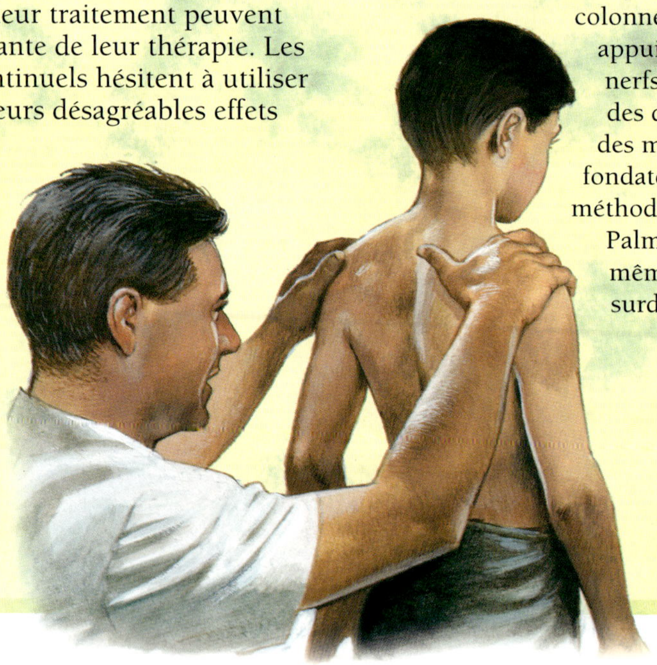

▼ LE CHIROPRATICIEN
Les chiropraticiens pensent que certaines parties de la colonne vertébrale appuient sur des nerfs, ce qui crée des douleurs et des maladies. Le fondateur de cette méthode, David Palmer, aurait même soigné la surdité.

plus du traitement prescrit par son médecin. La plupart des praticiens acceptent que les patients qu'ils soignent suivent des thérapies parallèles dans la mesure où celles-ci n'interfèrent pas avec les traitements conventionnels. Cependant, les thérapies alternatives peuvent conduire un malade à repousser une visite chez un médecin traditionnel, ce qui peut rendre son cas beaucoup plus difficile à soigner.

Certaines de ces thérapies sont délicates à définir. Les traitements à base de plantes, par exemple, sont considérés comme conventionnels s'ils contiennent des éléments médicalement actifs. Si leur efficacité n'est pas prouvée, ils sont classés parmi les thérapies alternatives.

L'acupuncture est une technique de traitement chinoise très ancienne qui consiste à piquer certains points du corps avec des aiguilles. La science ne reconnaît l'acupuncture comme technique médicale que depuis peu, c'est-à-dire à partir du moment où il a été prouvé que le fait de piquer certains points du corps pouvait soulager la douleur.

Le point commun à toutes ces formes de médecine parallèle et alternative est qu'elles n'ont pas encore d'explication scientifique. Certains croient qu'elles fonctionnent par effet placebo, l'action bénéfique d'origine psychologique d'un traitement. Les placebos sont souvent efficaces, probablement parce que le patient croit qu'ils vont le soigner.

▲ L'ACUPUNCTURE
La recherche scientifique a montré que l'acupuncture, la pratique chinoise consistant à piquer certains points du corps avec des aiguilles, soulageait réellement la souffrance. Des opérations lourdes ont eu lieu en Chine sans autre forme d'anesthésie que l'acupuncture.

▶ L'AROMATHÉRAPIE
Les odeurs exercent un puissant effet sur le corps et l'humeur. L'aromathérapeute masse le corps avec des huiles aromatiques, fait respirer les émanations d'huiles chauffées ou ingérer des essences de plantes médicinales.

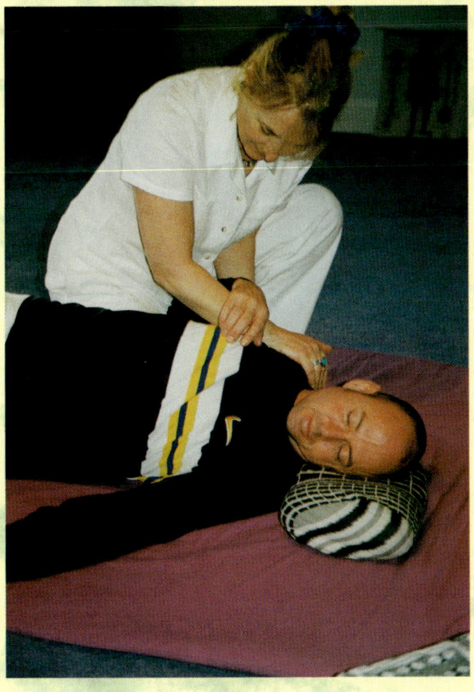

◀ SHIATSU
Il s'agit d'une technique pour soulager la douleur qui s'est développée au Japon au XXe siècle. Les praticiens du shiatsu se servent de leurs doigts pour appuyer fortement sur les points d'acupuncture.

▶ LES PIEDS D'ABORD
La réflexologie repose sur l'idée que les différentes zones des pieds représentent différentes parties du corps. Le massage et la stimulation de ces zones peuvent aider à soigner la maladie.

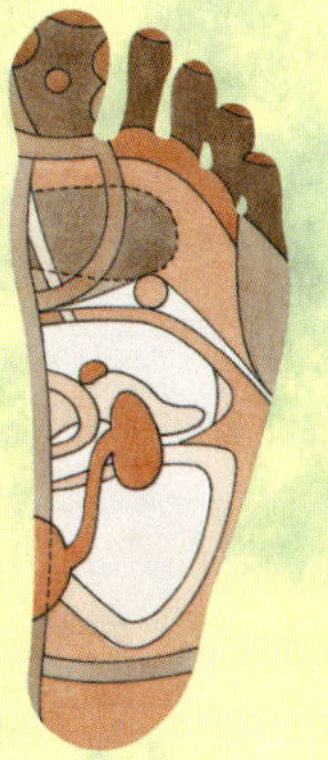

Dates clés

- 300 av. J.-C. Premières descriptions d'acupuncture dans le *Neijing*.
- 1601 apr. J.-C. L'acupuncture est décrite en détails par Yang Chi-chou.
- 1796 Samuel Hahnemann fonde en Allemagne l'homéopathie sur la « loi de similitude ».
- 1874 Le médecin Andrew Still introduit l'ostéopathie.
- 1895 David Palmer développe la chiropractie aux États-Unis.
- 1900 Développement du shiatsu.
- 1930 Eunice Ingham introduit la réflexologie.

Les médecines naturelles

▲ INTERDIT DE FUMER
Les médecines naturelles insistent sur la nécessité d'éviter les activités qui présentent un risque pour la santé, comme fumer.

Les formes les plus anciennes de la médecine font leur réapparition. Les médecines naturelles modernes traitent le patient dans sa globalité, et non uniquement sa maladie. Leur but est davantage de maintenir les gens en bonne santé que de soigner une maladie. Les influences les plus importantes des médecines naturelles d'aujourd'hui sont la médecine chinoise ancienne et la médecine ayurvédique indienne.

La naturothérapie combine en général un régime diététique, des exercices physiques et la relaxation avec d'autres techniques alternatives, comme la réflexologie, l'acupuncture et le traitement par les plantes. L'homéopathie est une forme de médecine naturelle largement pratiquée en Europe et aux États-Unis. Elle fut révélée en Allemagne, au début du XIXe siècle, par Samuel Hahnemann qui décrivit l'effet de très petites doses de substances médicamenteuses sur ses patients.

La méditation et la relaxation tiennent une place importante dans les médecines naturelles. Ces techniques ont été importées en Europe par des maîtres indiens qui combinèrent la médecine ayurvédique avec les pratiques occidentales. La méditation transcendantale est l'une des plus connues parmi ces techniques. Les gens récitent un mantra (chant) dans leur tête et atteignent ainsi un état de relaxation profonde.

◀ UNE NOURRITURE SAINE
Les gens sont de plus en plus conscients de ce qui constitue une alimentation équilibrée et de ses effets bénéfiques sur la santé. Beaucoup savent qu'ils doivent diminuer leur consommation en sucre, en sel et en graisses s'ils veulent réduire les risques de maladies. Les fruits et les légumes tiennent une place importante dans la diététique. Ils contiennent des vitamines qui aident le corps à assimiler les minéraux essentiels.

GÉRER LE STRESS

Le stress fait partie du mode de vie actuel. Il peut être à l'origine de l'hypertension, d'ulcères, et de dépressions nerveuses. La solution classique est de prendre des médicaments conçus pour traiter ces dysfonctionnements. Une approche naturelle consiste à soulager le stress grâce à des techniques de relaxation comme le yoga, le tai chi et la méditation.

◀ L'ART ORIENTAL
Le tai chi est un ancien art martial qui s'est développé en Chine au XVIIIe siècle. Il utilise les principes du yin et du yang pour équilibrer le corps et l'esprit grâce à des mouvements très lents.

▼ L'EXERCICE INDIEN
Le yoga est une discipline indienne ancienne destinée à exercer le corps et l'esprit. Il vise à libérer l'esprit des contraintes du corps par la maîtrise de ses mouvements et du souffle.

▲ LA MÉDITATION
Ce yogi médite dans la position du demi-lotus. La méditation a été rendue populaire en Occident par des Indiens comme le yogi Maharishi Mahesh et son mouvement pour la méditation transcendantale.

◀ UNE BONNE CONDITION PHYSIQUE
Les exercices physiques sont importants dans les médecines naturelles. Grâce à eux, le corps brûle son excédent en graisse et produit des muscles. De plus, il s'agit d'activité ludiques, et il est bien connu que le fait d'être heureux a des retombées positives sur la santé.

▼ LA VIE À LA BOURSE
La vie trépidante des affaires entraîne un stress permanent qui peut, à long terme, induire des changements dans le corps, engendrant des maladies comme l'anxiété, la dépression et les ulcères. Beaucoup de traitements naturels essaient de lutter contre ce stress.

Le mouvement des médecines naturelles a amené de nombreux praticiens conventionnels à considérer le patient dans sa globalité, et pas seulement sa maladie. Le mode de vie, les problèmes psychologiques et le régime alimentaire sont quelques-uns des facteurs affectant la santé d'un individu. Certaines cliniques proposent aujourd'hui des médecines naturelles en parallèle avec des traitements traditionnels, afin que leurs patients puissent choisir une combinaison de thérapies qui leur soit adaptée. L'un des problèmes rencontrés avec les médecines naturelles est de s'assurer du sérieux d'un thérapeute. Pour résoudre ce problème, nombre de pays souhaitent que les thérapeutes alternatifs se groupent en associations garantissant leurs qualités professionnelles.

stretching

massage

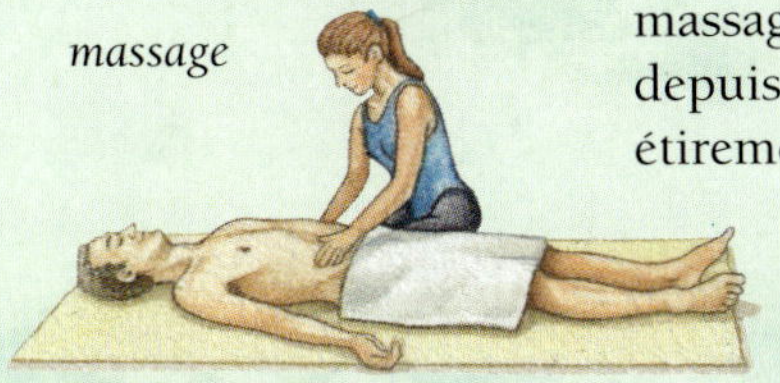

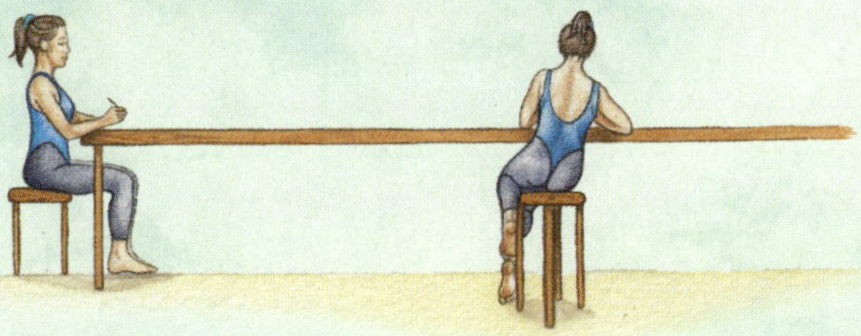

bonne position *mauvaise position*

◀ MASSAGE ET GYMNASTIQUE
Les bénéfices d'un exercice physique et du massage sont reconnus depuis toujours. Des étirements réguliers sont de bons exercices contre les troubles de la respiration.

▲ BIOANALYSE
Des capteurs électriques fixés sur le crâne permettent de mesurer l'activité du cerveau pendant la relaxation. Cette technique permet à la personne d'utiliser l'information recueillie par les capteurs pour améliorer son niveau de relaxation.

Dates clés

- 200 av. J.-C. Zuang Zi décrit l'importance de maintenir l'équilibre du Qi (énergie vitale) dans le corps.
- 200 av. J.-C. Le yoga se développe en Inde.
- 1700 apr. J.-C. Le tai chi se développe en Chine.
- 1959 Le premier tour du monde du yogi Maharishi Mahesh fait connaître la méditation transcendantale en Occident.
- 1968 Kenneth Cooper développe l'aérobic.

Les technologies modernes

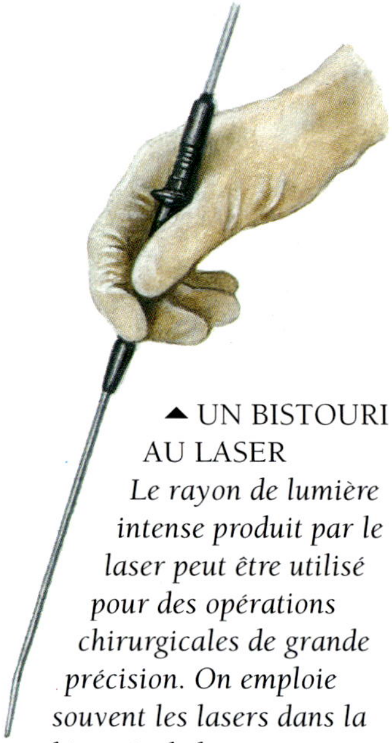

▲ UN BISTOURI AU LASER
Le rayon de lumière intense produit par le laser peut être utilisé pour des opérations chirurgicales de grande précision. On emploie souvent les lasers dans la chirurgie de la peau pour enlever les taches de naissance et les tatouages.

DEPUIS LES ANNÉES 1960, la technologie médicale a progressé plus vite qu'aucun médecin des générations antérieures aurait jamais pu l'imaginer. On a inventé le laser qui produit un rayon lumineux intense et sert de scalpel pour couper les tissus avec une extrême précision, enlever les tumeurs et pratiquer des opérations délicates de l'œil. Pour soulager la douleur, on a en général recours à des médicaments, mais parfois aussi à d'autres thérapies qui n'entraînent pas de

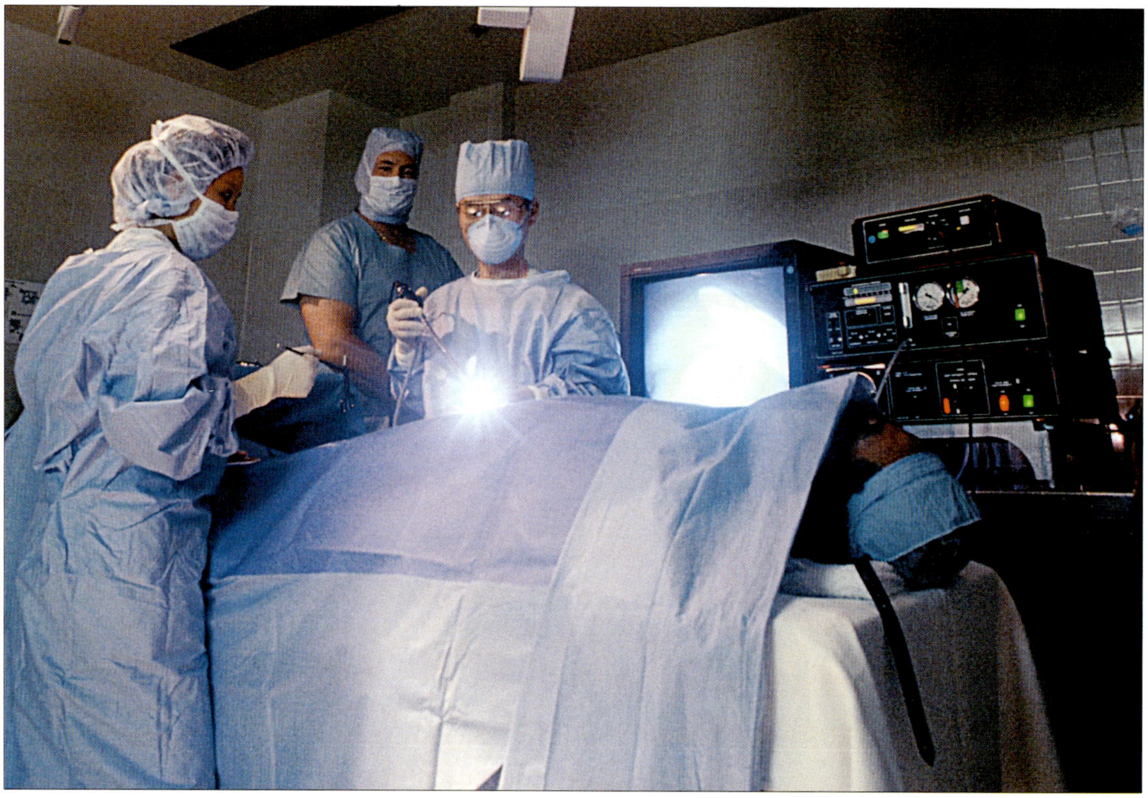

▶ L'ENDOSCOPIE
Certaines opérations modernes sont pratiquées à travers une petite ouverture effectuée dans le corps du patient. On y glisse une sonde qui transmet une image de l'intérieur du corps sur un grand écran.

LES TECHNIQUES LES PLUS RÉCENTES

La technologie progresse constamment, de même que la fabrication de médicaments toujours plus performants. Des instruments simples changent la vie d'un malade, comme un minuscule ressort inséré dans un vaisseau sanguin bouché pour le maintenir ouvert. Des technologies complexes, avec des appareils de surveillance informatiques, sont utilisées pour l'assistance cardiorespiratoire. Des techniques de pointe, comme l'endoscopie, permettent au patient de se remettre plus rapidement d'une opération.

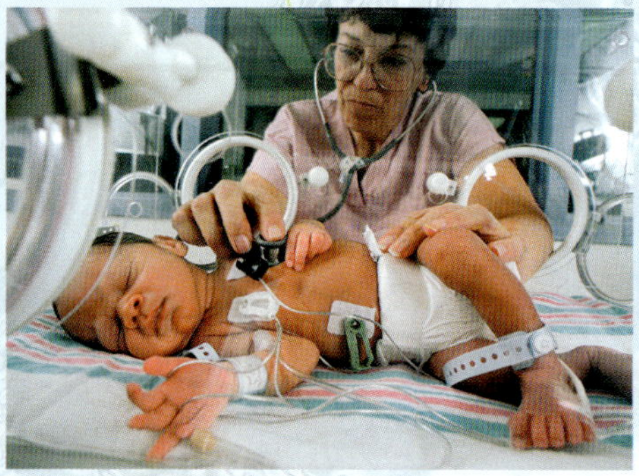

◀ LA CHANCE DE VIVRE
Autrefois, des bébés prématurés trop petits ne survivaient pas. Aujourd'hui, ils sont placés dans des services de réanimation néonatale. Ils respirent de l'air chaud filtré et toutes les fonctions de leur corps sont sous surveillance.

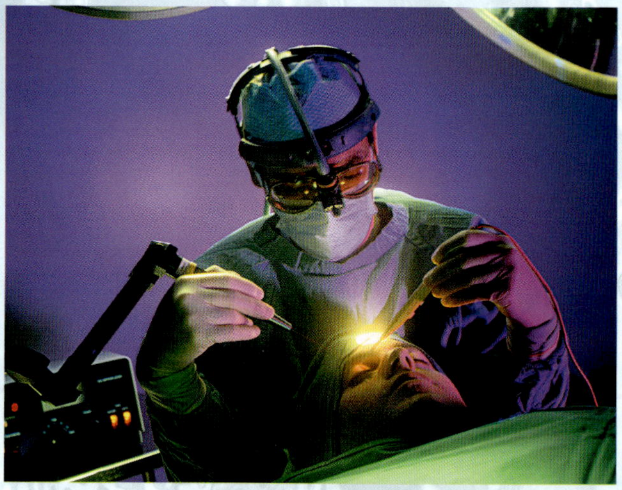

▲ LA CHIRURGIE OCULAIRE HI TECH
On a recours à des lasers pour opérer l'œil, sans avoir à ouvrir cet organe délicat. Le laser traverse la pupille et brûle de petites zones pour ressouder au bon endroit une rétine déplacée.

dépendance à ces calmants. L'efficacité de l'acupuncture pour contrôler la douleur a conduit à faire passer un faible courant électrique dans les aiguilles au niveau des nerfs périphériques induisant la douleur. Aujourd'hui, la neurostimulation transcutanée (NST) est devenue une pratique courante pour soulager les douleurs chroniques.

Les patients subissant d'atroces souffrances, par exemple dans le cas de cancers avancés, ont en permanence besoin d'analgésiques, produits soulageant la douleur. Pour cela, on leur implante une aiguille dans la zone concernée. Le produit est injecté par perfusion sous l'effet d'une minuscule pompe qui fonctionne avec une batterie que l'on peut porter à la ceinture.

Les bébés prématurés sont des sujets à risque, car leurs poumons ne sont pas encore complètement développés. Ils étaient autrefois placés dans des couveuses qui les maintenaient au chaud. Aujourd'hui, dans un service sophistiqué de réanimation néonatale, des ordinateurs contrôlent la quantité d'oxygène dans le sang du bébé, la température de son corps et sa respiration.

Les chocs électriques entraînent généralement la mort. Mais le défibrillateur est un instrument qui envoie une puissante décharge au cœur après une crise cardiaque. C'est maintenant un appareil essentiel de l'équipement d'urgence d'un hôpital moderne.

La dialyse est une méthode qui élimine les impuretés dans le sang des malades dont les reins ne fonctionnent plus. L'accumulation de ces déchets les empoisonnerait rapidement, mais une dialyse pratiquée plusieurs fois par semaine leur permet de mener une vie relativement normale, bien qu'une transplantation de rein reste leur seule chance de guérison totale.

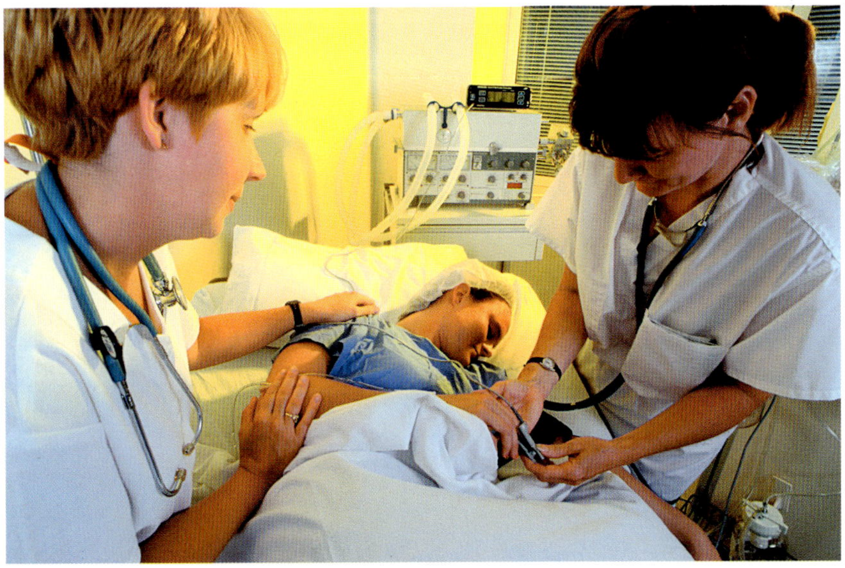

▸ UNE ASSISTANCE VITALE

Une assistance cardiorespiratoire peut remplacer de nombreuses fonctions du corps. Elle peut assister les personnes grièvement blessées dans un accident, ce qui donne au corps le temps de guérir. Des gens ayant subi des lésions cérébrales graves peuvent ainsi être maintenus en vie.

▾ LA NEUROCHIRURGIE

Le cerveau ne possède pas de sensibilité en surface. Ainsi, la neurochirurgie se pratique sur un patient conscient. On effectue une ouverture sous anesthésie locale. Ce cadre stéréotaxique permet au chirurgien de positionner les instruments avec précision.

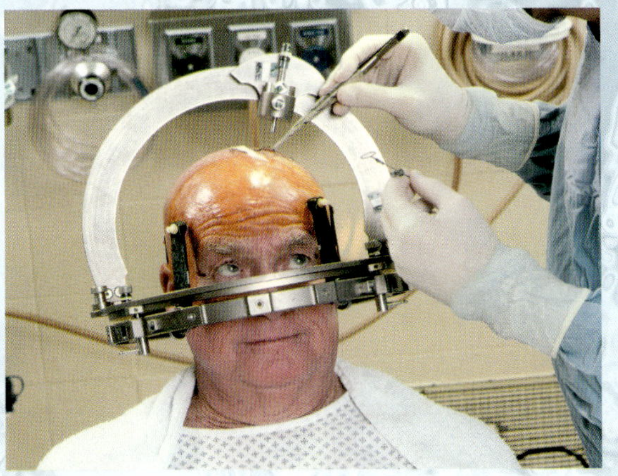

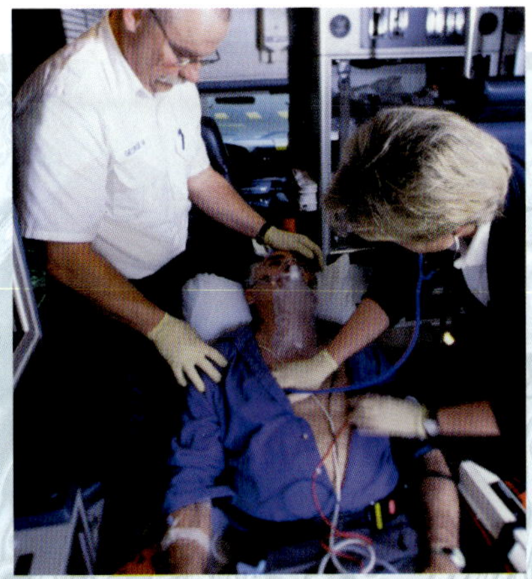

▴ LES PREMIERS SECOURS

L'ambulance transportait les blessés au plus vite à l'hôpital. Aujourd'hui, les soins commencent souvent pendant le trajet. Le personnel formé aux premiers secours sauve la vie de nombreuses personnes qui seraient mortes avant d'arriver à l'hôpital.

Dates clés

- 1928 On invente le « poumon d'acier » pour assister la respiration des patients paralysés par la polio. Il est largement utilisé jusque dans les années 1950.
- 1960 Invention du scalpel au laser.
- 1978 Naissance du premier « bébé éprouvette » suite aux recherches de P. Steptoe et R.G. Edwards. L'Église s'oppose à cette technique, mais celle-ci se développe largement.
- 1985 L'endoscopie devient pratique courante. Les patients se remettent plus facilement de ce genre de chirurgie.

Les images du corps

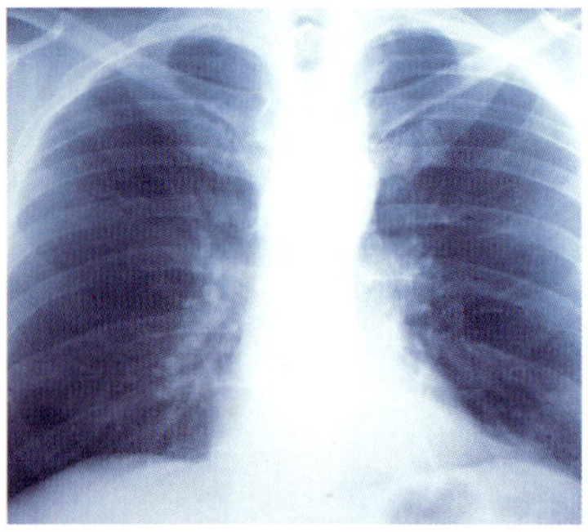

▲ RADIOGRAPHIE DES POUMONS
Les rayons X passent plus lentement à travers l'os qui est solide, qu'à travers le tissu mou. Ainsi, les os apparaissent-ils sur une radio, mais pas la chair. Ces rayons s'appellent X car Wilhelm Röntgen, qui les découvrit, ne savait pas exactement quelle était leur nature. On les utilise non seulement en médecine, mais aussi pour détecter des défauts dans des objets solides.

AUTREFOIS, LE SEUL MOYEN dont disposaient les médecins pour connaître le fonctionnement interne du corps humain était de l'ouvrir ou de regarder par les orifices naturels. Grâce au stéthoscope, ils purent prendre conscience du travail du cœur. Puis, les ophtalmoscopes leur permirent d'explorer l'intérieur de l'œil. Les endoscopes apparurent en 1805 et s'apparentaient davantage à un fin télescope. On les insérait par la bouche pour inspecter l'estomac ou dans l'anus pour examiner le rectum. Le fibroscope moderne, inventé en 1957, est une sonde souple composée de fibres optiques. Un faisceau projette de la lumière dans l'organisme, un autre transmet l'image sur un écran. Cette sonde transporte des bistouris, des pinces ou des

▼ L'UNE DES PREMIÈRES RADIOGRAPHIES
Wilhelm Röntgen, qui découvrit les rayons X, fit les premières radiographies. Sur celle-ci, on voit la main de sa femme. Sa bague est clairement visible, de même qu'une pièce de monnaie et un compas, car les rayons X ne traversent pas le métal.

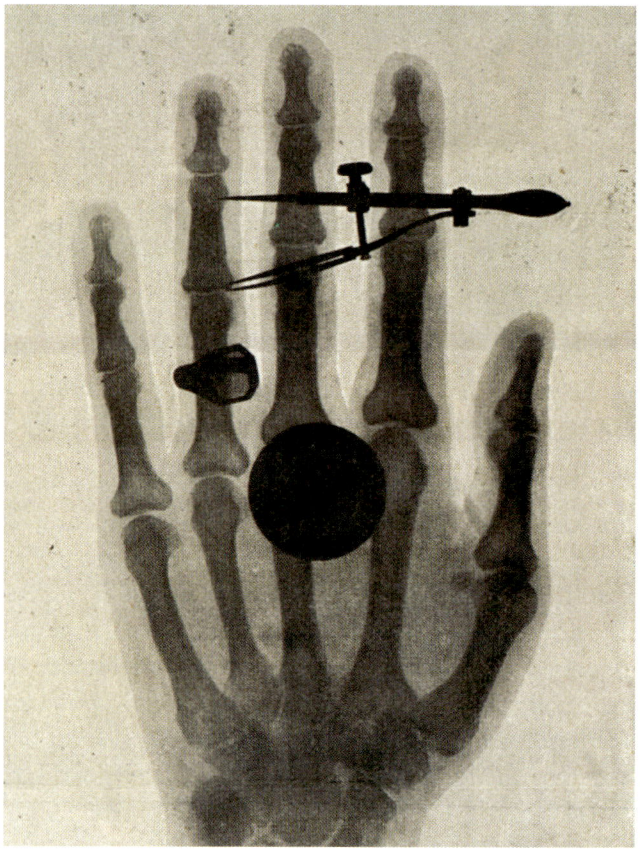

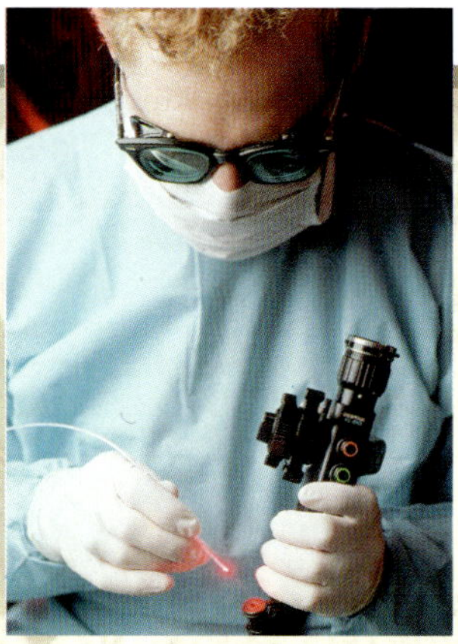

VUE DE L'INTÉRIEUR

L'imagerie médicale actuelle permet un diagnostic plus précis et réduit les risques de la chirurgie. On utilise des scanners pour des examens internes sans ouvrir le corps. L'endoscopie est aujourd'hui perfectionnée. Ainsi pour la laparoscopie, un minuscule dispositif optique est inséré dans une ouverture pratiquée dans l'abdomen, et permet d'explorer les organes internes pendant que le patient est sous anesthésie locale. Parfois, une chirurgie endoscopique est pratiquée à l'aide de très petits instruments fixés au dispositif d'exploration.

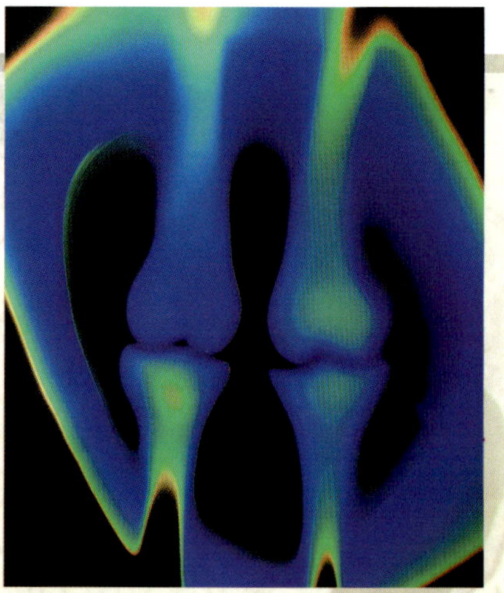

▲ L'ENDOSCOPE
L'endoscope est un tube optique muni d'un dispositif d'éclairage, qui est inséré dans le corps humain par un petit orifice. Il permet un examen et certains traitements.

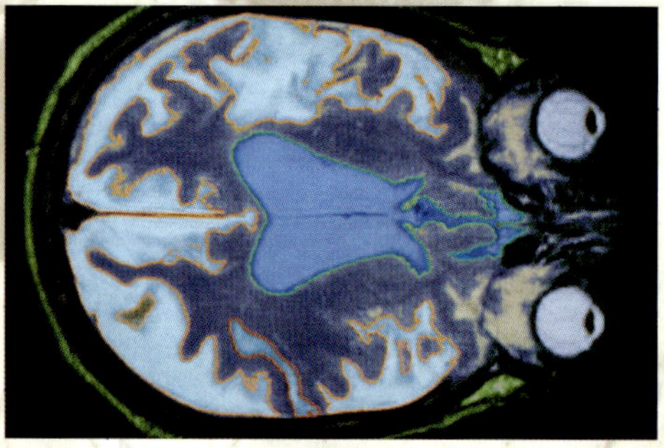

◀ L'IRM
L'imagerie par résonance magnétique permet d'obtenir des images précises d'organes et donne des informations sur les réactions chimiques dans le corps.

▲ LES POINTS CHAUDS
Une infection augmente la température de la zone du corps affectée. Des caméras thermiques détectent le rayonnement infrarouge de cette zone et réalisent un thermogramme.

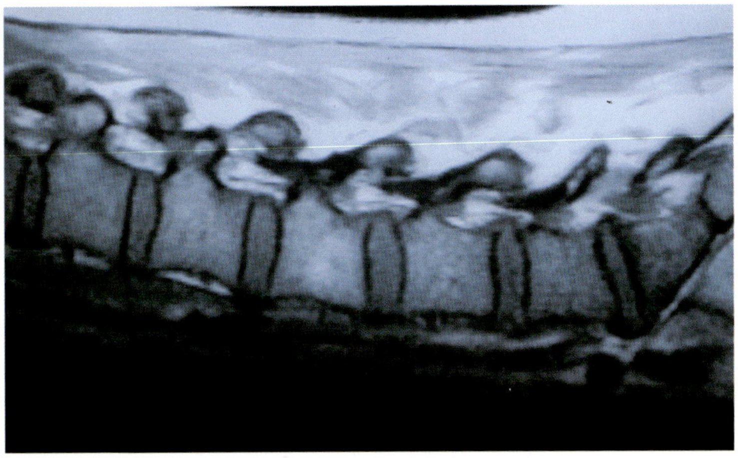

▲ SCANNER DU RACHIS DORSOLOMBAIRE
Le scanner est une machine faisant tourner un faisceau de rayons X autour du corps du patient et prenant différents clichés. Un ordinateur reconstruit ensuite des images de différentes sections du corps. Cette technique permet la visualisation de tissus non visibles aux rayons X.

rayons lasers pour de petites interventions locales.

La découverte qui permit aux médecins de visualiser l'intérieur du corps fut accidentelle. Le chercheur allemand Wilhelm Röntgen découvrit les rayons X, alors qu'il faisait des recherches sur les rayons cathodiques. Presque immédiatement, les médecins se rendirent compte de l'utilité des rayons X pour établir un diagnostic.

Dans les années 1950, suite à des recherches qui avaient eu lieu pendant la Deuxième Guerre mondiale, on développa une nouvelle méthode pour visualiser l'intérieur du corps. Le sonar est un appareil de détection sous-marine utilisant des ondes acoustiques de haute fréquence (des ultrasons) qui se réfléchissent sur des objets immergés, comme les sous-marins et sont enregistrées à la surface. En adaptant cette technique à la médecine, des ultrasons sont émis par une sonde et réfléchis par des organes et des tissus mous, comme certaines tumeurs, qui ne sont pas visibles sur une radiographie. Cette technique permet l'étude du fœtus dans l'utérus et l'échographie est aujourd'hui une procédure habituelle pendant la grossesse.

Les rayons X et l'échographie présentent des images planes, mais en 1967, Godfrey Hounsfield eut l'idée de produire des images de coupes du corps qui pourraient être rassemblées par un ordinateur pour créer une image en trois dimensions. Cette étude déboucha sur le développement du scanner, ou tomodensitomètre. Cet appareil de radiologie est composé d'un système émettant des rayons X autour du patient et d'un ordinateur reconstituant des images de coupes transversales du corps. Un produit de contraste est souvent utilisé pour obtenir des images plus précises.

L'imagerie par résonance magnétique (IRM) est une innovation plus récente. Elle présente moins de risques que les autres techniques de radiographie, car elle utilise les propriétés électromagnétiques de l'atome d'hydrogène abondant dans l'eau contenue dans le corps, et non un rayonnement nocif. Elle montre les réactions chimiques qui interviennent dans le corps. Elle peut, par exemple, mettre en évidence les parties du cerveau qui s'activent lorsque nous pensons, parlons ou bougeons.

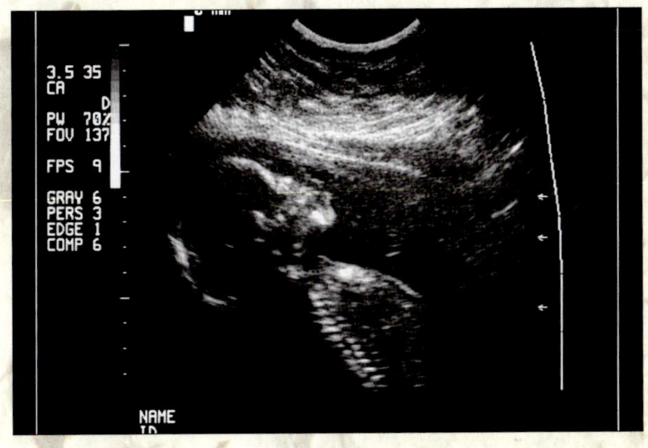

▲ L'ÉCHOGRAPHIE
On se sert des ultrasons pour contrôler la santé d'un bébé dans l'utérus. Ils produisent des images en mouvement.

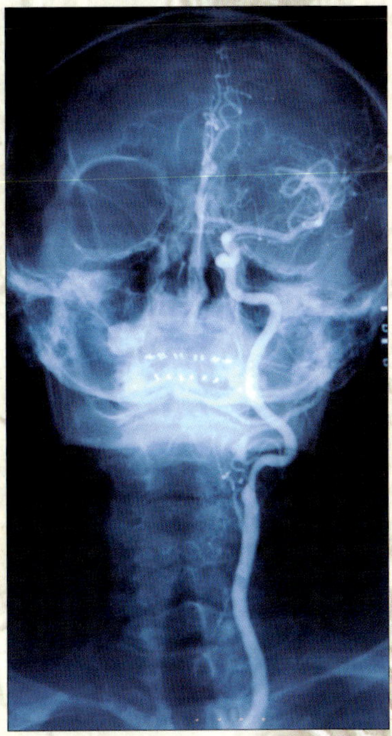

▶ L'ANGIOGRAPHIE
Les rayons X ne passent pas à travers les produits de contraste. Un tel produit injecté dans une artère permet un examen de cette dernière.

Dates clés

- 1805 A. J. Desormeaux crée le premier endoscope à Paris.
- 1895 Wilhelm Röntgen découvre les rayons X.
- 1950 Ian Donald invente l'échographie.
- 1953 L'angiographie se perfectionne.
- 1957 Première utilisation du fibroscope.
- 1967 Godfrey Hounsfield développe le scanner.
- 1971 Mise au point de la scanographie.
- 1980 Introduction des IRM.

Regard sur l'avenir

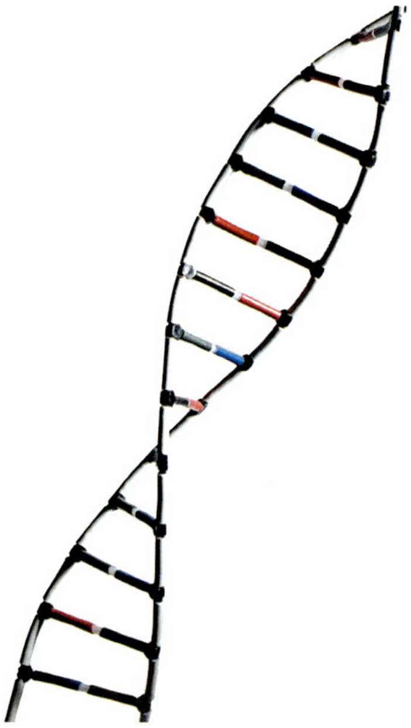

▲ LE CODE DE LA VIE
L'ADN porteur de l'information génétique, assure le contrôle de l'activité humaine.

La science et la médecine continuent à progresser à un rythme toujours plus rapide. Les innovations modernes sont issues du travail d'une équipe de chercheurs, chacun spécialisé dans un domaine particulier, plutôt que d'un individu isolé exceptionnellement doué. L'une des plus importantes innovations est la technique qui nous permet de lire la structure génétique de la cellule humaine. D'ici peu, chacun des millions de gènes qui constituent une cellule humaine sera répertorié et on comprendra la fonction de beaucoup d'entre eux. Ceci est très important, car de nombreuses maladies graves sont provoquées par des anomalies génétiques, des changements accidentels qui ont lieu dans les gènes à mesure que les cellules se reproduisent. Ces anomalies modifient le fonctionnement de l'organisme et provoquent des maladies. Il sera bientôt possible d'identifier les personnes porteuses de gènes défectueux héréditaires ; elles pourront alors décider de prendre le risque d'avoir ou non des enfants. Des recherches sont actuellement en cours en thérapie génique pour introduire dans les cellules une copie du gène manquant ou défectueux. Cette méthode est testée actuellement pour traiter le cancer, la mucoviscidose et la myopathie.

De nouveaux médicaments sont conçus par des ordinateurs qui construisent les images de

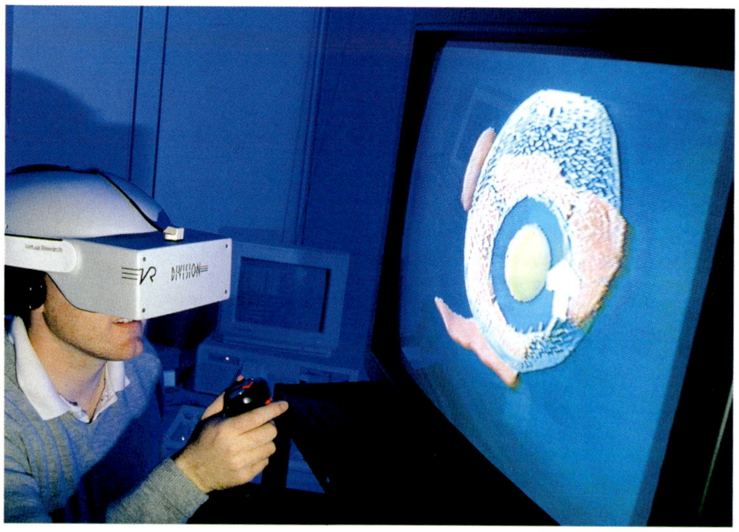

▶ LA CHIRURGIE VIRTUELLE
La réalité virtuelle permet aux étudiants et chirurgiens de pratiquer sans mettre en danger la vie d'un patient.

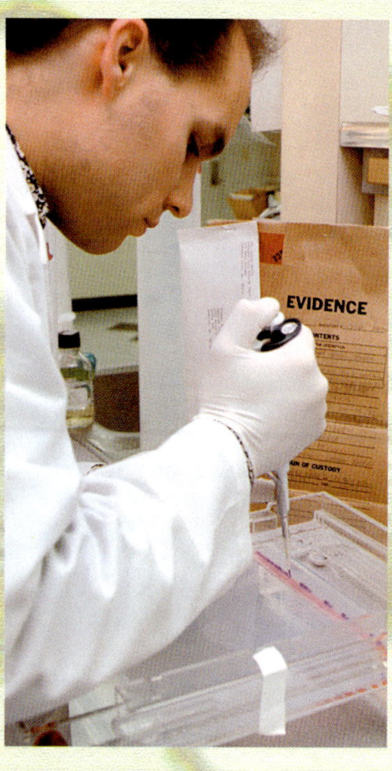

ET APRÈS ?
Les techniques médicales deviennent de plus en plus sophistiquées, mais aussi beaucoup plus chères. Certaines innovations médicales sont si onéreuses qu'il faudra en envisager une utilisation limitée si l'on veut continuer à pratiquer les soins médicaux courants. Il existe déjà de longues listes d'attente pour certaines opérations.

◀ LES OGM
Les ingénieurs en biologie savent déjà modifier génétiquement certains organismes. Peut-être qu'ils seront un jour capables de créer des aliments porteurs de médicaments pour la santé. Cependant, certaines personnes se demandent si les cultures génétiquement modifiées ne présentent pas des dangers.

◀ LE SYSTÈME IMMUNITAIRE
L'immunologie (étude du système immunitaire) constitue une branche importante des sciences médicales, car il faut encourager le corps à se protéger lui-même. Mais une mauvaise réaction immunitaire peut engendrer une maladie.

▶ POUR ATTAQUER
Les bactériophages sont des virus qui s'attaquent aux bactéries comme celle-ci. La génétique peut concevoir des bactériophages destinés à combattre des maladies spécifiques.

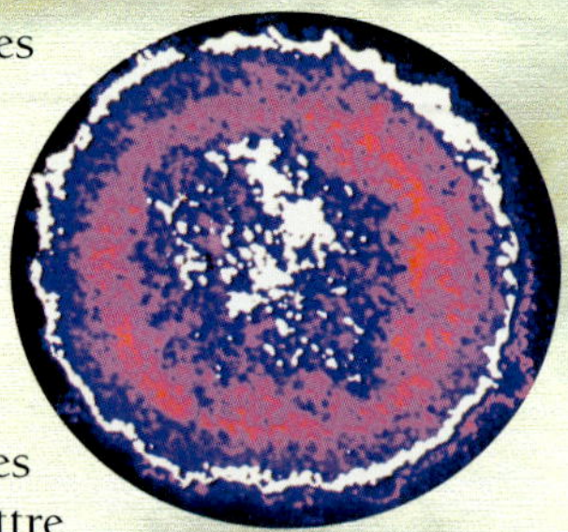

leur structure moléculaire. Les chercheurs peuvent ainsi modifier la molécule pour produire certains effets, avant même que le médicament n'ait été fabriqué.

Grâce à la vidéoconférence, un médecin converse directement avec un spécialiste qui peut se trouver dans un autre pays. Le spécialiste a la possibilité d'examiner le patient par une liaison vidéo. Pour une opération délicate, le chirurgien peut, grâce à la téléchirurgie, se faire assister par un expert qui prend, à distance, les commandes d'un robot manipulateur relié aux instruments.

La technologie médicale concerne essentiellement les pays développés. Des millions de gens dans le monde entier n'ont pas accès aux soins médicaux. L'amélioration du niveau de santé de tous les individus est un défi pour les médecins et les gouvernements. L'Organisation mondiale de la santé fait des efforts considérables pour mettre en place des programmes dans les pays en voie de développement.

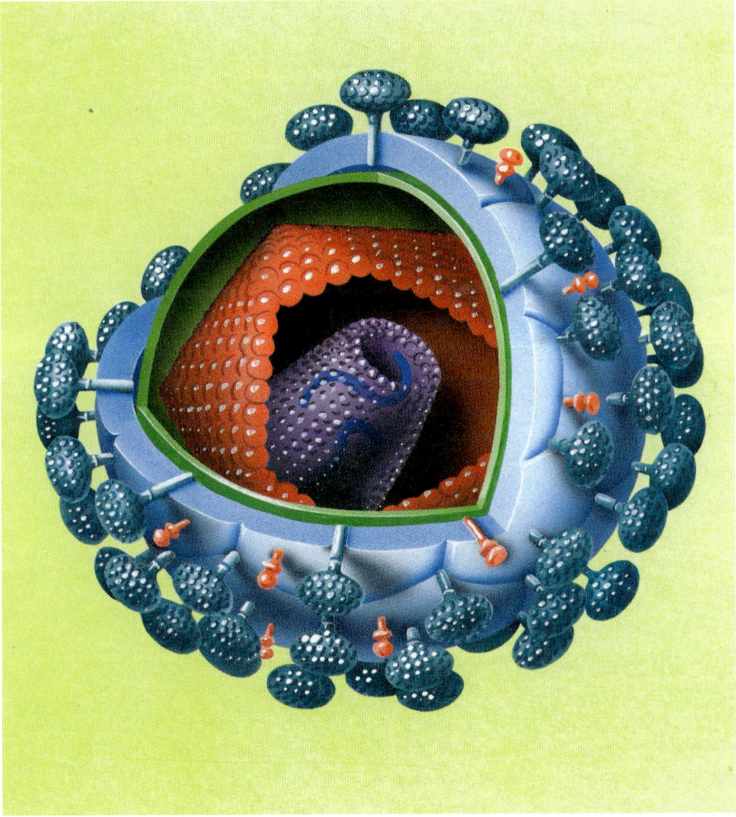

◂ LE VIRUS VIH
Le virus VIH associé au sida a été plus étudié qu'aucun autre virus, et sa structure est aujourd'hui bien comprise. Ce qui reste inconnu est la manière dont le virus change constamment pour éviter les attaques du système immunitaire. Des efforts considérables sont entrepris afin de trouver des traitements efficaces et des vaccins.

▸ DR WC
Au Japon des toilettes effectuent des diagnostics. Des détecteurs mesurent le contenu en graisses et en sucre des selles et de l'urine. Les résultats sont envoyés directement au médecin.

▾ EN APESANTEUR
Des recherches ont été effectuées dans l'espace pour purifier les médicaments. L'absence de pesanteur a de profonds effets sur l'organisme. Les gens souffrant de dégénérescence musculaire pourraient survivre plus longtemps en apesanteur.

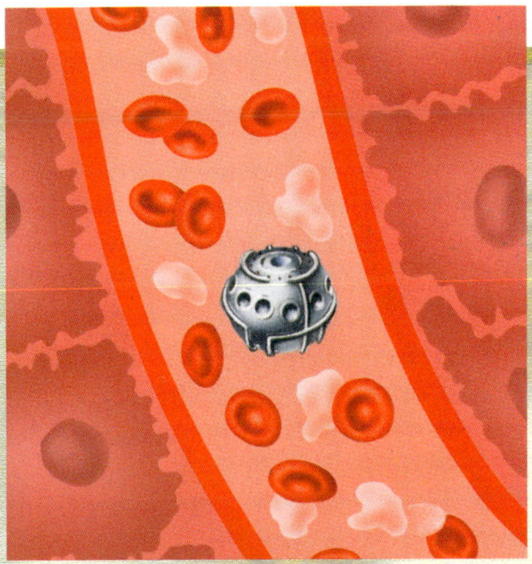

▴ LES NANO-ROBOTS
Des chercheurs envisagent de créer des robots suffisamment petits pour circuler à travers le corps dans le flux sanguin. Ils pourraient être programmés pour contrôler la santé d'une personne ou attaquer les tumeurs.

Dates clés

- 1869 Découverte de l'ADN.
- 1943 Les scientifiques découvrent que l'ADN transmet l'information génétique.
- 1953 James Watson et Francis Crick décrivent la structure à double hélice de l'ADN.
- 1970 Début du génie génétique.
- 1980 Développement de la réalité virtuelle.
- 1990 Début de la recherche médicale en apesanteur.
- 1990 Une levure génétiquement modifiée est commercialisée.

Glossaire

A

acupuncture : discipline médicale d'origine chinoise consistant à piquer des aiguilles spéciales en des points spécifiques du corps.

alchimie : forme ancienne de chimie, dont le but était de transformer des métaux ordinaires en métaux précieux, et de rechercher le moyen de donner à l'homme la vie éternelle.

amputation : ablation chirurgicale d'un membre malade ou blessé.

anatomie : en médecine, étude de la structure du corps humain.

anesthésiant : substance endormant la sensibilité dans tout ou partie du corps, afin d'empêcher la douleur pendant l'opération.

antibiotique : substance qui empêche le développement et la reproduction des microbes.

anticorps : substance produite par le système immunitaire du corps, qui tue ou affaiblit les microbes.

antisepsie : destruction des microbes capables de provoquer des infections, grâce à l'utilisation d'antiseptiques.

apothicaire : ancien nom donné au pharmacien.

asepsie : prévention de l'infection, obtenue en empêchant la présence de microbes.

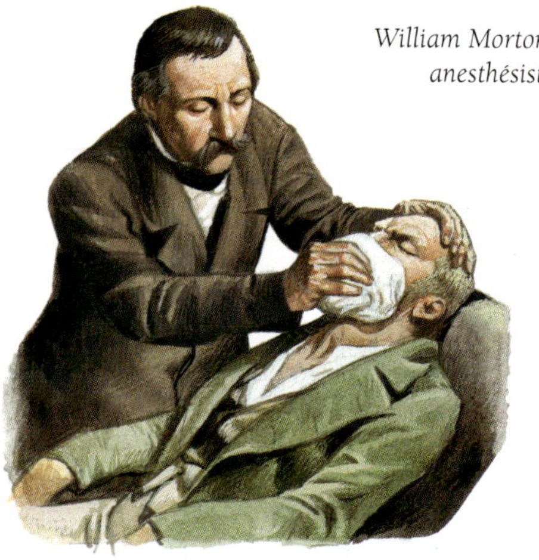

William Morton, anesthésiste

Apothicaires perses préparant un remède

asile : terme ancien attribué aux hôpitaux où étaient soignés, et généralement internés, les malades mentaux.

B

bactérie : micro-organisme présent dans tous les milieux et provoquant de nombreuses infections.

barbier : personne dont le métier était autrefois de faire la barbe, mais aussi des opérations de chirurgie.

C

cataplasme : onguent étalé sur une bande et placé sur une partie du corps enflammée ou blessée.

cautérisation : utilisation de la chaleur pour cicatriser les vaisseaux sanguins pendant une opération, autrefois pratiquée au fer rouge.

charlatan : personne qui trompe autrui, en vendant par exemple des remèdes sans efficacité.

chirurgien : médecin qui pratique une intervention, souvent interne, sur les organes malades ou blessés.

contrôle des naissances : limitation du nombre de naissances par la contraception.

D

diagnostic : identification d'une maladie par l'examen des symptômes.

dissection : action d'ouvrir un corps ou un organe pour connaître sa structure.

E

épidémie : propagation d'une maladie infectieuse.

G

greffe : transplantation d'un organe ou d'un tissu sur un individu, prélevé sur lui-même ou sur un autre individu.

Colonie de bactéries

H

herbier : livre répertoriant les plantes et leurs propriétés.

hygiène : partie de la médecine étudiant les moyens et les pratiques qui permettent de préserver ou de favoriser la santé.

I

immunité : état d'un organisme qui, s'étant défendu contre l'attaque d'un microbe, possède les anticorps pour le combattre une prochaine fois.

infection : pénétration et développement d'un microbe dans le corps.

inoculation : introduction d'un microbe dans le corps pour provoquer une infection contrôlée qui créera l'immunité à une maladie.

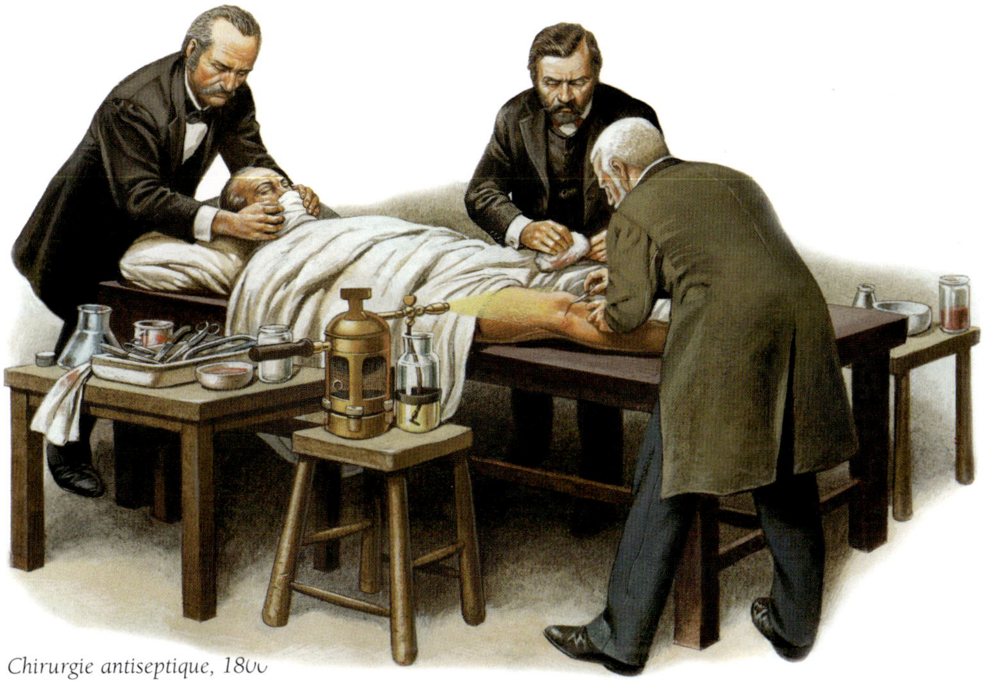

Chirurgie antiseptique, 1800

M

médecine alternative : médecine reposant sur des traitements non conventionnels, au lieu de remèdes prouvés scientifiquement.

microbe : organisme microscopique comme une bactérie, un virus ou un champignon.

mortalité : rapport du nombre de décès à l'effectif de la population, pendant une période donnée.

N

naturothérapie : ensemble des thérapies visant à restaurer des défenses immunitaires par des moyens naturels, dans la mesure du possible.

O

organisme : forme de vie animale ou végétale organisée ; plus spécialement le corps humain.

P

pharmacien : spécialiste formé à la préparation et à la vente des médicaments.

pronostic : déroulement ou issue prévus d'une maladie.

prothèse : pièce ou appareil destiné à remplacer un organe ou un membre, ou encore à rétablir une fonction.

psychiatre : médecin qui étudie et soigne les maladies mentales.

psychothérapie : utilisation de moyens psychologiques pour soigner une maladie mentale.

S

système immunitaire : système qui défend le corps contre la maladie en produisant des anticorps.

T

thérapie : traitement médical.

transfusion : injection d'un liquide, souvent du sang d'une autre personne, dans le flux sanguin.

trépaner : pratiquer une ouverture dans le crâne. Cette pratique était autrefois destinée à libérer des mauvais esprits, mais elle est toujours en usage, notamment pour effectuer une opération sur le cerveau.

V

vaccination : inoculer ou administrer oralement un vaccin composé de microbes morts ou affaiblis afin de créer l'immunité à une maladie.

virus : microbe qui ne se reproduit qu'en parasitant une cellule, et agent de nombreuses infections.

Écrits de Galien

Index

A
acupuncture 15, 54, 57, 62
ADN 60, 61
alchimiste 20, 21, 24, 51, 62
alternative (médecine) 52, 53
amérindienne (médecine) 10, 11
amputation 31, 62
anatomie 25, 62
anesthésiant 32, 33, 62
angiographie 59
antibiotique 42, 43, 62
antisepsie 32, 33, 62
apothicaire 21, 50, 51, 62
aqueduc 19
arabe (médecine) 20, 21, 30, 51
aromathérapie 53, 54
Asclépiade de Bithynie 18
Asclepios 16, 17
asepsie 33, 62
asile 48, 62
astrologie 22
Auenbrugger, Leopold 29
Avicenne 20, 21, 22, 25
ayurvédique (médecine) 12, 13, 31, 54

B
bactérie 32, 38
Banting, Frederick 47
barbier 23, 25, 30, 62
Barnard, Christiaan 47
Best, Charles 47
Blackwell, Dr Elizabeth 44, 45

C
caducée 16
cancer 35, 34
cautérisation 23, 25, 31, 62
Celse Cornelius 18, 19
Chadwick, John 36
Chain, Ernst 42, 43
chaman 10, 11
Charcot, Jean-Martin 49
charlatan 34, 35, 63
chinoise (médecine) 14, 15, 54
chiropractie 52, 53
chirurgie 23, 30, 31, 63
chloroforme 32
choléra 27, 36, 39
Crick, Francis 61
Curie, Marie 44, 45

D
dépression 48, 49, 54, 55
diabète 47
diagnostic 12, 28, 29, 62
dialyse rénale 47, 57
diphtérie 38, 39
dissection 24, 25, 62
Domagk, Gerhard 42, 43

E
eaux usées 37
échographie 59
égyptienne (médecine) 8, 9, 50
Ehrlich, Paul 42, 43
électrochoc 48
endoscopie 56, 58, 59
épidémie 26, 27, 62
épilepsie 9, 11, 22

F
Fabricius, Hieronymus 25
femme médecin 44, 45
fibroscope 58
Fleming, Alexander 42, 43
Florey, Howard 42, 43
Fracastoro, Girolamo 25
Freud, Sigmund 49

G
Galien, Claude 18, 19, 22, 23, 25, 28
gènes 60
grecque (médecine) 16-19, 51
greffe 13, 46, 47, 62
guerre (médecine de) 18

H
Hahnemann, Samuel 53, 54
Hammourabi, roi 8, 9
Harvey, William 24, 25
herbier 22, 54
Hildegarde 44, 45
Hippocrate 16, 17, 19, 22, 23, 28
homéopathie 52, 53, 54
hôpital 22, 23, 37, 45
Hounsfield, Godfrey 59
Huangdi, empereur 14
humeurs 12, 16, 17
Hunter, John 30, 31
hygiène 32, 60, 62
hypnose 34, 49, 62

I
imagerie médicale 58, 59
Imhotep 8, 9
immunologie 40, 41, 63
indienne (médecine) 12, 13, 30, 54
infection 32, 33, 36, 38
infirmière 44, 45
Ingham, Eunice 53
inoculation 40, 41, 63
IRM 58, 59

J
Jenner, Edward 40, 41
Jung, Karl 49

K
Kraepelin, Emil 49
Koch, Robert 38, 39

L
Laennec, René 28, 29
Landsteiner, Karl 47
laparotomie 58
Larrey, Dominique-Jean 31
laser 56, 57
lavement 23
lèpre 22, 23, 26, 36, 39
Lister, Joseph 32

M
magie 8, 12
Maimonide 20, 21
maladie mentale 18, 48, 49
maladies tropicales 38
Malpighi, Marcello 24, 25
manipulation 52
McDowell, Ephraïm 31
médicament 42, 43, 50, 51
méditation 12, 54
méridien de Qi 15
microbe 32, 38, 42
micro-organisme 38
microscope 38
Mondeville, Henri de 23
Morton, William 32, 33
moustique 39
moxibustion 52

N
naissance (contrôle) 44, 45, 62
naturelle (médecine) 54, 55
naturothérapie 54, 55, 63
néonatale (médecine) 56, 57
neurochirurgie 57
Nightingale, Florence 44, 45

O
œil (chirurgie) 20, 30, 31, 56
OGM 60
ophtalmoscope 28, 58
ostéopathie 52, 53

P
Palmer, David 52, 53
paludisme 38, 39, 42, 51
Paracelse 24
Paré, Ambroise 25, 31
Pasteur, Louis 32, 38 - 41
pénicilline 42, 43
peste 22, 26, 27, 36, 38
phrénologie 35
Pinel, Philippe 48, 49
plantes (médecine par les) 50, 53, 54, 62
Pline l'Ancien 19
poliomyélite 40, 41, 57
pouls 29
prématuré (bébé) 57
prothèse 46, 47, 63
psychanalyse 49
psychiatrie 48, 49
psychothérapie 48, 63

R
radiologie 58, 59
rage 38, 40, 41
Riva-Rocci, Scipione 29
rayons X 58, 59
réflexologie 53, 54
relaxation 54
Rhazès 20, 21
romaine (médecine) 18, 19, 30, 36
Röntgen, Wilhelm 29, 58, 59
Ross, Ronald 39

S
sage-femme 44
saignée 16, 17, 18, 23, 30
Salk, Jonas 41
Sanger, Margaret 44, 45
santé publique 19, 29, 36, 37
scanner 59
sédatif 18, 31, 51
Semmelweis, Ignac 32
Shennong, empereur 15
Snow, John 33, 36, 37, 39
Soranus 19
sorcier 10
sphygmomanomètre 29
Steptoe, Patrick 57
stéthoscope 28, 29, 58
Still, Andrew 53
Stopes, Marie 44, 45
stress 44, 55
Sushruta-samhita 12, 13, 31

T
téléchirurgie 61
thérapie génique 60
thermes 19
thermogramme 58
thermomètre 24, 28
transfusion sanguine 46, 47
transplantation 46, 47
trépanation 8, 9, 16, 30, 63
Treves, Frederic 31
Trotula 22, 23, 44
tuberculose 36, 38, 39, 43, 59
typhoïde 27, 36, 39

V
Vaca, Cabeza de 11
vaccination 15, 38, 40, 42, 63
Van Leeuwenhoek, A. 38, 39
variole 15, 40, 41
ventouse 18
Vésale, André 24, 25
VIH 35, 39, 40, 61
Vinci, Léonard de 25
Virchow, Rudolf 38, 39
virus 38, 39, 63
Von Helmhltz, Hermann 29

W
Waksman, Selman 43
Walker, Mary 44
Wang Shu-he 15
Warren, John Collins 32, 33
Watson, James 61
Wells, Horace 33
Wortley Montagu, Lady 40, 41

Y
yin et yang 14
yoga 12, 54

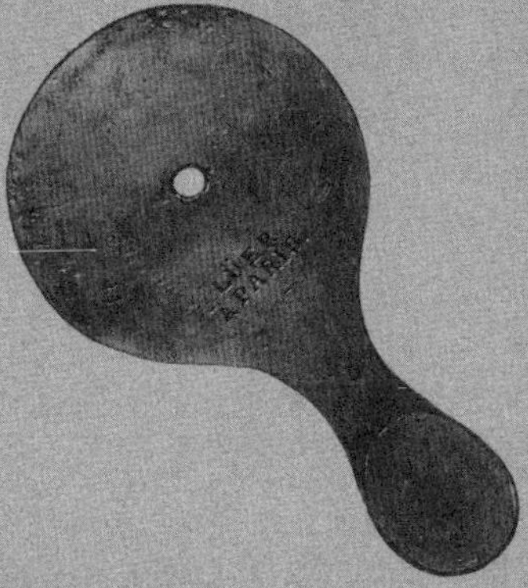

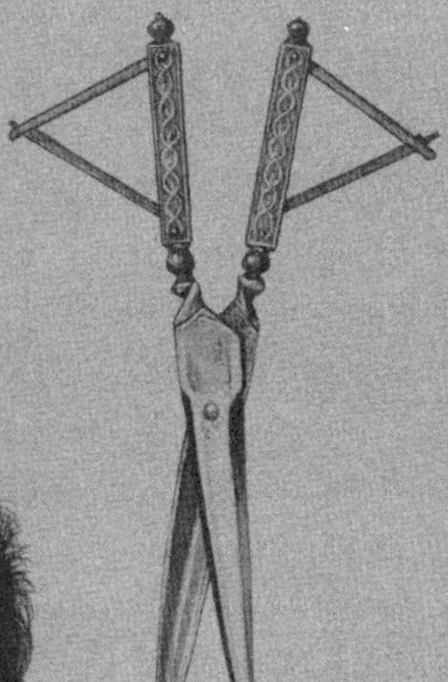